SCRIPTURAL TRACES:
CRITICAL PERSPECTIVES ON THE RECEPTION
AND INFLUENCE OF THE BIBLE

4

Editors

Claudia V. Camp, Texas Christian University
W. J. Lyons, University of Bristol
Andrew Mein, Westcott House, Cambridge

Published under

LIBRARY OF NEW TESTAMENT STUDIES

510

Formerly Journal for the Study of the Old Testament Supplement Series

Editor
Mark Goodacre

RECEPTION HISTORY, TRADITION AND BIBLICAL INTERPRETATION

Gadamer and Jauss in Current Practice

Robert Evans

B L O O M S B U R Y

LONDON • NEW DELHI • NEW YORK • SYDNEY

Bloomsbury T&T Clark
An imprint of Bloomsbury Publishing Plc

50 Bedford Square	1385 Broadway
London	New York
WC1B 3DP	NY 10018
UK	USA

www.bloomsbury.com
Bloomsbury is a registered trade mark of Bloomsbury Publishing Plc

First published 2014

© Robert Evans, 2014

British Library Cataloguing-in-Publication Data
A catalogue record for this book is available from the British Library.

ISBN:	HB:	978-0-56765-540-0
	ePDF:	978-0-56765-542-4

Library of Congress Cataloging-in-Publication Data
Evans, Robert
Reception History, Tradition and Biblical Interpretation/Robert Evans p.cm
Includes bibliographic references and index.
ISBN 978-0-567-65540-0 (hardcover)

Typeset by Forthcoming Publications Ltd (www.forthpub.com)
Printed and bound in Great Britain

To all the students with whom I have studied the New Testament through the last twenty years at the University of Chester. Don't worry, this is not required reading for any but the most hermeneutically inclined; but it owes a great deal to working with you on what the Bible means and how we read it. Grace to you and peace from God our Father and the Lord Jesus Christ.

CONTENTS

ABBREVIATIONS

ANF	*Ante-Nicene Fathers of the Christian Church*
CSEL	Corpus scriptorum ecclesiasticorum latinorum
EBR	*Encyclopedia of the Bible and its Reception*
JBL	*Journal of Biblical Literature*
JSNT	*Journal for the Study of the New Testament*
LCC	Library of Christian Classics. Philadelphia, 1953–
LCL	Loeb Classical Library
NPNF	*Nicene and Post-Nicene Fathers of the Christian Church*
NRSV	New Revised Standard Version
PCC-SGP	Patrologiae cursus completus, Series Graeca Prior
PCC-SL	Patrologiae cursus completus, Series Latina
SBL	*Society of Biblical Literature*
SJT	*Scottish Journal of Theology*
TDNT	*Theological Dictionary of the New Testament.* Edited by G. Kittel and G. Friedrich. Translated by G. W. Bromiley. 10 vols. Grand Rapids, 1964–76
ZNW	*Zeitschrift für die Neutestamentliche Wissenschaft*
ZTK	*Zeitschrift für Theologie und Kirche*

ACKNOWLEDGMENTS

I owe a great debt to Chris Rowland and Loveday Alexander whose wisdom and patience steered me through the whirlpools and doldrums of this project. Colleagues at the University of Chester have over several years offered me the encouragement and the means to undertake it. Particular students and colleagues made valuable suggestions of material: among them Andy Dawson, Fran Kenny, Michael Lakey, and Victor Morales; and stages of the project owe much to the intellectual generosity of Beth Swan, Gertrude Wright and Willard Swartley. Other colleagues offered wise evaluation: David Clough, Elaine Graham and Mat Collins. Parts of the case-study material reveal a long-standing debt to my tutors in Old English, Middle English and English literature at King's College London back in the 1970s. Most recently, the work and I profited greatly from the critical assessment and encouragement of Ian Boxall, Jonathan Roberts and Sean Winter. To all of the above, heartfelt thanks.

GLOSSARY OF KEY HERMENEUTICAL TERMS

The following German terms appear throughout this work. The glossary translations and definitions supplied here are offered partly to help the reader unfamiliar with the hermeneutical terminology, but in several cases because Gadamer's terms in particular can be misunderstood or are disputed. (Bracketed references following the hermeneutical term indicate location of first mention.)

Alterität (p.11)

Alterity or otherness: used by Jauss to describe how the otherness of the past can only be apprehended when the interpreter is able to separate what is different or 'alien' from their own 'horizon'. It is part of what Gadamer attributes to historical consciousness which is 'aware of its own otherness and hence foregrounds the horizon of the past from its own'.

Anwendung (p.6)

Application: for Gadamer, it is the 'central problem of hermeneutics' that 'understanding always involves something like applying the text to be understood to the interpreter's present situation'.

Auslegungsgeschichte (p.17)

History of interpretation or exegesis-history: there is some agreement that this usually refers to the scholarly accounts – rabbinic, patristic, mediaeval and modern – in commentaries and similar studies. There is not the same consensus concerning what is the argument of this work, that this cannot be seen as a body of reception methodologically different from an operation of *Wirkungsgeschichte*. *Auslegungsgeshcichte*, hermeneutically, should be seen as one expression of *Wirkungsgeschichte* – one that valorizes a particular range of sources received within a particular tradition or traditions.

Erwartungshorizont (p.10)

Horizon of expectation: Jauss added this concept to Gadamer's analysis of 'horizons' (see below). Each generation of readers interacts with the text in terms of a different framework of expectations. The *Erwartungs-horizont*, built up from earlier encounters with texts, is 'varied, corrected, altered', or even 'just reproduced' in successive historical periods.

Gipfeldialog der Autoren (p.123)
One of two terms (the other is *Höhenkamm der Autoren*) that Jauss uses to describe the idea of a 'summit conference' or 'summit dialogue' of authors. See §6.2 for some advocates of this construct in histories of reception.

Höhenkamm der Autoren (p. 183)
See *Gipfeldialog der Autoren.*

Horizont (p.5)
Horizon: Gadamer uses the concept *Horizont*, following Heidegger, to refer to a person's involvement in tradition. The 'prejudices that we bring with us' constitute the 'horizon of a particular present' because these represent 'that beyond which it is impossible to see'. He also uses it of the encounter with the past, experienced when reading a transmitted historical text. This involves the projection of an historical 'horizon' that is different from the horizon of the present. This is how the interpreter becomes aware of the distinctiveness of their own horizons, as against those of the text. Gadamer characterises this operation as one of both tension and fusion (see *Horizontverschmelzung*, below.)

Horizontabhebung (p.10)
Differentiation of horizons (lit. 'withdrawal of horizons'): Jauss proposed that this term carries 'an active sense', in place of Gadamer's *Horizontverschmelzung* (see below) seen as carrying 'a passive sense'. This is a distinction some biblical commentators have found persuasive, but this work argues for a dialectic of text and reader in both terms.

Horizontverschmelzung (p.10)
The fusion of horizons: the coming together of the horizons of a particular present (the reader's), and the projection of a different historical horizon (of the text) is not a formation of a single horizon, a naïve assimilation of the present with the past, but it involves experience of tension between the text and the present. Neither the horizon of the present reader nor of the historically-situated text exists in isolation: Gadamer writes, 'the horizon of the present cannot be formed without the past', and understanding 'is always the fusion of these horizons

supposedly existing by themselves'; and Jauss writes, 'If the horizon of our present did not always already include the original horizon of the past, historical understanding would be impossible... It is the task of historical understanding to take both horizons into account through conscious effort'.

Rezeptionsgeschichte (p.9)

Reception history: this is often used in English as synonymous with a 'history of reception'. However, where it is associated with Jauss and Gadamer, it carries the idea of the historical nature of responding to literature, and the role of historical consciousness (see *wirkungs- geschichtliches Bewusstsein*, below).

Traditionary text (p.34)

This is used in the revised 2004 translation of *Truth and Method* to translate both *überlieferten Text* ('transmitted text') and also, sometimes, *Überlieferung* ('tradition', see below) when this represents the historical object (a text) received through a tradition of interpretation (though the translators also translate this as 'what comes down to us from the past').

Überlieferung (p.5)

Tradition: we are limited and qualified in various ways, set within various traditions, and so subject to prejudices and limited in our free- dom. What we bring to the process of interpretation are not merely our individual concerns but the issues that have developed within the historical tradition to which we belong. Our understanding of a 'tradi- tionary work' is conditioned by the way that text has previously been understood in a tradition of interpretation, and our prejudgments are part of its legacy. However, the interpreter is not subject to tradition, but participates in it. *Überlieferung* is characterised by Gadamer as an 'ongoing conversation' where the text and the reader are both subjects and participants in a 'dialogue'.

Vorurteil (p.3)

Prejudice or pre-judgment: Heidegger had argued that interpretation begins with a 'structure of pre-judgment', a projection of meaning that derives from the interpreter's own situation, and Gadamer argues that all understanding inevitably involves some *Vorurteil*. Anticipations or pre-understandings are the conditions of the possibility of historical knowledge.

Wirkungsgeschichte (p.2)

In the first English edition of *Truth and Method* (1975), *Wirkungs-geschichte* is translated as 'effective history' and in later editions as 'history of effect'. Translation of this key term in Gadamer is a vexed issue where it is not distinguished from the pre-Gadamerian use of the term (see §1.1.a), or is appropriated in a shorthand way by English authors, or who reify it as 'a history of effects' or 'a history of influence'. It is not a history, nor a method, nor a type of reception, but a principle – that alongside the apparent immediacy with which we encounter a text from the past, we need a consciousness that we are already affected by history: 'Understanding is, essentially, an historically-effected [*wirkungs-geschichtliches*] event'. Gadamer's translators never (I think) give it an indefinite article: it is 'history of effect' or 'the history of effect'. Perhaps it needs hyphenating: 'the history-of-effect principle'. *Wirkung* is 'effect' or 'event', and in Gadamer, the 'event' in question is *understanding,* which is, essentially, *wirkungsgeschichtliches*, affected by history and effective in history. The meaning emerges best in conjunction with *Bewusstsein*, consciousness (see below).

Wirkungsgeschichtliches Bewusstsein (p.8)

In the translations of *Truth and Method* this was first 'effective historical consciousness', then 'historically-effected consciousness', and some-times, and perhaps most helpfully, 'consciousness of being affected by history'. *Wirkungsgeschichtliches Bewusstsein* is primarily conscious-ness of the hermeneutical *situation*, which understands both that a text is effective in history, and that human understanding is itself effected, constructed, by history. Gadamer writes (*Truth and Method*, p.300), 'If we are trying to understand a historical phenomenon from the historical distance that is characteristic of our hermeneutical situation, we are always already affected by history. It determines in advance both what seems to us worth enquiring about and what will appear as an object of investigation'. It is readiness to receive a new perspective, both of a text and of oneself, that distinguishes 'historically-effected consciousness'.

Chapter 1

INTRODUCTION:
IMPULSES AND PARAMETERS OF THIS STUDY

This book examines reception-historical approaches in biblical interpretation: it is an attempt to match some recent, flourishing practices in biblical studies with the reception theory that is often claimed for it. Its hermeneutical focus is the reception theory of Hans-Georg Gadamer and of Hans-Robert Jauss, and its textual focus is the New Testament texts exhorting 'submission', 'be subject'. It addresses the character of reception history, its application to the Bible and its relationship to historical criticism and to Christian hermeneutics.

The emergence and growth of interest in reception-historical methods in biblical studies in the last two decades have resulted in a wide range of strategies of selection, arrangement and evaluation of the post-history of biblical texts. The variety of method and the different claims made for hermeneutical principles raise a number of questions, which some critics interpret as inadequate engagement with reception theory. This work assesses a range of contemporary claims about the reception theory of Gadamer and Jauss applied in biblical interpretation; and it uses a case study to evaluate these claims and practices, to illustrate them and to test them.

The case study and related concerns of New Testament theology and ethics constitute the second springboard for this investigation. My own practice examines reception of a group of New Testament texts, and poses a number of exegetical and hermeneutical questions. The Pauline exhortations to 'submit' are widely cited and applied in theological, ethical and cultural contexts, and here the post-history of these verses is used in an engagement with arguments made about reception history. The pertinence of this for the aims of this study is that this theme from the Pauline corpus problematises key factors in the hermeneutical and methodological debates: the relative interpretative weight given to historical-critical analysis, ecclesial tradition, cultural context and theological hermeneutics in the evolution of various interpretations. The case study contributes to a critical evaluation of the role of these factors in reception history of biblical texts.

Together the analysis of the reception theory, the evaluation of emerging methodologies and reflection on my own practice contribute to an advocacy of Gadamer's hermeneutics. His analysis of how we receive historical texts offers, I suggest, an integrity to the whole discipline of biblical studies – which threatens in many quarters to fragment[1] into rival methodologies relating to historical, cultural and theological interests.

1.1. Reception history: the terms in use

The attention currently given to the afterlife or post-history of biblical texts is potentially part of a paradigm revolution in a discipline experiencing contesting and disputed methods; but the terminology, like the practice, is not at all uniform. This may be endemic to the field in question: 'One of the most striking qualities of Gadamer's *magnum opus* is its awareness that the history of language used obstructs any move towards an absolute definition of terms'.[2] Moreover, the origins of the terms in Gadamer and Jauss are sometimes barely reflected in the use that is made of them, even when a terminological preference is declared. I am attempting to discover or construct a conceptual clarity within this fragmented discourse. In the next two sections, therefore, I offer an outline of the reception theories of Gadamer and Jauss, with a focus on those principles and elements that are used and contested in the discussion and practice in subsequent chapters. I offer a glossary of some of the recurring words within an index of 'key hermeneutical terms' at the back.

1.1.a. Gadamer and *Wirkungsgeschichte*
Hans-Georg Gadamer describes his investigation (1960) as asking '(to put it in Kantian terms): How is understanding possible?'[3] The task of hermeneutics is, Gadamer maintains, 'not to develop a procedure of understanding, but to clarify the conditions in which understanding takes place'.[4] *Wirkungsgeschichte*, a key term and distinctively used in his

---

1. See, for example, Markus Bockmuehl's assessment where 'the troubled fortunes of New Testament scholarship' are characterised by the disappearance of method and criteria, an 'infinite library', and increasing specialisation and sub-specialisation: *Seeing the Word: Refocusing New Testament Study* (Grand Rapids: Baker Academic, 2006), pp.27–61.
2. Mark Knight, '*Wirkungsgeschichte*, Reception History, Reception Theory', *JSNT* 33 (2010), pp.137–46 (137).
3. Hans-Georg Gadamer, *Truth and Method* (trans. J. Weinsheimer and D.G. Marshall; London/New York: Continuum, 2nd rev. English edn, 2004), p.xxvii.
4. Gadamer, *Truth and Method*, p.295.

philosophical hermeneutics, is not a definition of a method but an analysis of a principle that operates universally in every act of understanding and interpretation: alongside the apparent immediacy with which we encounter a text from the past, we need a consciousness that we are already affected by history. '*Understanding is, essentially, an historically-effected [wirkungsgeschichtliches] event*'.[5]

His work concerns both the nature of understanding and the social, relational dimension of communication. He identifies *Verstehen* [understanding] as the fundamental mode of human existence,[6] and stresses its close connection with *Verständigung* ['coming to an understanding' with someone].[7] Understanding is achieved through the 'dialogue' or 'conversation' of two parties: this process, and the analogy of reading a text as engaging in a dialogue, is foundational for Gadamer's hermeneutics. When we talk with someone, some of what they say is familiar to us and we get it straight away. Sometimes we think, 'I'm not sure what you mean', or 'I'm not sure I would put it that way', or 'Why are you seeing it like that?' There is a sort of negotiation process where we come to terms with what is familiar and what is different about the ways someone else looks at things. We get to a point where we can say, 'I think I see what you mean'. Understanding is achieved in a process of 'coming to an understanding' with our conversation partner – and something like this is the case when that conversation partner is an historical text.

Martin Heidegger had argued that interpretation begins with the *Vorstruktur des Verstehens* ['fore-structure of understanding' or 'structure of pre-judgment'], a projection of meaning that derives from the interpreter's own situation.[8] Drawing on this, Gadamer argues that 'all understanding inevitably involves some prejudice [*Vorurteil*]'[9] and anticipations or pre-understandings are the conditions of the possibility of historical knowledge. All human existence, 'even the freest', is limited and qualified in various ways, 'set within various traditions', and thus

---

5. Gadamer, *Truth and Method*, p.299 (emphasis his); and *Wahrheit und Methode: Grundzüge einer philosophischen Hermeneutik* [1960] (Tübingen: Mohr, 1972), p.283.

6. 'Whereas hermeneutics had previously been involved with exegesis, the psychology of understanding (Friedrich Schleiermacher), or methodology in the human sciences ... (Wilhelm Dilthey), Gadamer claims for hermeneutics a universal status': Robert C. Holub, *Reception Theory: A Critical Introduction* (London: Methuen, 1984), p.36.

7. Cf. Joel Weinsheimer and Donald G. Marshall, 'Translators' Preface', in Gadamer, *Truth and Method*, p.xvi.

8. Martin Heidegger, *Sein und Zeit* (Tübingen: Max Niemeyer, 2006), pp.142–47.

9. Gadamer, *Truth and Method*, p.272; *Wahrheit und Methode*, p.254.

'subject to prejudices and limited in...freedom'.[10] Therefore the 'prejudices of the individual, far more than his judgments, constitute the historical reality of his being'.[11] Gadamer attributes the discrediting of prejudice to the Enlightenment.[12]

This is a critique both of the claims of subjective experience (referred by Gadamer to Immanuel Kant's development of 'reflective judgment')[13] and of the positivist claims of nineteenth-century historicism (which applied empirical methods to texts and language). Hermeneutics is 'neither subjective nor objective'.[14] *Historical distance* between subject and object is a crucial factor in understanding. This is not merely the epistemological paradox that 'objective knowledge can be achieved only if there has been a certain historical distance' and when the subjective involvement of the observer is removed – '[i]n other words, when it is dead enough to have only historical interest'.[15] Rather, historical consciousness should 'make conscious the prejudices governing our own understanding so that the text, as another's meaning, can be isolated and valued on its own'.[16]

Gadamer also seeks to rehabilitate the ideas of 'authority' and 'tradition'. He denies that authority is antithetical to 'reason':

> the authority of persons is based ultimately, not on the subjection and abdication of reason, but on an act of acknowledgment and knowledge – the knowledge, namely, that the other is superior to oneself in judgment and insight and that for this reason his judgment takes precedence, i.e., it has priority over one's own.[17]

Similarly he denies that 'tradition' is antithetical to 'freedom': 'in tradition is constantly an element of freedom... Even the most genuine and pure tradition does not persist because of the inertia of what once existed. It needs to be affirmed, embraced, cultivated.'[18] The interpreter is not subject to tradition, though it conditions her/his 'anticipation' of the meaning to be discovered, but participates in it. Understanding is the 'interplay' between 'the movement of tradition' and 'the movement of the interpreter':

10. Gadamer, *Truth and Method*, p.277.
11. Gadamer, *Truth and Method*, p.278.
12. E.g. Gadamer, *Truth and Method*, p.274.
13. E.g. Gadamer, *Truth and Method*, p.28.
14. Gadamer, *Truth and Method*, p.293.
15. Gadamer, *Truth and Method*, p.297.
16. Gadamer, *Truth and Method*, p.298.
17. Gadamer, *Truth and Method*, p.281.
18. Gadamer, *Truth and Method*, p.282.

> The anticipation of meaning that governs our understanding of a text is not an act of subjectivity, but proceeds from the commonality that binds us to the tradition. But this commonality is constantly being formed in our relation to tradition. Tradition is not simply a permanent precondition; rather we produce it ourselves inasmuch as we understand, participate in the evolution of tradition and hence further determine it ourselves.[19]

Gadamer uses the concept 'horizon' [*Horizont*], a metaphor used by Heidegger. The 'prejudices that we bring with us' constitute the 'horizon of a particular present' because our prejudgments represent 'that beyond which it is impossible to see'.[20] This horizon can change, in a comparable way to the changing of the physical horizon as we move to different standpoints. Gadamer uses the idea to refer to a person's involvement in tradition. The horizon of the present is continually being formed because 'the encounter with the past and the understanding of the tradition from which we come' tests our prejudgments. In the act of understanding an historical text, there is a 'fusion' of two 'horizons': the coming together of the horizon of the reader's particular present and (a projection of) the different historical horizon of the text.[21] The fusion of horizons [*Horizontverschmelzung*][22] is not a formation of a single horizon, but it involves experience of tension between the text and the present. It is neither a psychological manoeuvre placing the reader in the past, nor a 'naïve assimilation' of the past with the present. In fact, neither the horizon of the present reader nor of the historically situated text exists in isolation: 'the horizon of the present cannot be formed without the past... [U]nderstanding is always the fusion of these horizons supposedly existing by themselves'.[23] The bringing together of two 'horizons' brings about an adjustment of competing pre-judgments.

The fusion achieved by this consciousness does not become 'solidified into the self-alienation of a past consciousness', but is 'one phase in the process of understanding'.[24] The text and the reader are both subjects and participants in a 'dialogue' – and the tradition [*Überlieferung*] is the 'ongoing conversation'.[25] This foundational analogy is used (in a later essay) for the *challenge* a text makes to a reader:

19.   Gadamer, *Truth and Method*, p.293.
20.   Gadamer, *Truth and Method*, pp.304–5.
21.   Gadamer, *Truth and Method*, p.303.
22.   E.g. Gadamer, *Wahrheit und Methode*, p.290.
23.   Gadamer, *Truth and Method*, p.305.
24.   Gadamer, *Truth and Method*, p.305.
25.   Cf. Weinsheimer and Marshall in *Truth and Method*, p.xvi.

> The understanding of a text has not begun at all as long as the text remains mute... When it does begin to speak...it does not simply speak its word, always the same in lifeless rigidity, but gives ever new answers to the person who questions it and poses ever new questions to him who answers it. To understand a text is to understand oneself in a kind of dialogue.[26]

This last principle of reflexive criticism, that understanding is as much about self-understanding as it is about understanding a text, is often not well represented in accounts of Gadamer or in practice that refers to *Wirkungsgeschichte*. I shall argue that it is peculiarly well-suited to theory and practice of biblical interpretation in Christian traditions.

We cannot presuppose that the meaning we can discover in a written tradition agrees with that which its author intended.[27] Interpretation, the explicit expression of understanding, is not directed towards an authorial 'meaning' but toward the claim that the text makes on the interpreter.[28] Gadamer develops R.G. Collingwood's argument that 'We can understand a text only when we have understood the question to which it is an answer'.[29] This reconstructed question cannot stand within its original horizon (constituted by the 'prejudices' of 'a particular present') but is now included in the horizon of the new reader. It is a 'hermeneutical necessity' always to go beyond mere reconstruction. '[T]he text must be understood as an answer to a real question'[30] – 'real', that is, from the reader's perspective. For Gadamer, this leads to the 'central problem of hermeneutics', which is 'application' [*Anwendung*]:[31] 'understanding always involves something like applying the text to be understood to the interpreter's present situation'.[32]

Gadamer specifically argues (in the 1967 essay cited above) that this is 'in every respect true' in the case of *biblical interpretation in Christian proclamation*. The reader does not understand the biblical text 'if it does not seem to speak directly to him'.[33] It is through the sermon, not in a theologian's exegetical commentary, that the understanding and

---

26. Hans-Georg Gadamer, *Philosophical Hermeneutics* (ed. and trans. D. Linge; Berkeley: University of California Press, 1977), p.57. 'On the Problem of Self-understanding' was first published as one of the essays in *Kleine Schriften* (Tübingen: Mohr, 1967).

27. Gadamer, *Truth and Method*, p.365.

28. Cf. Jack Mendelson, 'The Habermas–Gadamer Debate', *New German Critique* 18 (1979), pp.44–73 (56).

29. Gadamer, *Truth and Method*, p.363.

30. Gadamer, *Truth and Method*, p.367.

31. E.g. Gadamer, *Wahrheit und Methode*, p.290.

32. Gadamer, *Truth and Method*, pp.306–7.

33. Gadamer, *Philosophical Hermeneutics*, p.58.

interpretation of the text 'first receives its full reality'; and more than this the 'actual completion of understanding does not take place in the sermon as such, but rather in its reception as an appeal that is directed to each person who hears it'.[34]

The English translations of Gadamer's terms have evolved, but, revealingly, without real resolution and leading to some misappropriation. In the first English edition of *Truth and Method* (1975), 'effective history' was used for *Wirkungsgeschichte*, and in later editions this is 'history of effect'. The English translation of Ulrich Luz's commentary (see 1.c. below) gives 'history of influence';[35] and John Sawyer suggests 'impact history'.[36] However, many writers in English reify it as 'a history of influence' (with an indefinite article) or as 'a history of effects' (with an indefinite article, and a plural). This is indeed what it could describe in a tradition of scholarship *before* Gadamer, where it was 'generally regarded as a mere supplement to historical enquiry'.[37] The earlier tradition, as Robert Holub notes, was concerned with 'the examination of an author's influence on later generations, especially subsequent writers'.[38] Gadamer distinguishes his use from the earlier tradition: 'To this extent, history of effect is not new', but with the attention given in his hermeneutics to historical consciousness as a hermeneutical principle, 'this is a new demand'. Translations such as 'a history of effects' or 'a history of influence' overlook this key distinction: as such, they do not contribute to clarity in theoretical discussion, and have a widespread and unexamined influence on some practice (see §§1.1.c and 6.3). The editors' introduction to the *Encyclopedia of the Bible and its Reception* translates *Wirkungsgeschichte* as 'the study of effects', and David Parris translates it as 'the history of the impact of a text':[39] neither is referring the term in those places to Gadamer, so are not incorrect, but these are not adequate as translations of Gadamer's principle.[40]

34. Gadamer, *Philosophical Hermeneutics*, p.58.

35. Ulrich Luz, *Matthew 1–7: A Commentary* (Edinburgh: T. & T. Clark, 1989), and *Matthew 8–20* (Philadelphia: Fortress, 2001), e.g. p.11.

36. John F.A. Sawyer, 'The Role of Reception Theory, Reader-Response Criticism and/or Impact History in the Study of the Bible: Definition and Evaluation' (http://bbibcomm.net/files/sawyer2004.pdf, accessed 2 August 2012), p.1.

37. Gadamer, *Truth and Method*, p.299.

38. Holub, *Reception Theory*, p.xii.

39. Klauck *et al.*, 'The Project, Introduction', *EBR* (http://www.degruyter.com/staticfiles/content/dbsup/EBR_02_Introduction.pdf, accessed 2 September 2012); David Paul Parris, *Reception Theory and Biblical Hermeneutics* (Eugene: Pickwick, 2009), p.117.

40. The phrase 'history of effects' occurs in one of Jauss's own works in English: Hans-Robert Jauss, 'The Identity of the Poetic Text in the Changing Horizon of

Wirkungsgeschichte in Gadamer is not a history, nor a method, nor a type of reception, but a principle – that alongside the apparent immediacy with which we encounter a text from the past, we need a consciousness that we are already affected by history. Gadamer's translators never (I think) give it an indefinite article: it is 'history of effect' or 'the history of effect'. *Wirkung* is 'effect' or 'event', and in Gadamer, the 'event' in question is *understanding*, which is, essentially, *wirkungsgeschicht-liches*, affected by history and effective in history. *Wirkungsgeschichte* is the 'history-of-effect principle', and the meaning emerges best in conjunction with *Bewusstsein*, 'consciousness'.

The translation of *wirkungsgeschichtliches Bewusstsein*, was first 'effective historical consciousness', then 'historically effected consciousness', and sometimes (perhaps most helpfully, in the 2004 translation) 'consciousness of being affected by history'.[41] Gadamer's English translators comment on trying to 'capture' Gadamer's meaning in these phrases.[42] A number of commentators claim distinctions of 'active' and 'passive' operations in these and other terms,[43] but to do this is to miss the dialectic, the double operation of text and reader in Gadamer's 'fusion' of 'horizons'. Gadamer's hermeneutics is 'dialectic' in both the general meanings of the term, 'a tension between two opposite entities' and 'a logical enquiry into truth'; and it 'seeks not only to preserve (without overcoming) oppositional terms but also to reveal such a tension as productive of the very process of understanding'.[44] *Wirkungs-geschichtliches Bewusstsein* therefore is 'primarily consciousness of the hermeneutical *situation*',[45] which understands both that a text is effective in history, and that human understanding is itself effected, constructed, by history. Its hallmark is *the readiness to receive a new perspective both of a text and of oneself*, and to have one's expectation thwarted.[46]

Understanding', in *Reception Study: From Literary Theory to Cultural Studies* (ed. James L. Machor and Philip Goldstein; New York/London: Routledge, 2001), pp.7–28 (7). (The essay was first published in *Identity of the Literary Text*, 1985.)

41. E.g. Gadamer, *Truth and Method*, p.301.

42. Weinsheimer and Marshall, 'Translators' Preface', p.xv.

43. See, e.g., Luz and Boer, §1.1.c below.

44. Lauren Swayne Barthold, *Gadamer's Dialectical Hermeneutics* (Plymouth: Lexington, 2010), p.xiv. 'Dialectic' is a slippery term, and Gadamer distinguishes, through Part II of *Truth and Method*, between early Platonic, later Platonic, and Hegelian dialectic. Barthold offers a helpful distinction: 'The use of "dialectic" evokes Gadamer's desire to preserve an in-betweenness characteristic of Platonic dialectic and to refuse the overcoming suggestive of Hegelian dialectic'.

45. Gadamer, *Truth and Method*, p.301 (emphasis his).

46. Gadamer, *Truth and Method*, pp.363–71, esp. 371.

This brief account indicates a number of key factors – prejudice, authority, tradition, authorial intention, application and self-understanding – which will recur in the theoretical debates in chapters below, and in the sampling of reception of the case study. Gadamer's analysis will be further explored and critiqued there.

Gadamer's philosophical hermeneutics was invoked in the rise of reader-response theory in literary criticism, which similarly makes the reader an active participant in interpretation. It specifically provides the foundation for the reception aesthetic of Jauss and of what has come to be termed *Rezeptionsgeschichte* or reception history.

1.1.b. Jauss, *Rezeptionsaesthetik* and *Rezeptionsgeschichte*

The terms *Rezeptionsaesthetik* and *Rezeptionsgeschichte* are used in reception theory, a branch of literary theory with a root, not always acknowledged, in philosophical hermeneutics. These German terms, used by the Konstanz School of literary studies, have a parallel in the anglophone term, 'Reader-Response Criticism', where the dialectic between text and reader remains key. However, the importance of *historical consciousness* distinguishes this reception theory from much Reader-Response theory,[47] and much of the current use of 'reception history' or *Rezeptionsgeschichte* makes reference to the work of Hans-Robert Jauss, a student of Gadamer. Indeed, a significant body of theory and practice in biblical interpretation expresses, explicitly or implicitly, a preference for Jauss over Gadamer (see §6.2).

Jauss was defending the place of mediaeval studies during a transformation of the German education system, and was concerned to establish *Literaturgeschichte* as the foundation discipline for literary studies (1967).[48] He was concerned with the relation between literature or art and 'pragmatic history', and to approach texts as both a result of social forces and the cause of social transformation.[49] His approach includes inserting an individual work into its 'literary series',[50] comparing the responses of readers of different periods. 'The meaning of a work...is extracted only during the progressive process of its reception',[51] through successive

47. See, e.g., Hans-Robert Jauss and Elizabeth Benzinger, 'Literary History as a Challenge to Literary Theory', *New Literary History* 2.1 (1970), pp.7–37.

48. His inaugural lecture in 1967 was 'Literaturgeschichte als Provokation für die Literaturwissenschaft'; this work was later published in Hans-Robert Jauss, *Toward an Aesthetic of Reception* (trans. T. Bahti; Brighton: Harvester Press, 1982), pp.3–45.

49. Jauss, *Aesthetic of Reception*, pp.45, 74.

50. Jauss, *Aesthetic of Reception*, p.32.

51. Jauss, *Aesthetic of Reception*, p.59.

engagements with generations of readers and their 'actualisations' of the potential meaning of the text. The model of a series of artistic instantiations as an illustration of 'the movement of tradition' derives from Gadamer, for whom the production of a play or a musical performance is not 'a mere variety of conceptions; rather, by constantly following models and developing them, a tradition is formed with which every new attempt must come to terms'.[52]

To Gadamer's analysis of 'horizons', Jauss introduced the concept of *Erwartungshorizont* ['horizon of expectation'] which varies from one historical period to another: the same text can be valued in one period and rejected in another. Each generation (or 'audience') interacts with the text in terms of a different framework of expectations. This does not exist as a set of openly stated or recorded propositions.[53] The horizon of expectation built up from earlier encounters with texts may become 'varied, corrected, altered', or even 'just reproduced'. Reception can result in a 'change of horizons'.[54] He later developed the concept of *Horizontabhebung* ['differentiation (*lit.* "withdrawal") of horizons']. He proposed that this carried 'an active sense', in place of Gadamer's *Horizontverschmelzung* ['fusion of horizons'], seen as carrying 'a passive sense'.[55] This is a distinction some biblical commentators have found persuasive, but which may be overstated and can be countered (see §§2.3 and 6.4).

To ground 'literary history' methodologically in a new way, Jauss proposed seven 'theses' (some of which have specifically been taken up by recent biblical interpreters).[56] The first thesis endorses Gadamer's rejection of historical objectivism: the 'historicity of literature' rests on the experience of a literary work by its readers. A literary work is not 'an object that stands by itself and that offers the same view to each reader in each period... The coherence of literature as an event is primarily mediated in the horizon of expectations of...contemporary and later readers.'[57]

---

52. Gadamer, *Truth and Method*, p.117.
53. Cf. de Man in Jauss, *Aesthetic of Reception*, p.xi.
54. Jauss, *Aesthetic of Reception*, p.23.
55. Hans-Robert Jauss, *Die Theorie der Rezeption: Rückschau auf ihre unerkannte Vorgeschichte: Ansprache anlässlich der Emeritierung von Hans-Robert Jauss am 11 Februar 1987* (Konstanz: Universitätsverlag Konstanz, 1987), p.17 (translation mine).
56. E.g. Parris, *Reception Theory*, pp.129–47.
57. Jauss, *Aesthetic of Reception*, pp.20–22.

The second calls for the reception and influence of a work to be described in relation to pre-understandings of the work and its genre. The author's anticipation of particular responses from the readership, and the horizon of expectation of the reader, derive in part from earlier works, and the work can subvert these expectations.[58] The third thesis develops this idea of a shifting horizon of expectation. Jauss uses the example of the changing reception of Flaubert's *Madame Bovary*, from being pilloried as an immoral book, on its publication in 1857, to a broad appreciation of it as marking a turning point in the history of the novel.[59] Anthony Thiselton applies this thesis to biblical interpretation, where 'the goal is also to move to new, formative horizons, which will correct and surpass former perceptions'.[60]

Jauss's fourth thesis focuses on the differences between the former and the current understanding of a work, because '[t]he reconstruction of the horizon of expectations in the face of which a work was created and received in the past enables one...to pose the questions that the text gave an answer to'.[61] He develops this in other writings: the reconstruction of *Wirkungsbedingungen* ['effective conditions'] for the first or early reception of a text always has a hypothetical status, and it does not determine the 'original meaning'.[62] The otherness [*Alterität*] of the past can only be apprehended by the interpreter being able to separate what is different, 'alien', from their own 'horizon'.[63] These elements are significant in my argument about the aims of historical-critical methods in biblical interpretation (Chapter 2).

His fifth thesis critiques and develops the Formalist theory of 'literary evolution' to focus on reading a text as part of a 'literary series'. Historical changes also occur within a system or series in the field of literature. A new work in an historical series may provide a 'solution' to the 'problem left behind' by an older text. The problem and solution may not have been recognisable in the first work, but the interpreter reads the old in the light of the new and asks 'to what degree this new element is

---

58. Jauss, *Aesthetic of Reception*, pp.23–34.

59. Jauss, *Aesthetic of Reception*, pp.27–28.

60. Anthony C. Thiselton, 'Reception Theory, H.R. Jauss, and the Formative Power of Scripture', *SJT* 65 (2012), pp.289–308 (293). The idea that later reception 'corrects' earlier reception is examined later, especially in §§6.1 and 9.2.b.

61. Jauss, *Aesthetic of Reception*, p.28.

62. See, e.g., Hans-Robert Jauss, *Alterität und Modernität der Mittelalterlichen Literatur: Gesammelte Aufsätze 1956–1976* (Munchen: Wilhelm Fink Verlag, 1977), p.129.

63. Jauss, 'Identity of the Poetic Text', pp.7–8.

already perceptible in the historical instant of its emergence'.[64] Parris develops this idea in an application of 'paradigm shifts' in biblical interpretation: new solutions to an epistemological crisis which answer questions the previous paradigm could not.[65]

The sixth thesis develops the strategy of identifying the 'epoch-making' moments in a literary series: a synchronic study of works contemporaneous with a particular work in the series, 'to make the literary horizon of a specific historical moment comprehensible'.[66] This is to be done within the framework of the diachronic series, with synchronic 'cross-sections' (see §2.3). The selection of these historical moments is neither by 'statistics nor the subjective wilfulness of the literary historian' but by the 'history of influence' [*Wirkungsgeschichte*] 'which results from the event' and 'from the perspective of the present'.[67] The interpretation of this aspect is central to my own argument (see, e.g., §9.3.b).

The seventh and final thesis of Jauss's inaugural work concerns the social function of literature, which properly occurs when the literary experience of a reader meets the horizon of expectation of their 'lived praxis'. It is a 'special history' with a challenge to 'general history':[68]

> The gap between literature and history, between aesthetic and historical knowledge, can be bridged, if literary history does not simply describe the process of general history in the reflection of its works one more time, but rather when it discovers in the course of 'literary evolution' that properly socially-formative function that belongs to literature as it competes with other arts and social forces in the emancipation of mankind from its natural, religious and social bonds.[69]

Texts, as works of art, are 'socially formative' and even 'emancipatory',[70] and it is through the reader that the purpose of the text is made effective. This last aspect is problematised by my case study, which is of texts that are explicitly hortatory and socially formative (discussed in §7.5).

Subsequently, Jauss developed three 'steps' of the hermeneutic process: understanding [*intellegere*], interpretation [*interpretare*], and application

---

64. Jauss, *Aesthetic of Reception*, p.35.
65. Parris, *Reception Theory*, p.190 (discussed in §6.2).
66. Jauss, *Aesthetic of Reception*, pp.36 and 37.
67. Jauss, *Aesthetic of Reception*, p.39.
68. Jauss, *Aesthetic of Reception*, p.39.
69. Jauss, *Aesthetic of Reception*, p.45.
70. An idea Jauss repeats later in 'Art History and Pragmatic History' in *Aesthetic of Reception*, p.74.

[*applicare*][71] (which we shall revisit in §2.4). The perceived practicality of aspects of Jauss's analysis, over against Gadamer's eschewal of describing his own work as a 'method', contributes to some of the differences in hermeneutical theory and practice among recent biblical interpreters. There are particular differences, which I hope to clarify, between those who see Jauss as adding something methodological and necessary for biblical interpretation which is not present in Gadamer (e.g. Parris: 'We must understand Gadamer as a prelude to Jauss')[72] and those (with whom I stand) who do not. Gadamer, indeed, sought to discredit the idea that any one 'method' could reveal the 'truth' of a text.[73] Jauss's own theoretical outlines, in fact, do not provide a consistent methodological pattern for Jauss himself;[74] and Gadamer's critique of Jauss was that he did not develop his theory in detail, but in particular that 'he never really ventured very far into the philosophical dimension'.[75]

1.1.c. Gadamer, Jauss and recent biblical interpretation

I have chosen to use 'reception history' (in the title and body of this book) as the portmanteau term which has gained currency in anglophone biblical studies – though this is a really a very recent phenomenon.[76] Different parts of my argument will consider distinctions between Gadamer and Jauss.

There is a considerable variety of method practised today and a range of different claims are made concerning hermeneutical principles. Some critics diagnose an inadequate engagement with Gadamer, Jauss and other reception theory: so Robin Parry observes, 'The world of biblical

71. Jauss, *Aesthetic of Reception*, p.139.

72. Parris, *Reception Theory*, p.2 (see §6.2).

73. 'The "and" in Gadamer's title [*Truth and Method*]...should be read...in its disjunctive sense': Holub, *Reception Theory*, p.36.

74. His accounts of the reception history of particular works are differently conceived: e.g. *The Book of Jonah: A Paradigm of the 'Hermeneutics of Strangeness'* (Minneapolis: University of Minnesota, 1987), and Baudelaire's *Fleurs du Mal* (*Aesthetic of Reception*, pp.170–82).

75. Hans-Georg Gadamer, *Gadamer in Conversation: Reflections and Commentary* (ed. and trans. Richard E. Palmer; New Haven: Yale University Press, 2001), p.63.

76. It is not, for example, included in any of these: R.J. Coggins and J.L. Houlden (eds.), *A Dictionary of Biblical Interpretation* (London: SCM, 1990); George Aichele and Fred W. Burnett (eds.), *The Postmodern Bible* (New Haven: Yale University Press, 1995); John Barton (ed.), *The Cambridge Companion to Biblical Interpretation* (Cambridge: Cambridge University Press, 1998); John H. Hayes (ed.), *Dictionary of Biblical Interpretation* (2 vols.; Nashville: Abingdon, 1999).

studies is now filled with many excellent books and articles on the reception history of various texts and motifs. However, what is usually lacking amongst biblical scholars is a clear grasp of the hermeneutical theory which underpins and justifies such studies'.[77] Conversely, Christopher Rowland observes that the theoretical literature on reception history provides limited assistance in determining the content of a compilation-history of reception or of evaluating it as a method of interpreting biblical texts.[78] Indeed, while works on reception theory and biblical interpretation have been relatively few, since 1990 there has been a 'veritable deluge' of *practice*:[79] studies, variously constructed, of the afterlives of biblical texts.[80] These include three huge systematic enterprises designed (variously) to address the reception through history of the whole Bible: the Blackwell Bible Commentaries, the *Evangelisch-Katholischer Kommentar* and the *Encyclopedia of the Bible and its Reception*.[81]

A key work that has promoted the practice of *Wirkungsgeschichte* in New Testament studies[82] is Luz's commentary on Matthew (1985–2002) in the *Evangelisch-Katholischer Kommentar* series. This makes a challenge concerning the *incompleteness* of interpretation by historical exegesis: 'One does not yet understand what the subject matter of the

77. Robin Parry, Review of David Paul Parris, *Reception Theory and Biblical Hermeneutics* (Eugene: Pickwick, 2009) (https://wipfandstock.com/store/Reception_Theory_and_Biblical_Hermeneutics, accessed 28 March 2012).

78. Christopher Rowland, 'A Pragmatic Approach to *Wirkungsgeschichte*: Reflections on the Blackwell Bible Commentary Series and on the Writing of its Commentary on the Apocalypse' [2004] (http://bbibcomm.net/downloads/rowland2004.pdf, accessed 7 April 2012), p.1.

79. Sawyer, 'Role of Reception History', p.11.

80. E.g. the different constructions in Yvonne Sherwood, *A Biblical Text and its Afterlives: The Survival of Jonah in Western Culture* (Cambridge: Cambridge University Press, 2000), and Judith L. Kovacs, *1 Corinthians: Interpreted by Early Christian Commentators* (Grand Rapids: Eerdmans, 2005).

81. J.F.A. Sawyer, J.L. Kovacs and C.C. Rowland (eds.), *Blackwell Bible Commentaries* (Oxford: Blackwell, from 2003); Joachim Gnilka *et al.* (eds.), *Evangelisch-Katholischer Kommentar zum Neuen Testament* (Düsseldorf/Zurich: Benziger, from 1978); Hans-Josef Klauck *et al.* (eds.), *Encyclopedia of the Bible and its Reception* (Berlin/New York: W. de Gruyter, 2009–).

82. Brevard Childs's programme of canonical reading preceded this, but in spite of some key similarities, he does not refer to Gadamer or Jauss. Childs argues for the recognition of historically conditioned readers, the hermeneutical task as 'interaction between text and reader' and 'a dialectical relationship…between the past and the present': *The New Testament as Canon: An Introduction* (London: SCM Press, 1984), p.40.

text *means* if one only understands what it *has meant*.[83] Luz understands *Wirkungsgeschichte* as a synonym of *Rezeptionsgeschichte*, but prefers the former term because of Gadamer's use, and also because the 'term "reception history" is formulated from the standpoint of the receivers and the term "history of effects" [*sic*, a plural] from the stand point of the original events or texts'.[84] This distinction is made by other authors: for example, Roland Boer claims (erroneously) to find the distinction in *Wahrheit und Methode* that *Rezeptionsgeschichte* marks 'the active task of interpreting, appropriating, and applying a text', while *Wirkungs-geschichte* designates 'a more passive and unwitting effect of the text on society and culture'.[85] Such distinctions reflect a curious judgment which is not (here) based on *method*: both *Wirkungsgeschichte* and *Rezeptions-geschichte* insist on a *dialectic*, a bi-directional operation between text and reader, neither of which is passive to the impulses of the other.

There is an emerging critique of some practices of biblical interpretation labelled 'reception history' or *Wirkungsgeschichte*, questioning their conformity with Gadamer's hermeneutics. For example, Mark Knight notes a substantial tension between Gadamer's clarification of 'the conditions in which understanding takes place'[86] and 'the very idea' of compilation histories modelled on Gadamer's 'history of influence';[87] and Luz, in a review of *The Oxford Handbook of Reception History*, suggests that Gadamer's 'interest was not the development of a new ancillary discipline called "history of effects" or "reception history"'.[88] As I suggested above (§1.1.a), the translation, 'history of effects', is part of the problem – which plays a role in the practices, and in the critique or defence of them – where Gadamer's distinctive use of *Wirkungs-geschichte*, the principle of history-of-effect, is not distinguished from 'a history of effects'. Where such terms or such practice make an equation of Gadamer's theory of understanding with a compilation of reception or 'effects', they contradict Gadamer, for whom 'historically-effected consciousness is something other than inquiry into…the trace a work

83. Luz, *Matthew 1–7*, p.98.

84. Ulrich Luz, 'The Contribution of Reception History', in *The Nature of New Testament Theology: Essays in Honour of Robert Morgan* (ed. C. Rowland and C. Tuckett; Oxford: Blackwell, 2006), pp.123–34 (124).

85. Roland Boer, 'Against "Reception History"' [May 2011] (http://www.bibleinterp.com/opeds/boe358008.shtml, accessed 3 July 2012).

86. E.g. Gadamer, *Truth and Method*, p.295 (cited above, §1.1.a).

87. Knight, '*Wirkungsgeschichte*', p.143.

88. Ulrich Luz, Review of *The Oxford Handbook of the Reception History of the Bible*, *JTS* 63.1 (2012), pp.273–76 (274).

leaves behind'.[89] (I am conscious of the irony of making this observation within a series bearing the title 'Scriptural Traces'.) Nor is Heikki Räisänen's distinction between 'effect' and 'use' available in Gadamer's hermeneutics.[90]

A similar slippage can occur with 'reception history' (meaning reception-historical approach to interpretation) and 'a history of reception' (meaning a compilation of reception, or a literary series). Here, however, there is more of a case to be made from Jauss's own account, and I shall discuss and demonstrate reception in a Jaussian construction of a literary series (Chapters 6, 7 and 8).

While I hope to clarify what is at stake in these distinctions, my own emphasis is not between what interpretation is and is not to be called *Wirkungsgeschichte*,[91] because, for Gadamer this is not one method among competing ones but is the way any transmitted text is read: it is not a type of reading, it is the very nature of reading. He describes the way we understand, and the key operation of historical consciousness in the way we understand transmitted texts. I shall, however, be identifying some practices as parts or 'phases' of a fuller, reflexive process that Gadamer describes, and I shall also consider differences in particular practices which refer themselves to a Jaussian method rather than to Gadamer's hermeneutics.

The practitioners may also have differing views on how radical a shift the new paradigm, or merely new fashion, of biblical interpretation will bring. The first commentary of the Blackwell series states that this starts from the assumption 'that what people believe the Bible means is as interesting and important as what it originally meant'.[92] This recognises that 'original meanings' might have value and validity (later reception is '*as* interesting and important'), but makes a challenge based on the limitation or incompleteness perceived in historical exegesis, the search for the meaning accessible to the first readers, sometimes equated with

89. Gadamer, *Truth and Method*, p.336.
90. Heikki Räisänen, *Challenge to Biblical Interpretation, Essays 1991–2001* (Leiden: Brill, 2001), p.270.
91. A different analysis is offered in a recent thesis by Richard Kueh, 'Reception History and the Hermeneutics of *Wirkungsgeschichte*: Critiquing the Use of Gadamerian Hermeneutics in Biblical Reception History' (unpublished doctoral dissertation, University of Cambridge, 2012): Kueh concludes that what is undertaken by biblical scholars 'must be understood' as *Rezeptionsgeschichte* and not *Wirkungsgeschichte*.
92. John Sawyer, Christopher Rowland and Judith Kovacs, 'Series Editors' Preface', in Judith Kovacs and Christopher Rowland, *Revelation Through the Centuries* (Oxford: Blackwell, 2004), p.xiii.

meaning 'intended' by the author.[93] Reflecting on recent publishing practice, Mark Knight identifies the collective impact of *Wirkungsgeschichte* and reception history as raising 'questions about the historical-critical method that continues to dominate NT studies';[94] and John Lyons suggests a terminological shift, *relabeling* historical-critical methodologies as 'reception history', which could lead to a modification of the historical critic's self-understanding, adjusting any perception or assertion that they simply 'seek historical answers', or even are 'in possession of the truth'.[95] This contested area is a key element in my own argument.

Another disputed term relating to reception history of biblical texts is *Auslegungsgeschichte* ['history of interpretation' or 'exegesis-history']. Luz, for example, wishes to restrict *Auslegungsgeschichte* to reception that 'occurs in the medium of language and has the aspect of a direct interpretation', a 'more restricted sphere' than *Wirkungsgeschichte*.[96] For him the body of theological accounts, such as commentaries, falls under the category of history of interpretation. Other parts of the 'legacy of the Church', hymns, prayers, art, confession, can be called *Wirkungsgeschichte* (translated as 'history of influence').[97] Among recent commentators on Paul, Wolfgang Schrage uses the phrase '*Auslegungs- und Wirkungs-geschichte*'.[98] These are distinctions a number of people want to make, and there is some agreement on 'history of interpretation' (or *Auslegungsgeschichte*) as the scholarly accounts from different historical periods in commentaries and similar studies. I shall argue that the terms do not represent a *methodological* distinction in Gadamer's hermeneutics (especially in §6.2.a).

A key challenge concerning a selection of reception in a literary series – and the nature of the 'legacy', and the 'tradition' of interpretation – has been developed most fully by David Parris. This is a trajectory

93. Limitations of historical-critical approaches are discussed in Chapter 2. The construct of 'authorial intention' in relation to Gadamer's hermeneutics is discussed in §9.2.

94. Knight, '*Wirkungsgeschichte*', p.137.

95. William John Lyons, 'Hope for a Troubled Discipline? Contributions to New Testament Studies from Reception History', *JSNT* 33 (2010), pp.207–20 (210).

96. Ulrich Luz, 'Wirkungsgeschichtliche Hermeneutik und kirchliche Auslegung der Schrift', in *Die prägende Kraft der Texte. Hermeneutik und Wirkungsgeschichte des Neuen Testaments: Ein Symposium zu Ehren von Ulrich Luz* (ed. M. Mayordomo-Marín; Stuttgart: Katholisches Bibelwerk, 2005), pp.15–37 (18) (translation mine).

97. Luz, *Matthew 1–7*, p.98, and *Matthew 8–20*, e.g. p.11.

98. Wolfgang Schrage, *Der erste Brief an die Korinther*, vol. 1 (Zurich: Neukirchener Verlag, 1991), e.g. pp.163–65.

that may be traced from Jauss through Luz (selecting 'typological' representations)[99] and Thiselton (charting 'continuities and discontinuities of interpretation with specific traditions')[100] to Parris (focusing on 'paradigm shifts' and a 'summit dialogue' of authors for defining moments of a tradition's contours)[101] and to other practitioners, such as John Riches (valorizing 'principal commentators' and their 'dialogue').[102]

Another contested matter in recent practice concerns (like Luz's distinction of *Auslegungsgeschichte*) the medium and location of reception. This is the claim that *Wirkungsgeschichte* not only contests the idea that exegesis should be 'confined to written explication of texts or to the views of a few academic exegetes' but it 'acknowledges literature, art, music and actualizations of the text as modes of exegesis just as important as the conventional explanatory writing of Judaism and Christian theology'.[103] This offers a particular challenge to the 'summit dialogue' of Parris and others; and both sets of claims raise the question: *which* realizations of a biblical text should be selected and valorized? – whether as reception that shapes the 'pre-understandings' of subsequent generations of interpreters, or that exhibits 'particular influence in theology in the history of the daily life of the church, or more broadly in the history of ideas'.[104]

The agenda offered by Jauss focuses on 'trajectories' of interpretation that legitimate 'possibilities of understanding, imitation, transformation, and continuation'.[105] However, the selection of reception involves categorical and value judgments about any one reader's tradition and their value within or in relation to a 'canon of exemplary commentators'.[106] Gadamer identifies the *conditions of understanding* a text in the *'traditions' to which readers belong*.[107] The role of 'tradition' in his hermeneutics, neglected in much practice and countered in some theory, is a core part of the examination undertaken here. *Theological agendas* in

---

99. Luz, *Matthew 1–7*, p.96.

100. Thiselton, *First Corinthians*, p.196.

101. Parris, *Reception Theory*, pp.170–202 and 216–22.

102. John Riches, *Galatians Through the Centuries* (Oxford: Blackwell, 2008), pp.11 and 2, respectively.

103. Jonathan Roberts and Christopher Rowland, 'Introduction', *JSNT* 33 (2010), pp.131–36 (132).

104. Thiselton, *First Corinthians*, p.196.

105. Hans-Robert Jauss, *Question and Answer: Forms of Dialogic Understanding* [1982] (trans. M. Hays; Minneapolis: University of Minnesota Press, 1989), pp.201–2.

106. Parris, *Reception Theory*, p.217.

107. Gadamer, *Truth and Method*, pp.278–85.

Christian interpretation of scripture are both problematised and ignored in examples of current discussion and practice: my own case study offers a focus for asking questions about the theology of the text and the reader. Robert Morgan suggests that the relevance of questions of theological interpretation of scripture to the 'new discipline' of reception history 'lies in its desire to understand what is going on in Christian reception of the Bible'.[108]

My aim in this work is to evaluate some of these contested terms, claims and practice in relation to the hermeneutics of Gadamer and Jauss, in three stages outlined below in §1.3. Alongside the hermeneutical analyses of Gadamer and Jauss, the second constraint and the second direction of investigation and evaluation are provided by the case study.

1.2. The case study

The case-study texts are a nexus of verses, widely cited and applied in theological, ethical and cultural contexts: the Pauline exhortations to 'submit'. I first undertook investigation of the post-history of these verses without a framework provided by the hermeneutical strategies indicated in this introductory chapter as contested claims and practice. This was partly motivated by an open-ended enquiry, to gain some understanding of a contemporary trend in biblical interpretation by means of my own practice. It was also motivated by a particular theological prejudgment[109] concerning Paul's teaching and the ethics of Christian subordination – a *theologia crucis*.[110] It is manifest that reception of these exhortations in history, and in a continuing legacy, does not reflect a uniform theological perspective, so this was from the beginning an enquiry in theological hermeneutics. The experience of discovering a range of locations and applications of these texts focused my questions about other practice and the implicit or explicit criteria operating in selecting and valorising reception of biblical texts. This drove me to a re-examination of Gadamer and Jauss, alongside recent

---

108. Robert Morgan, '*Sachkritik* in Reception History', *JSNT* 33 (2010), pp.175–90 (189).

109. See the role of 'prejudice' in Gadamer (above, §1.1.a).

110. See §10.5. In brief, my prejudgment concerns Paul's characterisation of the sacrificial death of Christ; for example, 'God chose what is weak in the world to shame the strong' (1 Cor. 1.27) as a radical transformation in his ethics of human relationships from the traditional structures of lordship to one where the superordinate 'strong' gives way to the subordinate 'weak', because the latter is a sister or brother 'for whom Christ died' (1 Cor. 8.11).

publications discussing the application of *Wirkungsgeschichte* and *Rezeptionsgeschichte* in biblical interpretation.[111]

The agenda that emerged (see §1.3 below) derives from key areas of contestation in recent publication and practice, and these are illustrated and tested by my own practice. My choice to explore the reception of paraenetic texts (rather than, say, narrative ones), and of a group of texts (rather than a single text), and of texts applied repeatedly in law, literature and doctrine, has proved to offer some clarity and some problematising of other claims and practice. (See particularly the case-study evaluations, at the ends of Chapters 4, 5, 7, 8 and 10.) Reception from my case study is therefore selected and arranged to evaluate the hermeneutical methods under discussion, which are claimed or demonstrated in practices of biblical interpretation referring themselves to the hermeneutics of Gadamer and Jauss.

1.2.a. The texts

The texts chosen are those with a paraenetic use of ὑποτάσσειν. Paul (and the deutero-Pauline tradition) uses it in exhortation relating to civil authorities, marriage partners and fellow Christians.[112] The principal texts used are these:

Rom. 13.1:   Let every person be subject to [ὑποτασσέσθω] the governing authorities.

Col. 3.18:   Wives, be subject to [ὑποτάσσεσθε] your husbands, as is fitting in the Lord.

Eph. 5.21-22:   Be subject to [Ὑποασσόμενοι] one another out of reverence for Christ. Wives, be subject [...][113] to your husbands as you are to the Lord.

---

111. E.g. Parris, *Reception Theory*; and the contributors to *JSNT* 33 (2010).

112. I have had to omit for the most part the subordination paraenesis relating to children and the young, and to servants and slaves. This does occasionally appear in illustrations from my sample where governance of the state is compared with household order, and where authority relating to servants or slaves is compared or contrasted with that relating to wives or women.

113. This clause in Greek must depend on the verb in the preceding clause if we follow the reading found in some significant early witnesses (including P46, B and Clement). The inclusion of ὑποτάσσεσθε or ὑποτασσέσθωσαν in other traditions is often judged to be best explained as scribal additions: see, e.g., Andrew Lincoln, *Ephesians* (Nashville: Word Books, 1990), p.351. The Vulgate gives *subiecti* in 5.21 and *subditae sint* in 5.22 (see §4.1). A tradition of English translation repeats the same verb chosen for the previous verse: either 'be subject' or 'submit'.

However, a persistent hermeneutical principle operates in patristic and mediaeval interpretation (and beyond) of a canonical univocality, where 'exegesis [is] slanted by the assumption that the scriptures formed a unity'.[114] This means that reception may well be not of a single text but of a number of texts which significant portions of readers and users have read collectively or in some relationship. There are particular canonical, and theological, *pre-understandings* at stake for some of the reception.

Consequently, the reception of the paraenesis to be subject to governing authorities may reference explicitly or implicitly, in addition to Romans 13, these two texts:

Tit. 3.1:   Remind them to be subject to [ὑποτάσσεσθαι] rulers and authorities, to be obedient, to be ready for every good work,

1 Pet. 2.13-14:   For the Lord's sake accept the authority [ὑποτάγητε] of every human institution [*or* creature, κτίσει], whether of the emperor as supreme, or of governors, as sent by him to punish those who do wrong and to praise those who do right.

The paraenesis to women or wives to be subject to men or to their husbands may reference, in addition to Col. 3.18 and Eph. 5.22, explicitly or implicitly, these texts:

1 Pet. 3.1:   Wives, in the same way, accept the authority [ὑποτασσόμεναι] of your husbands.

1 Cor. 14.34:   [W]omen should be silent in the churches. For they are not permitted to speak, but should be subordinate [ὑποτασσέσθωσαν].

1 Tim. 2.11:   Let a woman learn in silence with full submission [ὑποταγῇ].

Tit. 2.5:   …to be self-controlled, chaste, good managers of the household, kind, being submissive to [ὑποτασσομένας] their husbands, so that the word of God may not be discredited.

In the paraenesis to a mutual or reciprocal subordination (Eph. 5.21) another ὑποτάσσειν text is rarely drawn on:

1 Cor. 16.15–16:   They have devoted themselves to the service [εἰς διακονίαν… ἔταξαν ἑαυτούς] of the saints; I urge you to put yourselves at the service of [ὑποτάσσησθε] such people, and of everyone who works and toils with them.

---

114. Frances M. Young, *Biblical Exegesis and the Formation of Christian Culture* (Cambridge: Cambridge University Press, 1997), p.7.

However, it is particularly concerning this aspect of the paraenesis, *mutual* submission, that reception may link submission of believers to God in Christ with christological dimensions of (indicative use of) ὑποτάσσειν drawn from this text:[115]

> 1 Cor. 15.28:   When all things are subjected to [ὑποταγῇ] him, then the Son himself will also be subjected to [ὑποταγήσεται] the one who put all things in subjection [ὑποτάξαντι] under him, so that God may be all in all.

There are other New Testament texts that use the verb ὑποτάσσειν or the noun [ἡ] ὑποταγή. The relation of all of these to the three principal texts of the case study is considered within the semantic investigation of Chapter 4.

1.2.b. Their reception
Pauline texts have been sites of contestation in their interpretation and application in many periods of Christian history in Church and academy. So Harnack (1904) characterised Paul as 'a perennial reformer who continues in many and various ways to confront his successors';[116] Furnish (1994) suggests that 'understanding Paul turns out to be less a matter of trying to put him in his place than of engaging his thought, and considering how it may challenge ours and illumine the place where we are'.[117] Within this history of influence, the paraenetic texts of my case study have a formative and particularly diverse post-history. They have had a significant role in constructing, supporting or challenging social and political structures and attitudes in two millennia: for example, on the authority of the state, authority in the Church, the conduct of marriage and gender-relations, and institutions of slavery and roles of servants and workers.

Moreover, the verses are paraenetic—that is, *perlocutionary* utterances.[118] A perlocution is a speech act viewed in terms of its intention

115. Discussed in §§4.2 and 10.3.
116. This is William Baird's summary of Harnack's account of Paul's legacy, which is found in (e.g.) Adolf von Harnack, *What Is Christianity?* (trans. T.B. Saunders; New York: Harper, 1957), pp.178–92; W. Baird, 'The Fate of Paul in Nineteenth Century Liberalism', in *Theology and Ethics in Paul and his Interpreters: Essays in Honour of Victor Paul Furnish* (ed. E.H. Lovering and J.L. Sumney; Nashville: Abingdon, 1996), pp.254–74 (274).
117. Victor P. Furnish, 'On Putting Paul in his Place', *JBL* 113 (1994), pp.3–17 (17).
118. One of the terms and definitions of Searle's speech-act model: John Rogers Searle, *Speech Acts: An Essay in the Philosophy of Language* (Cambridge: Cambridge University Press, 1969), p.25.

and consequence; a locution that gets the correspondent to do something, or realise something. Paraenesis *intends* interaction with the receiver, and attempts to effect a change in the behaviour of the reader. These texts therefore provoke attention to hermeneutical concepts of reader and implied reader, and to the much disputed hermeneutical concept of the 'intention of the author'.

There is another feature of the texts that illustrates and problematises reception history in biblical interpretation: they are open to contested *theological* interpretation. On the one hand, ὑποτάσσειν in contemporary Greek literature was applied to social hierarchies and Paul's use may be held to reflect its 'general catechetical-type role in primitive Christian exhortation'[119] and an endorsement of rank (civic, domestic or ecclesial). In this trajectory it can lead to instantiations of involuntary subjection in coercive hierarchies. On the other hand, Paul also uses it in a key christological statement (1 Cor. 15.28) reflecting both the eschatological submission of all things to Christ and Christ's own submission to God. Engagement with this can lead to a different reception of the paraenetic texts, characterising submission as non-coercive and anti-hierarchical. Here Paul's theology of the cross, with its *reversals* of power and status, transforms the 'horizon of expectation' to a Christian ethos of mutual submission, or to a subversion of rank (with the 'strong' giving way to the 'weak') in the pattern of 'Christ crucified'.

These particular texts, therefore, lend themselves particularly well, though problematically, to a consideration of contested traditions and the life-application of texts.

1.3. The argument

Gadamer and Jauss do not themselves offer a full methodological framework, nor objective criteria for 'validity' of interpretation of what a text can be held to 'mean'. The concepts of *Wirkungsgeschichte* and *Rezeptionsgeschichte* as they are used by biblical interpreters in explicit or implicit constructs, and in challenges to other methodologies in biblical interpretation, vary in the place and value given to a number of elements:

- historical-critical exegesis;
- 'classic readings' of a text within a 'normative tradition' of interpretation, or the selection of a broader diversity of interpretation and application;

119. P. Carrington, *The Primitive Christian Catechism* (Cambridge: Cambridge University Press, 1940), p.49.

- concern for life-application of the paraenesis and the impact of the historical contingencies of the reader;
- theological or ideological prejudgments in acts of reception.

My discussion of these is shaped in the following three stages:

(1) *Reception history and historical-critical exegesis: Chapters 2, 3, 4 and 5.* Challenges to the priority given in biblical interpretation to historical-critical exegesis, and a perception of dichotomy between 'what the text meant' and 'what the text means', are reflected in some claims and practice of reception history of the Bible. Gadamer and Jauss both insist on engagement with the situation in which a text was created and first received as part of the hermeneutical process. This feature of their theory is often neglected or denied in contemporary discussion. I make the case that Gadamer and Jauss provide a very positive rationale for methodologies of historical-critical exegesis within a strategy of iterative engagement with a 'hypothetical first-reception'. The case study tests this with analysis focusing on genre, lexis and historical setting.

(2) *Reception history and the progressive process: Chapters 6, 7 and 8.* The insight expressed by Jauss that the meaning of a work 'is extracted only during the progressive process of its reception'[120] has been appropriated by recent theorists and practitioners in biblical interpretation with various constructions of such a progressive process. Some discussion problematises 'acceptable' limits of diversity. Some selections valorise a 'summit dialogue' of authors for defining moments of a tradition's contours. Some valorise the contingent particularity of each and every engagement with a text, which a summit-dialogue framework may compromise. I identify trends in contemporary practice, and argue that each may be defended as expressions of *Wirkungsgeschichte* and reception history as described by Gadamer and Jauss, though each trend offers a hermeneutical critique of the alternative practice. The case study tests two different constructs of a progressive process of reception as a contribution to the contestations.

(3) *Reception history and theological hermeneutics: Chapters 9 and 10.* A contested feature of Gadamer's hermeneutics focuses on his assessment of the role of 'prejudice' or prejudgments, the 'interestedness' of the reader and the reader's location within a tradition. Criticisms have focused, diversely, on 'subjectivism' and 'conservatism' in his hermeneutics. The critique and defence of Gadamer offered are evaluated in relation to issues of prejudgment, ideological and theological hermeneutics and an interpreter's location in a tradition, and in relation to the

---

120. Jauss, *Aesthetic of Reception*, p.59 (cited above, §1.1.c).

specifics of New Testament interpretation and the case study. Gadamerian hermeneutics calls for reflexive criticism within the process of understanding, which is also self-understanding.

These stages of argument are interdependent rather than sequential: it is not my claim that interpretation begins with historical-critical questions, to be followed by a progressive process and rounded off with some theological attention. The matters all impact on one another through every phase of interpretation. The *ordering* of the material in reception-historical approaches is one of the problems raised, and experienced, in what follows. I am attempting to articulate the nature of interpretation (using Gadamer) and see how different practices reflect this – not to reduce 'hermeneutics' to 'methodology',[121] and emphatically not to model or prescribe one single method.

Neither structural coherence nor conceptual clarity are easily achieved in the face of various factors: the deluge and variety of practice available, the terminological confusion apparent in much theory and practice, and, not least, the way Gadamer writes. His work has the reputation of being 'notoriously difficult',[122] and even one of the English translators of *Wahrheit und Methode* comments, 'No one, it is safe to say, finds Gadamer's work easy going'.[123] Therefore, interpretation of Gadamer, such as this attempt of mine, runs the risk of discovering or imposing an order or an emphasis in his analysis that Gadamer's own writing does not reflect. This study is nevertheless offered as a clarification of what Gadamer says, particularly as this applies to biblical interpretation; and, to a limited extent, of how Jauss confirms or differs from this. I engage with the theory because I am interested in the practice – a range of practices.

121. 'Gadamer proposes hermeneutics as a corrective and metacritical orientation to overcome the limitations of all methodological endeavour': Holub, *Reception Theory*, p.36.

122. E.g. Iain R. Torrance, 'Gadamer, Polyani and Ways of Being Closed', *SJT* 46 (1993), pp.497–506 (497).

123. Joel C. Weinsheimer, *Gadamer's Hermeneutics: A Reading of Truth and Method* (New Haven: Yale University Press, 1985), p.x.

Chapter 2

RECEPTION HISTORY AND HISTORICAL-CRITICAL EXEGESIS

2.1. Introduction: 'the end of historical-critical method'

> [The] collective effort [of *Wirkungsgeschichte* and reception history] is
> to raise questions about the historical-critical method that continues to
> dominate New Testament studies.[1]

As Mark Knight suggests here, the relation – and even the legitimacy –
of historical-critical approaches to biblical interpretation is a vexed
matter in much of the advocacy of reception-historical approaches.
Claims are made for a *dichotomy* of aims and method, with historical-
critical exegesis on the one side and contextual reception and application on the other. This chapter examines key issues in such claims and
practice, specifically in relation to Gadamer's hermeneutics and Jauss's
aesthetics of reception.

Such a dichotomy, attention either to the 'prehistory' or the 'post-
history' of the texts, has been highlighted by numerous commentators in
the last four decades, and has become axiomatic for some of the practitioners and theorists of reception history.[2] This may be referred to
Gadamer's insistence that we cannot restrict the meaning of any
historical text either to 'what the writer originally had in mind', or to 'the
horizon of the person to whom the text was originally addressed'.[3] He
argues,

> Every age has to understand transmitted text in its own way, for the text
> belongs to the whole tradition whose content interests the age and in
> which it seeks to understand itself. The real meaning of a text, as it speaks
> to the interpreter, does not depend on the contingencies of the author and
> his original audience. It certainly is not identical with them, for it is
> always co-determined also by the historical situation of the interpreter
> and hence by the totality of the objective course of history.[4]

1. Knight, '*Wirkungsgeschichte*', p.137 (cited in §1.1.c).
2. E.g. Luz, *Matthew 1–7*, p.98.
3. Gadamer, *Truth and Method*, p.396.
4. Gadamer, *Truth and Method*, p.296.

Gadamer issues a warning that the 'idea of the original reader is full of unexamined idealisation'. His principle that 'literature is defined by the will to hand on' contains a 'fundamental objection to the hermeneutical legitimacy of the idea of the original reader'. Determining the meaning of the text wholly in relation to such a construct 'does not get beyond an accidental delimitation'.[5]

Criticisms of *delimitation* in historical-critical methods in relation to the *whole* interpretative task have a significant history. Before the paradigms of *Wirkungsgeschichte* and *Rezeptionsgeschichte* were articulated, there was discourse and disagreement in the field of New Testament interpretation relating to historical consciousness and the distinction between 'what the text meant' and 'what the text means'. One of the key publishing events in the debate is Karl Barth's commentary on Romans (1919). In the Preface to the second edition (1921), Barth defends himself against the charge of being an 'enemy of historical criticism':

> I have nothing whatever to say against historical criticism. I recognize it and once more state quite definitely that it is both necessary and justified. My complaint is that recent commentators confine themselves to interpretation of the text which seems to me to be no commentary at all, but merely the first step to a commentary. Recent commentaries contain no more than a reconstruction of the text, a rendering of the Greek words and phrases by their precise equivalents, a number of additional notes in which archaeological and philological material is gathered together, and a more or less plausible arrangement of the subject matter in such a manner that it may be made historically and psychologically intelligible from the standpoint of pure pragmatism.[6]

Barth's complaint has some similarities with Gadamer's polemic against the textual applications of methods of natural science in nineteenth-century historicism. However, although Barth recognises that the 'differences between then and now, there and here...require careful investigation and consideration', his judgment is that 'the purpose of such investigation can only be to demonstrate that these differences are, in fact, purely trivial'.[7] This contracts to a vanishing point some strategies of both Gadamer and Jauss that might not lead to that conclusion. However, a further strand in Barth's account then adumbrates Gadamer's analogy of reading as a conversation, and he also describes, effectively,

---

5. Gadamer, *Truth and Method*, p.396.
6. Karl Barth, *The Epistle to the Romans* (trans. E.C. Hoskyns; London: Oxford University Press, 1933), p.6.
7. Barth, *Romans*, p.1.

the 'differentiation of horizons':[8] 'The conversation between the original record and the reader moves round the subject matter [*die Sache*], until a distinction between yesterday and today becomes possible'.[9]

A shortfall in historical-critical exegesis is a repeated concern in subsequent decades. Rudolf Bultmann in 1933 also[10] argued that historical-critical philology 'lost its real subject matter, the interpretation of texts for the sake of understanding them'.[11] In an essay published in 1950 on 'The Significance of the Critical Historical Method for Church and Theology in Protestantism', Gerhard Ebeling saw the question as touching on 'the deepest foundations and the most difficult interconnections of theological thinking and of the church situation'.[12]

There are formulations of the issue in the 1960s and 1970s in particular, contemporary with and subsequent to Gadamer's *Wahrheit und Methode* (1960) and Jauss's inaugural lecture (1967): biblical interpretation was likewise wrestling with the historical distance between a text and its interpreters. Krister Stendahl (in 1962) offered a phrasing of the dichotomy much used subsequently: he described the primary task as that of distinguishing between 'what the text meant' in its original setting and 'what the text means'.[13] Walter Wink (in 1973) introduced a book offering ways towards 'a new paradigm for Biblical study' with the statement that, 'historical biblical criticism is bankrupt', claiming that historical criticism has a tendency to cut the exegete off from the living community. It is 'incapable of achieving what most of its practitioners considered its purpose to be'. This purpose is to interpret the scriptures in such a way 'that the past becomes alive and illumines our present with new possibilities for personal and social transformation'.[14]

---

8. Jauss, *Theorie der Rezeption*, p.17 (cited in §1.1.b).

9. Barth, *Romans*, p.7. We return to matters concerning the *Sache* of biblical texts in §9.3.b.

10. 'The disagreements between [Bultmann and Barth] come so to dominate mid-twentieth-century theology that the extent of their agreement against most historical-critical scholarship (both before and after them) has generally been underestimated': Morgan, '*Sachkritik*', p.178.

11. Rudolf Bultmann, 'The Problem of Hermeneutics', in *Essays Philosophical and Theological* [1933] (trans. J.C. Grieg; London: SCM, 1955), p.237.

12. Gerhard Ebeling, *Word and Faith* (trans. J.W. Leitch; Philadelphia: Fortress, 1963), p.22.

13. Krister Stendahl, 'Biblical Theology, Contemporary', in *The Interpreter's Dictionary of the Bible*, vol. 1 (ed. G.A. Buttrick; Nashville: Abingdon, 1962), pp.418–32.

14. Walter Wink, *The Bible in Human Transformation: Towards a New Paradigm for Biblical Study* (Philadelphia: Fortress, 1973), pp.1 and 10–12.

Gerhard Maier's argument, under the title *Das Ende der Historische Kritischen Methode* (1974), is that historical-critical exegesis maintains 'human arbitrariness' in opposition to the demands of revelation, the true purpose of scripture: 'Therefore because this method is not suited to the subject, in fact even opposes its obvious tendency, we must reject it.'[15] Peter Stuhlmacher (in 1975) describes contemporary Protestant theology as 'hounded and harried' by fundamental problems of historical criticism: 'Just now the relevance of the entire historical-critical formulation of the questions is in part subject to serious doubt in theological and ecclesiastical circles'.[16] His positive evaluation of historical-critical exegesis for the Church is based on the understanding that it is not 'in and of itself' theological interpretation of scripture.[17]

In 1983, Willard Swartley, reviewing some of the publications noted here, suggests that the '1970s may well go down in the history of hermeneutics as the "decade of doubt" (some "disgust") about the historical-critical method'.[18] In the following decade (1986) Wayne Meeks describes the dichotomy in Stendahl's terms:

> the question is whether there can be any significant connection between 'then' and 'now'. New Testament Studies threatens to divide into two contrary ways of reading texts. One is a rigorously historical quest, in which all the early Christian documents…are treated as sources for reconstructing the diverse and curious varieties of the early Christian Movement. The other way of reading…by purely literary analysis… wishes to help text and reader to confront one another continually anew.[19]

Meeks' description of interpretative practice can be recognised in two kinds of publications today. There are commentaries whose parameters of interest share the limitations of Barth's 'recent commentators'. Markus Bockmuehl notes (in 1996) that the 'best modern commentary series continue to produce technical studies of books as ancient texts and as

15. Gerhard Maier, *The End of the Historical-Critical Method* [1974] (trans. E.W. Leverenz and F.R.F. Norden; St Louis: Concordia, 1977), p.25.

16. Peter Stuhlmacher, *Historical Criticism and Theological Interpretation of Scripture: Towards a Hermeneutics of Consent* (trans. R.A. Harrisville; London: SPCK, 1979), p.21.

17. Stuhlmacher, *Historical Criticism*, p.90.

18. Willard M. Swartley, *Slavery, Sabbath, War and Women: Case Issues in Biblical Interpretation* (Kitchener: Herald, 1983), p.328n.

19. Wayne A. Meeks, 'A Hermeneutics of Social Embodiment', in *Christians among Jews and Gentiles: Essays in Honor of Krister Stendahl on his Sixty-fifth Birthday* (ed. George W. Nickelsburg and George W. MacRae; Philadelphia: Fortress, 1986), pp.171–86 (176).

objects of detached critical analysis'.[20] For publications that expressly seek to 'help text and reader to confront one another…anew', Meeks probably had in mind, in 1986, those which espouse 'synchronic' strategies of literary analysis.[21] He characterises (or caricatures) these as demonstrating a way of reading that 'cares not at all where the texts came from or what they originally meant'. It is not (as I shall argue below, §2.2) Gadamer and Jauss who describe a method of reading that 'cares not at all' what the texts meant at first reception.

The disagreements continue into the twenty-first century, with a perceived fulfilment of the 'threat' predicted by Meeks: Aichele, Miscall and Walsh (in 2009) describe a divided discipline where historical-critical scholars attempt 'to produce assured and agreed-on interpretations',[22] while postmodernists espouse 'an anti-essentialist emphasis' denying the possibility of such interpretation.[23] John Barton and John Muddiman (in 2001) accept a 'chastening' of historical criticism by some postmodernist critiques, but only to the extent that those who use it should be aware that 'its sphere of operations, though vital, is not exhaustive'.[24]

Where Meeks noted the threat of a divided discipline, Swartley concluded (in 1983) that the consciousness of the shortfall in historical-critical exegesis for the full task of biblical interpretation has led to a range of attempts to *remedy* this:

20.   Markus Bockmuehl, 'A Commentator's Approach to the "Effective History" of Philippians', *JSNT* 18 (1996), pp.57–88 (57).

21.   E.g. Robert Alter, *The Art of Biblical Narrative* (London: George Allen & Unwin, 1981); and R. Alan Culpepper, *Anatomy of the Fourth Gospel: A Study in Literary Design* (Philadelphia: Fortress, 1983).

22.   I think it is true to say that the detractors of historical-critical analysis are more likely to characterise it as being 'assured' than are its current practitioners: '[F]ew historians still believe that a work of the past can be understood by reconstructing, on the basis of recorded evidence, the set of conventions, expectations, and beliefs that existed at the time of its elaboration': Paul de Man, 'Introduction', in Jauss, *Aesthetic of Reception*, p.xi.

23.   G. Aichele, P. Miscall and R. Walsh, 'An Elephant in the Room: Historical-Critical and Postmodern Interpretations of the Bible', *JBL* 128 (2009), pp.383–404 (384).

24.   John Barton and John Muddiman, 'General Introduction', in *Oxford Bible Commentary* (ed. John Barton and John Muddiman; Oxford: Oxford University Press, 2001), pp.1–5 (3). Cf. Lyons ('Troubled Discipline', pp.9–12) for the opposition of these two positions.

> More and more scholars are conceding that the historical-critical method, while assisting well the task of distancing the text from the biases of the interpreter, has not been able to prompt or manage well the rejoining of the text's message to the life-world of the interpreter... In its most critical form and by itself...the historical-critical method is inadequate.[25]

His 'inadequate' is closer to Barth's critique of the *deficiency* of comment confined to something he characterised as only 'the first step to a commentary'[26] than to Barton and Muddiman's characterisation of historical criticism as 'vital' but 'not exhaustive', though there is a commonality. Moreover, all three (in 1921, 1983 and 2001) explicitly identify *historical consciousness* as the key factor in the contribution of exegetical method:

> The differences between then and now, there and here, ...require careful investigation and consideration.[27]

> The historical-critical method...assist[s] well the task of distancing the text from the biases of the interpreter.[28]

> [H]istorical criticism [studies] biblical books...as anchored in their own time, not as...texts which we can read as though they were contemporary with us.[29]

There is also a recurring insistence in the theorists cited above concerning a *theological* interpretation and application of biblical texts in relation to historical-critical method,[30] which will be pursued in Chapter 9. Here I pursue the operation of *historical consciousness*, as a key element in Gadamer's hermeneutics, within the perceived dichotomy of 'what the text meant' and 'what the text means'.

2.2. 'One phase in the process of understanding'

There is a strand in the advocacy of reception history which subordinates or even separates historical-critical exegesis from the enterprise identified

---

25. Swartley, *Slavery, Sabbath*, p.219.
26. Barth, *Romans*, p.6 (cited above).
27. Barth, *Romans*, p.1.
28. Swartley, *Slavery, Sabbath*, p.219.
29. Barton and Muddiman, *Oxford Bible Commentary*, p.1.
30. E.g. 'interconnections of theological thinking and of the church situation' (Ebeling, *Word and Faith*, p.22); 'the demands of revelation' (Maier, *End of Historical-Critical Method*, p.25); 'theological interpretation of scripture' (Stuhlmacher, *Historical Criticism*, p.90).

as reception history. On the whole, perhaps, this is not a *hermeneutical* exclusion. In the Blackwell series, which represents itself as fulfilling a 'neglected dimension' in biblical interpretation, any subordination of exegetical material[31] is intended by the series editors as a corrective to the primary or exclusive goal of *traditional* commentaries, which they characterise as attempting to describe or construct 'one single meaning, normally identified with the author's original intention'.[32] This reflects Gadamer's *rejection of the meaning as depending solely* upon 'the contingencies of the author'.[33] Where it also reflects *rejection of attention to the first appearance* of the work, it can represent a partial reading of Gadamer and Jauss.

One contributor to the series, Mary Callaway,[34] in a paper given at the Blackwell Bible Commentary Meeting 2004, develops Luz's categorical distinction of commentaries as *Auslegungsgeschichte* and other parts of the 'legacy of the Church' as *Wirkungsgeschichte*,[35] into a methodological exclusion:

> the term History of Interpretation is used in general for studies that take an exegetical approach and have a theological interest. The…approach is exegetical and explores the hermeneutic by which the biblical text was interpreted. The term Reception History, as its origins in *Wirkungsgeschichte* imply, should describe studies that employ a mixture of historical, sociological and anthropological approaches to illuminate the mutual interplay of *effects* that a biblical text has had on a given culture and that a culture manages to encode in a biblical text.[36]

This is surely a misrepresentation of both *Wirkungsgeschichte* and also of what is often available in the contemporary 'exegetical approach'. Gadamer's hermeneutics does not exclude *any* approach or interest from the principle of history-of-effect (see §6.2.a for 'history of interpretation' as one form of *Wirkungsgeschichte*). And if historical-critical enquiry

31.   This varies considerably between individual volumes, and some commentaries in the Blackwell series may valorize exegetical interpretation in ways which give it a primary status (discussed in §6.2).

32.   Sawyer *et al.*, 'Series Editors' Preface', p.xi.

33.   Gadamer, *Truth and Method*, p.296 (cited in Chapter 2).

34.   Mary Callaway, *Jeremiah Through the Centuries* (Oxford: Blackwell, 2006).

35.   Luz, *Matthew 1–7*, p.98; and *Matthew 8–20*, e.g. p.11. (See §6.2.a for further consideration of this claimed distinction.)

36.   Mary Chilton Callaway, 'What's the Use of Reception History?', unpublished paper delivered at the annual meeting of the SBL, San Antonio, 2004 (http://bbibcomm.net/files/callaway2004.pdf, accessed 26 August 2012), pp.13–14.

may not employ historical, sociological[37] and anthropological[38] approaches it is hard to see what approaches it *could* use: some very limited philological strategies, perhaps, like those seen by Barth as offering 'no more than a reconstruction of the text'.[39] (I pursue the question of 'theological interest' in §9.3.b.)

The tendency to categorise exegesis as something hermeneutically apart from the endeavour of reception history cannot be justified using Gadamer and Jauss.[40] Rowland makes a different distinction concerning the character of the Blackwell Commentaries: 'The main difference about our commentary series is that the historical-critical exegesis is included as part of *Wirkungsgeschichte* rather than as a primary datum to which matters of *Wirkungsgeschichte* can be added'.[41] This is demonstrably right in terms of Gadamerian hermeneutics:[42] an act of historical-critical exegesis is a reception of the text, historically contingent, reflecting the interpreter's horizon of expectation. Bultmann articulated much the same insight in 1957: 'Since the exegete exists historically and must hear the word of Scripture as spoken in his special historical situation, he will always understand the old word anew'.[43]

Where I want to make a different approach to the question of a 'primary datum' and the role of historical-critical exegesis, is in the capacity of this approach to contribute to the reconstruction of 'the question to which [the text] is an answer'.[44] Gadamer discusses the necessity of engaging with the occasion of the origin of a text, and of the competences of its first readers:

---

37. E.g. R.F. Hock, *The Social Context of Paul's Ministry* (Philadelphia: Fortress, 1980); Gerd Theissen, *The Social Setting of Pauline Christianity* (Edinburgh: T. & T. Clark, 1982).

38. E.g. Atsuhiro Asano, *Community-Identity Construction in Galatians: Exegetical, Social-Anthropological and Socio-Historical Studies* (London: T&T Clark International, 2005); Bruce J. Malina, *The New Testament World: Insights from Cultural Anthropology* (Atlanta: John Knox, 1981); V.K. Robbins, *Jesus the Teacher: A Socio-Rhetorical Interpretation of Mark* (Minneapolis: Fortress, 1992).

39. Barth, *Romans*, p.6 (cited in §2.1).

40. Bockmuehl rightly asks, '[W]ho is to deny that exegetical work forms part of the effective history of the Bible?': 'Commentator's Approach', p.61.

41. Rowland, 'Pragmatic Approach', p.1.

42. In §2.4, the problem of 'first- and second-stage' interpretation is pursued.

43. 'Is Exegesis without Presuppositions Possible?', in *Existence and Faith: Shorter Writings of Rudolf Bultmann* (ed. and trans. S.M. Odgen; London: Hodder & Stoughton, 1960), pp.289–96 (296); cf. Parris, *Reception Theory*, p.156.

44. Gadamer, *Truth and Method*, p.363 (cited in §1.1.a).

> If we fail to transpose ourselves into the historical horizon from which the traditionary text[45] speaks, we will misunderstand the significance of what it has to say to us...
>
> This...is the clear hermeneutical demand: to understand a text in terms of the specific situation in which it was written.[46]

His inclusion of these strategies is curiously neglected in most discussion of Gadamer in relation to current practice. This may be attributable in part to the complexity of his argument, because these statements are from parts of the work where he first *distinguishes* 'historical scholarship' from the strategies of other readers such as literary critics. In historical scholarship, the understanding is 'one that involves keeping a hermeneutical distance... Hermeneutics and historical study...are clearly not the same thing.'[47] However, his second move is to insist on the 'universal' claim of 'historical consciousness';[48] that the 'problem of application... also characterises the more complicated situation of historical understanding', so 'what is true of every reader is also true of the historian'.[49]

Gadamer insists that, in the act of understanding, the 'fusion' of the two horizons ('the horizon in which the person seeking to understand lives and the historical horizon within which he places himself')[50] requires the projection of an historical horizon, as one 'phase' in the 'process' of understanding.[51] This projected horizon 'immediately recombines' with the life-horizon of the interpreter, because 'understanding always involves something like applying the text to be understood to the interpreter's present situation'.[52] As the historical horizon is 'projected', it is 'simultaneously superseded'. 'To bring about this fusion in a regulated way is the task of what we call historically effected consciousness [*wirkungsgeschichtliches Bewusstein*].'[53] He explains:

45.   In the revised translation of 2004, the neologism 'traditionary text' is sometimes used not only for *überlieferten Text* ('transmitted text') to maintain the active verbal implication, but sometimes also for *Überlieferung* ('tradition') when this represents the historical object (text). The translators also use 'what comes down to us from the past'.

46.   Gadamer, *Truth and Method*, pp.302 and 330. This must be held together with the insistence (discussed further in §2.4) that the 'horizon of understanding cannot be *limited*...by what the writer originally had in mind': Gadamer, *Truth and Method*, p.396 (emphasis mine).

47.   Gadamer, *Truth and Method*, pp.330–31.

48.   Gadamer, *Truth and Method*, p.333.

49.   Gadamer, *Truth and Method*, pp.334–35.

50.   Gadamer, *Truth and Method*, p.303.

51.   Gadamer, *Truth and Method*, p.305 (cited in §1.1.a).

52.   Gadamer, *Truth and Method*, pp.306–7 (cited in §1.1.a).

53.   Gadamer, *Truth and Method*, p.306.

Every encounter with tradition that takes place within historical consciousness involves the experience of tension between the text and the present.
The hermeneutic task consists in not covering up this tension by attempting
a naïve assimilation of the two but in consciously bringing it out. This is
why it is part of the hermeneutic approach to project an historical horizon
that is different from the horizon of the present. Historical consciousness is
aware of its own otherness and hence foregrounds the horizon of the past
from its own.[54]

However simultaneous this is, there is not a single horizon but a conscious 'fusion' of two, 'in a regulated way'. The *projection of the
horizon of the past* is a *phase in the process* of understanding. 'Historical
consciousness is aware of its own otherness and hence foregrounds the
horizon of the past from its own'; understanding follows a universal
process but also 'becomes a scholarly task...under special circumstances'.[55] This is where a case must be made for the distinctive scholarly
task comprised by historical-critical methods.

The full aims and precise methods of biblical exegesis are contested in
principle and practice: my purpose here is to identify some key correspondences in a broad range of contemporary practice, and the tools of a
particular 'scholarly task'. Much contemporary practice of exegetical
biblical commentary compares the text with its contemporaneous lexis
and literature. Much contemporary practice includes socio-historical
investigation into the 'original setting', and the cultural background of
terms used. Much contemporary practice includes socio-historical
investigation into the putative first readership; and some contemporary
practice (more on this question in §2.3 below) makes use of the concept
of the implied reader.[56]

Gadamer develops a particular concept of *Okkasionalität* in an argument that 'aesthetic' responses to works of art, literature, music or drama
cannot 'supersede the artwork's belonging to its [past] world'.[57] According
to Gadamer, 'Occasionality means that their meaning and content is
determined by the occasion for which they are intended'.[58] He uses the

54. Gadamer, *Truth and Method*, p.305.
55. Gadamer, *Truth and Method*, p.305.
56. E.g. Ulrich Luz, *Matthew in History: Interpretation, Influence and Effect*
(Minneapolis: Fortress, 1994), p.7: 'historical-critical research...uses both external
data – for example, from...language – and intratextual data such as information
about the implied readers...of the text'.
57. Gadamer, *Truth and Method*, p.158.
58. Gadamer, *Truth and Method*, p.138. 'Determined' was 'partly determined' in
Truth and Method (1979), p.127. Revisions in translation of Gadamer are discussed
in §6.4.

instance of portraiture as an example where a work has a 'determinable reference' to the person portrayed.[59] His argument is that the historical circumstances of the origin of a work remain embodied in it, part of its enduring meaning: 'The important thing is that this occasionality belongs to the work's own claim and not something forced on it by its interpreter... [I]t experiences a continued determination of its meaning from the 'occasion' of its coming-to-presentation'.[60] (Chapter 5 will include a range of historical-critical reception where such a consideration seeks to determine, or co-determine, the meaning of the case-study texts.)

Not only is Gadamer's inclusion of a projection of the historical horizon neglected in current discussion, his hermeneutics are held to be less adequate in this respect than Jauss's, by advocates of Jaussian methods. So Parris judges:

> This is one area in which the work of Hans Robert Jauss advanced the hermeneutical tradition he inherited from Gadamer. For Jauss, both forms of understanding are crucial; we not only need to pay careful attention to the subject-matter of the text, but we must also investigate the conditions in which the text was produced and first received if we...are to have an adequate understanding of it.

The possible correspondences between key elements of Jauss's theses (outlined in §1.1.b) and key aims of historical-critical methods are easier to identify than in Gadamer:

> Thesis 2: The analysis of the literary experience of the reader avoids the threatening pitfalls of psychology if it describes the reception and the influence of a work within the objectifiable system of expectations that arise for each work in the historical moment of its appearance, from a pre-understanding of the *genre*, from the *form and themes of already familiar works*.
> Thesis 3: Reconstructed in this way, the horizon of expectations of a work allows one to determine its artistic character by the kind and degree of its influence on *a presupposed audience*.
> Thesis 4: The reconstruction of the horizon of expectations, in the face of which a work was created and received in the past, enables one...to pose *questions that the text gave an answer to*, and thereby to discover how *the contemporary reader* could have viewed and understood the work.[61]

59. Gadamer, *Truth and Method*, p.140.
60. Gadamer, *Truth and Method*, pp.138, 141. (This too contains revisions in the English translation; see §6.4.)
61. Jauss, *Aesthetic of Reception*, pp.22, 25 and 28 (emphasis mine).

Whether the methodologies of historical-critical exegesis do indeed allow the interpreter confidently to reconstruct the horizon of expectations (in the face of which a work was created and received in the past) is, of course, put to question by some of the very different conclusions on the same text drawn by different exegetes (examples in Chapters 3, 4 and 5). Nevertheless, their investigations (as in Jauss's theses above) focus on the historical moment of the text's appearance, offer material that helps to characterise the kind and degree of its influence on a presupposed audience, consider questions that the text gave an answer to, and offer insights on how the (ancient) contemporary reader could have viewed and understood the work.

Examination of other texts contemporary with a biblical text (see Jauss's second thesis) is a particular strategy within historical-critical exegesis. Rowland makes a useful realignment of the terms 'diachronic' and 'synchronic'[62] in relation to historical-critical exegesis and reception history, and this has a particular resonance with another of Jauss's theses. Rowland recognises that the currency of these terms in biblical interpretation associates historical-critical study with a 'diachronic' perspective, and identifies as 'synchronic' those approaches which 'do not ask whence an idea comes but rather concentrate on how it functions or is part of a belief system or social matrix at a particular time and place'. However, in post-Enlightenment hermeneutics,

> there emerged an interpretation in which the exegesis of biblical texts was based on the relationship with texts which were contemporaneous with them rather than on the history of the way those texts had been interpreted within faith communities. In other words, it was a synchronic approach to the biblical texts as they were set in the context of that which was contemporary rather that which followed after them.[63]

The concern in exegetical method that examines the sources and antecedents of biblical texts is, Rowland concedes, a form of diachronicity, but the recognition of the synchronic impulse in exegesis allows a new distinction, a different diachronicity, and a recognition of 'the history of texts through time as a key to their interpretation'.[64]

---

62. The terms originated in the study of linguistics. Saussure distinguishes between synchronic linguistics (the study of language at a specific time) and diachronic linguistics (the study of the evolution of language): Ferdinand de Saussure, *Course in General Linguistics* (ed. C. Bally and A. Sechehaye; trans. W. Baskin; New York: McGraw-Hill, 1966).

63. Rowland, 'Pragmatic Approach', p.3.

64. Roberts and Rowland, 'Introduction', p.132.

Rowland makes no reference here to these terms in Jauss, but these can complement the case he makes. Jauss's sixth thesis valorizes the achievements made in linguistics, 'through the distinction and methodological interrelation of diachronic and synchronic analysis as the occasion for overcoming the diachronic perspective – previously the only one practised'.[65] These terms, in relation to German literary history,[66] rather than biblical interpretation, provide Jauss with a different, disparaging, use of 'diachronic' applied to his discipline. His argument was against the dominance of a particular historical method in literary studies in the 1960s,[67] with its 'diachronic view' of literature which characterised literary history as 'a chronological series of literary facts'.[68] His complaint was of 'a description of literature that follows an already sanctioned canon and simply sets the life and work of the writers in a chronological series…[without] judgments of quality'.[69]

However, it is the recognition of *a distinction of the operations of synchronic and diachronic study*, within the construction of reception as a 'series', that does correspond with Rowland's characterisation of exegesis as synchronic, and *Wirkungsgeschichte* or reception history as diachronic. Jauss describes a strategy of identifying the 'epoch-making' moments in a literary series: a synchronic study of works contemporaneous with a particular work in the literary series, 'to make the literary horizon of a specific historical moment comprehensible'.[70] This is to be done within the framework of the diachronic series, with synchronic 'cross-sections'. (It is this feature of Jauss's analysis that is appealed to by theorist-practitioners such as Thiselton and Parris, in constructions of reception that form a 'canon of exemplary commentators'[71] – to be discussed in §6.2).

Jauss does not in the theses refer to the first appearance and first reception of a text as one of the synchronic cross-sections of the diachronic line. However, Rowland's characterisation of the exegetical approach suggests how this might be viewed as another synchronic cross-section within a diachronic process. Jauss describes how synchronic analyses

---

65. Jauss, *Aesthetic of Reception*, p.36.
66. Jauss's critique of German literary history does not really speak to Anglo-American literary studies.
67. Hans-Robert Jauss, 'Limits and Tasks of Literary Hermeneutics', *Diogenes* 109 (1980), pp.92–119 (96).
68. Jauss, *Aesthetic of Reception*, p.36.
69. Jauss, *Aesthetic of Reception*, p.4–5.
70. Jauss, *Aesthetic of Reception*, pp.36 and 37.
71. Parris, *Reception Theory*, p.217.

are subsequently viewed in a diachronic perspective and a progressive process of the text's interpretation and application. The figure below is an attempt to represent these two, comparable synchronic explorations, described, severally, by Rowland and Jauss, in relation to the diachronic process of which, hermeneutically, they are also part.

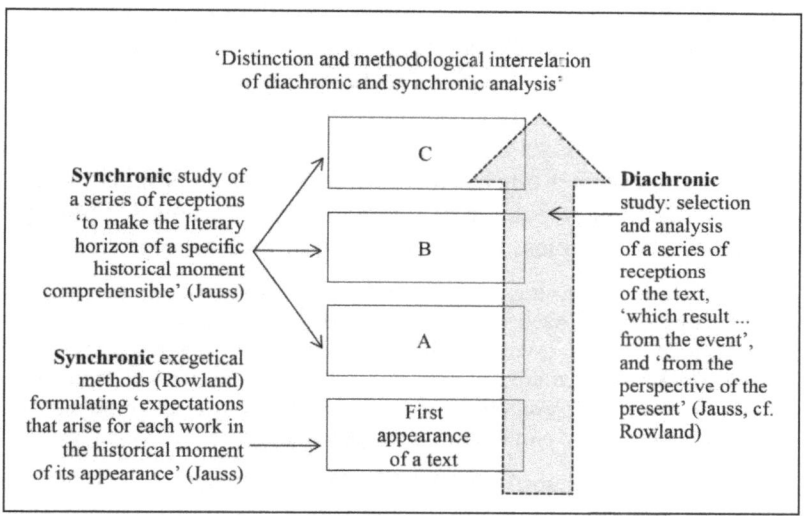

'Distinction and methodological interrelation
of diachronic and synchronic analysis'

Synchronic study of
a series of receptions
'to make the literary
horizon of a specific
historical moment
comprehensible' (Jauss)

Synchronic exegetical
methods (Rowland)
formulating 'expectations
that arise for each work in
the historical moment
of its appearance' (Jauss)

C

B

A

First
appearance
of a text

Diachronic
study: selection
and analysis
of a series of
receptions
of the text,
'which result ...
from the event',
and 'from the
perspective of the
present' (Jauss, cf.
Rowland)

Historical-critical investigation may thus be viewed within the methodo-logy of reception history as constituting one of the synchronic cross-sections of the diachronic line. Conceived in this way, historical-critical methods not only do not stand outside of the diachronic exercise of reception history, but may be represented as an (essential) operation within it. They do not produce the 'primary datum' in the sense of a single and unchallengeable 'meaning' of the text to which other mean-ings are later added (there is further consideration of this below in §2.4), but they contribute to the 'scholarly task' of a 'projection of the horizon of the past' which for Gadamer is 'one phase in the process of under-standing';[72] and for Jauss, this is a strategy to render the 'horizon of a specific historical moment comprehensible'.[73]

72. Gadamer, *Truth and Method*, p.305.
73. Jauss, *Aesthetic of Reception*, p.37.

2.3. The reconstruction of the 'horizon of expectation'

The criticism must be raised that we do not have access to the first reception – the interpretations, for example, of Roman Christians on the first reading-out in congregation of Paul's letter to them.[74] The construction that exegesis may make of this is hypothetical – and *the historical contingency of the exegete* always impinges on their representation. Such a criticism must apply to all operations of understanding. Anthropology – for example – requires strategies for the projection of a horizon that is different from the horizon of the observer. Clifford Geertz describes an anthropologist's analysis of a culture as a 'thick description', which provides 'whatever it is one has to know or believe' in order consciously to appropriate the perspective of its members.[75] Vernon Robbins compares a process in biblical interpretation with such an approach:

> I was intentionally trying to approach the Gospel of Mark like an anthropologist would approach a 'foreign' group of people in a 'foreign' land. It seems to me that our investigations badly need to confront the reality that New Testament texts are 'foreign' to our literature, society, economics, politics, and culture. Adopting the approach of a cultural anthropologist, then, is an important part of any investigation of a New Testament text.[76]

A 'thick description' too is a hypothetical construction: it is how we relate to an experience which is not our own, without (merely) identifying it with our own.

Gadamer argues that the interpreter at the same time becomes aware of the distinctiveness of their own horizons, as against those of the text. He characterises the experience as one of both tension and fusion. On the one hand,

> every encounter with tradition that takes place within historical conscious-ness involves the experience of the tensions between the text and the present. The hermeneutic task consists in not covering up this tension by attempting naïve assimilation of the two but in consciously bringing it out. This is why it is part of the hermeneutic approach to project an historical horizon that is different from the horizon of the present.[77]

---

74. Bockmuehl suggests that it is in the 'subapostolic period of living memory' that constitutes the first connection 'between readers actually addressed by the text and the readings it actually engendered': *Seeing the Word*, p.68.

75. Clifford Geertz, 'Thick Description: Toward an Interpretive Theory of Culture', in *The Interpretation of Cultures: Selected Essays* (New York: Basic Books, 1973), pp.3–30 (11), citing Ward Goodenough; he attributes the term itself (p. 6) to Gilbert Ryle, *Collected Papers*, vol. 2 (London: Hutchinson, 1971).

76. Robbins, *Jesus the Teacher*, p.xxi.

77. Gadamer, *Truth and Method*, p.305.

On the other hand, for understanding to take place, there must also occur a 'fusion'.[78] He compares this with a conversation with someone where,

> when we have discovered the other person's standpoint and horizon, his ideas become intelligible without our necessarily having to agree with him... When our historical consciousness transposes itself into historical horizons, this does not entail passing into alien worlds unconnected in any way with our own; instead, they together constitute the one great horizon.[79]

There are differences in the ways Gadamer and Jauss express how we process the partial and selective character of our perspective of the past. For both, understanding happens within the dialectic relation of the text and its historically conditioned readers. Some interpreters critique Gadamer's concept of the 'fusion of horizons' [*Horizontverschmelzung*] as singular,[80] or as a 'passive merging of two image fields into one field of vision'.[81] These sometimes see a remedy in Jauss's 'differentiation' [*Horizontabhebung*] of horizons of expectation,[82] because this is deemed to maintain the tension between the text of the past and the present experience of the reader: 'Only in this mediating of two different horizons, you arrive at a new experience, which changes the interpreter him/herself'.[83] This, however, is exactly what Gadamer's *Horizontverschmelzung* describes.

The reason for the emphasis on differentiation in Jauss's analysis is his key qualification of literary texts as 'aesthetic' objects: the *strangeness* of the work of art is a necessary condition to understanding it through the aesthetic pleasure or displeasure it provokes. The appearance of a new work of literature can negate familiar experiences or raise newly articulated experiences to consciousness, so its reception can result in a 'change of horizons': 'The way in which a literary work, at the historical moment of its appearance, satisfies, surpasses, disappoints, or refutes the expectation of its first audience obviously provides a criterion of its aesthetic value'.[84] Jauss therefore advocates 'first' and 'second' (and successive) readings. The 'aesthetic' response of a reader from their

78. Gadamer, *Truth and Method*, e.g. p.305.

79. Gadamer, *Truth and Method*, pp.302–3.

80. E.g. Rachel Nicholls: 'Instead of one fusion of horizons in the act of reading the biblical text, I seek many "fusions"': *'Walking on the Water': Reading Matthew 14. 22-33 in the Light of its Wirkungsgeschichte* (Leiden: Brill, 2008), p.14.

81. Parris, *Reception Theory*, p.152.

82. Jauss, *Theorie der Rezeption*, p.17 (cited in §1.1.b).

83. Brigid Merriman, 'Minutes of the colloquy of 27 February 1983', in *Protocol of the Colloquy of the Center for Hermeneutical Studies in Hellenistic and Modern Culture* (ed. W.R. Herzog; Berkeley: University of California Press, 1983), p.52.

84. Jauss, *Aesthetic of Reception*, p.25.

own historical contingency, where the work can be received in its pleasing or displeasing strangeness, is countered by a second which considers the text in the light of (a reconstruction of) the aesthetic experience of its first readers. This provokes the 'differentiation' of horizons.

Gadamer's metaphor of the 'fusion' of 'horizons' is focused not on *aesthetic* experience but on the construction of 'tradition' and oneself as interpreter within a tradition. Neither the horizon of the present reader nor of the historically situated text truly exists in isolation: 'the horizon of the present cannot be formed without the past... Understanding...is always the fusion of these horizons supposedly existing by themselves.'[85] 'Tension' is thus built into the 'fusion', and Jauss's articulation does not add something hermeneutically distinctive. Jauss, in a later work, echoes Gadamer very closely:

> If the horizon of our present did not always already include the original horizon of the past, historical understanding would be impossible, since the past in its otherness may only be grasped in so far as the interpreter is able to separate the alien from his own horizon. It is the task of historical understanding to take both horizons into account through conscious effort.[86]

Whether *Horizontverschmelzung* or *Horizontabhebung* is the preferred term,[87] both Gadamer and Jauss seek to avoid a 'naïve' fusion of horizons, and both describe a 'mediation' in the process of understanding, the 'interplay' of text and reader. The dialectic process in Gadamer, and the 'reconstruction of the horizon of expectations in the face of which a work was created and received in the past' in Jauss,[88] are strategies that allow for the interestedness and historical contingencies of the reader, and for the hypothetical character of reception constructed through exegetical methods focusing on original setting and the context and competences of the first readers.

The focus in such an examination, and in the subsequent dialectic with other readings and other readers, is on 'the reader'.[89] A key aim of

85. Gadamer, *Truth and Method*, p.305 (cited in §1.1.a).

86. Jauss, 'Identity of the Poetic Text', pp.7–8. I revisit this in §6.4.

87. I discuss further the different emphases in Jauss and Gadamer concerning fusion or mediation of horizon in §6.4. I discuss challenges to Gadamer's analysis of the 'fusion of horizons' as either an appropriation by the interpreter of the prejudgments of the text, or an imposition on the text of the interpreter's prejudgments in §9.3.

88. Jauss, *Aesthetic of Reception*, p.28 (cited in §2.2).

89. See §9.2 for discussion of locating meaning in the author or 'authorial intention'.

exegesis within this strategy is to elucidate 'how the [ancient] contemporary reader could have viewed and understood the work'.[90] The first readers are 'constructed' partly from the historical investigations of setting and contemporaneous culture, but also through the immanent literary devices of the work. (Both historical and literary investigations, of course, are subject to indeterminacies, and to the interpreter's horizon of expectation.) John Lyons notes the 'growing emphasis on audiences' in biblical studies: 'most recent proposals involve a posited audience imaginatively crafted with the aim of strengthening the critic's interpretation'. Moreover, much historical-critical exegesis has a common purpose with reception history in that it 'aims to understand the interaction between a text, a context and an audience's response'.[91] Historical-critical exegetes may not self-consciously articulate this construct of reader through immanent literary devices,[92] but typically they examine the text for clues to the culture, situation, assumptions of the first readers, and the text's rhetoric influencing their possible responses. A framework of the first readers' contingencies and competences corresponds closely to Geertz's 'thick description' of a culture providing 'whatever it is one has to know or believe' in order consciously to appropriate the perspective of its members.[93] The term that best describes the object of this endeavour (using the tools of historical-critical exegesis, within the perspective of a reader-oriented approach demanded by reception history) is 'hypothetical first-reception' [*hypothetische Erst-Rezeption*], which I derive from Moisés Mayordomo-Marín's 1997 doctoral thesis, supervised by Ulrich Luz.[94]

90. Jauss, *Aesthetic of Reception*, p.28 (cited in §2.2).

91. Lyons, 'Troubled Discipline', p.213. Lyons's argument is for a wholesale re-labelling of historical-critical methodologies with the terminology of 'reception history' (though this is made without reference to Gadamer or Jauss). Mine is an attempt to articulate the *distinctive* and significant role of historical-critical methodologies *within* the dialectic of a reception-historical approach.

92. Some exegetes are explicit about such a construct: e.g. Luz includes the 'intratextual data' of 'information about the implied readers and the implied author' in the methods of historical-critical research: *Matthew in History*, p.7.

93. Geertz, 'Thick Description', p.11 (cited above).

94. Moisés Mayordomo-Marín, *Den Anfang Hören: Leseorientierte Evangelienexegese am Beispiel von Matthaeus 1–2* (Göttingen: Vandenhoeck & Ruprecht, 1998). This is published in a prestigious series but has not been translated, and is not cited in any works I have discovered, with two recent exceptions. One is Victor Manuel Morales Vásquez, *Contours of a Biblical Reception Theory: Studies in the Rezeptionsgeschichte of Romans 13.1-7* (Göttingen: VandR unipress, 2012), pp.55–63. I discuss this further in §3.1 and in §6.2. (It is to Victor Morales Vásquez, during his preparation for the doctoral thesis that forms the basis of his book, that I owe my

Mayordomo-Marín's work is a conscious synthesis of approaches including Jauss's reception theory and Iser's term, *implizite Leser.* Wolfgang Iser was co-founder with Jauss of *Rezeptionsaesthetik* at the University of Konstanz. The 'encoded' or 'implied reader' is the reader created by the text: the text invites particular responses and predisposes a reader to read in particular ways:[95]

> The concept of the implied reader is a textual structure anticipating the presence of a recipient without necessarily defining him: this concept pre-structures the role to be assumed by each recipient... [T]he concept... designates a network of response – inviting structures, which impel the reader to grasp the text.[96]

> This term incorporates both the prestructuring of the potential meaning by the text, and the reader's actualization of this potential through the reading process. It refers to the active nature of this process.[97]

Mayordomo-Marín's aim is to develop and apply a method in which reader-oriented impulses in recent literary criticism are fruitful for the exegesis of the Gospels. His use of reader-oriented approaches is undertaken not to supplant methods of historical-critical exegesis, which he also employs, but to bring together perceptions of divergent approaches.[98] He operates with Jauss's framework, where the reader first examines the

---

introduction to Mayordomo-Marín's work.) The second is a brief reference in Mark Elliott, 'Effective-History and the Hermeneutics of Ulrich Luz', *JSNT* 33 (2010), pp.161–73 (165). John Nolland made a (very positive) review of *Den Anfang Hören* in 2000, noting its strengths as 'those of critical evaluation and synthesis rather than originality': Review of Moisés Mayordomo-Marín, *Den Anfang Hören: Leser-orientierte Evangelienexegese am Beispiel von Matthäus 1–2, Review of Biblical Literature* (2000) (http://www.bookreviews.org/pdf/492_312.pdf, accessed 28 March 2012).

95. I am employing Iser's terms because of their use by Mayordomo-Marín and because of Iser's association with Jauss, but comparable terms are used for the textual encoding of such a reader, such as Umberto Eco's 'model reader': *The Role of the Reader: Explorations in the Semiotics of Texts* (ed. Thomas Sebeok; Bloomington: Indiana University Press, 1979), pp.7–10. Developments of these terms in relation to biblical interpretation are discussed in Anthony C. Thiselton, *New Horizons in Hermeneutics* (London: Harper Collins, 1992), pp.516–29.

96. Wolfgang Iser, *The Act of Reading: A Theory of Aesthetic Response* (Baltimore: The Johns Hopkins University Press, 1978), p.34.

97. Wolfgang Iser, *The Implied Reader: Patterns of Communication in Prose Fiction from Bunyan to Beckett* (Baltimore: The Johns Hopkins University Press, 1974), p.xii.

98. Mayordomo-Marín, *Anfang Hören*, pp.11–26.

text in terms of the reader's own 'horizon of meaning' [*Sinnhorizont*],[99] her/his location and response. Sustained attention is then given to the 'horizon of meaning' of the hypothetical first-readers which includes an analysis of their situation and an exploration of the encyclopaedic competences of these readers.[100] (The absence of questions concerning *sources* in this part of the process is confirmation of the 'synchronic' focus, as characterised in §2.2 above, that this stage of analysis may be perceived to have.) The process moves into one stage of Jauss's dialectic, the interaction between the reader's own location and the challenges to this from the text.

Mayordomo-Marín's method is one articulated example of how tools of historical-critical exegesis are components in constructing the *possibilities* of the first reception, an understanding of 'the questions to which [the text] is an answer'.[101] This reconstructed question stands, in Gadamerian terms, within its original horizon, but it is included in the horizon of the new reader.[102] Hypothetical first-reception can characterise this phase in understanding as preliminary, plural and iterative – 'applications' rather than a claim for a definitive, singular 'meaning'. They are, in Lyons' phrase, 'exercises in plausibility'.[103]

One tendency in appropriating the language of *Wirkungsgeschichte* in biblical studies is the assertion that Gadamer repudiates the locus of meaning in the author or in a hypothetical first-reception: 'The real meaning of the text, as it speaks to the interpreter, does not depend on the contingencies of the author and his original audience. It certainly is *not identical* with them…' However, this is only half the story. This tendency often fails to identify Gadamer's inclusion of these as co-determinants of the 'real meaning', in a mediation/fusion with the horizon/contingencies of the reader: such meaning 'is always *co-determined also* by the historical situation of the interpreter'.[104]

2.4. The contested 'priority' of historical-critical interpretation

Beginning with historical exegesis and then addressing the role of the contemporary reader has its merits, but it fails to question the priority of exegetical interpretation.[105]

99. Mayordomo-Marín, *Anfang Hören*, e.g. p.196.
100. Mayordomo-Marín, *Anfang Hören*, e.g. p.151.
101. Gadamer, *Truth and Method*, p.363.
102. Gadamer, *Truth and Method*, p.367.
103. Lyons, 'Troubled Discipline', p.213.
104. Gadamer, *Truth and Method*, p.296 (emphasis mine; cited in §2.1).
105. Knight, '*Wirkungsgeschichte*', p.142.

A contestation outstanding in the account above is whether such a strategy, of hypothesising first-reception, makes the scholar's reconstruction of the reception-possibilities the 'primary datum' to which later meanings are added. There are many advocates of just such a staging. John Ashton writes that 'study of the meaning of an ancient text is not only a legitimate object of enquiry but the essential prerequisite *before* the exegete embarks on contemporary application'.[106] John Barton explicitly articulates 'stages' of interpretation: 'The first-stage is a perception of the text's meaning; the second, an evaluation of that meaning in relation to what we already believe to be the case. This operation cannot be collapsed into a single process, in which meaning is perceived and evaluated at one and the same time and by the same operation.'[107]

Such articulation of historical-critical methods as essential components in constructing the possibilities of the first reception will not accord with Gadamer's hermeneutics if it is represented as a (temporal) *pre*-condition for understanding, rather than *co*-determinant in the process of understanding an historic text. There is a division – and in some quarters a lack of clarity – on this question in recent biblical interpretation where reference is made to Gadamer and Jauss.

On one side, Rowland contests the division of 'original meaning' and secondary 'evaluation': 'Following Hans-Georg Gadamer, text and interpreter can be seen as co-participants in a conversation that constitutes meaning rather than being secondary to some prior, original meaning'.[108] Lyons refers to the 'virtual inability' of reception history to 'insist on notions of first- and second-stage interpretations'.[109]

On the other hand, Luz expresses the process as one where reception history refers to what follows *after* exegesis rather than being intrinsic to all interpretation including historical-critical reading. Knight points out that although Luz tells us that the 'history of influence' will be given

---

106. John Ashton, *Studying John: Approaches to the Fourth Gospel* (Oxford: Oxford University Press, 1994), p.207 (emphasis his). This also expresses the contested distinction between 'meaning' and 'application', not available according to Gadamer; cf. one of the earliest commentators on *Truth and Method*, E.D. Hirsch: *Validity in Interpretation* (New Haven: Yale University Press, 1967), p.8 (and discussed in §9.2).

107. John Barton, *The Nature of Biblical Criticism* (Louisville: Westminster, John Knox, 2007), p.159.

108. Christopher Rowland, 'Re-imagining Biblical Exegesis', in *Religion, Literature and the Imagination: Sacred Worlds* (ed. Mark Knight and Louise Lee; London: Continuum, 2010), pp.140–49 (143).

109. Lyons, 'Troubled Discipline', p.214.

weight in his commentary and 'will be placed in the midst of the interpretation',[110] in fact his 'analysis' (a traditional form of exegesis) and 'the
history of influence' are located in discrete sections, 'with the former
typically preceding the latter'.[111] Similarly, Thiselton valorizes a capacity
of reception history to add dimensions of meaning to *previous* exegetical
insights: 'Wrestling with *Wirkungsgeschichte* or reception history opens
the door to exegesis as explication: an explication that permits us to see
a dimension of meaning that *successive contexts of reading* bring into
sharper focus for our attention'.[112] Rachel Nicholls's suggestion and
practice is explicitly that *Wirkungsgeschichte* is best 'regulated' as
'secondary acts' of interpretation in a series of encounters scheduled
after historical exegesis.[113] 'After exegesis comes reception history' is
also part of Roland Boer's attack on the 'primacy of that strange guild of
biblical exegetes' within the enterprise of 'reception history' of the
Bible.[114]

It is surely this lack of consensus and, in a number of cases, lack of
clarity concerning what Gadamer and Jauss actually say about accessing
the 'horizon of the past', that lays the discipline open to such partially
informed critiques. The defences offered can also be deficient in precisely
this respect: Chris Heard's response to Boer (on the Blackwell Bible
Commentaries web pages) validates the role of the *reader* in reception
theory but is silent on the role of historically effected consciousness,
which is key to the distinction between mere 'reader-response' and
Rezeptionsgeschichte.[115]

Gadamer describes the *nature* of understanding, not the *stages* in which
it can be achieved. His critique of Schleiermacher is illuminating in this
respect. For Schleiermacher, in the case of an historical text when 'a gulf
of time has to be bridged', there is a 'special task' to be undertaken that
he describes as 'identifying with the original reader'. For Schleiermacher,
this is *preliminary* to the act of understanding, not – as for Gadamer –
'bound up with it'. The 'process of identifying' is for Schleiermacher
'only an ideal precondition for the actual act of understanding'.[116]

110. Luz, *Matthew 1–7*, p.95.
111. Knight, *Wirkungsgeschichte*', p.142. (Luz may have been constrained by the
format of the EKK series; see §6.3.a.)
112. Anthony C. Thiselton, *Thiselton on Hermeneutics: Collected Works with
New Essays* (Grand Rapids: Eerdmans, 2006), p.304 (emphasis his).
113. Nicholls, 'Walking on Water', pp.13–14.
114. Boer, 'Against "Reception History"' (see §1.1.c).
115. Chris Heard, 'In Defense of Reception History' (12 June 2011) (http://
bbibcomm.net/?p=216#more-216, accessed 3 July 2012).
116. Gadamer, *Truth and Method*, p.190.

However, it is not the fact that this construction of the competences of the first reader is undertaken *temporally first* that distinguishes Gadamer's hermeneutics from Schleiermacher's, but the fact that Schleiermacher locates the meaning to be discovered in the author, and not in a fusion of horizons: 'which for him does not consist of identifying with the original reader, but in putting oneself on the same level as the author, whereby the text is revealed as a unique manifestation of the author's life'.[117]

Jauss's own practice can be quarried for some, limited, justification of scheduling analysis in stages. He developed three 'steps' of interpretation, 'grounded in the theory that the hermeneutic process is to be conceived as a unity of the three moments of understanding [*intellegere*], interpretation [*interpretare*], and application [*applicare*]'.[118] He credits Gadamer with having brought 'back to light' the 'significance of this triadic unity of the hermeneutic process'.[119] They are posed as a unity, and in Gadamer they are precisely that, and indeed a 'fusion': 'Interpretation is not an occasional, post facto supplement to understanding; rather, understanding is always interpretation, and hence interpretation is the explicit form of understanding'.[120] In Jauss's framework, however, in practice,[121] they can become three stages. The first 'moment' has a 'pre-reflective' quality based on the reader's aesthetic experience. The second seeks to reconstruct the (aesthetic) experience of the first or early readers in the light of their encyclopaedic competences. The third stage of analysis is historical reflection, and considers the successive readings in the reception of the text, the progressive process to which Jauss's own interpretation also belongs.[122] Thiselton identifies the 'second stage' reading as 'akin to exegesis in biblical studies',[123] but Parris identifies the 'third level of reading' as the one that involves 'the historical-reconstructive reading of the text'.[124]

The steps, Jauss notes, do not need to be undertaken in this order: 'The priority of aesthetic perception in the triad of literary hermeneutics requires the *horizon* but not the *temporal priority* of the first [aesthetic]

117. Gadamer, *Truth and Method*, p.190. In §9.2, the location of meaning in 'the author' or in concepts of 'authorial intention' is discussed.

118. Jauss, *Aesthetic of Reception*, p.139 (cited in §1.1.b).

119. Jauss, *Aesthetic of Reception*, p.139.

120. Gadamer, *Truth and Method*, p.306.

121. E.g. his analysis of Baudelaire's 'Spleen II' in *Aesthetic of Reception*, pp.139–85.

122. Hans-Robert Jauss, *Ästhetische Ehrfahrung und litarische Hermeneutik* (Frankfurt: Suhrkamp, 1997), pp.836 and 846.

123. Thiselton, 'Reception Theory', p.299; and see the discussion in §2.2.

124. Parris, *Reception Theory*, p.163, citing Jauss, *Aesthetic of Reception*, 146.

reading'.[125] However, for Jauss, they *can* be successive. Lyons's analysis, of reception history's virtual inability to insist on notions of first- and second-stage interpretations,[126] is therefore challengeable, if we follow Jauss. It is harder to challenge using Gadamer: 'the ideal pre-condition of placing oneself on the same level as the original reader cannot be realized before the actual attempt of understanding, but is wholly bound up with it'.[127] Gadamer would be unlikely to refer to any reading as 'pre-reflective' (as Jauss, above). Nevertheless, as we have seen, he does describe the projection of an historical horizon as 'one phase in the process of understanding', which 'under special circumstances' becomes 'a scholarly task.[128]

Both Gadamer and Jauss, then, proscribe 'naïve fusion' and the 'objectivist illusion'.[129] Therefore, an historical-critical reading is an historically contingent reception of the text, and the projected horizon, the hypothetical first-reception, 'immediately recombines'[130] with the life-horizon of the interpreter as it is constructed:

> To believe that it is possible to gain access to the alien horizon of the past simply by leaving out one's own horizon of the present is to fail to recognize that subjective criteria, such as choice, perspective and evaluation, have been introduced into a supposedly objective reconstruction of the past.[131]

But Gadamer and Jauss also insist, as a phase in the full process of understanding, on the reader's transposition 'into the historical horizon from which the traditionary text speaks'.[132] Crucially, there is a self-conscious, reflexive character to the process, *centred on 'historical consciousness'*.

Jauss attributes the acquisition of the 'horizon of perceptive comprehension' to either '*historical* comprehension' or '*repeated* reading'.[133] In these two terms is the pragmatic reality of how the fusion or mediation of horizons is accomplished with the inclusion of scholarly construct of

---

125. Jauss, 'Limits and Tasks', p.119 (emphasis mine).

126. Lyons, 'Troubled Discipline', p.214 (cited above).

127. Gadamer, *Truth and Method*, p.190.

128. Gadamer, *Truth and Method*, p.305 (cited in §2.2).

129. Jauss, 'Identity of the Poetic Text', pp.7–8.

130. Gadamer, *Truth and Method*, p.305 (cited in §2.2).

131. Jauss, 'Identity of the Poetic Text', pp.7–8 (to be revisited in §6.4).

132. Gadamer, *Truth and Method*, pp.302 and 330. This must be held together with the insistence (discussed further in §2.4) that the 'horizon of understanding cannot be *limited*…by what the writer originally had in mind': Gadamer, *Truth and Method*, p.396 (emphasis mine).

133. Jauss, 'Limits and Tasks', p.119 (emphasis mine).

the horizon of 'first reception'. It is *wirkungsgeschichtliches Bewusstsein* that does not cover up the 'tensions between the text and the present', and where the resulting 'fusion' is not merely 'naïve assimilation of the two'.[134] It is *iterative* reading that enables meaning to be 'perceived and evaluated' within the same process, without being 'collapsed' into a single operation.[135] The reconstruction of the earliest reception-possibilities is not achieved as a prior act establishing 'assured and agreed-on interpretations',[136] but iteratively, within the dialectic of understanding an historical text, with an historical consciousness that is 'aware of its own otherness and hence foregrounds the horizon of the past from its own'.[137]

I have postponed to Chapter 9 a more thorough-going examination of the role of prejudgments. I shall pursue there Gadamer's argument that the interpreter may not share the views constituting the first horizon of the text, but that nevertheless those views form an integral part of the interpreter's self-understanding, which 'proceeds from the commonality that binds us to the tradition'.[138]

2.5. Interim summary

Claims for a hermeneutical deficiency in historical biblical criticism – that in 'its most critical form and by itself' it is 'inadequate', and that it is 'incapable of achieving what most of its practitioners considered its purpose to be'[139] – are claims which do indeed draw support from Gadamer and Jauss. However, Gadamer's hermeneutics and Jauss's aesthetics of reception do not offer real support for claims of, merely, a *dichotomy* of method between historical-critical exegesis on the one side and other forms of reception and application on the other. Where Swartley notes that the efforts to 'remedy' the 'deficiency' in historical-critical interpretation have either concerned the framework of exegetical method itself, or introduced considerations that alter the method,[140] my analysis identifies a particular role for standard historical-critical methodologies as an integral part of the paradigm of understanding texts, described by *Wirkungsgeschichte* and reception history.

134. Gadamer, *Truth and Method*, p.305 (cited in §2.3).
135. Barton, *Nature of Biblical Criticism*, p.159 (cited above).
136. Aichele *et al.*, 'Elephant in the Room', p.384 (cited in §2.1).
137. Gadamer, *Truth and Method*, p.305 (cited in §2.2).
138. Gadamer, *Truth and Method*, p.293.
139. As above: Swartley, *Slavery, Sabbath*, p.219; Wink, *Bible in Human Transformation*, pp.10–12.
140. Swartley, *Slavery, Sabbath*, p.219.

Both Gadamer and Jauss demand a dialectic engagement with (hypo-thetical) first-reception because of the necessity, within a process of understanding the text, of a 'reconstruction of the horizon of expectations in the face of which a work was created and received in the past'.[141] Hypothetical first-reception can be conceived, within the methodologies of reception history, as constituting one of the synchronic cross-sections of the diachronic perspective in which other instantiations of a text are viewed. In this respect, it is *one* construction of reception among others, a perception of meaning like any other that is discovered with a con-sciousness of the hermeneutical situation, of being 'affected by history'.[142]

However, historical-critical methods contribute, distinctively, to the whole process of understanding as 'the scholarly task' of a 'projection of the horizon of the past', which for Gadamer is 'one phase in the process of understanding'.[143] Any such projected horizon, as it is projected, is 'simultaneously superseded' in a fusion with the life-horizon of the interpreter.[144] Some critics claim that this is to 'collapse...into a single process' what can only be undertaken in two stages: so, 'after exegesis comes reception history'.[145] Such a hermeneutics underestimates the principle of historical consciousness, that is 'aware of its own otherness and...foregrounds the horizon of the past from its own.'[146] It also over-looks the pragmatic strategies of iterative reading where partial, provi-sional and plural analyses, 'exercises in plausibility',[147] contribute to the constructed horizon. It is self-consciously undertaken: interpretation is 'the explicit form of understanding'.[148] It may even be *positioned* in stages and phases, if these are revisited and not permanently enshrined as the 'primary datum': 'To bring about this fusion in a *regulated* way is the task of what we call' *wirkungsgeschichtliches Bewusstein.*[149]

Chapters 3, 4 and 5 will sample the case study in relation to recon-structions of hypothetical first-reception using some historical-critical methods, testing these arguments and illustrating how exegetical read-ings are themselves receptions characterised by prejudgments, tradition and historical contingency. Readers wanting to move directly to the

141. Jauss, *Aesthetic of Reception*, p.28.
142. Gadamer, *Truth and Method*, p.301.
143. Gadamer, *Truth and Method*, p.305.
144. Gadamer, *Truth and Method*, p.306.
145. Barton, *Nature of Biblical Criticism*, p.159, and Boer, 'Against "Reception History"'.
146. Gadamer, *Truth and Method*, p.305.
147. Lyons, 'Troubled Discipline', p.213.
148. Gadamer, *Truth and Method*, p.306.
149. Gadamer, *Truth and Method*, p.306 (emphasis mine).

second nexus of theoretical issues might go next to Chapter 6. Some issues touched but left aside here in Chapter 2 are addressed further in Chapters 6 and 9: the claims of exegetical readings as *normative* in a tradition of interpretation, the appeal to the author's 'intention' as definitive, and the theological character of the texts.

Chapter 3

THE CASE STUDY AND HISTORICAL-CRITICAL TOOLS:
GENRE AND THE *ERWARTUNGSHORIZONT*

3.1. Introduction

In this first selection, arrangement and discussion of reception of my
case-study texts (in Chapters 3, 4 and 5) we are focussing on the consideration given to the semantic competences and historical contingencies
of the first readers. This is offered not as a reconstruction of any plausible applications that emerge as a 'primary datum'[1] establishing 'assured
and agreed-on interpretations',[2] but in order to reflect on the projection of
an historical horizon as 'one phase in the process of understanding'.[3]

Both Mayordomo-Marín's work (on Mt. 1 and 2) and Morales
Vásquez's work (on one of my own texts, Rom. 13.1-7) provide constructions of this process. We all (Mayordomo-Marín leading the way)
examine the historical setting, and encyclopaedic competences, in relation to genre and semantics, of the first readers. However, the intention
of those two authors is primarily to demonstrate a model or a method,
where mine is primarily to test the way particular approaches reflect the
hermeneutics of Gadamer and Jauss.

Both these authors begin, as I do not, with the Jaussian 'first reading'
in relation to their own contemporary location. In Jauss, this is the 'pre-
reflective stage', *intellegere* without *interpretare* and *applicare*, and not
'fused' as Gadamer would have it (see §2.2). Morales Vásquez makes
this stage (Jauss's *intellegere*, though in no way 'pre-reflective') a selection of contemporary academic reception; and this is followed by
constructions of hypothetical early reception' (Jauss's *interpretare*).
Thiselton makes the same parallel of this 'second stage' reading as 'akin
to exegesis in biblical studies'.[4] Morales Vásquez offers a series of

---

1. Rowland, 'Pragmatic Approach', p.1 (cited in §2.3).
2. Aichele *et al.*, 'Elephant in the Room', p.384 (cited in §§2.1 and 2.4).
3. Gadamer, *Truth and Method*, p.305 (cited in §2.2).
4. Thiselton, 'Reception Theory', p.299; and see the discussion in §2.2.

historical reception subsequently (Jauss's *applicare*): he says this is to go a 'step further' (than Mayordomo-Marín and Thiselton) 'in the integration of the exegesis of the Scriptures with their history of reception'.[5] This is a common distinction (exegesis as something other than *wirkungsgeschichtliches* reception)[6] but in Gadamerian hermeneutics all exegesis stands within, not before or outside of, the process of historically effected understanding (see §2.4).

I have therefore attempted to demonstrate how historical-critical approaches are characterised like all constructions of meaning by the dialectic of Gadamerian hermeneutics: all meaning is *co-determined* by the historical situation of the interpreter.[7] The intention of this analysis is not to establish a definitive horizon of expectation for any of my texts, but is a sampling of different attempts in the process, to illustrate how these considerations contribute to meaning-possibilities accessible to the earliest readers. In the dialectic of reception history, attempts to reconstruct the horizon of meaning in which the texts were first received are provisional, plural, and iterative (see §2.4). The sample is diverse in its historical periods: the questions posed by historical-critical approaches concerning the *Erwartungshorizont*, the horizon of expectation of the first readers, are not confined to recent centuries though richly present there. It is my intention to show that the different constructions can be 'perceived and evaluated' without being 'collapsed' into a single operation of understanding the text.[8]

This material is presented in Chapters 3, 4, and 5 using areas of exegetical investigation that contribute to construction(s) of hypothetical first-reception. In Chapter 2, these factors were identified in both historical-critical method and the hermeneutics of Gadamer and Jauss:

1.   Insights from contemporary literature, and the semantic competences of the first readers: these are part of 'the objectifiable system of expectations that arise for each work in the historical moment of its appearance, from a pre-understanding of the genre, from the form and themes of already familiar works'; 'how the contemporary reader could have viewed and understood the work'.[9]

---

5.   Morales Vásquez, *Contours of a Biblical Reception Theory*, p.63.

6.   I shall suggest (§6.3.a) that this distinction is made by the *Encyclopedia of the Bible and its Reception*, implicitly in its structure.

7.   Gadamer, *Truth and Method*, p.296 (cited in §§2.1 and 2.4).

8.   Barton, *Nature of Biblical Criticism*, p.159 (cited §2.4).

9.   Jauss, *Aesthetic of Reception*, pp.22 and 28 (cited in §2.3).

2. Socio-historical setting and occasion: identification of these responds to 'the clear hermeneutical demand: to understand a text in terms of the specific situation in which it was written'.[10]

The present chapter, therefore, examines expectations based on 'genre'; Chapter 4 examines the key words and the possibilities of meaning they carried to the first readers (their 'semantic competences'); and Chapter 5 examines attempts to engage with 'historical setting and occasion'. (A further factor, the contested objective of authorial intention, will sometimes appear within the discussion of the semantic competences, in relation to claims of a distinctively Pauline theology. Further discussion of this in relation to Gadamerian hermeneutics is principally reserved until Chapter 9, and illustrated from the case study in Chapter 10.)

I comment within the sampling of material on how the exegetical analysis here is characterised by and contributes to the dialectic of *Wirkungsgeschichte*. The material offers elements of reconstruction of *Wirkungsbedingungen* ['effective conditions'] for the first or early reception of a text, and identification of its *Alterität* [the 'otherness' of past, 'alien' from the later reader's 'horizon']. As such, it contributes to the *Horizontabhebung* offering a comparison or differentiation with the contemporary horizon of expectation of other 'historically conditioned' readers.[11]

The horizon of expectation of a text's first or early readers may be formed in part by their experience of Graeco-Roman conventions in discourse and literature. All Pauline uses of ὑποτάσσειν and ὑποταγή occur within the genre of the Graeco-Roman 'letter' (§3.2). All three main case-study texts, Rom. 13.1, Col. 3.18, Eph. 5.21-22, are in the genre of 'paraenesis' (§3.3). Two of these are in the genre identified as the *Haustafel* (§3.4).

3.2. The genre of letter, with a focus on Romans

Expectations, in Jaussian terms, can be confirmed or reconfigured: a text 'satisfies, surpasses, disappoints or refutes the expectations of its first audience'.[12] The genre of 'letter' was particularly flexible,[13] and the early

10. Gadamer, *Truth and Method*, p.330 (cited in §2.3).
11. Jauss, *Alterität und Modernität*, p.129, and *Theorie der Rezeption*, p.17 (cited in §1.1.b).
12. Jauss, *Aesthetic of Reception*, p.25.
13. D. Aune, *The New Testament in its Literary Environment* (Philadelphia: Westminster, 1987), p.159.

Church exhibits varieties of the form, and Paul was a particularly creative and eclectic letter writer.[14] James Dunn suggests that the 'familiar
forms and idioms' of Paul's letter to the Romans 'made it more readily
hearable and assimilable for the recipients',[15] but if this is so, we still
have to consider quite what forms and idioms were familiar, and what
use Paul might be making of such familiarity. It might not be in order to
conform to the familiar.

A genre question relevant to reception of Rom. 13.1 is how far it
should be categorised as Paul's theological treatise, a 'non-historical
christianae religionis compendium'[16] rather than occasional, written to
meet the needs of a particular situation and issue (see also Chapter 5).
The former was a traditional view until Ferdinand Baur's 're-historici-
sation' of Romans,[17] and is one which continues to have proponents. So
Bornkamm says that no knowledge of internal conflicts in the Roman
congregations will shed light on the purpose of Romans,[18] and Luz says
that 'the subject-matter discussed in it is the key to understanding its
structure, not the specific circumstances which occasioned it'.[19]

J.A. Fitzmyer considers the category of *Lehrbrief* (a didactic, philosophical treatise with the opening framework of a letter) and suggests for
Romans the category 'essay letter', in preference to 'letter-essay' – 'to
put stress on its missive character'.[20] This illustrates well Aune's caveat
on the *limits of genre-analysis* in determining the first or any reader's
'expectation':

14. Cf. Aune, *Literary Environment*, p.203.

15. James Dunn, *Romans 1–8* (WBC, 38a; Dallas: Word, 1988), p. lix.

16. C. Bryan, *A Preface to Romans: Notes on the Epistle in its Literary and
Cultural Setting* (Oxford: Oxford University Press, 2000), p.17 (raising this as a
question).

17. F.C. Baur, *Paul the Apostle of Jesus Christ: His Life and Work, his Epistles
and his Doctrine: A Contribution to a Critical History of Primitive Christianity*
(trans. A. Menzies; London: Williams & Norgate, 2nd edn, 1876), e.g. vol. 1,
pp.313–15.

18. G. Bornkamm, *Paul* (trans. M.G. Stalker; London: Hodder & Stoughton,
1971), p.93.

19. Ulrich Luz, '*Zum Aufbau von Röm. 1–8*', *Theologische Zeitschrift* 25 (1969),
pp.161–81 (162–63); trans. from A. Wedderburn, *Reasons for Romans* (London/
New York: Continuum, 2004), p.7.

20. J.A. Fitzmyer, *Romans: A New Translation with Introduction and Commentary* (London: Geoffrey Chapman, 1992), p.69.

> Early Christian letters tend to resist classification…in terms of the many
> categories listed by epistolary theorists. Most early Christian letters are
> multi-functional and have a 'mixed' character, combining elements from
> two or more epistolary types. In short, each early Christian letter must be
> analysed on its own terms.[21]

Paul, then, was able to draw on various types of epistolary communication available to him – personal letter, official letter, letter-essay.[22] Two
factors complicate further the question of genre and expectation. First,
the oral, public performance of the letters, read out in one or more house-
churches where additional oral messages might be appended, is a
significant condition. M.L. Stirewalt suggests: 'Paul is writing letters
socially and theologically bound to the oral word. He does not conceive
of a context in which, on reception, his word is not reanimated by oral
speech.'[23] Second, there is the possibility or likelihood that as well as
being targeted for particular audiences, the letters quickly circulated
more widely among a group of Christian congregations: this is suggested
by the early reference (2 Pet. 3.16) to a body of Paul's letters. These
factors leave at least *a considerable flexibility in the horizon of expectation* establishable by genre.

3.3. The genre of paraenesis

This genre question presents a key illustration of the 'negotiability' of
horizons of expectation, and of how far the appropriation of a genre will
fulfil expectation and confirm prejudgments or move the reader 'to new,
formative horizons, which will correct and surpass former perceptions'.[24]
With 'paraenesis', no less than 'letter', a focus on genre presents a contestable contribution to the *Erwartungshorizont*.

   In twentieth-century reception of my texts, the account given by Hans
Lietzmann and Martin Dibelius[25] of the Christian appropriation of a
Graeco-Roman literary form has been very influential, and interpreters
compare the texts with letters of popular Hellenist moral philoso-
phers. Paraenesis, generically, describes 'a text which strings together
admonitions of general ethical content…in the form of a command or a

21. Aune, *Literary Environment*, p.203.
22. Cf. M.L. Stirewalt, *Paul, the Letter Writer* (Grand Rapids: Eerdmans, 2003),
p.107.
23. Stirewalt, *Letter Writer*, p.108.
24. Thiselton, 'Reception Theory' (cited in §1.1.b).
25. Hans Lietzmann, *An die Römer* (Tübingen: Mohr Siebeck 1906); Martin
Dibelius, *James: A Commentary on the Epistle of James* [1921] (trans. M.A.
Williams; Philadelphia: Fortress, 1975).

summons'. They are general admonitions that 'do not apply to a single audience and a single set of circumstances' but reproduce the 'popular ethics of antiquity'.[26] In this respect, and in more recent studies, it is sometimes generically distinguished from 'deliberative rhetoric' which represents advice about specific occasion.[27]

Andrew Pitts characterises this enterprise – comparing sections of Pauline letters with the philosophical letters of popular moralists – as 'misguided', because literary features, claimed to have a uniquely philosophical origin, 'do not conform to patterns of usage found among the Hellenistic moralists, are not distinctively philosophical or may be accounted for more convincingly within other social and literary contexts'.[28] In particular, many interpreters account for the content and ethos of the exhortations as a legacy from Judaism.[29]

In Jaussian terms, the genre-focused analysis views New Testament paraenesis as a reception of an earlier work where, in the new encounter, the horizon of expectation does not become 'varied, corrected, altered', but 'just reproduced'.[30] The meaning is attributable to the sources, and not to a distinctive authorial voice or theological perspective. So Dibelius argues that 'the hortatory sections of the Pauline epistles have nothing to do with the theoretic foundation of the ethics of the apostle, and very little to do with other ideas peculiar to him. Rather they belong to tradition.'[31] In this perspective, ὑποτασσέσθω in Rom. 13.1-3 (for example) would be read as part of a catalogue of generic virtues and vices: ὑποτασσέσθω and ἀγαθος represent social virtues against the corresponding social vices, ἀνθέστηκεν and κακος.[32]

Conversely, the horizon is represented as 'mediated' rather than merely 'reproduced' if the parenesis is seen as a combination of borrowed

---

26. Dibelius, *James*, pp.3, 11 and 5.

27. E.g. Aune, *Literary Environment*, p.191, and Margaret M. Mitchell, *Paul and the Rhetoric of Reconciliation: An Exegetical Investigation of the Language and Composition of 1 Corinthians* (Westminster: John Knox, 1992), p.53.

28. Andrew W. Pitts, 'Philosophical and Epistolary Contexts for Pauline Paraenesis', in *Paul and the Ancient Letter Form* (ed. Stanley E. Porter and Sean A. Adams; Leiden: Brill, 2010), pp.270–306 (270–71).

29. E.g. Jerome D. Quinn, 'Paraenesis and the Pastoral Epistles: Lexical Observations Bearing on the Nature of the Sub-genre and Soundings on its Role in Socialization and Liturgies', in *Paraenesis: Act and Form* (ed. John Gammie and Leo Perdue; Semeia 50; Atlanta: SBL, 1990), pp.189–210 (201).

30. Jauss, *Aesthetic of Reception*, p.23 (cited in §1.1.b).

31. Martin Dibelius, *From Tradition to Gospel* (ed. W. Barclay; trans. B.L. Woolf; New York: Scribner, 1965), p.239.

32. Cf. Aune, *Literary Environment*, p.195.

injunctions from Hellenism or Hellenistic Judaism with distinctively Christian elements. For example, P. Carrington and E.G. Selwyn attempted to reconstruct a pattern of teaching behind the New Testament letters which includes both unique Christian elements and borrowed paraenetic material.[33]

This becomes thorough 'transformation' of the horizon of expectation in some interpretations. C.H. Dodd recognises that the paraenetic material is not specifically Christian but argues that 'ethical ideas are transformed by being brought into a context which is religious through and through'.[34] W.D. Davies describes this as Paul 'baptising' the traditional material into Christ.[35] J.D. Quinn suggests that traditional paraenetic material, when used in 'the service of an essentially new social phenomenon, the Christian churches', would be regarded in contemporaneous culture as 'subversive, if not revolutionary'.[36]

Gadamer describes this mediation or transformation of an inherited legacy. The interpreter (here it is Paul, offering a reception of some Hellenistic-Jewish paraenesis) is not subject to tradition, but participates in it. Understanding is the 'interplay' between 'the movement of tradition' and 'the movement of the interpreter'. What the reader of Paul's text then receives is an evolution of the tradition which Paul has participated in[37] and not merely passed on. This is an issue of some significance in the Christian tradition(s) of reception of my case-study texts. They can be received as bearing the perspective of the sources of the words or ideas in Hellenistic social mores, or they can be received as bearing a transformative theological significance deriving from Paul and the *kerygma*. This can be illustrated in the exegetical discussion of the paraenesis of household relationships that follows.

3.4. The genre of *Haustafel*[38]

The *Haustafel* or Household Code can be represented as a subset of the paraenesis genre. The structure of paired exhortations to three pairs of

33. Carrington, *Catechism*, p.31; E.G. Selwyn, *The First Epistle of Peter* (London: Macmillan 1969), pp.17–23.

34. C.H. Dodd, *Gospel and Law: The Relation of Faith and Ethics in Early Christianity* (Cambridge: Cambridge University Press, 1951), p.25.

35. W.D. Davies, *Paul and Rabbinic Judaism* (London: SPCK, 1948), p.136.

36. Quinn, 'Paraenesis and the Pastoral Epistles', p.201.

37. Cf. Gadamer, *Truth and Method*, p.293 (cited in §1.1.a).

38. This term derives from the heading to Luther's *Kleinen Katechismus* (1529): B.J. Kidd, *Documents Illustrative of the Continental Reformation* (Oxford: Clarendon, 1911), p.220.

agents in the household[39] is found in Col. 3.18–4.1 and Eph. 5.21–6.9. Wives, children and slaves are mentioned first in each pairing, and they are exhorted to 'submission' (wives) or 'obedience' (children and slaves). There is similar material, not in the same structure, in 1 Tim. 2.8-15; 5.1-2; 6.1-2; Tit. 2.1-10; 3.1, and 1 Pet. 2.18–3.7.

These may borrow from patterns of the common rhetorical topic, *peri oikonomias*, adapted for moral instruction among Christians. Studies in the 1970s (by David Balch and others) argued that this way of thinking about patterns of social obligation was 'much older and broader than had previously been suspected'.[40] Balch traces the 'axiomatic' pattern of social hierarchy from Plato, and an exact outline of the three pairings in Aristotle, and then subsequent appearances in Stoic, Hellenistic-Jewish and Neo-Pythagorean contexts.[41] He concludes that these were available in the Roman Empire in the first century C.E., with the probability that Jewish-Christian authors (such as Paul and the author of 1 Peter) would be aware of the ethic and 'its apologetic purposes' through Hellenistic Judaism rather than from pagan sources of Greek political thought.[42] (In fact, 'submission' is not applied to wives in these sources.)

The pre-existence of such a pattern has been questioned. Lars Hartman argues that there is no evidence of a literary form of 'household code' lying ready to hand for early Christians to use, and that Colossians 3 and Ephesians 5 owe more to the Graeco-Roman world for the attitudes and social convention they reflect than for their literary form.[43] The precise origins have not yet been explained according to Angela Standhartinger, who suggests that the closest parallels in genre to the Colossians *Haustafel* are 'popular-philosophical collections of laws'.[44]

---

39.   The hierarchical ordering of the household in antiquity, and the influence of household roles in house churches and the subsequent tradition, are pertinent matters, and will be discussed in §5.3.a.

40.   Wayne Meeks, 'The *"Haustafeln"* and American Slavery: The Hermeneutical Challenge', in Lovering *et al.*, *Theology and Ethics*, pp.232–53 (242).

41.   David L. Balch, *Let Wives Be Submissive: The Domestic Code in 1 Peter* (SBLMS, 26; Chico: Scholars Press, 1981), e.g. pp.61–62; citing Plato, *Laws* 3.690 A–D, and Aristotle, *Politics* 1.1253b 1–14.

42.   Balch, *Let Wives*, p.120.

43.   Lars Hartman, 'Some Unorthodox Thoughts on the "Household Code" Form', in *The Social World of Formative Christianity and Judaism* (ed. J. Neusner *et al.*; Philadelphia: Fortress, 1988), pp.219–32.

44.   A. Standhartinger, 'The Origin and Intention of the Household Code in the Letter to the Colossians', *JSNT* 23 (2001), pp.117–30 (117).

Scholars who accept the use of an existing genre differ in how such a use *confirms*, or *transforms*, the horizon of expectation of early readers.[45] A.J.M. Wedderburn, for example, argues that they confirm expectation and the impact is 'merely conventional'. He suggests that the conventions adopted (in Colossians) were not universally accepted, but represent a humane middle way between the other options current in the first century, which are either aspirations of emancipation or an assertion of domineering patriarchal rights. The use of the conventions merely to endorse the *status quo* would only be avoided if there is a radical reappraisal of them, a questioning of whether these relationships 'reflected the character of the Lord', and Wedderburn suggests:

> There is little sign in Colossians of that happening (it lacks even the mutual subordination found in Eph. 5.21), except perhaps in the call for husbands to love their wives; yet even this…is merely conventional. When this questioning does not occur the consequences are calamitous… what should be a common subjection of all to their one Lord turns into a fixed, hierarchical and patriarchal order.[46]

Wedderburn asks if the appeals to such conduct as 'fitting in the Lord' (etc.) does more than lend 'a Christian endorsement to the thoroughly patriarchal norms of society of the day'.

Conversely, Ben Witherington argues that in the *Haustafeln*, 'Paul[47] is not urging conformity to society's norms, or what is seen as natural, but rather conformity to Christ'. They are the author's attempts to *start* with the existing social structures, but to 'reform' the patriarchal structure of the family:

> If his exhortations were fully implemented, and if a household 'head' indeed acted as head servant in self-sacrificial service to others, would ancients have recognised such as a 'traditional patriarchal family'? I think not. It would not look like modern egalitarian models of the family, but in its own way and time it would have been novel, indeed in some respects radical… [H]is call for the husband to act as a servant toward other members of the family would have been offensive, especially among the Graeco-Roman social elite.[48]

---

45. The question is related to the semantic impact of ὑποτάσσεσθε etc. (§4.2).

46. Wedderburn in A.T. Lincoln and A.J.M. Wedderburn, *The Theology of the Later Pauline Letters* (Cambridge: Cambridge University Press, 1993), p.57.

47. The effect of reading the letters as deutero-Pauline is discussed in §4.5.a.

48. Ben Witherington, *The Paul Quest: The Renewed Search for the Jew of Tarsus* (Leicester: InterVarsity, 1998), pp.189–90.

Andrew Lincoln describes (in effect) a 'mediation' of horizons, which neither merely reproduces nor wholly transforms the horizon of the genre. He characterises the paraenesis of women's submission (in Ephesians) as 'an essential part' of the author's attempt to help the churches 'assimilate to life in society while preserving their distinctive identity': 'The patriarchal structuring of household management, which was seen as crucial for the stability of society, is taken over, but to it the writer brings his Christian vision of relationships'.[49]

If it *is* the goal of traditional commentaries to describe or construct 'one single meaning...identified with the author's original intention',[50] that is not what is achieved here. The different conclusions drawn are themselves part of the variety of 'effect' which is the legacy of the texts. These three, recent, instances assessing the use of the *Haustafel* genre on 'how the contemporary reader could have viewed and understood the work',[51] illustrate an operation of an historical-critical method that has an appropriate role within a reception-history approach to biblical interpretation. The 'meaning' remains contested, in a dialectic with different reception of the text and with other impulses in the process of understanding a traditionary text.[52]

The 'interestedness' and historical contingencies of the readers are factors in their exegesis (further illustrated in §§4.4.a and 4.5.b). The identification of the genre as 'merely' a reflection of Hellenistic society's norms can be an *unacknowledged* hermeneutical tactic, dismissing the ethical force of the text for the interpreter's own life-horizon. This can be associated with a hermeneutics that selects a theological imperative, or a canonical principle, or 'authorial intention' as determinative for interpreting and applying a Pauline text (discussed in §9.3.b). Gadamer insists on a self-consciousness in this process.

The interim case-study evaluation at the close of Chapter 4 reflects on this material along with the reception (focussed on lexis and 'semantic competences') in that chapter.

49. Lincoln, *Later Pauline Letters*, p.141.
50. Sawyer *et al.*, 'Series Editors' Preface', p.xi (cited in §2.3).
51. Jauss, *Aesthetic of Reception*, p.28 (cited above).
52. This translation of *Überlieferung* was noted in §2.2.

Chapter 4

THE CASE STUDY AND HISTORICAL-CRITICAL TOOLS: LEXIS AND THE *ERWARTUNGSHORIZONT*

4.1. Introduction

This sampling of the case study continues the focus on the semantic possibilities of the texts for the first readers. In the pursuit of 'how the contemporary reader could have viewed and understood the work',[1] historical-critical analysis regularly seeks insights from contemporary literature (a 'synchronic' strategy, see §2.2) to inform the lexical range of the words used.[2] This includes other uses by the same author, and uses in other biblical texts. The hermeneutical principle of canonical univocality,[3] which often operates in the reception of these texts, also requires examination of the other instances of the verb ὑποτάσσειν and the noun ὑποταγή in Pauline and other New Testament texts.

The reception principally sampled in my case study is in Greek, Latin and English, with some in German and Middle English. In translation, there is not a tradition of, nor agreement about, the semantic and theological specificity of these words in Paul's use. Latin translation of ὑποτάσσειν is consistent, using *subditus* or *subiectus*. However, this does not really represent identification of a distinctive frame of reference for the terms: the Vulgate uses these to translate other Greek terms too, for example, *subditus* for ὑπόδικος in Rom. 3.19 and *subiectus* for δεδού-λωται in 1 Cor. 7.15.

This is significant in later reception. When, for example, Hincmar (c. 806–882) concedes that an archbishop should submit to the Pope,[4]

---

1. Jauss, *Aesthetic of Reception*, p.28 (cited in the introduction to Chapter 3).

2. The focus in this chapter on lexis responds to the nature of the case-study texts (iterations of one Greek word and cognates) and to observable patterns of their reception, and does not represent the 'false assumption...that the word, rather than the sentence or speech-act, constitutes the basic unit of meaning to be investigated': Thiselton, *On Hermeneutics*, p.193.

3. E.g. Young, *Biblical Exegesis*, p.7 (see §1.2.a).

4. Hincmarus, *Epistola II, ad Nicolaum Papam de vacatione sedis Cameracensis* (ed. J.P. Migne; *PCC-SL* 126; Paris, 1870), pp.32 and 33.

both Leon Strieder and George Tavard suggest that 'as well as drawing on canonical terms' ('holy canons', 'holy laws'), Hincmar uses 'feudal' terms in this argument.[5] *Subditas* and *subiectos* are indeed feudal terms, but they are also the Vulgate words in Pauline texts on submission (e.g. Rom. 13.1; 1 Cor. 15.27). It is a recurring feature in the reception of the texts that commentators may refer the language used to the cultural ideology of the day rather than to a distinctive Pauline use.[6] It is a view that extends to the language of the primary texts themselves and their perceived reflection of prevalent culture, as with some commentators above (§§3.3 and 3.4) or Peter Davids who sees the subordination paraenesis as reflecting 'the commonplaces of secular culture'.[7]

The absence of a distinct frame of reference of these words in Latin sets the trend for subsequent translation, and the English tradition of translation does not keep a consistent distinction. For example, though KJV gives 'submit' for ὑποτάσσησθε in 1 Cor. 16.16, the NRSV translates this as 'put yourselves at the service of'; and translates ὑποτασ-σόμεναι in 1 Pet. 3.1 as 'accept the authority of'. It is still more clearly evident in the use of 'submit' or 'subject' for a number of other Greek expressions. For ὑπόδικος (Rom. 3.19), the Geneva Bible has 'subject to judgement'. For δογματίζεσθε (Col. 2.20), KJV has 'subject to ordinances', followed by NRSV with 'submit to regulations'. For ἐνέχεσθε (Gal. 5.1) and ἀνέχεσθε (2 Cor. 11.4), NRSV has 'submit'. Exegetes, as this suggests, take different views on the relative force of the lexicon of 'obedience' (e.g. πειθαρχεῖν, πείθεσθαι, ὑπακούειν) and 'submission'.

4.2. *Hupotassein* in Greek literature; and the influence of Psalm 8.6

Ὑποτάσσειν indicates in the active to 'place under', 'subordinate'; and in the middle voice to 'subject oneself', 'acknowledge [someone's] dominion', 'order oneself under [a leader]'. It appears in this sense in Josephus.[8] The middle can carry the meaning to 'subject oneself' out of, for example, fear, or to 'submit oneself voluntarily'. The root can apply

5.   Leon F. Strieder, *The Promise of Obedience: A Ritual History* (Collegeville: Liturgical Press, 2001), p.13; cf. George Tavard, 'Episcopacy and Apostolic Succession according to Hincmar of Reims', *Theological Studies* 34 (1973), pp.594–623.

6.   E.g. Christopher Hill (ed.), *The English Revolution 1640: Three Essays in Interpretation* (London: Lawrence & Wishart, 1940), p.12.

7.   Peter Davids, *The First Epistle of Peter, New International Commentary* (Grand Rapids: Eerdmans, 1990), p.98.

8.   E.g. Flavius Josephus, *The Jewish War* 2.566, 2.578 and 5.309, in *The Works of Josephus* (trans. William Whiston; Peabody: Hendrickson, 1995), pp.633–34 and 712.

to military troops.[9] The image of troops arranged in lines of battle does seem to lie behind the language of 1 Cor. 15.23: 'each in his own order [τάγματι]'; and behind the antithesis in Rom. 13.1-2: ὑποτασσέσθω / ὁ ἀντιτασσόμενος.

It appears in Greek literature relatively late. Although the call for wives to obey husbands was common in Hellenistic Judaism (as noted in §3.4), wives are not exhorted with ὑποτάσσεσθαι in such parallels: for example, Josephus, who uses ὑπακούειν, and Philo, who uses δουλεύειν.[10] There are only two extant examples from other Greek authors, Pseudo-Callisthenes and Plutarch, of the use of the actual verb (not in exhortation) for the wife's attitude toward her husband.[11]

In the Septuagint the word is not common. In the active, it is used to mean 'place under', 'subordinate', especially by God who makes other creatures subject to humans (Ps. 8.6), and the people subject to the anointed king (Ps. 18.47 = LXX 17.47). The middle voice can refer to the acknowledgment of God's power, and the power of his people (e.g. 1 Chron. 22.18). Cranfield judges that in only one of the uses in the Septuagint is 'obedience' prominent, with the corollary in the New Testament that 'sometimes the specific idea of obedience is prominent (e.g. Rom. 8.7); but in the majority of cases, while it may well be included, it is not clear that it is the predominant thought'.[12]

There are possibilities of a *confirmatory* effect, in relation to a horizon of expectation of early readers, where the word carries the 'normative' context of military rank and social hierarchies, or a *transformatory* effect, where the word is associated with a 'distinctive' context of theological statements. Carrington suggest the former: it represents an appropriation of an established idea used widely in the early Church. So, he says, ὑποτάσσεσθε and ὑποτασσέσθων have a 'general catechetical-type role in primitive Christian exhortation'.[13] Such an analysis takes too little account of the role of Old Testament scripture for the concept

9. Cf. David J. Williams, *Paul's Metaphors: Their Context and Character* (Cambridge: Henderson, 1999), p.177.

10. E.g. Josephus, *Against Apion* 2.24 and 2.201, in Josephus, *The Life, Against Apion* (ed. H.St.J. Thackeray; LCL 1; Cambridge, Mass.: Harvard University Press, 1926), p.372; Philo, *Hypothetica* 7.3 in *Philo* (ed. F.H. Colson; LCL 9; London: William Heinemann, 1941), p.424.

11. Plutarch, *Conjugalia Praecepta* 33 (*Moralia* 142e), and Pseudo-Callisthenes, *Historia Alexandri Magni* 1.22.4; cf. Lincoln, *Ephesians*, p.367.

12. C.E.B. Cranfield, *A Commentary on Romans 12–13* (Edinburgh/London: Oliver & Boyd, 1965), p.661. (Cranfield's reception is discussed further below, §§4.4.a and 4.4.b.)

13. Carrington, *Catechism*, p.49.

of submission in early Christianity, and a distinctive horizon of expectation of 'submission' or 'subjection' in the light, particularly, of Ps. 8.6. (Applying the full context for the semantic range of a word to other instances such as this runs the risk, of course, of 'illegitimate totality transfer'.)[14]

The citations of Ps. 8.6 in the New Testament, in the Pauline tradition (1 Cor. 15.27; Eph. 1.22; Phil. 3.21) and beyond it (Heb. 2.8; 1 Pet. 3.22) give the word a constituent role in early Christian confession or apologetic, describing the role of Christ in salvation.[15] All but one instance in the New Testament of the active voice of ὑποτάσσειν (the exception is Rom. 8.20) are christological and stand in express relationship to Ps. 8.6. This represents a potentially *transformative* use, a christological mediation of horizons, which changes the horizon of expectation from one with, for example, a role in military ranking and social stratification, to a new 'order' in Christ.

Paul's citation of Ps. 8.6 in 1 Corinthians 15 is close to the Septuagint rendering, using the same form of ὑποτάσσειν but with a shift from second to third person:

Ps. 8.6 [= LXX 8.7]:   πάντα ὑπέταξας ὑποκάτω τῶν ποδῶν αὐτοῦ

1 Cor. 15.27:   πάντα [γὰρ] ὑπέταξεν ὑπὸ τοὺς πόδας αὐτοῦ.

The christological and eschatological statement of 1 Cor. 15.27-28, with an eschatological submission of all things to Christ and Christ's own submission to God, suggests a transformative theological appropriation of the term:

> For 'God has put all things in subjection [ὑπέταξεν] under his feet'. But when it says, 'All things are put in subjection [ὑποτέτακται]', it is plain that this does not include the one who put all things in subjection under [ὑποτά-ξαντος] him. When all things are subjected to [ὑποταγῇ] him, then the Son himself will also be subjected to [ὑποταγήσεται] the one who put all things in subjection [ὑποτάξαντι] under him, so that God may be all in all.

There is a very probable allusion to Ps. 8.6 in Phil. 3.21: 'He will transform the body of our humiliation that it may be conformed to the body of his glory, by the power that also enables him to make all things [τὰ πάντα] subject to [ὑποτάξαι] himself'. The 'humiliation' [ταπεινώσεως]

---

14. James Barr, *The Semantics of Biblical Language* (London: SCM, 1961), p.218.

15. Paul 'assumes that his audience accepts the applicability of these passages to the Christ events... [T]hey are already deeply embedded in Christian teaching and liturgy': Martin C. Albl, *'And Scripture cannot be broken': The Form and Function of the Early Christian Testimonia Collections* (Leiden: Brill, 1999), p.225.

echoes Phil. 2.3 [ταπεινοφροσύνη]. This offers an association of a pattern of submission to Christ and of Christ's own self-submission in Phil. 3.21 with an exhortation to what is effectively (though without the use of ὑποτάσσειν) mutual submission in Phil. 2.3: 'in humility regard others [ἀλλήλους] as better than yourselves'.

Ephesians 1.22 cites Ps. 8.6 more fully: 'And he has put [ὑπέταξεν] all things [πάντα] under his feet and has made him the head over all things for the church'. Some commentators see this as informing the paraenesis later in the letter (see §4.6.a below).

The spread of allusions to Ps. 8.6 (linked to Ps. 110.1) may suggest that this became a constituent part of the primitive Christian confession (Carrington's 'general catechetical-type role'),[16] but the occurrences of ὑποτάσσειν and ὑποταγή are principally in the Pauline and deutero-Pauline tradition, and the paraenetic dimension of the Pauline use is distinctive. The paraenetic uses occur in the middle voice or passive-middle form, which opens up a question of how far the subject is a free agent, choosing to make this reflexive action, and how far positioned in an involuntary stratification. The middle can also contribute to an uncertainty, when there is no indirect object to the verb (e.g. 1 Cor. 14.34), as to whom or to what those exhorted should submit themselves. Gerhard Delling, in the *Theological Dictionary of the New Testament*, judges the submission in the middle voice of ὑποτάσσειν as demanding 'readiness to renounce one's own will for the sake of others, i.e. ἀγάπη, and to give precedence to others'.[17] He relates this to his view that being subordinate [ὑποτάσσομαι] bears a semantic relationship to Christian humility [ταπεινοφροσύνη],[18] but makes no reference to the theological framework in Pauline teaching that connects the kerygma of 'Christ crucified' with these exhortations.[19]

It is the universal and reciprocal exhortation Ὑποτασσόμενοι ἀλλήλοις ἐν φόβῳ Χριστοῦ (Eph. 5.21) that most obviously challenges the reception of the word as merely repeating a traditional social and political hierarchy. Yet the latter view is prevalent in the history of reception: for example, Davids sees the subordination paraenesis as reflecting 'commonplaces of secular culture', in which '[s]ubmission to God, of course, would be an assumption of Christianity' but not 'submitting to people'.[20]

16. Carrington, *Catechism*, p.49 (cited above).
17. Gerhard Delling, 'Hupotassein', in *TDNT* VIII (1972), pp.39–46 (45).
18. Cf. E. Kamlah, 'Ὑποτασσέσθαι in den neutestmentlichen Haustafeln', in *Verborum Veritas: Festschrift für G. Stählin zum 70 Geburtstag* (ed. O. Bocher and K. Haacker; Wuppertal: Brockhaus, 1970), pp.237–43.
19. This is developed and critiqued in §10.5.
20. Davids, *Peter*, p.98.

My own theological prejudgment here (§1.2.b; see also §10.5) is that Paul's characterisation of the sacrificial death of Christ, for example, 'God chose what is weak in the world to shame the strong' (1 Cor. 1.27), radically transforms his ethics of human relationships from traditional structures of lordship to one where the super-ordinate 'strong' gives way to the subordinate 'weak', because she or he is a sister or brother for whom Christ died (e.g. 1 Cor. 8.11). The semantic relationship of this to ὑποτάσσειν is not transparent. It may be expressed in the exhortation to reciprocal or mutual submission and in the christological formulation of 1 Cor. 15.28. However, the other uses of the word are never applied to a person whose social status is higher than the person they are urged to submit to: that is, it is wives and not husbands who are urged to 'submit'. This suggests a not-wholly-resolved 'mediation of horizons' between a meaning embodying the expectations of social stratification, and a transformative value arising from a pattern of humility and obedience that does not 'conform to this world' (Rom. 12.2).

There are thus various questions of semantic analysis seeking the plausibilities of meaning for early reception, contributing to the construction of a horizon of expectation for 'hypothetical first-reception'. There are various attempts at answers from a broad sweep of exegetical tradition and this material is discussed in the following sequence:

§4.3. Ὑποτάσσειν and [ἡ] ὑποταγή in indicative statements
§4.4. Be subject to the governing authorities
§4.5. Wives, be subject
§4.6. Be subject to one another
§4.7. Ὑποτάσσειν and [ἡ] ὑποταγή in the rest of the New Testament

Although the threefold focus remains Rom. 13.1, Col. 3.18 and Eph. 5.21-22, the lexical questions call for some examination of each occurrence of ὑποτάσσειν and ὑποταγή in the New Testament, and these are all included in the different sections.

4.3. *Hupotassein* and indicative statements in Pauline texts

Paul uses ὑποτάσσειν and ὑποταγή in indicative statements as well as in the paraenetic uses that are the focus of the case study. I noted above what may be one of the most significant for a mediation of meaning – 1 Cor. 15.27-28 (with Phil. 3.21 and Eph. 1.22).

In Gal. 2.5, ἡ ὑποταγή is used with an active verb to describe refusal of submission to false believers: 'we did not submit [οὐδὲ εἴξαμεν τῇ ὑποταγῇ] to them'. The *transformatory* horizon is present here in the reference to 'the freedom we have in Christ Jesus' (2.4). The outworking of this in anti-hierarchical relations (in the community of believers) is apparent in the verse (2.6) that immediately follows: 'those who were supposed to be acknowledged leaders (what they actually were makes no difference to me; God shows no partiality) – those leaders contributed nothing to me'.

In 1 Cor. 14.32 there is a statement in the passive indicative: 'the spirits of prophets are subject to [ὑποτάσσεται] the prophets'. It is in close proximity to a paraenesis to women who 'should be subordinate [ὑποτασσέσθωσαν]' (14.34). Both these prophets and 'women' are exhorted to silence, for the needs of the community in worship:

1 Cor. 14.30:   If a revelation is made to someone else...let the first person be silent [σιγάτω].

1 Cor. 14.34:   women should be silent [σιγάτωσαν] in the churches.

The prophets are exercising control: the REB translates, 'it is for prophets to control prophetic inspiration'.[21] How far the women are to be understood as exercising control or required to be under control is variously received (see §4.5.b).

In Romans, there are two indicative statements (one a middle-passive, the other passive) concerning the submission of human beings to God, God's law or righteousness. These are framed as negative statements, about the refusal to submit by 'those who live according to the flesh' and by Israel:

Rom 8.7:   For this reason the mind that is set on the flesh is hostile to God; it does not submit to [ὑποτάσσεται] God's law – indeed it cannot.

Rom. 10.3:   For, being ignorant of the righteousness that comes from God, and seeking to establish their own, they have not submitted to [ὑπετάγησαν] God's righteousness.

Romans also includes a use (passive indicative) not paralleled elsewhere in Paul or in the rest of the New Testament[22] where God has submitted creation to 'futility'. This submission is explicitly involuntary. The transformatory potential of submission, patterned in 1 Corinthians 15, is hinted in the 'hope' of the act of subjection:

21. '[A]n acceptable rendering of Paul's point', though not reflecting the vocabulary: Thiselton, *First Corinthians*, p.1144n.

22. 8.20b was noted above as the only instance of the active voice of ὑποτάσσειν that is not christological and alluding to Ps. 8.6.

Rom. 8.20:   for the creation was subjected [ὑποτάγη] to futility, not of its own will but by the will of the one who subjected it [ὑποτάξαντα] in hope.

Karl Barth, exceptionally, appeals to this instance of ὑποτάσσειν (and to no other instances), which he sees as semantically determinative, governing the range of the word in the paraenetic use in Rom. 13.1.[23] It is an example of a transformation of the horizon of understanding, but, I think, unique in using Rom. 8.20 as the catalyst of mediation.[24] Barth argues:

> Though subjection may assume from time to time any various concrete forms, as an ethical conception it is here purely negative. It means to withdraw and make way; it means to have no resentment, and not to overthrow... To *be in subjection* is, when it is rightly understood, an action void of purpose, an action, that is to say, which can spring only from obedience to God. Its meaning is that men have encountered God, and are thereby compelled to leave the judgement to Him.[25]

The semantic range is governed by Rom. 8.20 and the theology of submission to God, and by the ethical horizon of Romans 12, especially Rom. 12.19: 'never avenge yourselves, but leave room for the wrath of God'. Barth summarises: 'Our subjection means, therefore, no more than that vengeance is not our affair'.[26] He therefore characterises the person who 'resists authority' as a 'rebel' and 'revolutionary'[27] and their conflict with the ruling powers as an example of what is discouraged in Rom. 12.17, 'Do not repay anyone evil for evil'. To disapprove of rebellion against the governing authorities is not to approve the authorities themselves:

> There is here no word of approval of the existing order; but there is endless disapproval of every enemy of it. It is God who wishes to be recognised as He that *overcometh* the unrighteousness of the existing order. This is the meaning of the commandment; it is also the meaning of the Thirteenth Chapter of the Epistle to the Romans.[28]

---

23. Barth, *Romans*, p.485.

24. Neil Elliott, however, notes 'thematic correspondences between Romans 8 and 13' which suggest a 'similar structure of thought undergirding Paul's talk of "subjection" in Romans 8–11 and in Romans 13': *Liberating Paul: The Justice of God and the Politics of the Apostle* (Sheffield: Sheffield Academic, 1994), pp.193–95.

25. Barth, *Romans*, pp.481 and 483.

26. Barth, *Romans*, p.485.

27. Barth, *Romans*, pp.481 and 485.

28. Barth, *Romans*, p.481.

Barth, then, does have a problem, and a differentiation of horizons between two juxtaposed texts, with Rom. 13.1b, 'the powers that be are ordained of God', which has to defer to his reading of submission: 'Here a positive, affirmative authority seems to be assigned to the existing government. This would, however, directly contradict the basis of *subjection* which has been set forth above'.[29] Barth's own historical context and ideological commitments (as a critic of the way conservative and liberal 'Culture-Protestantism' accommodated Christianity to political movements that led to the Third Reich[30]) are surely operating in this reception.

4.4. Be subject to the governing authorities

There is a wealth of exegetical discussion, hinging on the semantic force of ὑποτάσσειν and its association with contested secular or theological frameworks of reference, in relation to Rom. 13.1, 13.5 and Tit. 3.1.

4.4.a. 'Submit', 'obey', and the semantic range

A good proportion of contemporary scholarship holds that Titus is deutero-Pauline, authored in the form it appears by followers of Paul.[31] This means that the text of Tit. 3.1, 'Remind them to be subject to rulers and authorities [ἀρχαῖς ἐξουσίαις ὑποτάσσεσθαι]', may be interpreted as early reception of Rom. 13.1. Even as an early reception, this may constitute a realignment of the meaning, a mediation of the horizons of the earlier text. There is a concern for the authority or command [μετὰ πάσης ἐπιταγῆς] of Titus himself in the congregation which introduces this exhortation (2.15). *Ecclesial* authorities – a disputed matter in reception of Rom. 13.1[32] – are in view in Titus (but not termed ἐξουσίαι). The positive reference to rulers and authorities [ἀρχαῖς ἐξουσίαις] offers a possible tension with the eschatological framework of 1 Cor. 15.24, where πᾶσαν ἀρχὴν καὶ πᾶσαν ἐξουσίαν will be 'destroyed' by Christ.

Because the earlier tradition did not see Tit. 3.1 as a reception of Romans 13, the later text has had an influence on the interpretation

29. Barth, *Romans*, p.484.

30. See, e.g., Arne Rasmusson, 'Historiography and Theology: Theology in the Weimar Republic and the Beginning of the Third Reich', *Kirchliche Zeitgeschichte* 20.1 (2007), pp.155–80 (155).

31. See, e.g., a summary of positions held in Robert M. Karris, 'The Pastoral Letters', in *The Oxford Companion to the Bible* (ed. Bruce Metzger and Michael D. Coogan; New York: Oxford University Press, 1993), pp.573–76 (574).

32. See §§5.2.a and 7.2.b. Submission to elders or individuals in the churches is part of the paraenesis in 1 Cor. 16.16 and 1 Pet. 5.5.

of Romans, in a reverse trajectory (and in the canonical hermeneutic). This is particularly apparent in an English tradition of translation of πειθαρχεῖν in Tit. 3.1 as 'to obey magistrates', which emerges in the Geneva Bible, the Bishop's Bible and the KJV.[33] The Geneva Bible gives Romans 13 the heading, 'He willeth that we submit ourselves to Magistrates', and the notes for Rom. 13.1-7 in the 1599 edition use the word 'magistrate' or 'magistrates' nine times.[34] Barrett's commentary in 1957 uses the phrase 'obedience to magistrates' as its section heading for Rom. 13.1-7.[35]

Origen in two places shows that he assumes a 'plain sense' reading of ὑποτάσσειν in Romans 13, effectively an undifferentiating fusion of horizons. In *Contra Celsum*, he says he need only take the words of Rom. 13.1-2 'in their more obvious and generally received acceptation'[36] in order to refute what Celsus has said concerning the tendency of Christians to rebellion and lawlessness.[37] He contrasts this with his treatment of Rom. 13.1-2 in his *Commentary on Romans* where he offered a longer explanation of the words, and 'various applications'.[38] However, his treatment of ὑποτάσσειν there is also very brief: Paul 'does not say merely obey, but be subject'.[39] Chrysostom in his (late fourth century) interpretation of Rom. 13.1-7 makes this same distinction of 'be subject' from (simply) 'obey'.[40] Such distinction between ὑποτάσσειν

33. The Vulgate has 'oboedire'; Wycliffe has 'obeische to that that is said'; Tyndale has 'obey the *officers*'; the Rheims New Testament has 'obey at a word'.

34. Foster and DeMar, *1599 Geneva Bible*: heading and notes to Rom. 13.1–7.

35. C.K. Barrett, *The Epistle to the Romans* (London: A. & C. Black, 1957), p.244.

36. Origen, *Contra Celsum* 8.65, in H. Chadwick, *Origen, Contra Celsum* (Cambridge: Cambridge University Press, 1965), p.502. (Hereafter bracketed page references to *Contra Celsum* refer to Chadwick's edition.)

37. Origen, *Contra Celsum* 8.65 and 8.68 (pp.502 and 504).

38. For example, his discussion of the nature of human law and God's law. This, for Origen, provides a restriction of Paul's exhortation for submission to the authorities when civil authorities do not act as God's servants: Origen, *Commentaria in Epistolam Pauli ad Romanos* 9.28, in J.P. Migne (ed.), *PCC-SGP* 14 (Paris, 1862), pp.1227–28. (Hereafter bracketed page references to *Commentaria in Epistolam Pauli ad Romanos* refer to Migne's edition.) It is a recurring feature of the reception that interpreters seek to define limits to this injunction (see, e.g., Gregory in §7.2.f).

39. Origen, *ad Romanos* 9.28, p.1227. This brevity contrasts with the more detailed semantic attention he gives to ψυχή, in Rom. 13.1, and its distinctiveness from both πνεῦμα and σῶμα: Origen, *ad Romanos* 9.25, in *PCC* XIV, p.1226.

40. John Chrysostom, 'Homily on Romans XXIII', in *Homilies on the Acts of the Apostles and the Epistle to the Romans* (ed. P. Schaff; rev. Oxford translation; NPNF 1.11; Grand Rapids: Eerdmans, 1969), p.511.

and ὑπακούειν remains a contested one in several parts of subsequent reception. For a number of twentieth-century commentators (e.g. William Sanday with Arthur Headlam, and C.K. Barrett) ὑποτάσσεσθαι means 'to obey'.[41] Charles Cranfield questions their assumption on the grounds that there are 'three perfectly good Greek verbs meaning obey' (πειθαρχεῖν, πείθεσθαι, ὑπακούειν).[42]

For Ernst Käsemann, 'obedience' is voluntary but 'submission', in a divinely ordered world, is not. He reaches this conclusion through an examination of the contemporary vocabulary of Hellenistic administration, which he regards as '[o]ne of the surest and most fruitful results of the [lexical] discussion':

> When the imperial authority issues orders, it is given this task by God, so that it becomes itself a divine διαταγή. This does not mean an abstract order as such, but concrete 'regulation'. The relation of subjects to it is often described as ὑποτάσσεσθαι in correspondence with ὑπερέχοντες, and it is defined in terms of 'obligation'.[43]

His conclusion places submission in the frame of involuntary stratification: 'Whereas ὑπακούειν usually designates free obedience, ὑποτάσσεσθαι emphasises more strongly the fact that a divine order rules in the divinely established world and that this entails super- and sub-ordination…, disregard of which is destructive of life in society'.[44]

For John Murray too ὑποτασσέσθω in the middle or passive is stronger than ὑπάκουω, and is a term 'more inclusive than that for obedience': 'It implies obedience when ordinances to be obeyed are in view, but there is more involved. Subjection indicates the recognition of our subordination in the whole realm of the magistrates' jurisdiction and willing subservience to their authority'.[45] Romans 13 therefore exhorts 'active participation in the duty of subjection'.

41. William Sanday and Arthur C. Headlam, *A Critical and Exegetical Commentary on the Epistle to the Romans* [1st edn 1895] (Edinburgh: T. & T. Clark, 5th edn, 1902), p.365; C.K. Barrett, *The Epistle to the Romans* (London: A. & C. Black, 1957), p.244.

42. C.E.B. Cranfield, *A Critical and Exegetical Commentary on the Epistle to the Romans*, vol. 2 (Edinburgh: T. & T. Clark, 1975), p.660. (For more on Cranfield's semantic analysis, see below.)

43. E. Käsemann, *Commentary on Romans* [1973] (trans. and ed. G.W. Bromiley; Grand Rapids: Eerdmans 1980), p.353, citing A. Strobel, 'Zum Verständnis von Römer 13:7', *ZNW* 47 (1956), pp.67–93 (87–88), and Delling, *TDNT* VIII, pp.43–44.

44. Käsemann, *Romans*, p.351, citing Delling, *Römer*, pp.13, 49ff. and *TDNT* VIII, p.36.

45. J. Murray, *The Epistle to the Romans: The English Text with Introduction, Exposition and Notes* (Grand Rapids: Eerdmans, 1990), p.148.

Swartley's analysis, while agreeing that subjection should not be confused with obedience, reaches a conclusion that is the reverse of this:

> Christians are to be subject to the order that in turn is ordered by God. This distinction recognizes that Christians sometimes need to refuse to obey the authorities because of their higher allegiance to God (Acts 5:29); subjection then means not rebelling nor resisting with evil (i.e. with violence), but bearing rather the consequences of disobedience.[46]

For Witherington, too, submission may encompass disobedience:

> Submitting to the governing powers, which among other things means recognizing that they have God-given authority, is not quite the same as obeying them. In other words, this text would not rule out a civil disobedience undertaken with due respect of government's authority, for instance if the government should require the worship of the emperor.[47]

Gadamer's insight that interpretation begins with the *Vorstruktur des Verstehens*, a projection of meaning which derives from the interpreter's own situation, can be considered in these variations of semantic analysis. Murray's conclusion (that ἐξουσίαις ὑπερεχούσαις ὑποτασσέσθω means willing subservience to the authority of rulers) and Swartley's (that it means not using violence to resist but that it encompasses civil disobedience) are related to some different prejudgments. Murray valorizes the Westminster Confession of Faith, citing its account of a magistrate's just and legal authority, with approval.[48] On the other hand, Swartley, in a Mennonite tradition, and writing for a journal targeted at 'Christians for Justice and Peace', has the stated intention to counter reception where the text 'has generated more uncritical acceptance of the powers, indeed specific governments, than any other'.[49] The engagement of the commentator with a reconstructed horizon of expectation of the first readers does not take place before or separate from an engagement with the text from the perspective of *their own* horizon of expectation. The lexical sifting which is part of historical-critical method should thus be seen not as a 'primary datum' but as part of the dialectic of *Wirkungsgeschichte*.

46.   Willard M. Swartley, 'How to Interpret the Bible: A Case Study of Romans 13.1–7 and the Payment of Taxes Used for War', *Seeds* 3 (1984), pp.28–31 (29).

47.   Witherington, *Paul Quest*, p.178.

48.   Murray, *Romans*, p.148.

49.   Swartley, 'How to Interpret', p.32.

4.4.b. A Pauline theological frame of reference

While the commentators above looked at contemporaneous vocabulary *outside* of the New Testament, other Pauline texts also provide exegetes with possible insights into the semantic range of ὑποτάσσειν. I first sample some commentators who look at Pauline eschatology for the semantic framework for ὑποτασσέσθω in Romans 13, and then at some who look at Pauline christology. (This separate categorisation will be artificial in some cases, especially where 1 Cor. 15.24-28 is in view.)

Some examples express an interpretative uncertainty, which may express a tension of *irreconcilable* horizons of meaning. I noted (§4.4.a) that the positive reference in Tit. 3.1 to rulers and authorities offers a possible tension with the eschatological framework of 1 Cor. 15.24. Rowland notes the same tension with respect to Romans 13 – 'that there is very little, if anything, in the Pauline letters with which one may compare this passage'.[50] It is the absence of the eschatological tension, Paul's conviction of the ultimate subordination of all powers in heaven and earth to God in Christ as expressed in 1 Corinthians 15, that makes Romans 13 such a problem to interpret:

> there does appear, at first sight, to be a certain conflict between Paul's con- viction that a new order has come with a new lord and new demands which would replace the old, and a passage like Romans 13, where there seems to be little concern with the transforming power of the eschato- logical spirit in the attitudes of those in Christ, with regard to what was, in Paul's day, perhaps the most obvious power opposed to the ways of God.[51]

Commentators have wrestled variously with this. The destruction of authorities in Pauline eschatology (1 Cor. 15.24) impacts on Augustine's interpretation of the Romans paraenesis. He concludes that because social order must give way to the eschatological order, submission to governing authorities is best seen as obedience rendered to God, rather than to the office holders: 'until we have reached that world where every principality and power will be voided let us endure our condition for the sake of everyday social order…rendering obedience not so much to people as to God, who commands these things'.[52]

---

50. Christopher Rowland, *Christian Origins* (Cambridge: Cambridge University Press, 1985), p.281.

51. Rowland, *Origins*, pp.281–82.

52. Augustine, *Expositio Quarumdam Propositionum ex Epistola ad Romanos* 72.6, in Paula Fredriksen Landes, *Augustine on Romans: Propositions from the Epistle to the Romans and Unfinished Commentary on the Epistle to the Romans* (Chico: Scholars Press, 1982), p.42.

Barrett describes Rom. 13.1-7 as 'a self-contained treatment of a special theme'.[53] Dodd distinguishes the thought-world of Rom. 13.1-7 from 'the usual apocalyptic circles with which Paul is ordinarily associated', and the passage therefore demonstrates how Paul 'repudiated apocalyptic tradition', finding in the Roman Empire an instrument of God's providence.[54] James Kallas argues from the uniqueness of the subordination paraenesis in Rom. 13.1-7 that Paul cannot have intended to say what these verses say. Rejecting an unresolved differentiation of horizons, Kallas concludes that these verses must be a later interpolation 'at a time when the church was obliged, by the failure of the end to come, to re-evaluate the nature of the worlds'.[55]

John Ziesler notes the absence in Romans 13 of the Pauline vision of a thoroughly christological eschatology: 'there is nothing in vv1-7 about Christ, nor about the realm of redemption. Yet we must remember that Paul now looks at everything, creation included, from the perspective of the lordship of Christ'.[56] Cranfield (earlier) asks, 'is it true to say that this passage is non-christological?'[57] He agrees with Morrison[58] that christology is central here as elsewhere in Paul's understanding of God[59] (but not that ἐχουσίαις ὑπερεχούσαις are spiritual powers: they are 'probably' civil authorities).

Cranfield's exegesis of Rom. 13.1-7[60] pays particular, unusual, attention to ὑποτάσσειν, which is 'quite clearly a key word in this section',[61] to its translation and its scope and function elsewhere in Paul. He reviews the use of ὑποτάσσειν outside of the New Testament, noting that in only one of the uses in the Septuagint is obedience prominent; and in the New Testament, 'sometimes the specific idea of obedience is prominent

53. Barrett, *Romans*, p.244.

54. C.H. Dodd, *The Epistle to the Romans* (London: Fontana, 1959), p.202.

55. James Kallas, 'Romans XIII.1-7: An Interpolation', *NTS* 11 (1965), pp.365–74 (370).

56. John Ziesler, *Paul's Letter to the Romans* (London: SCM, 1989), p.311.

57. Cranfield, *Romans*, vol. 2, p.653.

58. Clinton D. Morrison, *The Powers That Be: Earthly Rulers and Demonic Powers in Romans 13.1–7* (London: SCM, 1960).

59. Reception reflecting Pauline theology will be considered more fully in Chapter 9.

60. C.E.B. Cranfield, 'Some Observations on Romans 13: 1-7', *NTS* 6.3 (1960), pp.241–48; *The Service of God* (London: Epworth Press, 1965); *Commentary on Romans 12–13*; *Critical and Exegetical Commentary on the Epistle to the Romans*, vol. 2.

61. Cranfield, *Romans*, vol. 2, p.660.

(e.g. Rom. 8.7); but in the majority of cases, while it may well be included, it is not clear that it is the predominant thought'.[62] He connects the use in the Romans paraenesis with the paraenesis in Eph. 5.21 where it is used of *reciprocal* obligations. 'Mutual obedience' is not a coherent idea, and he argues that the problem is solved 'by recognising that the word does not mean obey'. He compares the theology with Rom. 12.10 ('outdo one another in showing honour') and with Phil. 2.3 ('in humility regard others as better than yourselves'), and concludes that 'ὑπο-τάσσεσθαι τινι in the NT can denote the recognition that the other person, as Christ's representative to one, has an infinitely greater claim upon one than one has upon oneself'.[63] It may be easier to see how Cranfield's understanding fits Eph. 5.21 than Rom. 13.1.

James Dunn, indeed, believes that Cranfield tries to 'import too much theological freight in to the word'.[64] He finds 'submission' a secular more than a theological term. Dunn and Cranfield arrive at a similar horizon of understanding but by attention to different factors, both grounded in specifically Pauline contexts. Dunn's linguistic analysis of ὑποτασσέσθω counters Cranfield's argument that it has the sense of 'recognising that one is placed below the authority by God'.[65] He agrees with Cranfield that the subjection is limited by the terms of the ruler's God-given authority, but holds that this is not to be found in the import of the word itself, but is the point of the clauses that follow: '"Be subject" is the principle...to which the qualifications are added'.[66] (We shall return to 'theological freight' especially in §9.3.b and §10.4.)

4.5. Wives, be subject

There was very much less *lexical* attention focused on the paraenesis addressed to wives than on the submission to civil authorities until comparatively recently. Where Romans 13 raised questions about the appropriateness of authority and obedience, there were fewer challenges for many centuries to what a wife's submission meant in its 'more obvious and generally received acceptation'.[67]

---

62. Cranfield, *Romans*, vol. 2, p.661.
63. Cranfield, *Romans*, vol. 2, pp.661–62.
64. Dunn, *Romans 9–16*, p.760.
65. Cranfield, *Romans*, vol. 2, p.660.
66. Dunn, *Romans 9–16*, p.760.
67. Origen, *Contra Celsum* 8.65, p.502 (cited in §4.4.a above).

4.5.a. A 'social norm' or an 'adaptation'

In the discourse on gender that predates the texts, Aristotle's biology – identifying the male with perfected and active 'form', and the female with 'defective' and passive 'matter'[68] – had pervasive and tenacious social and political consequences[69] with a long legacy in the Church. In the thirteenth century, Thomas Aquinas joined Augustinian theology with an Aristotelian world order of natural hierarchies. There was therefore, for many, no need for a negotiation or mediation of the horizon of expectation between the legacy of ὑποτάσσειν in Hellenism and their own world order and life experience. With this paraenesis, unlike Rom. 13.1, there is a greater complacency about a common semantic range of 'submission' and 'obedience': 'the terms are frequently synonymous. 'Submit' is a broader term but may entail being willing to obey that person and such obedience would certainly have been seen as the wife's role in most parts of the ancient world'.[70]

The lexis of ὑποτάσσειν in marriage and domestic contexts is bound up with the inheritance and use of the *Haustafel* genre. We saw that Wedderburn suggests the reception of submission (in Colossians) is one that confirms expectation, and the impact is 'merely conventional', with little sign of a mutual subjection reflecting 'the character of the Lord' (§3.4). Witherington sees it, transformatively, as an exhortation to 'conformity to Christ'. Lincoln describes a 'mediation' of horizons, in which the author, not wholly successfully, 'brings his Christian vision of relationships' to the 'patriarchal structuring of household management'.[71] Other commentators see no shift in the word from its legacy in Hellenism: for example, for Delling, ὑποτάσσειν in Colossians 'simply denotes the status of women as such'.[72]

Where Colossians and/or Ephesians are seen as deutero-Pauline, like Titus they may be viewed as *early reception* of Paul's earlier teaching. This perspective can identify two distinct horizons of expectation being mediated: on the one hand, Paul's realignment of relationships 'in

---

68. Aristotle, *Physics* 1.9 192a, 20–24, in Aristotle, *Physics* (trans. R. Waterfield; Oxford: Oxford University Press, 1996), p.31. (Hereafter bracketed page references to *Physics* refer to Waterfield's edition.)

69. Cf. Margaret King and Albert Rabil, 'The Other Voice in Early Modern Europe: Editors' Introduction to the Series', in Jaun Luis Vives, *The Education of a Christian Woman: A Sixteenth Century Manual* (ed. and trans. C. Fantazzi; Chicago: University of Chicago Press, 2000), pp.ix–xxviii (xi).

70. Lincoln, *Later Pauline Letters*, pp.366–67.

71. Wedderburn, *Later Pauline Letters*, p.57; Witherington, *Paul Quest*, p.189; Lincoln, *Later Pauline Letters*, p.141 (cited in §3.4).

72. Delling, 'Hupotassein', p.43 (cited in §4.5.a).

Christ' (e.g. 'there is no longer male and female', Gal. 3.28) and on the other a social norm. For example, Wedderburn sees the Colossians *Haustafel* as evidence of a 'more pronouncedly Greek point of view' in comparison to Paul's perspective, but holds that Paul's teachings may be counted as one of the most important factors in the author's background.[73] That a tradition of household duties was adopted is understandable in view of the importance of the household as the focus of early Christian life and worship (see discussion of the socio-historical setting, §5.3.b). 'However, it is important to note that the tradition needed to be adapted':[74] 'It is the risk in all such borrowings that the borrowed material does not fit altogether comfortably into its new context…and the thought of Colossians is witness to the sort of tensions and strains that such adaptations provoke'.[75]

The Ephesians *Haustafel* presents a particular juxtaposition of the frameworks to be mediated because it is introduced by an exhortation to the mutual submission of believers, immediately followed by a particular exhortation of wives to husbands, syntactically dependent on the verb used in the first statement:[76]

> Eph. 5.21-22:   Be subject ['Υποτασσόμενοι] to one another out of reverence for Christ. Wives, …to your husbands as you are to the Lord.

The letter itself has framed a universal submission where all things are subject to Christ – 'he has put [ὑπέταξεν] all things under his feet' (Eph. 1.22). However, the submission of believers to Christ is made a specific model of submission of wife to husband:

> Eph. 5.24:   Just as the church is subject [ὑποτάσσεται] to Christ, so also wives ought to be, in everything, to their husbands.

This, Elisabeth Schüssler Fiorenza believes, is a *transformation* of the semantic range of the word, not from secular patriarchy into a pattern of freedom and mutual subordination in Christ, but in a *theologising* of patriarchal domination. With the exhortation to wives to be subject to their husbands 'as [they] are to the Lord' (Eph. 5.22), the cultural-social structures are theologised and reinforced.[77] They consequently

73. Wedderburn, *Later Pauline Letters*, p.12.
74. Wedderburn, *Later Pauline Letters*, p.21.
75. Wedderburn, *Later Pauline Letters*, p.22.
76. See note (§1.2.a) on textual variants.
77. Elisabeth Schüssler Fiorenza, *In Memory of Her: A Feminist Theological Reconstruction of Christians Origins* (London: SCM, 1983), p.269.

express a domination which *exceeds* that of the secular semantic horizon.[78]

The lexis appears in the instructions for behaviour in 1 Timothy and Titus. It is not in paraenetic form and not *addressed to* the (young) wives, children and slaves who are to submit.

1 Tim. 2.11:   Let a woman learn in silence with full [ἐν πάσῃ] submission [ὑποταγῇ].

1 Tim. 3.4:   [A bishop] must manage his own household well, keeping his children submissive [ἐν ὑποταγῇ] and respectful in every way.

Tit. 2.3-5:   [T]ell the older women to be reverent...so that they may encourage the young women...to be self-controlled, chaste, good managers of the household, kind, being submissive to [ὑποτασσομένας] their husbands.

Tit. 2.9:   Tell slaves to be submissive to [ὑποτάσσεθαι] their masters and to give satisfaction in every respect; they are not to talk back.

Where contemporary scholarship holds that these texts are deutero-Pauline or post-Pauline,[79] these instances can be interpreted as an early reception of Colossians and Ephesians, or of 1 Cor. 14.34 (this text is discussed in §4.5.b below), and may constitute a realignment of the meaning, a mediation of the horizons of the text. However, even if they do not share common authorship, some interpreters assume a common semantic range and uniform praxis, a common horizon.[80]

4.5.b. Prejudgments and the horizon of the interpreter

Peter O'Brien believes that analyses which see exploitation, oppression and tyranny as the corollary of words for 'submission' reflect the horizon of the interpreter and 'a world which prizes permissiveness and free-dom', and not the horizon of the text. He makes an apologia for an ethic of wifely submission: 'The idea of subordination to authority in general, as well as in the family, is out of favour. Christians are often affected by these attitudes... But authority is not synonymous with tyranny, and the submission to which the apostle refers does not imply inferiority.'[81]

---

78. G.E.M. de Sainte Croix makes a comparable argument concerning Rom. 13.1: *The Class Struggle in the Ancient Greek World: From the Archaic Age to the Arab Conquests* (London: Duckworth, 1981), p.452.

79. E.g. Karris, 'Pastoral Letters', p.574 (cf. §4.4.a).

80. E.g. B. Gerhardsson, *The Ethos of the Bible* (Philadelphia: Fortress, 1982), pp.84–85 (see §5.3.a).

81. Peter T. O'Brien, *The Letter to the Ephesians* (Grand Rapids: Eerdmans, 1999), p.412.

Indeed, here again, the prejudgments and life-commitments, the conscious or unconscious interests of commentators, operate in the exegetical analyses made. Meeks notes that, 'Schüssler Fiorenza and some other feminists…are quite candid in advocating an honest and overt adoption of an ideological position against the perceived patriarchy in any of the texts as well as in the tradition that interprets them'.[82]

The legitimacy or illegitimacy of 'reading back' the meaning of the words into earlier texts is pertinent to 1 Cor. 14.34 (the final instance to be noted of the paraenesis to women or wives in Pauline texts): 'women should be silent in the churches. For they are not permitted to speak, but should be subordinate [ὑποτασσέσθωσαν], as the law also says.'

There is a repeated lexis[83] of ὑποτάσσω and σιγάω in relation both to prophecy in worship and to these women (noted in §4.3). Attention to this immediate context may lead to interpretation of submission in both cases as submitting 'to the needs of the community', and a theological ethic of freedom and mutual submission.[84] Conversely, attention to the use in the *Haustafeln* and the Pastorals may lead to interpreting the submission of women as submission to men or husbands and a patriarchal ethos. (The 'solution' to the tension of removing 1 Cor. 14.33b-36 from its context, as an interpolation, has more advocates[85] than does a similar strategy for Rom. 13.1-7.)[86]

4.6. Be subject to one another

The position of the paraenesis to wives in Eph. 5.22, juxtaposed with the exhortation to mutual submission in 5.21, means that much of the semantic comment hinges on the tension or resolution of these two occurrences. Ephesians 5.21, 'Be subject to [Ὑποτασσόμενοι] one another

---

82. Meeks, 'American Slavery', p.248.

83. The verses 1 Cor. 14.34–35 get 'a large amount of significant vocabulary' from the immediately preceding verses: Ben Witherington, *Women in the Earliest Churches* (SNTSMS, 59; Cambridge: Cambridge University Press, 1988), p.91.

84. E.g. E.E. Ellis, 'The Silenced Wives of Corinth', in *New Testament Textual Criticism* (ed. E.J. Epp and G.D. Fee; London: Oxford University Press, 1981), pp.213–20 (218); Witherington, *Earliest Churches*, p.103; Thiselton, *First Corinthians*, p.1155.

85. E.g. H. Conzelmann, *1 Corinthians: A Commentary on the First Epistle to the Corinthians* (Philadelphia: Fortress, 1975), p.246; Schrage, *Der erste Brief*, vol. 3, pp.481–87; C.K. Barrett, *The First Epistle to the Corinthians* (London: A. & C. Black, 2nd edn, 1971), pp.330–33.

86. E.g. Kallas, 'Interpolation', p.370 (cited in §4.4.b above).

out of reverence for Christ', introduces the *Haustafel,* and is itself preceded by the citation of Ps. 8.6 (Eph. 1.22).

Lincoln argues that the exhortation to *mutual submission* is the unique contribution of Ephesians: it is 'only here in the Pauline corpus is the actual verb "to submit" employed for mutual relationships among believers';[87] elsewhere the notion is used only for the attitude of specific groups, for example, women or children or slaves, or the attitude of believers to the state. This is contestable. I suggest that there are two other instances in Paul's letters of ὑποτάσσειν or ὑποταγή in a reciprocal, non-hierarchical context. In 1 Cor. 16.15-16, Paul urges the congregation to 'submit' to Stephanas and others. This can be read as hierarchical submission to church leaders, but the exhortation is grounded in their service of the community of believers. The NRSV brings out lexical symmetry (τάσσειν / ὑποτάσσειν), though at the expense of losing the lexical parallel with other submission paraenesis:

> 1 Cor. 16.15-16:   you know that members of the household of Stephanas were the first converts in Achaia, and they have devoted themselves to the service [εἰς διακονίαν τοῖς ἁγίοις ἔταξαν ἑαυτούς] of the saints; I urge you to put yourselves at the service of [ὑποτάσσησθε] such people, and of everyone who works and toils with them.

The submission paraenesis here is in the framework of reciprocity of service and submission, which Paul expresses in a number of ways.[88] It may also, arguably, be detected in 2 Cor. 9.13 (my second instance), where generous, self-sacrificial sharing is the outworking of submission [ὑποταγῇ] to Christ:

> 2 Cor. 9.13   Through the testing of this ministry you glorify God by your obedience [ὑποταγῇ] to the confession of the gospel of Christ and by the generosity of your sharing with them and with all others.

Franz Leenhardt is one of the very few commentators (on Rom. 13.1) to refer to the use of ὑποτάσσησθε in 1 Cor. 16.16 'in regard to the mutual respect and submission' of Christians. He compares the frame of reference in Romans 13 with the κοινωνία of mutual submission (also seen in 1 Cor. 14.32 and 34 where both women and the spirits of prophets are

---

87. Lincoln, *Later Pauline Letters,* p.365.
88. E.g. Gal. 6.2, 'Bear one another's burdens, and in this way you will fulfill the law of Christ'; Phil. 2.3, 'in humility regard others as better than yourselves'. This theological ethic is pursued in relation to the submission paraenesis in §10.2.

among those who submit to the needs of the community): 'Such submission implies a positive obedience to common need, incumbent on an
individual in view of the position he [*sic*] occupies in a collective whole
whose good he is obliged to promote'.[89]

4.6.a. A transformative meaning for other uses

For Jerome, ὑποτασσόμενοι ἀλλήλοις governs the semantic force of the
verb in the other paraenesis. (This accords too with his translation of
1 Pet. 2.13, '*subiecti estote omni humanae creaturae*'; see §4.7.) He
opens his comment on Eph. 5.21 with a commendation of the teaching to
bishops, presbyters and 'every order of teachers…that they be subjected
to those who are subjected to themselves'.[90] He writes:

> Another will interpret 'subjected to one another'…so that not only is a
> wife subject to her husband, and children to their parents, and servants to
> their masters, but also husbands are to be subject to their wives according
> to the duty which is commanded, and fathers to children so that they do
> not provoke them to wrath, and masters to servants that they may abstain
> from threats… They should be subject to one another and do this from
> 'the fear of Christ' so that as he was subject to his servants, so also these
> who appear to be greater may be subject to those lesser than themselves
> by rendering the duties which are commanded.[91]

This is remarkable in the early tradition. J. Armitage Robinson (see
§4.6.b below) deprecates this radical application of the higher being
subject to the lower as a 'fanaticism', and sees it as an imposition onto
the text from Jerome's life-world horizon, specifically his collisions with
bishops.[92]

Gilbert Bilezikian argues that the semantic transformation occurs in
the addition of ἀλλήλοις. Although the natural meaning of ὑποτάσσειν
in the New Testament is 'to make oneself subordinate to the authority
of a higher power…to yield to rulership', the addition of the reciprocal
pronoun *to each other* in Eph. 5.21 'changes its meaning entirely… By
definition, mutual submission rules out hierarchical differences'.[93]

89. Franz J. Leenhardt, *The Epistle to the Romans* [1957] (trans. H. Knight;
London: Lutterworth, 1961), p.327.

90. Jerome, 'Commentary on Ephesians', in *The Commentaries of Origen and
Jerome on St Paul's Epistle to the Ephesians* (ed. R. Heine; Oxford: Oxford University Press, 2002), p.231.

91. Jerome, 'Ephesians', p.232.

92. J. Armitage Robinson, *St Paul's Epistle to the Ephesians, an Exposition*
(London: Macmillan, 1909), pp.170–71.

93. G. Bilezikian, *Beyond Sex Roles: What the Bible Says about a Woman's
Place in Church and Family* (Grand Rapids: Baker, 1985), p.154.

Bilezikian uses the phrase 'mutual subjection' and believes that this 'suggests horizontal lines of interaction among equals'. As a result, 5.21 controls the understanding of 5.22–6.9. Mutual submission requires that all Christians, regardless of status, function, sex or rank, are to serve one another in love (Gal. 5.13). This is the framework in Ephesians itself (4.1-4): 'I…beg you to lead a life worthy of the calling to which you have been called, with all humility and gentleness, with patience, bearing with one another in love, making every effort to maintain the unity of the Spirit in the bond of peace. There is one body and one Spirit.' All become subordinate to one another, and 'there remains no justification for distinctions among them of ruler and subordinate'.[94] This therefore is also the pattern of Christ's love for the church which is held out for husbands to follow in 5.25-31, and it is this that does justice to the reciprocal pronoun '[submitting] to one another' – so husbands are to submit to wives in exactly the same way.

4.6.b. A conformity to hierarchies

For Armitage Robinson, the number of occurrences indicating a confirmation of social hierarchies in Paul's letters outweighs the mutual submission of Christians in Eph. 5.21. It is 'used twenty-three times by St Paul'. If we take out the references in 1 Peter, which 'is not independent of St Paul's epistles', it occurs only nine times in the rest of the New Testament. This is an example of a 'statistical argument', which can be used over against a 'canonical' argument in which one or more key verses can be offered as a hermeneutical κανών by which other occurrences of the word should be judged (see §10.2).

For Armitage Robinson the 'recognition of the sacred principles of authority and obedience' is the 'key note of subordination'.[95] He writes:

> Recognise, says the Apostle, that in the Divine ordering of Human life one is subject to another. We must not press this to mean that even the highest is in some sense subject to those who are beneath him. St Jerome indeed takes this view, and proceeds to commend the passage to bishops, with whom he sometimes found himself in collision. But the Apostle is careful in what follows to make his meaning abundantly clear, and does not stultify his precept by telling husbands to be subject to their wives, but to love them; nor parents to be subject to their children, but to nurture them in the discipline of the Lord.[96]

---

94. Bilezikian, *Beyond Sex Roles*, p.154.
95. Robinson, *Ephesians*, p.172.
96. Robinson, *Ephesians*, pp.170–71.

The christological use of ὑποτάσσειν does not suggest, *pace* Jerome (§4.6.a above), that 'even the highest is in some sense subject to those who are beneath him'. Rather, 'the authority which corresponds to natural relationships finds its pattern and its sanction in the authority of Christ over His Church'. Although 'subordination must be met by love', which is defined by a theology of the cross (Eph. 5.2),[97] and although love is defined as 'the love of self-surrender',[98] this does not have the outworking of the husband/master 'subject to those who are beneath him'. Armitage Robinson's own life-world horizon corresponds to the ethos of the *Haustafel*, and he sees this as a pattern of social life that is 'divinely founded' and 'unchanging'. The 'unchanging institution of family' in England in 1909 includes, in his words, 'servants and masters'[99] – which makes a claim for a common horizon much less likely to be shared in England a century later (and subject to considerable contestation even a decade later).

S.B. Clark also measures the occasional, 'isolated' statements of Paul that suggest an egalitarian perspective, against the subordination passages by which they are 'outnumbered'. Ephesians 5.21 is therefore *not* an appeal for mutual submission: what is meant is, 'let each of you subordinate himself or herself to the one he or she should be subordinate to'.[100] The introductory verse says that there is to be appropriate subjection of one to another, and then the specific subjection meant is spelled out as wives to husbands, children to parents and slaves to their owners.

Wayne Grudem believes that the pronoun ἀλλήλους is not always fully reciprocal and should not be read as such in Eph. 5.21.[101] Sometimes it is; and indeed it is in the closest instance, Eph. 4.25 ('members of one another'). But in other contexts a symmetrical relationship cannot be in view, as, for instance, in Rev. 6.4 ('slaughter one another'), or in 1 Cor. 11.33 ('wait for one another'). Dawes counters that Grudem fails to mention that in each of the cases cited, there is something about the

97. For subordination and a *theologia crucis*, see §10.5.

98. Robinson, *Ephesians*, p.173.

99. Robinson, *Ephesians*, p.170.

100. S.B. Clark, *Man and Woman in Christ: An Examination of the Roles of Men and Women in the Light of Scripture and the Social Sciences* (Ann Arbor: Servant Books, 1980), pp.74–76.

101. Wayne Grudem, 'Wives Like Sarah, and the Husbands Who Honor Them', in *Recovering Biblical Manhood and Womanhood: A Response to Evangelical Feminism* (ed. John Piper and Wayne Grudem; Wheaton: Crossway, 1991), pp.193–210 (207n); cf., in the same volume, George W. Knight, 'Husbands and Wives as Analogues of Christ and the Church', pp.161–75 (173n).

context that justifies reading ἀλλήλους in a more restricted sense, and that he fails to demonstrate that here too the context demands the restricted sense.[102]

O'Brien criticises G.W. Dawes for not appreciating that ὑποτάσσομαι is dealing with submission within ordered relationships and 'therefore his criticisms of Grudem are wide of the mark'. He uses the Pauline reciprocity of Gal. 6.2 to support Grudem's case: '"Bear *one another's* burdens", does not signify that *everyone* should exchange burdens with *everyone* else, but that some who are more able should help bear the burdens of *others* who are less able'.[103]

He argues against Bilezikian (§4.6.a above) and others concerning the 'widely held view' that Eph. 5.21 states a general principle of mutual submission by all Christians to all others in the Body of Christ. His position, like Clark's above, is that in the *Haustafel* the focus is on specific kinds of mutual submission 'in the light of' this general principle. He advocates a different interpretation, which 'recognises' that 5.21 is a general heading urging believers to be submissive or subordinate, and the particular ways in which Christians are to submit to others are then specified in the household table for wives, children and servants: 'The apostle is not speaking of *mutual* submission in the sense of a reciprocal subordination, but submission to those who are in authority over them [or earlier: "to appropriate authorities"]'.[104] He argues semantically that the word does not describe a 'symmetrical' relationship, but one in 'an ordered array'; none of the relationships where this verb appears is reversed: 'husbands are not told to be subject to their wives, nor parents to children, nor the government to citizens'.

4.6.c. Reference to an alternative lexis of service and humility
Dawes (§4.6.b above) concedes to Grudem that there is something *puzzling* about Eph. 5.21: 'It is not so much the *idea* of mutual subordination in itself, which…is a gracious ideal for Christian living. What is truly puzzling is the relationship of v21 with the verses which follow… There is a certain *Widerspruch* between the language of mutual subordination in v21 and that of female subordination in vv 22-24.'[105] His hermeneutical strategy is to interpret these verses 'within the context of the letter as a whole'. This means that the injunctions to love and to

102. G.W. Dawes, *The Body in Question: Metaphor and Meaning in the Inter-pretation of Ephesians 5.21–33* (Leiden: Brill, 1998), p.214.

103. O'Brien, *Ephesians*, p.404 (emphasis his).

104. O'Brien, *Ephesians*, p.404.

105. O'Brien, *Ephesians*, pp.232–33.

submit must be applied to both partners, because each is directed to all believers elsewhere in the letter, and therefore that what emerges is a much more 'symmetrical', reciprocal ethic than appears at first sight (a transformed horizon of expectation). This is described as an examination of context, but it has some of the characteristics of a prejudgment, or an exercise of *Sachkritik*.[106]

Appeals to a broader framework than the *Haustafel* are common, and from early in the tradition. Origen understands submission to one another in Eph. 5.21 in terms of the humility and service of Christ and the apostles (citing 1 Cor. 9.19; Gal. 5.13; Phil. 2.7; Jn 13.14; Mt. 20.26-27) where to be voluntarily 'enslaved' is a command 'given to all'.[107] To be subject to one another 'destroys all desire to rule and be first'. However he then makes no reference to this mutual subjection in the comment on the injunctions to husbands and wives.

John Chrysostom cites the closest parallel in the alternative lexis, δουλεύετε ἀλλήλοις (Gal. 5.13), in comment on Ephesians, in an anti-hierarchical application: 'Let no one sit down in the rank of a freeman, and the other in the rank of a slave; rather it were better that both masters and slaves be [slaves] to one another'.[108] However in a Homily on Romans he argues that God has made many forms of rule and subordination because 'equality of rank often breeds strife'. Subjects are set 'under their rulers as household servants are under their masters'.[109] Here the two horizons of Eph. 5.21 and Rom. 13.1 are not brought together. The semantic framework of ὑποτασσέσθω in the latter is Aristotelian stratification in the 'natural' order.

Rudolf Schnackenberg argues that the 'misleading' subordination of wife to husband loses all sense of 'the oppressive or degrading' because in the transition to the *Haustafel* (Eph. 5.21) all members of the congregation are urged to mutual subordination to one another in reverence to Christ. More important than 'subordination' is 'the mutual ordering to each other': 'The "allocation of roles" for husband and wife is seen according to the social conditions and view which pertained at that time, but in a reciprocal relation which relativizes the differences and raises to a higher unity'.[110]

---

106. See §§9.3.b, and 10.3 and 10.5.

107. Origen, 'Commentary on Ephesians', in Heine, *Commentaries*, p.231.

108. Chrysostom, 'Homily on the Epistle to the Ephesians XIX', in *Homilies*, p.142 (translation slightly modified).

109. John Chrysostom, 'Homily on Romans 23', in *Homilies*, p.511.

110. Rudolf Schnackenburg, *The Epistle to the Ephesians, a Commentary* (trans. H. Heron; Edinburgh: T. & T. Clark, 1991), pp.257 and 246.

Again, support comes from the different lexis used elsewhere. While the command to submit remains 'for the most part' limited to individual groups (women, slaves, children, younger people) or is concerned with the subordination of the Christian to the governing powers, there are in Paul exhortations 'materially comparable' to the command to all to subordinate themselves to one another – though without the verb ὑποτάσσειν. Schnackenburg cites Rom. 12.16, Phil. 2.3 and Gal. 6.2: 'Subordination in this sense becomes an embracing expression for the behaviour of Christians in community... For the author it is not an external legal category but an attitude demanded by love, urging to "service" ("humility") for which every Christian must be willing.'[111]

If the ethos of the *Haustafel* is less than mutual in its principle of subordination, this is an *external* pollution and a dissonance of the semantic framework: 'Hence if certain anthropological-social ideas of that time creep in[,] in the exhortation to wives (cf. vv. 22f.), this is a contemporary limitation which does not question the fundamental claim on all Christian to be subordinate to one another'.[112]

Witherington (see §3.4) argues for the paraenesis as urging 'conformity to Christ', not 'to society's norms'.[113] He refers the concept of mutual submission to the pattern of Christ (and references 1 Cor. 15): 'clearly it does not imply anything about the inherent inferiority of the subordinate member' because the term is 'also used to speak of Christ in relationship to God in 1 Cor. 15.28'.[114] Submissiveness does not (*pace* Delling) denote the status of women 'as such'[115] but is 'relational, not ontological, in character', and is 'the shape of Christian humble service', which 'in Colossians 3 is especially predicated of the wife, but in Eph. 5.21-22 can be seen as appropriate for husband and wife toward each other'.[116] This is Pauline theology, but seems like special pleading for the *Haustafeln*. Witherington finds in Ephesians 5 a 'new approach to marriage' which is 'Paul's deliberate attempt to reform the patriarchal structure of his day'.[117]

---

111. Schnackenburg, *Ephesians*, p.244.
112. Schnackenburg, *Ephesians*, p.244.
113. Witherington, *Paul Quest*, pp.189–90.
114. Witherington, *Paul Quest*, p.188.
115. Delling, 'Hupotassein', p.43 (cited in §4.5.a).
116. Witherington, *Paul Quest*, p.188.
117. Ben Witherington, *Women and the Genesis of Christianity* (Cambridge: Cambridge University Press, 1990), p.156.

A different attempt (to resolve the perceived tension between the mutual injunctions and the submissions that confirm a stratified hierarchy) looks outside of the New Testament for the semantic range of ὑποτάσσειν. Kroeger uses three instances from Polybius' *Histories* to argue that the word may imply 'to relate one thing to another in a meaningful fashion' or 'to classify one thing in terms of another'.[118] This particular strategy to reconcile the tension is not successful: it is not referred to the rest of Paul's use, and the translation offered, for most commentators, falls outside the semantic range of the word.[119]

The last three sections (§§4.6.a, 4.6.b and 4.6.c) have focused on the different semantic concepts of subordination, which reflects conformity or dissonance of relationships in Christian households with those in the wider society. In Chapter 5, the Christian 'household' will be explored further in an examination of different constructions of the socio-historical setting.

4.7. *Hupotassein* and the rest of the New Testament

There are some significant parallels with Pauline paraenesis in 1 Peter, which make it a plausible instance of early reception of Pauline or deutero-Pauline texts.[120] If it is not a direct effect of Pauline texts, the subjection material – both to civil authorities and of wives to husbands – would derive from some common tradition.[121] Lohse suggests that though 1 Peter is not dependent on any Pauline letters, it is influenced by Pauline theology'.[122] Of course much reception assumes a semantic and theological univocality (see §1.2.a). Like the Pauline texts, 1 Pet. 3.22 reflects the influence of Ps. 8.6: powers and authorities are eschatologically subject [ὑποταγέντων] to Christ.

---

118. Catherine Kroeger, 'The Classical Concept of Head as Source', App. III in Gretchen Gabelein Hull, *Equal to Serve: Women and Men in the Church and Home* (London: Scripture Union, 1987), p.281.

119. E.g. Dawes, *Body in Question*, p.210; and O'Brien, *Ephesians*, p.400n.

120. So for Oscar Cullman, for example, 1 Peter 'offers, so to speak, the first exegesis of this Pauline passage': *Christ and Time: The Primitive Christian Conception of Time and History* (trans. F. Filson; London: SCM, 1951), pp.196–97.

121. Selwyn posits an early oral substratum, a catechism: *First Peter*, pp.369–75. Others reject the hypothesis that teaching on submission was a common element on the horizon of the early Church: e.g. W. Monro, *Authority in Peter and Paul: The Identification of a Pastoral Substratum in the Pauline Corpus and 1 Peter* (Cambridge: Cambridge University Press, 1983), p.3.

122. Eduard Lohse, 'Paraenese und Kerygma im 1 Petrusbrief', *ZNW* 45 (1954), pp.68–89 (83–85).

An extended *Haustafel* pattern is introduced by a general exhortation of submission to human authorities:

> 1 Pet. 2.13-14:   For the Lord's sake accept the authority [ὑποτάγητε] of every human institution [πάσῃ ἀνθρωπίνῃ κτίσει], whether of the emperor as supreme, or of governors, as sent by him to punish those who do wrong and to praise those who do right.

This tradition of translation – and the examples of emperor and governors – suggests a parallel with Rom. 13.1. Jerome, however, translated '*omni humanae creaturae*'; he was followed by exegetes using the Vulgate, and followed in English by the Douay-Rheims Bible (1582–1610): 'to every human creature'. Martin Luther, for example, cites the Vulgate of this phrase to express mutual submission,[123] though elsewhere and in his own translation of the Bible (1545), he gives, '*Seid untertan aller menschlichen Ordnung*'.

First Peter has only one of the pairs of the *Haustafel*, husbands and wives. Wives are urged to submit:

> 1 Pet. 3.1:   Wives, in the same way, accept the authority [ὑποτασσόμεναι] of your husbands, so that, even if some of them do not obey the word, they may be won over without a word by their wives' conduct.

> 1 Pet. 3.5:   It was in this way long ago that the holy women who hoped in God used to adorn themselves by accepting the authority [ὑποτασσόμεναι] of their husbands.

Slaves, not masters are included – and slaves are urged to submit in contrast to 'obey' in Colossians and Ephesians:

> 1 Pet. 2.18:   Slaves, accept the authority [ὑποτασσόμενοι] of your masters with all deference, not only those who are kind and gentle but also those who are harsh.

The children/fathers pairing does not appear. The νεώτεροι who are urged to submit might mean young people or all the 'flock' of the elders:

> 1 Pet. 5.5a: In the same way, you who are younger must accept the authority of [ὑποτάγητε] the elders [*or* those who are older].

The code is followed by commands to 'all of you' – in a parallel with the mutual submission of Eph. 5.21 but expressed with ταπεινοφροσύνην:

---

123. Martin Luther, *Lectures on Romans* (trans. W. Pauck; London: SCM, 1961), p.362.

1 Pet. 5.5b: And all of you must clothe yourselves with humility in your
dealings with one another [ἀλλήλοις τὴν ταπεινοφροσύνην
ἐγκομβώσασθε].

The KJV draws the parallel much closer: 'ye younger, submit yourselves
unto the elder. Yea, all of you be subject one to another'.

The words are otherwise not frequent in the rest of the New Testament, raising the possibility of a distinctiveness of the Pauline use. In
Lk. 10.17 and 20, spirits submit to Jesus' followers (cf. 1 Cor. 14.32) –
or to Jesus through them: 'Lord, in your name even the demons submit
[ὑποτάσσεται] to us'. Luke 2.51 also uses the word of the submission of
the child Jesus to his parents: ἦν ὑποτασσόμενος αὐτοῖς (KJV, 'he was
subject unto them'; NRSV, 'he was obedient to them').

In Jas 4.7, the exhortation is submission to God (cf. Rom. 8.7):
'Submit [ὑποτάγητε] yourselves therefore to God. Resist [ἀντίστητε] the
devil, and he will flee from you.' There is a parallel with Rom. 13.1-2
where the reverse of 'submission' to authorities appointed by God is
described as 'resisting' [ἀνθέστηκεν, ἀνθεστηκότες].

In Hebrews, the use of Ps. 8.6 is explicit. The *syntactic* parallels with
Pauline texts are not close:

Heb. 2.5:   Now God did not subject [ὑπέταξεν] the coming world...to
angels.

Heb. 2.8:   '...subjecting [ὑπέταξας] all things under their feet'. Now in
subjecting [ὑποτάξαι] all things to them, God left nothing
outside their control. As it is, we do not yet see everything
in subjection [ὑποτεταγμένα] to them.

There are two references in Hebrews that bear some comparison to the
application of ὑποτάσσειν to household and ecclesial order respectively.
One compares submission to God to the submission of children to
parents:

Heb. 12.9:   Moreover, we had human parents to discipline us, and we
respected them. Should we not be even more willing to be
subject [ὑποταγησόμεθα] to the Father of spirits and live?

The second exhorts obedience to church leaders but does not use
ὑποτάσσειν:

Heb. 13.17:   Obey your leaders and submit to [ὑπείκετε] them, for they are
keeping watch over your souls and will give an account. Let
them do this with joy and not with sighing – for that would
be harmful to you.

As noted (at the beginning of this chapter), there is not a clear tradition of translation or interpretation acknowledging ὑποτάσσειν as having a distinctive frame of reference. For example, Hincmar reflects reception of subordination paraenesis as applied to ecclesial authorities and cites, not the Pauline texts (see the reception by Ignatius, §7.2.b), but Heb. 13.17 (from the Vulgate using *subiacete* for ὑπείκετε) and Lk. 2.51.[124]

4.8. Interim case-study evaluation (Chapters 3 and 4)

Historical-critical methods reflecting on 'how the contemporary reader could have viewed and understood the work'[125] in terms of genre (Chapter 3) and semantic competences (Chapter 4) appear richly in the history of reception of the case-study texts: they are part of the herme-neutical paradigm of *Wirkungsgeschichte*. Claims for singularity and certainty that appear in some characterisations of historical-critical exegesis are not much in evidence, collectively, here. The historical-critical attention to genre and lexis exhibits contested and indeterminable features, which suggest that these methods do not offer final resolutions of the meaning or meanings accessible to the first readers. They may, however, offer some, contestable, constraints on the range of meanings and applications the text may give rise to, in a hermeneutical strategy consonant with Gadamer's paradigm.[126]

The role of cultural and theological *prejudgments* in assessments of the genre and lexis has been evidenced (and see later, §10.5). This appears in the construction of the horizon of the past *fused* with contemporary horizon of expectation of the interpreter.[127]

I am not offering the practice here as a model of method, but as a way to examine how these particular approaches reflect the hermeneutics of Gadamer and Jauss. Nevertheless, the iterative pattern offers one demon-stration of Jauss's 'repeated reading' which might lead to an acquisition of the 'horizon of perceptive comprehension'.[128]

---

124. Hincmarus, *Epistola II*, p.33.

125. Jauss, *Aesthetic of Reception*, p.28 (cited in §2.3).

126. Cf. the mediation of horizons implicit in Klaus Berger's assessment that 'Exegesis can never confirm the correctness of any application. What it can do is to assess the *degree* to which a given application deviates from the original meaning of the text': Klaus Berger, *Hermeneutik des Neuen Testaments* (Gütersloh: Gerd Mohn, 1988), pp.120–21; trans. from Räisänen, *Beyond New Testament Theology*, p.78. There are, of course, evaluations here ('correctness', 'deviates', 'original meaning') which are not the articulations of Gadamer's paradigm.

127. Examples include those in §§4.4.a and 4.4.b, above.

128. Jauss, 'Limits and Tasks', p.119 (cited in §2.4).

My case study is particularly rich in reception which assumes or argues for the use of ὑποτάσσειν in one text to be understood in terms of its occurrence in another. The frequency of use in the Pauline and post-Pauline tradition, and the infrequency of the word in Christian texts outside of this tradition – and preference for other words for similar exhortation (e.g. Heb. 13.17) – may suggest that the Pauline use is not merely drawing on a common Christian stock,[129] but engenders distinctive semantic competences, new horizons.

This raises questions for some exegetes in the later reception history (which includes my own reception: §4.2 above) concerning how far the paraenesis should be read explicitly in terms of Pauline theology. We shall pursue the hermeneutics of this further in Chapter 9 and its outworking in the case study in Chapter 10.

---

129. *Pace*, e.g., Carrington, *Catechism*, p.49 (cited in §4.2 above).

Chapter 5

THE CASE STUDY AND HISTORICAL-CRITICAL TOOLS:
SOCIO-HISTORICAL SETTING
AND THE *ERWARTUNGSHORIZONT*

5.1. Introduction

> The reconstruction of the horizon of expectations in the face of which a
> work was created and received…enables one…to pose the questions that
> the text gave an answer to.[1]

The sampling from the case study in this chapter examines the sort of
reconstruction Jauss describes here; and different responses to 'the clear
hermeneutical demand: to understand a text in terms of the specific situation in which it was written'.[2] It continues the investigation of exegetical
methods, both as they contribute to constructions of hypothetical first-
reception, and as they illustrate the cultural and theological prejudgments
embodied in such readings. Therefore the historical contingencies and
the life-horizon, of the interpreters and their impact on their prejudgments, occasionally highlighted in Chapters 3 and 4, are particularly in
evidence here.

Chapter 4 needed to include all the occurrences of ὑποτάσσειν in the
New Testament, because of the various appeals made to reading the texts
collectively or in some relationship. This chapter, however, can focus
more exclusively on my three principal texts: Rom. 13.1 (§5.2); Col.
3.18 and Eph. 5.21-22 (§5.3).

5.2. Romans 13.1

5.2.a. 'Ordained by the natural order'

There is an absence of reference to the historical situation of the first
readers in most patristic and scholastic reception. This may represent an
assumption of little tension in the *Horizontverschmelzung* – the fusion of

---

1. Jauss, *Aesthetic of Reception*, p.28 (cited in §1.1.b).
2. Gadamer, *Truth and Method*, p.330 (cited in §1.1.c).

the horizons of past and present – and of a *commonality* of social and political order. The 'universal' framework of authority and submission is more likely to be referred to 'the order of nature' or to Aristotle than to particularities in Pauline theology and the setting of his congregations. In an explanation of 'dominion' Aquinas cites, as all speaking with one voice, 1 Pet. 4.10, Aristotle and the tradition of 'natural order' handed on by Augustine:

> And therefore the Philosopher says that when many are geared to one thing, you will always find one of them to be principal or director... Secondly, because if one man greatly surpassed another in knowledge and justice, it would be all wrong if he did not perform this function (of being principal or director) for the benefit of others; as it says in 1 Peter... So Augustine too says that the just do not rule out of a lust to dominate, but out of the duty to look after things; this is what the order of nature prescribes. This is how God constituted man.[3]

There are several references in the early patristic literature (e.g. Clement, Polycarp) to the requirement to pray for those in authority, and this becomes a common feature in apologists (e.g. Justin Martyr, Athenagoras, Tertullian).[4] Political and social conservatism before Constantine reflects the anxiety that the Church should not be seen as rebellious.[5] After Constantine, with Christians in public office, this can be manifested in the explanation of texts that might be seen as subversive or antinomian.

Pelagius' commentary on Rom. 13.1 does relate the paraenesis (and also the teaching on humility in Eph. 5.16 and Col. 4.5) to particular circumstances, a particular social and political ethos, and a theology of 'freedom':

> This is an argument against those who thought they were obliged to use their Christian freedom in such a way that they rendered honour or paid taxes to no one. Paul wishes, therefore, to humble them in whatever way possible, lest perchance they suffer reproach on account of God. Thus he teaches them to redeem the time with humility.[6]

---

3.   Aquinas, *Summa Theologiae* 1a.96, 4, in Thomas Aquinas, *The Summa Theologiae*, vol. 13 (trans. Edmund Hill; Cambridge: Cambridge University Press, 2006), p.135; and citing Aristotle, *Politics* 1.1254a.28, 1 Pet. 4.10 and Augustine, *City of God* 19.14. (Hereafter bracketed page references to *Summa Theologiae* refer to Hill's edition.)

4.   See §7.2.a.

5.   E.g. Origen's rebuttal of Celsus' accusation of sedition against Christians: *Contra Celsum* 8.65 (p.502).

6.   Pelagius, *Commentary on St Paul's Epistle to the Romans* (trans. Theodore de Bruyn; Oxford: Clarendon, 1998), pp.136–37.

(Christian freedom and taxation in the Roman setting are both taken up by other commentators later, see §5.2.b). Pelagius also makes a tantalisingly brief suggestion of a different reading, 'Alternatively: "Higher authorities" can mean ecclesiastical authorities',[7] but he makes no reference to the historical situation of these in the Roman congregation.

Chrysostom is explicit that the specifics of the historical situation in Rome are *not* part of Paul's message. Paul's assertion of God's appointment of rulers is not about each ruler individually, but about the institution of government, the 'power', not the person: 'Hence he does not say, "for there is no ruler but of God"; but it is the *thing* he speaks of, and says, there is no power but of God.' He paraphrases Paul: 'Nor am I [Paul] now speaking about individual rulers but about the thing in itself for that there should be rulers, and some should rule and others be ruled, and that all things should not just be carried on in all confusion'.[8] Chrysostom's support of secular authority may be referred to his own historical situation: he was brought to Constantinople as a churchman whose authority was intended to enhance that of the civil authority in its capital city. When Christianity under Theodosius became the official state religion (Council of Constantinople, 381 C.E.), the Church could be seen as effectively a single, universal institution, like the Empire.[9]

5.2.b. 'Jewish impatience and the Gentile yoke'

Jean Calvin stands near the head of generations of interpreters[10] who have sought in the special circumstances of Paul's exhortation to the Christians in Rome, a reason why he might have urged their submission to the governing authorities. Calvin's suggestion is that the Jewish Christians of Rome might share the sense of 'Jewish impatience' under a 'Gentile yoke'.[11]

If Romans was written c. 57 C.E., Jewish Christians were in an inhospitable but uncertain period, after Claudius' expulsion of Jews

---

7. Pelagius, *Romans*, p.137. Joseph Stevenson will later (1834) run with this idea (see §7.4.c).

8. Chrysostom, 'Homily on Romans 23', p.511 (emphasis mine).

9. Cf. Edmund Hill, *Ministry and Authority in the Catholic Church* (London: Chapman, 1988), p.41.

10. See, e.g., the tradition, and a construction of the historical circumstances, documented in J. Friedrich, W. Pöhlmann and P. Stuhlmacher, 'Zur historischen Situation und Intention von Rom. 13. 1-7', *ZTK* 73 (1967), pp.131–66.

11. John Calvin, *Commentary upon the Epistle of Saint Paul to the Romans* [1539] (ed. H. Beveridge; trans. C. Rosdell; Edinburgh, 1844), p.364.

from Rome, 49 C.E.;[12] they were in the first years of the new Emperor Nero, and before his persecution of Christians in 64 C.E.[13] There were 'persistent public complaints about Nero's taxes.[14] Commentators speculate, like Calvin, on the nature of Jewish and Jewish-Christian 'impatience' in these circumstances.

For Anthony Guerra, it is 'obvious' that Paul is 'addressing specifically *Roman* Gentile and Jewish Christians', and that it is 'this factor that has been ignored in the exegesis of Romans and the results have been nowhere more distorting'.[15] For him, the 'concrete historical situation' is the issue of taxation, and Paul is 'probably' also aware of strained relations between the Jewish community and the wider populace.[16] Elliott identifies Paul's appeal to subjection to authorities in 13.1-7 within the overall rhetorical purpose of Romans 'to advocate for the safety of the Jewish community in Rome'. Paul wrote Romans to oppose gentile-Christian 'boasting' over Israel, and the 'corresponding indifference to the plight of real Jews in Rome in the wake of the Claudian expulsion'.[17]

Swartley is among those who identify complaints against taxation as key. Romans 13.7 urges compliance with two different forms of taxation: φόρος, which is to be identified with the 'tributa', a fixed poll tax, collected by government officials, and τέλος, identified as the commission tax collected by agents, who bid for the office – a system that led to extortion and exploitation. Swartley interprets Rom. 13.1-7 as an exhortation not to join the revolt engendered particularly by resentment against the second of these, the commission levies: 'In light of the emphases in chapters 12–13, it is clear that Paul considered this counsel to serve best the expression of love, that he considered the early reign of

---

12. Gaius Suetonius Tranquillus, *De Vitis Caesarum* 5.25, in Suetonius, *The Lives of Twelve Caesars* (trans. J.C. Rolfe; LCL, Latin Series, 148; Cambridge, Mass.: Harvard University Press, 1959), p.53; and referred to in Acts 18.1-2.

13. P. Cornelius Tacitus, *Annales* 15.44, in Tacitus, *The Annals of Imperial Rome* (trans. M. Grant; Harmondsworth: Penguin, 1975), p.365. (Hereafter bracketed page references to *Annales* refer to Grant's edition.)

14. Tacitus, *Annales* 13.1 (p.308).

15. Anthony J. Guerra, *Romans and the Apologetic Tradition: The Purpose, Genre and Audience of Paul's Letter* (Cambridge: Cambridge University Press, 1995), pp.160–61.

16. Guerra, *Romans*, p.164.

17. Neil Elliott, 'Romans 13: 1-7 in the Context of Imperial Propaganda', in *Paul and Empire: Religion and Power in Roman Imperial Society* (ed. Richard A. Horsley; Harrisburg, PA: Trinity Press International, 1997), pp.184–205 (190–91); cf. Elliott, *Liberating Paul*, pp.22–26.

Nero as favourable for good to flourish, and that he hoped the Christian church in Rome would flourish'.[18]

There is no scholarly consensus, however, on the impact of the context of persecution or Jewish rebellion. Where Marcus Borg, for example, speculates that Jewish nationalism had reached violent levels in Rome,[19] Delling maintains that Christians did not support Jewish nationalistic claims or rebellion against Rome (because their perspective on acknowledging the rule of God but living under a foreign government was modelled on Jesus, e.g. Mk 12.13-17).[20] For Delling as for Chrysostom, the historical circumstances of the first readers are not significant for the message. Thomas Schreiner similarly minimises Zealot activity in the impact of persecution as factors, and sees the key element in Rome's position as capital of the empire, so that 'the relation of believers to governing authorities was a natural subject of discussion'.[21]

Pelagius, we saw, referred to the *mistaken* application of Christian freedom as meaning 'that they rendered honour or paid taxes to no one'.[22] Schreiner plays down such a context of a 'spiritual enthusiasm' that dismissed the need for any governmental power. Conversely, this is the key factor in the context for Käsemann. (His linguistic judgment that 'submit' indicates hierarchical stratification and lacks the voluntarism of 'obey' was included in §4.4.a.)[23] For him, the paraenesis was directed against emancipatory tendencies on the part of Christian slaves and women 'who demand equality'.[24]

Dunn argues for a 'context-specific' reading of the passage, dependent on Paul's 'knowledge of current affairs in Rome', including the situation of the Jews there, and that Paul 'writes with the reality of his readers' political context very much in view'.[25] This contrasts with Käsemann, who posits that Christian contacts with political authorities were few.[26] For Dunn, Paul is redrawing the boundaries of the new people of God in non-ethnic terms, and as such, in their particular context, he is putting the

18. Swartley, 'How to Interpret', p.30.

19. Marcus Borg, 'A New Context for Romans XIII', *NTS* 19 (1972), pp.205–18.

20. Gerhard Delling, *Römer 13, 1-7 innerhalb der Briefe des Neuen Testaments* (Berlin: Evangelische Verlagsanstalt, 1962).

21. Thomas R. Schreiner, *Romans: Baker Exegetical Commentary on the New Testament* (Grand Rapids: Baker Books, 1998), p.678.

22. Pelagius, *Romans*, p.136 (cited in §5.2.a).

23. Käsemann, *Romans*, p.13.

24. Käsemann, *Romans*, p.351.

25. Dunn, *Romans 9–16*, pp.761 and 768; see also 'Romans 13: 1-7 – A Charter for Political Quietism?', *Ex Auditu* 2 (1986), pp.55–68.

26. Käsemann, *Romans*, p.350.

political status of the new congregations at risk. He therefore reads Rom. 13.1-7 as a 'reminder' to the congregation of expedience, and extrapolates the exhortation and application: 'since you cannot change the terms under which you live, and since your position is already hazardous, remember the political realities of the politically powerless and live accordingly'.[27]

T.L. Carter finds a similar application of the exhortation in the circumstances of its first readers, that 'to resort to rebellion or violent revolution would...have been futile' (and would also have entailed being overcome by evil, rather than overcoming evil with good – Rom. 12.21).[28] Carter, too, argues that Paul's meaning is thoroughly dependent on the historical contingencies, but this is because the 'lack of congruence between Paul's commendation of the authorities and the reality of what was actually taking place in Rome'[29] was so great that his first readers would have received the text as ironic. If this is so, 'Paul's ironic meaning has generally been missed', as Carter notes. However, my own case study shows that commentators, while not discovering an ironic meaning, variously argue that Paul, in some other way, 'cannot mean' what his words appear to mean: for example Luther (§7.3.c) argues that 'St Paul cannot possibly be speaking of any obedience except where there can be corresponding authority'.[30]

5.2.c. 'Pagans' and 'tyrants'

The broad context of Christians under pagan rule, and superficially under cruel and tyrannical regimes, is an important factor, variously, in the reception. Article XXXV of the Articles of Religion drawn up by the Church of England in 1563 prescribes the reading of Homilies, to provide 'a godly and wholesome doctrine, and necessary for these times'.[31] The Homily 'Against Disobedience and Wilful Rebellion' (a repeated preoccupation in this period)[32] notes this characteristic of Paul's historical context in Rom. 13.1-7 and 1 Tim. 2.1-3: 'And who I pray you, was

27. Dunn, *Romans 9–16*, pp.690–70.

28. T.L. Carter, 'The Irony of Romans 13', *Novum Testamentum* 46.3 (2004), pp.209–28 (227).

29. Carter, 'The Irony of Romans 13', p.227.

30. Luther, 'Part 2', p.265.

31. Article 35, in The Church of England, *Sermons or Homilies, Appointed to Be Read in Churches in the Time of Queen Elizabeth of Famous Memory: To Which Are Added, the Articles of Religion* (London: Ellerton & Henderson for The Prayer-book and Homily Society, 1824), p.632.

32. The Book of Homilies ends with a 'Thanksgiving for the Suppression of the Last Rebellion': in Church of England, *Homilies*, pp.615–16.

Prince over the most part of the Christians, when GODS holy spirit by Saint Pauls pen gave them this lesson? Forsooth, Caligula, Claudius or Nero: who were not only no Christians, but Pagans, and also either foolish rulers, or most cruel tyrants.'[33] The application is in obedience to kings, and 'all that are in authority' and the submission of servants even to 'froward' masters. The life-world horizon of the Church of England in the sixteenth and seventeenth centuries included its opposition to Anabaptist teaching and groups such as the Mennonites (principally in the Netherlands but in contact with English exiles such as John Smyth) who rejected Christian participation in the magistracy and taught non-resistance.

For Thomas Hobbes in 1651, the context of Christians in Rome under pagan rule is viewed in relation to the life-world horizon of the contested authority of clergy to contravene monarchical or Commonwealth rule. If Paul's readers were required to be subject to pagan rulers and pagan masters, clergy in Hobbes' day must be required to be subject to civil rule:

> These princes and powers whereof St. Peter and St. Paul here speak were all infidels: much more therefore we are to obey those Christians whom God hath ordained to have sovereign power over us. How then can we be obliged to obey any minister of Christ if he should command us to do anything contrary to the command of the king or other sovereign representant of the Commonwealth whereof we are members, and by whom we look to be protected?[34]

Conversely, in the same period, John Milton uses the historical context of Romans 13 to support religious freedom from civil authority. He writes in 1659, during the nine-month succession of Oliver Cromwell's son as Lord Protector, 'A Treatise of Civil Power in Ecclesiastical Causes: shewing that it is not lawfull for any power on earth to compel in matters of Religion'. The context of pagan rulers – who did not 'meddle' in matters of religion except in the illegitimate role of tyrant and persecutor – is determinative for exegesis of the paraenesis: 'how prove they that the apostle means other powers then such as they to whom he writes were then under; who medld not at all in ecclesiasticall causes,

---

33. John Jewel, 'Against Disobedience and Wilful Rebellion', in Church of England, *Homilies*, p.571. (Bishop Jewel authored all but two of the twenty-one homilies.)

34. Thomas Hobbes, *Leviathan: The Matter, Form and Power of a Commonwealth* [1651] (ed. R. Tuck; Cambridge Texts in the History of Political Thought; Cambridge: Cambridge University Press, 1991), p.341.

unless as tyrants and persecutors'.[35] He challenges interpreters who draw the opposite conclusion and 'for want of other prooff will needs wrest that place of S Paul Rom 13 to set up civil inquisition, and give power to the magistrate both of civil judgment and punishment in causes ecclesiastical'.[36] Milton does not here cite Calvin, who had similarly insisted that the higher authorities known to the Roman Christians were secular not spiritual, and who had applied this to his own context: 'This whole disputation is of civil government; therefore, in vain go they about by this place to establish their abominable tyranny, which exercise authority over men's consciences'.[37]

In 1939, when Klausner identifies the context as one under tyrannical Emperors, he characterises the paraenesis as appeasement. In Rom. 13.1-5 he finds 'complete opportunism' with regard to the state and its authority:

> When one considers all the shameful deeds of oppression…of the Roman government…particularly in the provinces where Paul lived and travelled, one cannot escape a feeling of resentment and protest against this recital of praise for the tyranny of Caligula and Nero… One is forced to see in it flattery of the rulers, on the one hand, and yielding to force, on the other hand.[38]

Kallas objects that Klausner 'leaves us with the inference that Paul is both hypocritical and servile'.[39] Klausner is conscious of the different horizon he brings to the text: 'my particular viewpoint as a Jew…is different from that of the Christian investigators'.[40] He made his doctoral studies in Germany, and wrote *Jesus and Paul* in the 1930s. Each reader asks questions of the text that are, in Jauss's words, 'decided first and foremost by an interest that arises out of the present situation'.[41]

35. John Milton, 'A Treatise of Civil Power in Ecclesiastical Causes', in *John Milton: Selected Prose* (ed. C.A. Patrides; Harmondsworth: Penguin, 1974), pp.305–6.

36. Milton, 'Civil Power', p.305.

37. Calvin, *Epistle of Saint Paul to the Romans*, p.368. He has a high view of civil authority (see §7.3.d).

38. Joseph Klausner, *From Jesus to Paul* [1939] (London: Allen & Unwin, 1942), pp.565–66.

39. Kallas, 'Interpolation', p.369. (His reception figures in §4.4.b.)

40. Klausner, *From Jesus to Paul*, p.xi.

41. Jauss, *Aesthetic of Reception*, p.65.

5.2.d. 'Good reasons, unknown to us'

There is thus no consensus on the historical context of the paraenesis, though considerable agreement – *pace* Chrysostom – that it has one. Barrett asserts the importance of the occasionality of Rom. 13.1-7, but without being able to identify the nature of the occasion. He treats it as a self-contained treatment of a special theme: it is still a bit of a puzzle, but the answer lies in the occasion and context, 'and there may well have been good reasons, unknown to us... why this example should have been chosen'.[42] Minear similarly admits defeat: 'I am unable to find particular reasons in the Roman situation for Paul's including of this teaching'.[43]

If the exhortation is in any way specific to context and boundaried by occasion, it is a remarkable operation of *Horizontverschmelzung* that interpreters are able to apply it to very diverse life-world horizons. Elliott expresses surprise, for instance, at Dunn's insistence (§5.2.b above) that 'the discussion in these verses is context-specific' when he nevertheless explains the passage as the expression of Paul's view of 'a divinely ordered society', and thus 'a theology of political power', and Paul's 'political realism',[44] and comments: 'but this perhaps shows the resilience of the generalized convention of reading this passage'.[45] This endorses Käsemann's epigrammatic complaint: 'The basis of what [Paul] demands is reduced to a minimum, while exegesis usually seeks to take from it a maximum'.[46] Käsemann writes that while it 'cannot be denied that Paul's intention is to set up a valid order', he does it 'in a way which is thoroughly tied to time and situation'.[47] He argues, to the converse of Dunn and others, that Paul is not making an exhaustive statement about the relation to authorities, in spite of this tendency in its interpretation:

> Throughout church history our passage has been regarded as the classic statement of the Pauline and indeed the New Testament and Christian doctrine of the state, and has been made binding. Almost inevitably then, the exhortation has stood in the shadow of metaphysics of the state or an interrelating of church and state in salvation history. The doors have thus been opened in Christianity not only to conservative but also to reactionary views even to the point of political fanaticism.[48]

42. Barrett, *Romans*, p.244.

43. Paul Minear, *The Obedience of Faith: The Purpose of Paul in the Epistle to the Romans* (London: SCM, 1971), p.88.

44. Dunn, *Romans 9–16*, p.773; Elliott, *Liberating Paul*, p.289n.

45. Elliott, *Liberating Paul*, p.288 n.

46. Käsemann, *Romans*, p.354.

47. Käsemann, *Romans*, p.357. He uses the instance of ὑποτασσέσθωσαν in 1 Cor. 14.34 to confirm his view that the context of the exhortation limits its frame of reference.

48. Käsemann, *Romans*, p.354.

James Hollingshead at the end of the twentieth century summarised scholarship on Rom. 13.1-7 as generally finding three different characters of Paul, and reflecting national trends in doing so:

> when scholars read Rom. 13.1-7, they find three different Pauls: there is Paul the good citizen, champion of the rights of the state; Paul the revolutionary, the leader of a rebellious Christian underground; Paul the pragmatist, resigned to Roman rule... It is interesting to note that this split is divided along the national lines of the commentators involved; British scholars tend to see Paul as defending the state; Germans tend to see him as a radical; and Americans see Paul as a pragmatist (with Yoder as a partial exception).[49]

5.3. Colossians 3.18 and Ephesians 5.21-22

The material in Chapters 3 and 4 concerning the genre and lexis of the *Haustafeln* fulfils a double duty here, contributing also to the construction of the domestic *setting* of these relationships, as part of the horizon of expectation of the first readers. The use of pairs of injunctions, repeating an 'axiomatic' pattern of social hierarchy,[50] was seen as reflecting a social context which (variously interpreted) endorses 'a fixed, hierarchical and patriarchal order', or attempts assimilation to 'life in society while preserving their distinctive identity', or embodies a radical reformation of the patriarchal structure of the family model of family 'offensive' to the Graeco-Roman social elite.[51] The introduction of the household code in Ephesians with ὑποτασσόμενοι ἀλλήλοις was seen as encoding a social setting where those 'who appear to be greater may be subject to those lesser than themselves', and a society with 'horizontal lines of interaction among equals'; or a setting reflecting the 'social conditions and view which pertained at that time', but in a way that 'relativizes the differences in a reciprocal relation'; or conversely, it encodes the 'unchanging institution of family' with its 'recognition of the sacred principles of authority and obedience'.[52] The sampling of comment that follows is further contribution to these constructions,

---

49. James R. Hollingshead, *The Household of Caesar and the Body of Christ: A Political Interpretation of the Letters from Paul* (Lanham, Md.: University Press of America, 1998), pp.xii and xix–xx (n).

50. Balch, *Let Wives*, p.61 (cited in §3.4).

51. Wedderburn, *Later Pauline Letters*, p.57; Lincoln, *Later Pauline Letters*, p.141; Witherington, *Paul Quest*, pp.189–90 (cited in §§3.4 and 4.5.a).

52. Jerome, 'Ephesians', p.232 (cited in §4.6.a); Bilezikian, *Beyond Sex Roles*, p.154 (§4.6.a); Schnackenburg, *Ephesians*, p.246 (§4.6.c); Robinson, *Ephesians*, p.172 (§4.6.b).

particularly in relation to the question (posed in §3.4), how far the use of such a genre *replicates* the ethos and social context of the hypothetical first-reception, and how far it represents a *different* horizon of expectation.

5.3.a. 'Ordained by the natural order'

There is even less reference in patristic and scholastic reception to specifics of a socio-historical situation in Colossae or Ephesus than there was concerning the socio-political situation of Christians in Rome. Christian assumptions about the structure of the family changed very little:[53] 'Indeed, though the family has generally been considered to be a major social institution, Christian theology has rarely addressed it with the same attention as it has the state'.[54] The discourses of household and state in early reception could be combined. Cicero had described the state as a patriarchy: 'The name of the king is like that of a father to us' and the subjects are 'best sustained by the care of the one man who is the most virtuous and the most eminent'.[55]

There was an early charge that Christian households did not conform to accepted household order. In the mid-second century, Celsus makes a critique (known through Origen's rebuttal) of early Christianity as a revolutionary movement, because they had created a social group that promoted its own laws and its own patterns of behaviour. He makes an attack that relates their sedition in terms both of civil authority[56] and of disruption of accepted household order. Celsus argues that religion, which should properly be linked to affairs of the city and state (i.e. the male domain),[57] among the early Christians had become a private affair, in domestic settings, and among women. Christians urge children to go 'with the women...to the wooldresser's shop or to the cobbler's, or to the washerwoman's shop'.[58] The proselytising tactics of the Christians include the attempt to dupe women and children and to teach them to be

---

53. Cf. Armitage Robinson's claim in 1909 that the 'institution of family' is 'unchanging': Robinson, *Ephesians*, p.170 (cited in §4.6.b).

54. A. Farley, 'Family', in *A New Dictionary of Catholic Social Thought* (ed. Judith A. Dwyer; Collegeville: Liturgical Press, 1994), p.371.

55. Marcus Tullius Cicero, *De Re Publica* 1.54–55 (35), in Cicero, *De Re Publica, De Legibus* (trans. C. W. Keyes; LCL, 16; Cambridge, Mass.: Harvard University Press, 1928), p.83.

56. Origen, *Contra Celsum* 8.68 (p.504).

57. Cf. Margaret Macdonald, 'Rereading Paul: Early Interpreters of Paul on Women and Gender', in *Women and Christians Origins* (ed. Ross Shephard Kraemar and Mary Rose D'Angelo; Oxford: Oxford University Press, 1999), p.242.

58. Origen, *Contra Celsum* 3.55 (p.166).

disrespectful of authority: 'whenever they get hold of children in private and some stupid women that talk nonsense and have no understanding, they let out some astounding statements, as, for example, that they must not pay attention to their father and to their teachers, but must obey them'.[59]

The domestic setting and circumstances that form the background of this (hostile) account may resemble some of the social context of the congregations in Colossae and Ephesus, and the *Haustafeln* may have been used to counter similar criticisms, and witness that Christian domestic life supported the *status quo*. Roman society had its own rhetoric of the *polis* integrating its inhabitants on the basis of equal rights, but 'in fact large sections of the population did not have equal rights at all – neither women, nor *peregrini*, nor slaves; and this often meant the greater part of the population'.[60]

When Aquinas marries Augustinian theology with an Aristotelian world order of natural hierarchies (cf. §4.5.a), patriarchal authority continues to be referred to nature rather than to the *Haustafeln*. It is the prime authority and the only natural dominion: in natural law, everyone is free apart from the exercise of dominion by father and husbands over their children and wives.[61] If the male principle was superior and the female inferior, then in the household, as in the state, men should rule and women must be subordinate.[62] The paraenetic texts then continued to be received in contexts where very similar forms of discourse, legislation and economy were perpetuated. Indeed, they are still; though there are now also established traditions of reception where the interpreters' historical condition and horizons of expectation are revisionally or radically different from those embodied in the writings of Aristotle, Cicero and Aquinas. From both perspectives there are bodies of comment that have continued to construct the domestic setting of the paraenesis as conforming to the subordination of women and wives in the wider society of the first-century Roman Empire. (Two examples above were from Wedderburn and Armitage Robinson: §§3.4 and 4.6.a.)

---

59. Origen, *Contra Celsum* 3.55 (p.165).

60. Gerd Theissen, *Social Reality and the Early Christian: Theology, Ethics, and the World of the New Testament* (trans. Margaret Kohl; Minneapolis: Fortress, 1992), pp.276–77.

61. Aquinas, *Summa* 1a.92, 1, 1a.96, 4 and 2a-2ae.10, 10 (vol. 13, pp.35–38, 133–37 and vol. 32, pp.66–70).

62. The relation of male to female is naturally that of the superior to the inferior, of the ruling to the ruled': *Politics* 1.1254b; in Aristotle, *Politics* (trans. Ernest Barker, rev. R.F. Stalley; Oxford: Oxford University Press, 2009), p.16.

Crouch compares the view of the status of women in the Colossians *Haustafel* with those held by pagan contemporaries, and concludes that it represents a 'lower' view: 'It is difficult to imagine a Stoic or even a wandering popular philosopher making this statement'.[63] He suggests that the lower view of women can be ascribed to the influence of Hellenistic Judaism, which had 'reacted to the moral laxity of the Hellenistic culture by intensifying [its] distrust of women'.[64] This tradition impacts not only in the formulations of the *Haustafeln* but also Paul's reference to the 'law' in 1 Cor. 14.34 supporting the subordination of wives.

There are interesting resonances of the idea that Christian teaching continues to go beyond the pattern of secular culture in its household hierarchy and the subordination of women. Florence Nightingale complains that the duties of service to their families, urged upon women by the 'Evangelical Party' of the second half of the nineteenth century, represents a move beyond the secular culture of the day: 'the degree to which they have raised the claims upon women of "family" – the idol they have made of it. It is a kind of Fetichism [*sic*].'[65] Charles Gore illustrates some of the substance of Nightingale's complaint in his comment on Eph. 5.21 (in 'a practical exposition' in 1898). He sees a stronger principle of subordination operating in a Pauline or a Victorian *congregation* than in secular society: 'St Paul mentions submission as required, in a sense, from all Christians towards all others – "submitting yourselves one to another". But it is plain that in any community and most of all in a Christian community where order is a divine principle, some will be specially "under authority"'.[66] The divine principle of order for Gore seems to be a principle of social stratification and patriarchy: his role in the development of Christian Socialism might suggest an unresolved *Horizontabhebung* of text and life.[67] In the same

---

63. J.E. Crouch, *The Origin and Intention of the Colossian Haustafel* (Göttingen: Vandenhoeck & Ruprecht, 1972), p.107.

64. Crouch, *Colossian Haustafel*, p.108.

65. In A.M. Alchin, *Silent Rebellion: Anglican Religious Communities 1845–1900* (London: SCM, 1958), p.209.

66. Charles Gore, *St Paul's Epistle to the Ephesians: A Practical Exposition* (London: John Murray, 1898), p.211.

67. In a companion volume, in a 'practical exposition' of Rom. 13, Gore comments that, in England, this passage has often been put to 'two conspicuously unjustifiable uses'. The first is its use in the debate about the 'divine right of kings' and 'passive obedience', whereas 'it asserts the divine right of civil authority, but not of any particular kind of civil authority'. The second is their use to justify a claim on behalf of the state to 'coerce' and govern the Church: Charles Gore, *St Paul's Epistle to the Romans: A Practical Exposition* (London: John Murray, 1900), p.123.

period, and in the politicised environment of the women's rights movement, Elizabeth Cady Stanton believed the ethos of Col. 3.18 and Eph. 5.22 (and 1 Tim. 2) to be so antithetical to 'women of this generation' that the texts 'should no longer be read in our churches... All these old ideas should be relegated to the ancient mythologies as mere allegories, having no application whatever to the women of this generation.'[68]

Some more recent analyses have identified in Colossians 3 and Ephesians 5 circumstances that produced advocates contesting social patterns within the community. Käsemann (see above, §5.2.b) sees the *Haustafel* as a corrective to an interpretation of a theology of freedom. It is directed against emancipatory tendencies on the part of Christian slaves and women 'who demand equality'.[69] Theissen sees some of the same tensions operating in respect of household order as were at work in the paraenesis on submission to governing authorities. There was a revolution of values whereby those with no access to authority in the social hierarchy gained authority not previously available to them, and at the same time 'there are unmistakable signs of repression':

> An almost violent effort was made to repress any consequences of the new values which would have called in question the ability of the early Christian groups to survive in the society of the time. Paradoxically enough, 'evolutionary' and 'repressive' tendencies can be found in close proximity to each other; the acquisition of upper-class values (which meant a value revolution) released expectations that were repressed, and often survive only in the form of a utopian hope.[70]

In relation to slaves Theissen detects 'considerable tension';[71] and in its paraenesis for the subordination of women, early Christianity goes 'even beyond the average patriarchal consensus'. This is part of the same 'contradiction', and is related to the claims of and experience of women's authority in (some of) the earliest Christian communities:

---

68. E.C. Stanton, 'An Expurgated Edition of the Bible', *Free Thought Magazine* 20 (1902), p.704, cited by Carolyn de Swarte Gifford, 'Politicizing the Sacred Texts: Elizabeth Cady Stanton and *The Woman's Bible*', in *Searching the Scriptures: A Feminist Introduction*, vol. 1 (ed. E. Schüssler Fiorenza; London: SCM, 1993), pp.52–63 (60).
69. Käsemann, *Romans*, p.351 (cited in §5.2.b).
70. Theissen, *Social Reality*, p.279.
71. Theissen, *Social Reality*, p.284.

Women are not merely declared equal in principle (Gal. 3.28). There are also still many traces in early Christian texts showing that in Christianity's beginnings they had an importance that must not be underestimated. Monogamy, the prohibition of divorce, and the ascetic control of sexuality were all to women's advantage.[72]

5.3.b. The household and the 'household of God'

A large body of comment in recent decades has focused on the social setting of Pauline Christianity, including feminist, socio-historical and socio-rhetorical criticism. However, in exegetical commentaries there is not a great proportion of exegetical attention given to local *specifics* of historical context, the occasionality of Col. 3.18 or Eph. 5.21-22.[73] Commentaries regularly consider the occasions of the letters as a whole. The occasion of Colossians is attributed typically to a report from Epaphras (1.9) of false teaching (2.8) being adopted in the congregation, with characteristics of asceticism (2.21) and mysticism (2.18), possibly from a Jewish tradition (2.16).[74] The exhortatory section 3.5–4.6 is typically discussed as having characteristics of early Christian catechesis rather than being generated from local circumstances.[75] Ephesians is typically seen as written for more than one congregation (there are no personal greetings or references to contextual circumstances[76]) and possibly not shaped by the occasions and needs of a specific congregation.[77]

With Col. 3.18 and Eph. 5.21-22, the specifics of the situation are principally investigated in terms of the nature of the household, and the replication or transformation of this in the membership of the 'household of God' (Eph. 2.19). Paul's congregations met in private houses. How far these should be seen as conforming to the stratifications of an accepted secular household, and how far transformed by a new identity with revisionist or radical social implications, is debated. There are many

---

72. Theissen, *Social Reality*, pp.284–85. See also my discussion of a changing post-Pauline church in the constructions of Meeks, Fiorenza and Lincoln (§5.3.b).

73. This may reflect the genre distinction noted above (§3.3) that paraenesis is held to embody universal advice, rather than advice for specific occasions (Dibelius, *James*, p.11; Aune, *Literary Environment*, p.191).

74. E.g. Peter T. O'Brien, *Colossians, Philemon* (WBC 44; Dallas: Word Books, 1982), pp.xxxi–xxxiii.

75. O'Brien, *Colossians*, p. lxii ('though we have not direct evidence for this').

76. E.g. Markus Barth, *Ephesians* (AB 34A; New Haven: Yale University Press, 1974), p.10.

77. E.g. Lincoln suggests it is 'hazardous' to propose specific settings for this letter: *Ephesians*, p. lxxi.

analyses of the setting that identify a tension between two semantic concepts of subordination, and two constructs of domestic relations. So Lincoln writes that the author of Ephesians,

> accepts and even reinforces the basic structures of the patriarchal house-
> hold, but then within them brings to bear Christian motivations of love
> and service. His unique contribution…to early Christian household codes
> [is] his exhortation to all the members of the household to submit to one
> another (5.21), though for him this is quite compatible with the following
> exhortations for particular subordination.[78]

Like Schnackenberg (see §4.6.c), both J. Paul Sampley and Ernest Best express this dissonance as the effect of importing or imposing the alien ethos of the *Haustafel* onto a new, Christian ethos of mutual standing. Sampley argues that the exhortation to mutual submission in Eph. 5.21 is to be understood as completely relativising what follows, a critique of the domestic paraenesis. He even (effectively) suggests that this new horizon of understanding creates a dissonance in the author's reception – and reproduction – of the *Haustafel*. The *Haustafel* contains a viewpoint of unequal application of submission with which the writer of Ephesians does not entirely agree.[79] Sampley fails to explain why the writer makes quite such extended use of the code when it does not really represent his ethical teaching.

Best notes the same dissonance between Eph. 5.21 and the *Haustafel* as Sampley, but the different frame of reference of the former does not impinge on the submission that follows: 'sometimes commentators describe the relationship as mutual and reciprocal, but this is incorrect'.[80] The origin of the *Haustafel* form as a piece of tradition, used independ-ently in Colossians and Ephesians (an argument confirmed by the easy way in which the *Haustafel* of Colossians can be detached from its con-text), means that the beginning of the *Haustafel* of Ephesians is *grafted* into its context through 5.21: 'but though this verse promises a mutual relationship between members of a household, this is not the way in which it is developed; 5.21 is therefore a verse constructed to permit the transition from what preceded to the section of tradition'.[81]

---

78.   Lincoln, *Later Pauline Letters*, p.123.

79.   J.P. Sampley, *'And the Two Shall Become One Flesh': A Study of Traditions in Ephesians 5.21-33* (Cambridge: Cambridge University Press, 1971), p.117.

80.   Ernest Best, *Essays on Ephesians* (Edinburgh: T. & T. Clark, 1997), p.190.

81.   Best, *Essays*, p.195.

This is a mediation of horizons with an established place in the analysis of Pauline language and of the social structure of his churches. Ernst Troeltsch marks the beginning of the articulation of Christian ethics characterised as 'the patriarchalism of love', which he sees as a construct of Paul's teaching and practice, and with the role of the household codes as key to the process.[82] '[I]nner religious equality' is affirmed', while maintaining 'the willing acceptance of given [social] inequalities':

> This...type of Christian patriarchalism...receives its special colour from the warmth of the Christian idea of love, through the inclusion of all in the Body of Christ... It is undeniable that this ideal is dimly perceived by Paul, and only by means of this ideal does he desire to alter given conditions from within outwards, without touching their external aspect at all.[83]

Christianity should be 'very cautious towards any attempt to carry over this [religious] equality into the sphere of secular relationships and institutions'.[84] This has been a very influential view: 'Troeltsch and Schweitzer have cast giant shadows across Pauline interpretation...and their explanations of Paul's "social conservatism" continue to enjoy wide currency'.[85] The resulting *fusion* is by later writers termed 'love-patriarchalism' or 'benevolent patriarchalism'.[86] My own judgment is that these are apt descriptions of the ethos of the Pastoral Letters,[87] but difficult to fuse with the more radical theology and ethics expressed in the other Pauline or deutero-Pauline texts (see §§10.2 and 10.5). Lincoln comments: 'The clear note of reciprocity in the admonition by the author of Ephesians to parents and to children, to masters and to slaves, is not sustained into the later tradition'.[88]

---

82. Ernst Troeltsch, *The Social Teaching of the Christian Churches*, vol. 1 [1912] (trans. Olive Wyon; New York: Macmillan, 1931), pp.286–87.

83. Troeltsch, *Social Teaching*, p.78.

84. Troeltsch, *Social Teaching*, pp.69–79.

85. Elliott, *Liberating Paul*, pp.61–62.

86. Theissen, *Social Setting*, p.107; Dale Martin, *Slavery as Salvation: The Metaphor of Slavery in Pauline Christianity* (New Haven: Yale University Press, 1990), p.128.

87. Cf. Martin Dibelius who writes that the Pastorals are characterized by '*Bürgerlichkeit*' which 'describes the attitude of the good, honest, decent, ordinary citizen. Household rules appear, though the family is now the church rather than the natural family': *Die Pastoralbriefe* (Tübingen: Mohr-Siebeck, 1955), p.7, cited by C.K. Barrett, 'Deuteropauline Ethics', in Lovering *et al.*, *Theology and Ethics*, pp.161–72 (163–64).

88. Lincoln, *Later Pauline Letters*, p.141.

Such a view is countered by Birger Gerhardsson, for example, who sees the subordination of women in the deutero-Pauline letters (citing Eph. 5.22-24; Col. 3.18-19; 1 Tim. 2.8-15; Tit. 2.1-5) as an ethical pattern *derived from and mirroring the earliest Pauline communities*, and he claims that '[e]arly Christianity seems to have maintained a quite uniform praxis in these matters'.[89] It is supported, however, by a number of other commentators, for example, Meeks, Schüssler Fiorenza and Lincoln, who construct a developing social pattern in Pauline and post-Pauline churches.

Meeks detects tensions or a 'clash' between Pauline teaching (leadership of women, a charismatic style of leadership, Gal. 3.28 and the transformative constitution of a 'new family of God, where all without exception are "sisters and brothers"'[90]) and the 'traditional expectations of the householder's own power and authority' which the *Haustafeln* in the classical and Hellenistic and Jewish-Hellenistic traditions reinforced.[91] He argues that the context of the household was a strongly contributing factor to the conflicts in the allocation of power and the understanding of roles in the first and early Christian communities:

> The head of the household, by normal expectations of the society, would exercise some authority over the group and would have some legal responsibility for it. The structure of the *oikos* was hierarchical, and contemporary political and moral thought regarded the structure of superior and inferior roles as basic to the well-being of the whole society. Yet... there were certain countervailing modes and centres of authority in the Christian movement that ran contrary to the power of the *paterfamilias*, and certain egalitarian beliefs and attitudes that conflicted with the hierarchical structure.[92]

The use of the *Haustafeln* adapted for moral instruction among Christians is significant in this development: 'In time, in circles that appealed to the memory of Paul as an authority..., the whole church would be construed as "the household of God", with great stress upon the hierarchical order of the various roles peculiar to the ecclesiastical organization'.[93]

---

89. Gerhardsson, *Ethos of the Bible*, pp.84–85 (cited in §4.5.a).
90. Wayne A. Meeks, *The First Urban Christians* (New Haven: Yale University Press, 1983), p.199.
91. Meeks, 'American Slavery', p.244.
92. Meeks, *First Urban Christians*, p.76.
93. Meeks, *First Urban Christians*, p.77.

Schüssler Fiorenza argues that the ethos of the *Haustafeln* and the Pastorals should not be *read back* into the earlier letters of Paul. In reconstructions of Paul's early communities (such as that represented in 1 Corinthians) and of the later developments of the post-Pauline tradition (such as those presented in Colossians and Ephesians, and later again in 1 and 2 Timothy and Titus), she argues that Paul promoted an egalitarian vision but also modified it. He feared 'orgiastic' behaviour in worship and so restricted the role of women and paved the way for the transferral of patriarchal structures to the community, which led to the complete subordination of women. The Pastorals then take the development into the gradual exclusion of women from ecclesial office and towards the gradual patriarchalisation of the whole church: 'the church is now stratified according to "natural" age and gender divisions. Though still the new "family", it is clearly understood in terms of the patriarchal household. The church is understood as the household of God.'[94]

Lincoln characterises the paraenesis of women's submission in Ephesians as 'an essential part' of the author's attempt to help the churches 'assimilate to life in society while preserving their distinctive identity': 'The patriarchal structuring of household management, which was seen as crucial for the stability of society, is taken over, but to it the writer brings his Christian vision of relationships'.[95] The 'benefits' of the strategy are mixed: while there must be a process of adjustment of the Pauline churches to life in society with its necessary increasing institutionalisation, the distinctive behaviour called for by the letter in respect of life in the household must have created modifications within the dominant ethos of the surrounding world. The results are particularly mixed for the women themselves:

> while the writer's adaptation of the code would have resulted in gains for some women within marriage, the instructions about subordination would have had implications for the role of women in the general life of the churches and contributed to identification of positions with any authority as male prerogatives.[96]

As with Schüssler Fiorenza's trajectory above, Lincoln argues that it is in the Pastorals that some of the results of this tendency can be seen: as the household became the dominant model for the Church, 'women were excluded from authoritative teaching roles'.

---

94. Fiorenza. *In Memory*, p.288.
95. Lincoln, *Later Pauline Letters*, p.141 (cited in §3.4).
96. Lincoln, *Later Pauline Letters*, p.141.

5.4. Interim case-study evaluation

Historical-critical methods reflecting on historical setting and occasion are demonstrated in the reception of these texts, and contribute variously to how their 'meaning and content is determined by the occasion for which they are intended'[97] in the hermeneutical paradigm of *Wirkungs-geschichte*. As with the historical-critical attention to genre and lexis, the claims for singularity and certainty appearing in some characterisations of historical-critical exegesis are not evidenced by, collectively, the contested and indeterminate features here. These suggest that the methods do not offer final resolutions of the meaning or meanings accessible to the first readers: they contribute to constructions which are co-determinants of meaning, in a mediation with the horizons of the interpreters.

Again, the nature of my case-study texts raises some particular issues. The texts are paraenetic and therefore perlocutionary – interacting directly with the receiver, and attempting to effect a change in the behaviour of the reader. This foregrounds the *differentiation* of horizons (*Horizontabhebung*) in Jauss's model,[98] and the readiness to receive a new perspective of a text in the adjusting 'fusion' of two horizons in Gadamer's articulation.[99] There are some powerful examples in the sample of a perceived *Alterität*[100] in the contingencies of hypothetical first-reception over against the interpreters' different historical contingencies (e.g. in §§5.2.c and 5.3.b above). If the social conditions of a Colossian household or the political situation of the Roman Christians are characterised as differing from the conditions of the (later) reader, what is the impact of this in the *perlocutionary* effect of the text on the reader? If the socio-political conditions no longer apply, in what way does the paraenesis apply? There are pertinent hermeneutical principles of lived affinity, solidarity in tradition, and theological prejudgments operating. The discussion of these principles (in Chapter 9) will be followed by further sampling from the case study (in Chapter 10), including reception that foregrounds the *Alterität* in the horizon and historical circumstances of text and reader.

---

97. Gadamer, *Truth and Method*, p.138.
98. Jauss, *Theorie der Rezeption*, p.17.
99. Gadamer, *Truth and Method*, p.305.
100. Jauss, *Alterität und Modernität*, p.129.

Chapter 6

RECEPTION HISTORY AND THE PROGRESSIVE PROCESS

6.1. Introduction: what process?

> *Wirkungsgeschichte* is an attempt to…appreciate the history of texts
> through time as a key to their interpretation.[1]

The present study turns now to a different focus of issues in reception
history of biblical texts, and this chapter examines recent approaches in
relation to features of Gadamer's hermeneutics and to Jauss's argument
that the meaning of a work 'is extracted only during the progressive
process of its reception'.[2] What sort of progressive process? A biblical
text is interpreted over time and in relation to previous interpretation.
The idea has been pursued by recent theorists and practitioners in biblical
interpretation with various constructions of such a 'process'. In doing so,
there has been little apparent agreement on the selection of reception, and
a great variety in the level of engagement with the hermeneutical theory
of Gadamer and Jauss.[3] Indeed, neither Gadamer nor Jauss provides
objective methodological criteria for constructing or valorizing a particular trajectory of interpretation in preference to another.

Current practice, particularly in structures of a compilation-history of
reception, reveals very different judgments about *which* realizations of a
biblical text should be selected or valorised as those that shape the 'pre-
understandings' of subsequent generations of interpreters. This chapter
considers principles of selection and exclusion that operate, particularly
in relation to continuities and pluralities, the limits of diversity, and the
value given to contingent particularity and life-application.

What I am pursuing are emerging patterns of practice and explicit
claims about the hermeneutics, which constitute a second group of
contested issues in the reception of biblical texts. There is no attempt

---

1. Roberts and Rowland, 'Introduction', p.132.
2. Jauss, *Aesthetic of Reception*, p.5 (cited in §1.1.c).
3. Cf. Parry, 'Review of Parris'; and Rowland, 'Pragmatic Approach', p.1 (cited
in §1.1.c).

here to be exhaustive in this survey of practice or even fully representative; and the taxonomy I make is rather a polarised one. Though it may indeed represent some polarisation in the practice, its purpose is to clarify what is at stake, hermeneutically, in different forms of practice. The cross-over with my first group of questions (concerning historical-critical approaches) appears in various places: such as in §6.2.a, reflecting on *Auslegungsgeschichte* and the nature of the material sampled; and in section 3, reflecting on historical contingency in the horizons of past and present.

Some particular patterns are emerging. On the one hand, there is discourse and practice that valorise trajectories of interpretative tradition, which may be seen as significant, exemplary or normative within an ecclesial or theological tradition. Selection of reception reveals (or constructs) 'structures of exemplary character that condition the process of the formation of literary tradition'[4] and potentially form a 'canon of exemplary commentators'.[5] This trend is examined in §6.2.

On the other hand, there is discourse and practice that sees in reception history a method of recovering neglected aspects of the interpretation of a text, and/or a method of challenging conservative traditions. This trend is examined in §6.3.

Among theorists and practitioners of both of these perceived trends, there can be attention to application and lived praxis, a feature central to Gadamerian hermeneutics and to a long tradition of Christian hermeneutics. This gives rise to questions about the *relative weight* given on the one hand to a tradition of interpretation in a progressive process, and on the other to the contingent particularity of each engagement with a text. This aspect is examined in §6.4.

6.2. 'Structures of exemplary character'
The use of Gadamer and Jauss in an argument concerning the selection of moments in a literary series has been developed most fully by David Parris in a trajectory that may be traced from Jauss through Luz and Thiselton, to students of Thiselton such as Parris and Morales Vásquez and to other practitioners such as John Riches.[6]

---

4. Jauss, *Question and Answer*, p.202.
5. Parris, *Reception Theory*, p.217.
6. Luz, *Matthew 1–7* and *Matthew 8–20*; Thiselton, *First Corinthians*; Parris, *Reception Theory*; Morales Vásquez, *Contours of a Biblical Reception Theory*; Riches, *Galatians*.

In his commentary on Matthew, Luz makes a selection of interpretations in the 'confessing traditions' within the 'legacy of the Church',[7] which have influenced subsequent readers in their pre-understandings of the text. Each reader comes to biblical texts with interpretative presuppositions formed in different, definable, ecclesial traditions. Luz's preference is for earlier examples of these representations, which are judged more 'effective' than modern reception. This judgment rests to a degree on a tautology: older readings, which have survived through history, can be credited with having 'effects' not yet observable for more recent readings.

Luz outlines a specifically interdenominational approach (also reflected in the aims and scope of the *Evangelisch-Katholischer Kommentar*). The reception of a text in one ecclesial tradition informs, enriches, and may offer a 'corrective' to interpretation of the text in a different denominational tradition. There are two main hermeneutical impulses [*Stossrichtungen*]. In the first, 'the "Church" is present from the outset in a prominent way'. 'Our own' denominational churches are 'mothers' of the readings which they guide, or at least 'a point of reference without which the biblical texts, since they are their canonical texts, cannot be perceived'.[8] In the second, 'It shows us what Roman Catholics or Orthodox, Pentecostals or secular people, Africans, monks or Anabaptist peasants became through the Bible... The texts are theirs as well as ours!'[9] Rowland comments on the manifestation of specific 'traditions' in interpretation (in its appearance in Parris' work):

> There is much rhetoric around about Catholic, Anglican, and Reformed patterns of interpretation, but actual interpreters are formed by traditions much more diverse and eclectic than can be easily encapsulated by this or that theological label... [A tradition is] inevitably a fluid constellation of ideas and events at a particular time and place that condition particular readings of biblical texts.[10]

Luz argues that the engagement with confessional, denominational processes of interpretation refreshes the meaning for the reader with new hermeneutical questions. This reflects Gadamer's insight of how readers

---

7. Luz, *Matthew 1–7*, pp.96 and 11, respectively.

8. Luz, '*Wirkungsgeschichtliche Hermeneutic*', pp.15–16 (translation mine).

9. Luz, 'Contribution of Reception History', p.131; cf. Luz, '*Wirkungsgeschichtliche Hermeneutic*', p.16.

10. Christopher Rowland, Review of David Parris, *Reception Theory and Biblical Hermeneutics*, *Review of Biblical Literature* 2010 (http://www.bookreviews.org/pdf/7129_7747.pdf, accessed 27 July 2010).

are shaped by their historicity and tradition. If tradition conditions our thinking, the disorientation provided by a challenging perspective provides a way more clearly to understand our own reading perspective.[11] This is a feature that Parris will characterise in Jaussian terms as paradigm shifts. Mark Elliot suggests that Luz's understanding of ecclesial reception of the Bible, and his aim of explicating 'what the text says devotionally', means that his construction of the progressive process is likely to lead to 'a range of "ecclesial messages", each of them rather bland or abstract' rather than ones which 'sharpen the message'.[12] The boundaries are pre-determined: Jonathan Roberts observes that Luz's belief in the 'trajectory' of biblical texts, and his identification of parameters for separating 'valid' from 'false' interpretations, means that his parameters are 'shaped by the very tradition that he then uses them to define'.[13]

Some critics perceive the 'risk of locking up the Bible once again within the churches' to be endemic to this role of *tradition* in Gadamer's hermeneutics. Dunn suggests that where 'meaning is thought to reside (only?) in a reading within a continuum and continuity of meaning', the corollary is that it is unable to be heard or understood by the world beyond the Church:

> Christians belong not only to diverse and overlapping communities, of workplace or residence or leisure; and unless they want to live a schizophrenic existence of two disconnected language-worlds, they must learn to speak a common language. A hermeneutic which effectively denies the possibility of the biblical message being heard outside the churches and in the forums of the world's discourses is a hermeneutic of irresponsibility and despair.[14]

(I shall return to questions of solidarity with an ecclesial tradition, and of 'responsible interpretation' in §9.3)

---

11. Cf. Rachel Nicholls, 'Is *Wirkungsgeschichte* (or Reception History) a Kind of Intellectual *Parkour* (or Freerunning)?', British New Testament Conference, September 2005 (http://issuu.com/revrach/docs/wirkungsgeschichte, accessed 2 August 2012), p.10 (and cited below, §6.3).

12. Elliott, 'Hermeneutics of Ulrich Luz', p.171.

13. Jonathan Roberts, 'Introduction', in *The Oxford Handbook of the Reception History of the Bible* (ed. Michael Lieb, Emma Mason and Jonathan Roberts; Oxford/New York: Oxford University Press, 2011), pp.1–8 (5).

14. James Dunn, 'Criteria for a Wise Reading of a Biblical Text', in *Reading Texts, Seeking Wisdom: Scripture and Theology* (ed. David F. Ford and Graham Stanton; Grand Rapids: Eerdmans, 2003), p.49.

Thiselton describes his principle of selection of histories 'of effects' of texts, and refers it explicitly to 'the theoretical model proposed by H.R. Jauss': 'A dialectic between textual controls or constraints and interpretative creativity can most readily be sustained (as Jauss suggests) by comparing a stable core of continuity within tradition with more disruptive paradigms introduced by fresh hermeneutical questions'.[15]

Sometimes the examples are, he claims, explicitly distinguished as 'influence and effects' and not allowed to 'become dissipated into a mere history of interpretation'.[16] The distinctions are not hermeneutically clear. Sometimes, they are 'integrated into the exegesis as contributions from the patristic and other periods'.[17] Thiselton cites Luz's judgment that any account of the post-history of a text must inevitably be selective[18] and outlines three defining characteristics of the sample he has himself selected: examples that instantiate

i.   continuities and discontinuities of interpretation with specific traditions which influence interpretation;
ii. the influence and history of effects...which shape the 'pre-understand-ings' of subsequent generations of interpreters (i.e. predispose them to address a certain agenda, but do not determine their agenda); and...
iii. effects which have held particular influence in theology in the history of the daily life of the church, or more broadly in the history of ideas.[19]

The value-judgments to be exercised in the application of these principles must lead to contestable choices concerning the 'agenda' of interpreters, and influence in theology or society, and contestable defini-tion or valorization of 'specific traditions'. I shall pursue these with particular reference to David Parris's analysis and case study, and John Riches' volume for the Blackwell series. It is the first two of these principles which are developed by Parris, and the second and third which emerge from Riches' discussion and practice. (The third is also pursued in the arguments of §6.4 below, and later in §9.3.a)

Parris, like Thiselton, refers to Jauss. He is explicit about this agenda, to 'understand Gadamer as a prelude to Jauss',[20] and that 'more is needed

---

15. Thiselton, *First Corinthians*, p.xvii. Cf. the account of Jauss as the 'main founder' of reception history in A.C. Thiselton, *1 and 2 Thessalonians Through the Centuries* (Oxford: Blackwell, 2010), pp.1–3.

16. This is a distinction I cannot reconcile with Gadamerian hermeneutics (see §6.2.a below).

17. Thiselton, *First Corinthians*, p.196.

18. Thiselton, *First Corinthians*, p.196, citing Luz, *Matthew 1–7*, p.95.

19. Thiselton, *First Corinthians*, p.196, and citing Jauss, *Aesthetic of Reception*.

20. Parris, *Reception Theory*, p.2.

if we are going to…apply Gadamer's hermeneutics to biblical interpretation. We really need some form of methodological framework'.[21] The method Jauss develops includes inserting 'the individual work into its literary series to recognise its historical position and significance'.[22] To a degree, a formulation of such a methodology contrasts with Gadamer's avoidance of describing his hermeneutics as a scientific method.[23] It may also be redefining the concept of a 'canon', which for Gadamer is in a continuous process of redefinition: as Chris Lawn writes, 'Gadamer's canon, as a partner in dialogue, is constantly changing. Gadamer's canon is made up of texts, the voices of which draw the reader into conversation.'[24]

Jauss subsequently elaborated on the theses of his earlier work and described how subsequent receptions of a text in the course of history produce 'trajectories' of interpretation that legitimate 'possibilities of understanding, imitation, transformation, and continuation'.[25] These trajectories of interpretation may be seen as 'structures of exemplary character that condition the process of the formation of literary tradition'.[26] Jauss appropriated the idea of paradigm shifts from Kuhn's analysis of problem-solutions from changing historical periods of science evaluated by reference to different 'paradigms'.[27]

Parris develops the idea of paradigm shifts using Alasdair MacIntyre's work,[28] which he judges 'a more constructive and useful model for reception theory than Jauss's appropriation of Kuhn's work'.[29] These

21. Parris, *Reception Theory*, p.114. This perceived need for a 'methodological framework' seems to be about 'validity' and this is 'tradition-constituted' (*Reception Theory*, p.193). This is discussed in §9.3.b.

22. Jauss, *Aesthetic of Reception*, p.32.

23. Cf. Knight, '*Wirkungsgeschichte*', p.139: '*Truth and Method*…is more interested in contributing to an unruly and ongoing dialogue than it is in establishing a clear technique or fixed methodology… The practicality of Jauss's work helps explain his appeal for New Testament scholars wanting to incorporate the insights of the hermeneutic tradition into their own discipline.'

24. Chris Lawn, *Gadamer: A Guide for the Perplexed* (London: Continuum, 2006), p.128. (Implications of this are explored further in §9.3.)

25. Jauss, *Question and Answer*, pp.201–2 (cited in §1.1.c).

26. Jauss, *Question and Answer*, p.202.

27. Thomas Kuhn, *The Structure of Scientific Revolutions* (Chicago: University of Chicago Press, 1962).

28. Particularly Alasdair MacIntyre, 'Epistemological Crisis, Dramatic Narrative and the Philosophy of Science', in *Paradigms and Revolutions* (ed. Gary Gutting; Notre Dame: University Press, 1980), pp.54–74, and *Whose Justice, Which Rationality?* (Notre Dame: University Press, 1985), pp.356–63.

29. Parris, *Reception Theory*, p.188.

may be 'macro' (methodological paradigm) shifts: new solutions to an epistemological crisis, which answer questions the previous paradigm could not.[30] They may be 'micro' (or semiotic) shifts in the use and definition of concepts.[31] So Parris seeks to offer, and argues that reception history properly offers, 'defining moments of a tradition's contours'.[32]

How far one may properly describe the course and parameters of a tradition so as to be confident of measuring its contours is a point at issue. In Parris' theoretical discussion, the key illustration of 'epistemological crisis' concerns Reformation reception:

> The fact that an epistemological crisis can only be recognized in retrospect may explain why the Catholic tradition did not recognize the questions Luther did; they did not go through the same epistemological crisis and paradigm shift, and thus did not recognize it. But for the Protestants the questions that Luther raised are a defining moment in the formation of the Protestant tradition.[33]

This (rather unnuanced) description of a dichotomy is illustrative of the judgments to be made in using the concept of 'tradition', and of the validity of Rowland's critique, above. In his case study, Parris does not in fact uncover such shifts: for example, 'Luther's cursing of the allegorical method employed by the fathers...appears to give the impression that he was making a strong break from patristic and mediaeval exegetical practices. But in many respects he is quite hospitable to their allegorical interpretations.'[34] The Reformation reception in my own case study similarly suggests continuity rather than paradigm shift (see particularly §7.3.e). However, Riches's reception history of Galatians (discussed below) concerns a text that offers a specifically denominational contest in reception hinging on Luther's reading.

Jauss's analysis is framed in the history of literary studies, a field in which 'paradigms' of literary theory have been identified, not unchallenged but with some measure of scholarly consensus.[35] The same generalisations cannot be made in biblical studies: if there are paradigm shifts, they may be localised, partial, plural, and their application undeclared and debatable. Parris indeed concedes that in biblical studies

---

30. Parris, *Reception Theory*, p.190.
31. Parris, *Reception Theory*, p.198.
32. Parris, *Reception Theory*, p.217.
33. Parris, *Reception Theory*, p.191.
34. Parris, *Reception Theory*, p.257.
35. E.g. Terry Eagleton, *Literary Theory: An Introduction* (Oxford: Blackwell, 1983), p.74.

they are 'not...sharply defined'[36] and that a tradition of interpretation is 'a serpentine path, with twists, turns, and dead ends' rather than 'a steady march towards a higher, "truer" understanding of a text or the past'.[37] In his case study, however, he is able to use literary paradigms for the reception of Mt. 22.1-14, the parable of the wedding feast: parables 'are closer to Jauss's concern with literary or poetical forms of texts'.[38] Where his case studies *illustrate* this methodology, as they were designed to do,[39] my own case study of paraenetic texts, not having the same 'fictional or internally representative' nature, *tests* it (Chapters 7 and 8).

Reception in a particular literary history is a key factor in Riches's selection of reception of Galatians. In an introduction discussing his aims and method, he explains that (although the Blackwell Bible Commentary series is interested in how texts of the Bible exert influence in various cultural expressions) his volume in the series 'takes the form almost exclusively of a literary history...dominated by the commentary form'.[40] The nature of the letter and its reception influences this choice: particularly the role of Galatians in denominational contestation – both as 'the book that Luther prized above all others'[41] and its subsequent use to contest Luther's influential readings. Riches selects some of the 'principal commentators' on a biblical text, and he heads the reception with discussion of the historical setting of nine of these, 'to introduce to the reader the commentators...*whom I have chosen to emphasize*' (Marcion, Augustine, Chrysostom, Aquinas, Luther, Calvin, Perkins, Baur and Lightfoot).[42] The selection – and the preference for the commentary form of reception – is modelled to the agenda, which is to show the engagement in close dialogue with other readers in the 'tradition'.[43]

Riches states that in this presentation of reception he does not additionally offer his own interpretation of the texts or set out his own views; but acknowledges that 'portrayal of the literary history of a text...

---

36. Parris, *Reception Theory*, p.176. He makes a careful identification and application of particular 'paradigms', because in biblical studies the paradigm shifts must be spoken of in 'localized terms' (p.193).
36. Parris, *Reception Theory*, p.176.
37. Parris, *Reception Theory*, pp.19–20.
38. Parris, *Reception Theory*, p.222.
39. Parris, *Reception Theory*, pp.222–23.
40. Riches, *Galatians*, p.2.
41. Riches, *Galatians*, p.4.
42. Riches, *Galatians*, pp.63 and 11–58, respectively (emphasis mine).
43. Riches, *Galatians*, p.2.

is itself an account of the text'. He uses an analogy of the compiler as resembling the director of a play, whose role is not 'to provide the audience with an account of what the play means'. He recognises the shortcoming in the analogy: what he is presenting is not 'a single performance' but like a 'dialogue' of interpreters. This is 'quite clearly more than a purely descriptive task; it is an interpretative one'.[44] The qualification is important: selection and organization of reception does not allow for an avoidance of historical contingency and ideological interest.[45] He offers the reception that he has 'chosen to emphasize'. Judgments about what constitutes the body of principal commentators, or its significant impact, are contestable (see §6.3, below). For example, the very limited representation of reception by women authors is ascribed to their absence from the tradition he is sampling ('there are few female commentators').[46] A different assessment of important areas of the impact of the text, weighted less to a history of denominational doctrine and more to (for example) feminist hermeneutics and contemporary ecclesial issues, might see the impact of Gal. 3.28 as of greater signifi- cance than it is given here[47] (and indeed the feminist analysis of the 1980s as marking a 'paradigm shift' in its reception with a considerable influence and legacy). The reception of Galatians that Riches charts is unquestionably impactful, but it does not represent the only selection available that could claim this: such selection and organization is partly determined by the agenda of the compiler.

We see the same sort of choices, reflecting a theological tradition and a Jaussian literary series, operating in Morales Vásquez's selection of reception of Rom. 13.1-7 (Clement of Rome, Martyrdom of Polycarp, Chrysostom, Ambrosiaster, and Aquinas). The intention is to demon- strate 'how important it is for contemporary readers to interact with the instances of reception by past readers whose legacy is still influential'. The 'debt' to patristic and scholastic traditions reflects 'the need for systematic theological formulations'.[48] The roles of 'tradition' and reflex- ive criticism, the commentator's 'self-understanding', in Gadamerian hermeneutics are not examined by these practitioners (see Chapter 9).

44. Riches, *Galatians*, pp.64–65.
45. Cf. V. Henry T. Nguyen, Review of John Riches, *Galatians Through the Centuries*, *The Bible and Critical Theory* 6.1 (2010), 15.1–15.3 (15.2): 'Does Riches wield his influence on his presentation of the text's reception history through his choice of which themes merit his focus, and which…commentators warrant more attention than others?'
46. Riches, *Galatians*, p.2.
47. Riches, *Galatians*, pp.209–13.
48. Morales Vásquez, *Contours of a Biblical Reception Theory*, pp.233–34.

The selections of reception in a Jaussian series have a tendency to be offered as if self-explanatory.

Parris also espouses the idea of a *Gipfeldialog der Autoren*: the identification of 'paradigm shifts' in the interpretation of a text offer a 'summit conference' or 'summit dialogue'[49] of authors for defining moments of a tradition's contours. Parris offers four reasons for espousing this as a principle of selection.

First, the authors chosen represent 'the more significant interpreters because of the impact they have had on their contemporaries, the influence they exerted on later readers, or their innovative interpretation that was later recognized and accepted into the canon of exemplary commentators'. Second, the summit dialogue preserves the questions and answers that 'served as boundary markers...for what counted as valid readings of a text' in their various historical periods. Third, 'a disproportionate percentage of the best evidence that has been historically preserved for how a passage has been interpreted, taught and applied is located at the summit-dialogue level'. Fourth, it often preserves and reveals 'the major defining points in an interpretive tradition'.[50]

Parris's case study matches this in its consideration of patterns of reception of Mt. 22.1-14 in the patristic period and then the influence of Augustine's interpretation through the early mediaeval period and down to Luther and Calvin. He claims, 'The norm-forming power of texts helps to explain how the reception of biblical texts and previous interpretations of the Bible have shaped church history'.[51] The end point for Parris is not contested meaning, or disrupted process or subverted tradition but 'continuity': 'The summit-dialogue is a heuristic tool that allows us to identify the competing trajectories of interpretation and at the same time observe the history of mediation within that tradition that creates continuity'.[52]

Rowland describes this as the approach that is 'becoming typical in much biblical scholarship: tradition is largely determined by the major voices of the Christian theological tradition'.[53] It is programmatically characteristic of the *Evangelisch-Katholischer Kommentar*. The concept of a 'summit dialogue' may provide a clear principle of selection and

49. The English term 'summit dialogue' translates two terms that Jauss uses: *der Gipfeldialog der Autoren*, and *der Höhenkamm der Autoren*: Jauss, 'Der Leser als Instanz einen Neue Geschichte der Literatur', *Poetica* 7 (1975), pp.326–40.

50. Parris, *Reception Theory*, pp.217–19.

51. Parris, *Reception Theory*, p.301.

52. Parris, *Reception Theory*, p.221.

53. Rowland, Review of David Parris, *Reception Theory and Biblical Hermeneutics*.

judgment for these defining moments, but it may make 'tradition' into, in Rowland's words, 'a kind of academic theological equivalent of the *magisterium*'.[54] The selection and identification of 'defining moments' or 'exemplary commentators' involve categorical and value judgments about any one reader's tradition. This will be considered later (§9.3) in relation to Gadamer's analysis concerning the interrogation of a text both in continuity and discontinuity with a tradition, and the role of theological prejudgments.

6.2.a. Reception history and history of interpretation

> We must acknowledge a certain distinction between *Wirkungsgeschichte* and *Auslegungsgeschichte*, that is, the history of interpretation. In other words, the effective history of a text is not the same as the mere account of its treatment in the annals of interpretation.[55]

The distinction made here by Bockmuehl was also implied by Thiselton, but is not in fact apparent, as a distinction of method, in the practices discussed above (which predominantly chart the progressive process of biblical interpretation in Church history using exegetical commentaries). Though the distinction is commonly made, I would argue that *Auslegungsgeschichte* [history of interpretation or exegesis-history] should be seen as in fact one expression of *Wirkungsgeschichte* – one that valorises a particular range of sources within a particular tradition or traditions.

Luz focuses the distinction on the *types of source material* used, reflecting a convention that *Auslegungsgeschichte* usually or properly refers to the history of scholarship to be found in theological commentaries on the text. It is other parts of the 'legacy of the Church', hymns, prayers, art and confession, that can be called *Wirkungsgeschichte*.[56] Luz says that he is following his teacher Gerhard Ebeling, who defined Church history as 'the history of the exposition of scripture';[57] and the 'exposition of scripture', writes Luz, 'was for him what we call "reception history" today', including 'interpretations of the Bible in non-verbal media such as art, music, dancing, prayer' and also 'in political actions, wars, peace-making, suffering, institutions'.[58]

---

54. Rowland, Review of David Parris, *Reception Theory and Biblical Hermeneutics*.

55. Bockmuehl, 'Commentator's Approach', p.61.

56. Luz, *Matthew 1–7*, p.98, and *Matthew 8–20*, e.g. p.11 (cited in §1.1.c).

57. Gerhard Ebeling, *The Word of God and Tradition* (London: Collins, 1968), p.28.

58. Luz, 'Contribution of Reception History', p.123; cf. Elliott, 'Hermeneutics of Ulrich Luz', p.170.

The distinction is not fully resolved in Luz[59] or across the range of available practice.[60] Heikki Räisänen criticises Luz for insufficient precision in the distinction of *Auslegungsgeschichte* and *Wirkungsgeschichte*.[61] Bockmuehl then criticises Räisänen for overlooking Luz's acceptance of a relationship of 'concentric circles' between *Wirkungsgeschichte* and *Auslegungsgeschichte*,[62] and for Räisänen's own distinction between reception which is and is not 'effective': 'these categories themselves seem somewhat woolly'.[63]

Wirkungsgeschichte and *Auslegungsgeschichte* can indeed be presented without methodological distinction. Thiselton was able to incorporate into his exegetical commentary on 1 Corinthians (in 'an abbreviated form') much of the post-history he had assembled.[64] Riches presents reception of Galatians almost exclusively from written sources and almost wholly belonging to *Auslegungsgeschichte*, exegesis history in its relationship to Church history. In my own case study it would be hard to distinguish the nature of some of the material from a range of sources, from material in *commentaries* of the same periods.[65] What is at stake here is not in fact methodological. *Wirkungsgeschichte* describes the way in which we understand texts from the past, and forms of *Auslegungsgeschichte* conform to that description. These are traditions of reception of biblical texts which continue 'to influence modern debates upon the theological sense and purpose of church history'.[66] Exponents of *Wirkungsgeschichte* cannot (methodologically) contest the inclusion of exegesis, theology and traditions of interpretation in the Church. However, they can contest 'the idea that exegesis should be *confined* to written explication of texts or to the views of a few academic exegetes':[67]

59. '[I]n his commentary this distinction is by no means consistently carried through': Bockmuehl, 'Commentator's Approach', p.61.

60. E.g. Callaway's different attempt (judged unsuccessful in §2.2) to distinguish them not by source, nor the medium of language, but by exegetical 'approach' and theological interest.

61. H. Räisänen, *Challenge to Biblical Interpretation, Essays 1991–2001* (Leiden: Brill, 2001), p.271.

62. The history of influence and the history of interpretation are related to each other like two concentric circles so that 'history of influence' is inclusive of 'history of interpretation' (Luz, *Matthew 1–7*, p.95).

63. Bockmuehl, 'Commentator's Approach', p.62n.

64. Thiselton, *First Corinthians*, p.xvii.

65. For example, political propaganda: William Fleetwood's pamphlet itself provoked by a sermon (§7.4.b), and the *Kairos* document (§7.4.d).

66. Klauck *et al.*, 'The Project, Introduction', *EBR*.

67. Roberts and Rowland, 'Introduction', p.132 (emphasis mine).

> What becomes clear on reading *Truth and Method* is that [the list of sources offered by Luz]…is indicative rather than definitive: nothing is to be excluded from what we understand within the history of effect. Thus, in the case of New Testament studies, *Wirkungsgeschichte* is as concerned with political or economic appropriations of the Bible as it is with literary or musical re-imaginings, and everyday application of Scripture by the Christian laity is to be considered along the more focused insights of specialist scholars.[68]

Hermeneutically, what this problematises is the *ground of the value judgments* involved with identifying a tradition, valorizing 'influential' reception in a progressive process of interpretation, and choosing 'defining moments of a tradition's contours'. *Wirkungsgeschichte*, a number of theorists and practitioners contend, presents a *challenge* to tradition that is 'largely determined by the major voices of the Christian theological tradition'.[69] Bockmuehl, for example, acknowledges that 'it is certainly true that the Bible's practical effect on history and culture often becomes most clearly visible where it moves out of the hands of the scribes and scholars into the life of Church and society'. He adds, 'The scope of this field is thus potentially very far reaching',[70] and, indeed, there is a range of reception-historical approaches which reflects this interest and impact.

6.3. 'Acceptable limits of diversity'

In contrast to the selection of reception that seeks to construct a 'canon of exemplary commentators',[71] there is current discourse and practice that seeks to recover neglected interpretation of a text, and/or challenge conservative traditions. The impetus may be attributed to imperatives within *Wirkungsgeschichte*. It may also be characterised (as by Dunn, above) as an imperative from Christianity's engagement with the world beyond the Church. In Dunn's case, he sees this as a *challenge* to Gadamer, who, he thinks, 'effectively denies the possibility of the biblical message being heard outside the churches'.[72]

Contemporary practice that specifically advocates diversity in reception is easily found. It is harder to uncover advocacy of the practice that clearly demonstrates the *imperative* in Gadamer's hermeneutics

68. Knight, '*Wirkungsgeschichte*', pp.138–39.
69. Rowland, Review of David Parris, *Reception Theory and Biblical Hermeneutics*.
70. Bockmuehl, 'Commentator's Approach', p.62.
71. Parris, *Reception Theory*, p.217 (cited in §§6.1 and 6.2, above).
72. Dunn, 'Criteria for a Wise Reading', p.49 (cited in §6.2). Reception 'outside the churches' of my case-study texts is offered in Chapter 8, testing this claim.

to do so.[73] The imperatives of Wire, Watson, May and Meyer, and Sherwood, for example, like Dunn's, have different foundations.

Antoinette Wire derives her advocacy of listening to diverse reception from Paul himself: 'If we take on the role of the reader that Paul sets up and locate the Bible's authority not in given dogmas or individual authors but in the event where the persuasive word meets conviction, this event may occur where we do not expect... [V]oices from outside the canon may speak with authority.'[74]

Francis Watson looks for a mediation in biblical interpretation between 'the ecclesial and non-ecclesial spheres', on the grounds of the universal truth-claims of Christianity: 'the sphere of the church and its proclamation are not hermetically sealed against the rest of the world, and to confine the significance of...[canonical texts] within narrowly communal limits would betray the universality of their truth-claim'.[75]

Melanie May and Lauree Hersch Meyer make a challenge, from an approach in feminist hermeneutics, against associating 'authentic interpretation' only with particular communities of faith:

> If we attempt to establish the acceptable limits of diversity with reference to an already given deposit of faith, we serve a dominator tradition. Each of us will then seek to set the terms for unity in our own image and tend to identify the Tradition with our own tradition... A crucial choice is before us: whether we will continue to invest authority in...already established confessional traditions as if they were the Tradition, or whether we can recognize authority whenever and wherever the divine Word finds flesh.[76]

This is motivated by a liberative theological agenda for 'the birth of a new orality among all peoples whose voices have been silenced or stifled' and a commitment to 'God's liberating and life-giving presence among all people and in all creation'.[77]

Yvonne Sherwood makes a plea for 'expanding our definitions' in biblical studies:

73. But see the discussion on the reflexive character of *Wirkungsgeschichte* in §9.3.

74. Antoinette Clark Wire, *The Corinthian Women Prophets: A Reconstruction through Paul's Rhetoric* (Minneapolis: Fortress, 1990), p.11. I made a comparable argument in a work on Paul's exercise of 'dialectic authority' in 1 Corinthians: Robert Evans, *Judge for Yourselves: Reading 1 Corinthians* (London: Darton, Longman & Todd, 2003).

75. Francis Watson, *Text and Truth: Redefining Biblical Theology* (Edinburgh: T. & T. Clark, 1997), p.51.

76. Melanie May and Lauree Hersch Meyer, 'Unity of the Bible, Unity of the Church: Confessionalism, Ecumenism and Feminist Hermeneutics', in Schüssler Fiorenza (ed.), *Searching the Scriptures*, vol. 1, pp.140–53 (148).

77. May and Meyer, 'Unity of the Bible', p.149.

so that we can pay attention to all mutations of the biblical in Culture, including those that the Mainstream may well regard as monstrous or deviant. By circumscribing the discipline and protecting it, Biblical Studies may well be closing its eyes to one of the vibrant uses of the 'biblical' in Western culture: a use that, as a reflection of the paradoxical post-Christian times in which we live, animates biblical texts precisely by questioning their relevance.[78]

The instances of reception of the book of Jonah that she selects include a large proportion of what she terms 'backwaters and underbellies' – the traditions that use the text in ways subversive to a mainstream Christian tradition of reception. Her aim is to 'revivify' biblical studies as a component of cultural studies.

Thus there may be various foundation principles on the basis of which biblical interpreters may advocate diversity and the recovery of neglected reception. The rationale may not be rooted in Gadamer and Jauss, *any more than* a rationale for a 'canon of exemplary commentators' may be. These are not, perhaps, inevitable constructs from Gadamer's hermeneutics (though the 'canon' as a literary series has some support in Jauss's methodology). Rachel Nicholls, for example, embraces a principle of engaging with diversity in reception, but recognises that though this may correspond to a feature of Gadamer's writing, it is not in fact represented in it:

> It could be that the best way to explore the historicity, both of oneself and the text being interpreted, is to view it from a number of different historical vantage points, provided by a range of its interpreters who belong to different times and places. This is not a suggestion that Gadamer makes, but it is one practical response to his assertion that we are shaped by tradition… Perhaps we need to experience the disorientation of finding ourselves in a totally different place in relation to the text.[79]

This is comparable to the motive in Luz's work, that engagement with differing denominational interpretations 'refreshes' the meaning for the reader.

Some recent theorists and practitioners who do make a specific claim of an imperative for diversity *in Gadamer's hermeneutics* are Räisänen, Bockmuehl, Rowland and Roberts. Räisänen made a particular claim for newness of meaning as the defining feature of 'effective history': 'If it can be shown that a particular…interpretation had actually brought about a new idea or a new practice, and not just legitimated an existing one,

78. Sherwood, *Afterlives*, p.208.
79. Nicholls, *'Parkour'*, p.10.

that would belong to effective history'.[80] In this view, *pace* Thiselton, Parris *et al.*, a reception of a biblical text with the effect of repetition or backing up pre-existing views 'will not qualify'.[81] This is not what Gadamer says, though, crucially in his hermeneutics, every act of interpretation is a new application. In a changing world, the horizon of expectation of a reader is not stable and not singular. To elucidate the rejection of *a single, definitive interpretation*, Gadamer uses the analogy of music performance: 'we would regard the canonisation of a particular interpretation – e.g. in a recorded performance conducted by the composer, or the detailed notes on performance which come from the canonized first performance – as a failure to understand the actual task of interpretation'.[82]

The methods examined in section 1 above might be claiming such a 'canonisation of a particular interpretation' in their construct of a 'canon of exemplary commentators'. For Gadamer, each time the text is read is a new 'performance', and a different act of interpretation arrives at a different understanding of a text: 'It is enough to say that we understand in a different way, if we understand at all'.[83] The task of interpreting a text is repeated, and when it is, no 'performance' can be identical.

Bockmuehl agrees with Räisänen that *Wirkungsgeschichte* is not to be restricted to mere legitimation of the *status quo*: 'The effective history of the Bible cannot be reduced to its effect on the formation of the traditions of creedal orthodoxy. Nor must it be seen as merely a way to legitimize certain conservative interpretations.'[84] However, *pace* Räisänen, Bockmuehl holds that *Wirkungsgeschichte* concerns not just 'the generation of new ideas and practices' but also 'the legitimation and confirmation of existing ones'.[85] This is undoubtedly right, if Gadamer's own analysis is the touchstone. There is no distinction in Gadamer between repeated reception, new interpretation and something called an 'effect' – it is *understanding* that is the *Wirkung* [effect] of a text (see below).

Similarly, the series editors of the Blackwell Bible Commentary Series do not characterise *Wirkungsgeschichte* with Räisänen's restriction, but do express a 'determination to recover aspects of traditions of interpretation which are less prominent'.[86] Christopher Rowland and Jonathan

80. Räisänen, *Challenge*, p.270.
81. Räisänen, *Challenge*, p.271.
82. Gadamer, *Truth and Method*, p.118.
83. Gadamer, *Truth and Method*, p.296.
84. Bockmuehl, 'Commentator's Approach', p.61, citing Räisänen, above.
85. Bockmuehl, 'Commentator's Approach', p.62.
86. Rowland, 'Pragmatic Approach', p.5.

Roberts claim that *Wirkungsgeschichte* 'contests the idea that exegesis should be confined to...the views of a few academic exegetes... It... entails acknowledgment that...there is a rich tradition of biblical interpretation which lies unstudied and perhaps unread in libraries and archives.'[87] I consider further in a later chapter (§9.3.b) whether there are impulses, including theological imperatives, *external* to Gadamerian hermeneutics for this inclusion of neglected reception.

Roberts roots a critique of 'certitudes of the past' in Gadamer's hermeneutics, in an account of Gadamer's legacy in biblical interpretation. Although, he suggests, biblical interpreters who are 'disaffected by poststructuralism' may be attracted by Gadamer's attempt to rehabilitate tradition as something that may embody truth, in fact this is 'a double-edged sword', because 'the reclamation of tradition as a dialogue partner also demands the relinquishment of a foundationalist dream that the meaning of biblical...texts can be settled once and for all'.[88]

Even so, it is 'if one is sure of one's own tradition' that 'the reception enterprise works well'.[89] The case he then makes for the range and diversity of engagement in the *Oxford Handbook of Reception History of the Bible* is the historical contingency of interpreters, or editors of reception: this is in a multi-cultural, multi-disciplinary, multi-faith environment. (The journal *Relegere* expresses a comparable agenda, 'to promote and disseminate academic research on reception history, broadly understood, both within and across religious traditions'.)[90] This foregrounds the question: what are 'the parameters of "validity" to be' where the 'religious tradition' is 'completely open-ended'?[91] The impulse for the diversity here has a foundation in one response to 'the question of who owns the Bible'.[92]

I noted above that a question raised by volumes of reception such as *Galatians Through the Centuries* is the agenda of the editor: collating reception is 'quite clearly more than a purely descriptive task; it is an interpretative one'. Editors of reception offer the reception which they have 'chosen to emphasize'.[93] So Roberts problematises the enterprise:

87. Roberts and Rowland, 'Introduction', p.132.
88. Roberts, *Oxford Handbook*, p.3.
89. Roberts, *Oxford Handbook*, p.5.
90. James E. Harding, Eric Repphun and Will Sweetman, 'Focus and Scope', *Relegere: Studies in Religion and Reception* (http://www.relegere.org/index.php/relegere/about/editorialPolicies#focusAndScope, accessed 3 April 2012).
91. Roberts, 'Introduction', p.5.
92. Roberts, 'Introduction', p.6.
93. Riches, *Galatians*, pp.64–65 (cited above).

'What material do we decide to interest ourselves in?', '*whose* responses do [we] deem to be of importance?... [H]ow is the choice of material to be justified, and to what end is it being marshalled?'[94] Within the *Oxford Handbook*, the material collectively serves the principle that 'no individual, school, or group does or can own biblical reception';[95] though a common 'tradition' of 'scholarly post-Enlightenment readings of form and content' is identified as providing an initial 'panoramic view'. An element common with the Thiselton/Parris model appears in the selection of books that 'have been influential in the history of interpretation',[96] and it raises the same question as it does in their constructs: 'Influential to whom?'

Karlfried Froehlich warns that the 'tracing of random texts in their history of exposition yields at best interesting details and the impression of a bewildering zigzag course'.[97] Random to whom? If the pursuit of the less-studied reception of texts or the collation of a 'heteroglossic chorus of interpreters'[98] offer a *critique* of the reception of traditionary texts within a reader's tradition, to this extent these too are operations of *Wirkungsgeschichte*. Bewildering to whom? If texts do indeed have a complex, convoluted, multi-faceted legacy to the reader, whose tradition is partly formed by this legacy, this too is an operation of *Wirkungsgeschichte*. Readers are shaped by their historicity and tradition, and if this, for them, is a heteroglossic chorus, then they receive the text with that legacy. So Rowland writes:

> It is a crucial insight to acknowledge the extent to which we are formed socially, culturally, and psychologically, but that which is handed down, tradition, is extremely varied. Though many religious traditions make an attempt to form those who will lead it by a process of inculturation, most readers of biblical texts are not so formed and that which we receive is a much more complex amalgam that is peculiarly historically contingent.[99]

94. Roberts, 'Introduction', pp.5 and 1, respectively.

95. Roberts, 'Introduction', p.7.

96. Roberts, 'Introduction', p.6.

97. Karlfried Froehlich, 'Church History and the Bible', in *Biblical Hermeneutics in Historical Perspective* (ed. M.S. Burrows and P. Rorem; Grand Rapids: Eerdmans, 1991), p.10, also cited by Parris, *Reception Theory*, p.xiii.

98. David B. Gowler, 'Socio-Rhetorical Interpretation: Textures of a Text and its Reception', *JSNT* 33 (2010), pp.191–206 (203).

99. Rowland, Review of David Parris, *Reception Theory and Biblical Hermeneutics*. More discussion of the nature and role of 'tradition' in Chapter 9.

It remains true, as Roberts notes, that it is 'if one is sure of one's own tradition' that 'the reception enterprise works well' or appears to, to those engaged within it.[100] In a review of the huge project being undertaken by the *Encyclopedia of the Bible and Its Reception*, Roberts and Rowland see its plenitude as providing 'liberation from the boundary setting of any single tradition' for scholars of reception who adopt 'a methodologically and historically agnostic position'. They locate the impulse for this in the hermeneutics of reception history, which 'by its essence requires the relinquishment of the hermeneutic parameters established by a given tradition'. But, they ask, if those are relinquished, what parameters take their place? – 'we have all this material, but what should we do with it?'[101] Their answer points to 'new hermeneutical paradigms' not established by a given tradition, but Gadamer's emphasis on tradition and prejudgments in the negotiation of meaning may not be an obvious fit for 'agnostic' positions. (This is revisited in §9.3: how Gadamer's hermeneutics describes the possibility of understanding traditions in which the reader does not already participate.) This methodologically collective term, 'agnostic', might cover a range of ideological investments: for example, those discernible in individual chapters of the *Oxford Handbook*.[102] Elsewhere, Rowland comments, 'Commitment of one kind or another is likely to confront anyone who reads the Bible in the light of the needs of the world'.[103]

However, compilations of reception that define tradition (or 'canon', or 'commentator') differently from the 'canon of exemplary commentators', or that consciously seek out neglected or subversive interpretation of a text, offer a particular critique of the self-limiting summit-dialogue construct. They offer a considerable challenge to the value given to a set of readings which we have chosen because we limited our investigation to what was most supportive of our position – or, even, to what was most readily available. We may be 'sure of our own tradition', but Gadamer's

---

100. In Chapter 9, I shall pursue the ability of a tradition to critique itself.

101. Jonathan Roberts and Christopher Rowland, 'Review Essay: *Encyclopedia of the Bible and Its Reception*', *Relegere: Studies in Religion and Reception* 1.2 (2011) (http://www.relegere.org/index.php/relegere/article/viewFile/473/452, accessed 3 April 2012).

102. Two chapters with some resonances in the traditions of my own case study are Ann Loades, 'Elizabeth Cady Stanton's *The Woman's Bible*', and Brad Braxton, 'Preaching, Politics and Paul in Contemporary African American Christianity', in Lieb *et al.*, *Oxford Handbook*, pp.307–22 and 557–75.

103. Christopher Rowland, '"Open thy Mouth for the Dumb": A Task for the Exegete of Holy Scripture', *Biblical Interpretation* 1 (1993), pp.228–45 (244).

hermeneutics calls for awareness of the pre-judgments transmitted by that tradition, rather than interpretation that merely preserves one's own position.[104]

Parris defends a particular selective method partly on the grounds that 'a disproportionate percentage of the best evidence...for how a passage has been interpreted...is located at the summit-dialogue level'. To this unsubstantiated qualitative measure ('best evidence') he appends an important qualification: 'Given the overwhelming amount of material that has been preserved,... our primary consideration, in many instances, should be given to the most influential interpretations. This is especially true if we only have a limited amount of time to invest in this type of study'.[105] Alongside the further qualitative measure of 'most influential', there are two quantitative measures: the 'amount of material', the 'limited...time'. As a pragmatic imperative these priorities may have merit, but they represent a considerable qualification of 'the progressive process' of reception and do not represent a judgment drawn from Gadamer and Jauss. Such a construct of selection does not have a *hermeneutical* foundation.

The discussion of cultural artefacts as reception of biblical texts has become a particular feature of some contemporary practice[106] but there is little or no discussion rooting this in specifics of Gadamer or Jauss. Roberts and Rowland claim that *Wirkungsgeschichte* contests the idea that exegesis should be confined to written explication of texts, but rather it 'acknowledges literature, art, music and actualizations of the text as modes of exegesis just as important as the conventional explanatory writing of Judaism and Christian theology'.[107] This claim is repeatedly made, or the idea assumed, but I have never found it substantiated. The location in *Truth and Method* of the full substance of it could in fact be contested. Although Gadamer uses a number of analogies from art and music[108] to reflect on the universals of historical consciousness and

104. Gadamer, 'Philosophical Journey', p.17 (see §9.3).

105. Parris, *Reception Theory*, p.219.

106. E.g. the first Blackwell commentary includes an illustration by Blake of Babylon and the Beast of the Apocalypse: Kovacs and Rowland, *Revelation*, Plate 1; Sherwood's study includes the representation of Jonah in thirteenth-century windows in Cologne cathedral: *Jonah*, Figures 3a and b.

107. Roberts and Rowland, 'Introduction', p.132; Luz and Knight make comparable statements: Luz, '*Wirkungsgeschichtliche Hermeneutik*', p.18 (cited in §1.1.c); Knight, '*Wirkungsgeschichte*', pp.138–39 (cited in §6.2.a).

108. E.g. Gadamer, *Truth and Method*, pp.130–52.

human understanding,[109] the work concludes with a long section on *language* as the medium of the hermeneutic experience.[110] Gadamer's hermeneutics concern the ability to understand, and it is this 'endowment' of humanity that sustains 'communal life with others' and 'above all' it takes place 'by way of language and the partnership of conversation'.[111] The claims made here by Roberts and Rowland, and the comparable claims and practice, may nevertheless be valid inferences drawn from the *universality* of historical consciousness in human experience according to Gadamer's theory of understanding.[112]

We noted (in §1.1.c) a recurring lack of distinction of Gadamer's history-of-effect principle (understanding as an historically effected event) from 'history of effects' (plural),[113] and this may be compounded, in the recognition of events and artefacts as instantiations of texts, into a reification of the idea of 'effect'. In Gadamer, *Wirkung* ['effect' or 'impact'] refers principally to reflexive *understanding*: 'Understanding proves to be a kind of *effect* and knows itself as such... [H]istorically-effected consciousness is something other than inquiry into...the trace a work leaves behind. *Wirkung* is, rather, a *consciousness of the work* itself, and hence itself has an effect'.[114] That traditions of interpretation of texts may be *expressed in events and artefacts*, however, is not in dispute: in my own case study (§8.4.a) I discuss the 'scold's bridle' as a brutally physical instantiation of the exhortation to submission in 1 Tim. 2.11.

109. 'Play is perhaps second only to the concept of the fusion of horizons in *Truth and Method*. Gadamer uses this concept not only to overcome some of the conceptual weaknesses in other hermeneutical theories but also as an apologetic for the universality of hermeneutics and to keep the role of method in its proper place': Parris, *Reception Theory*, p.65.

110. Gadamer, *Truth and Method*, pp.385–484, esp. 453. 'Language is the *Vermittlung*, the communicative mediation which establishes common ground': Weinsheimer and Marshall, 'Translator's Preface', p.xvii.

111. Hans-Georg Gadamer, 'Text and Interpretation' (trans. D.J. Schmidt and R. Palmer), in *Dialogue and Deconstruction: The Gadamer–Derrida Encounter* (eds Michelle P. Michelfelder and Richard E. Palmer; Albany: State University of New York Press, 1989), pp.21–51 (21).

112. Gadamer, *Truth and Method*, p.333.

113. E.g. Thiselton, *First Corinthians*, p.196; Nicholls, *'Walking on the Water'*, p.21.

114. Gadamer, *Truth and Method*, p.336 (emphasis mine; cited in §1.1.c).

6.3.a. Selection and organization

> Anyone who has attempted any form of reception history will quickly
> come up against the enormity of the task and the need to create some kind
> of bound to what may seem to be a potentially limitless task.[115]

Where the progressive process of the reception of a biblical text is
constructed from a legacy in literary history principally in the form of
commentaries ('its treatment in the annals of interpretation'),[116] the
selection and organization of material may not be very problematic:

> the genre of the commentary is particularly well suited to a running
> account of the place and presence of biblical books within the history of
> our civilization, which could provide...tools for the construction of a
> hermeneutical bridge from the world of the text to the world of the
> Christian reader and his or her community.[117]

However, the challenge and justification of selection and organization is
very different if the approach of reception history is understood to reject
'narrowly communal limits', or a 'rigid classification of reception' or
service of 'a dominator tradition'; and is understood to challenge 'the
acceptable limits of diversity', recover 'aspects of traditions of interpretation which are less prominent' and even to animate biblical texts
'precisely by questioning their relevance'.[118]

The huge enterprise of *Encyclopedia of the Bible and Its Reception*
demonstrates that even the most ambitious and inclusive scheme – one
that seeks to 'summarize...and synthesize...the vast current knowledge
of biblical studies and allied disciplines while creating links, identifying
problematic areas and lacunae in scholarship'[119] – is defining its parameters in principle and practice. In practice, the intention to be, precisely,
encyclopaedic, means that very little space can be allocated to the
'minor' figures listed.[120] In principle, the aspiration is to '*completeness*

115. Rowland, Review of David Parris, *Reception Theory and Biblical Hermeneutics*. It is precisely 'limitless'; reception history is subject to the 'Shandean dilemma'
concerning historical recording, that the present becomes the past at a rate faster than
the past can be retrieved into the present: Laurence Sterne, *The Life and Opinions of
Tristram Shandy, Gentleman* [1759–67] (Harmondsworth: Penguin, 1967), esp. p.286.
116. Bockmuehl, 'Commentator's Approach', p.61 (cited in §6.2).
117. Bockmuehl, 'Commentator's Approach', p.88.
118. Watson, *Text and Truth*, p.51; Eric S. Christianson, *Ecclesiastes Through
the Centuries* (Oxford: Blackwell, 2007), p.262; May and Meyer, 'Unity of the
Bible', pp.148–49; Rowland, 'Pragmatic Approach', p.5; Sherwood, *Afterlives*,
p.208 (all cited in §6.3 above).
119. Klauck *et al.*, 'Project, Introduction', *EBR*.
120. Cf. Roberts and Rowland, 'Review Essay: *EBR*'.

only in…coverage of the scriptures themselves and their formation', and a *partial* account of their reception and influence 'in ways that pragmatically account for the *major* themes and issues'.[121] The decisions about what is 'major' are subject to the same questions that we have directed to 'exemplary, 'influential' and 'canon'. The separate, more 'complete', treatment of the 'scriptures themselves' apart from their 'reception' is very problematic for a reception-historical hermeneutic, which does not offer the possibility of 'access to the alien horizon of the past simply by leaving out one's own horizon of the present'.[122]

The *Encyclopedia* arranges its material with separately edited 'domains'. Two of these concern the contextual history of surrounding events, society, religion and culture in relation to the formation of the Hebrew Bible and New Testament. To match a reception-historical approach, this would need to be seen as contributing to reconstruction of *Wirkungsbedingungen* [effective conditions] for the first or early reception of a text, and identification of its *Alterität*,[123] in order to offer a comparison or differentiation with the contemporary horizon of expectation of other 'historically-conditioned' readers.

Jewish and Christian and 'cultural' reception are then edited separately: 'Two more domains cover the influence of the Bible in the Judaic and Christian traditions respectively, while the fifth domain encompasses biblical reception and influence in literature, art, music, and film, as well as in Islam and in other religions'.[124] This separation is also problematic.[125] Eric Christianson, as a contributor to the Blackwell series, reflects on the nature of the material and suggests that this

> should cause us to blur our often rigid classification of reception as 'in the church/synagogue' or 'in culture'… Of course the church and the synagogue have never existed in some cultural vacuum, and some of the most provocative readers are those who inhabit what we perceive as the realms of religion and of culture.[126]

121. Klauck *et al.*, 'Project, Introduction' (emphasis mine).
122. Jauss, 'Identity of the Poetic Text', p.8 (cited in §2.3).
123. Jauss, *Alterität und Modernität*, p.129, and *Theorie der Rezeption*, p.17 (cited in §1.1.b; and used to introduce my own attempts at this in Chapters 3, 4 and 5).
124. Klauck *et al.*, 'Project, Introduction'.
125. Callaway's methodological distinction, of cultural reception as part of *Wirkungsgeschichte* and reception with a 'theological interest' as *Auslegungsgeschichte*, was judged unsuccessful (cited in §2.2).
126. Christianson, *Ecclesiastes*, p.262.

Just as Callaway's methodological distinction, of (a) cultural reception as part of *Wirkungsgeschichte* and (b) reception with a 'theological interest' as *Auslegungsgeschichte*, was judged unsuccessful (§2.2), so the division in *EBR* of reception into Christian or Jewish 'tradition' and then 'cultural' expression is methodologically, categorically, flawed. The integration of ecclesial, theological, legal and literary frameworks in reception of Pauline ethics in my own case-study problematises this (see especially the evaluations in §§7.5 and 8.7).

The *Encyclopedia* is collating immensely useful material – and any understanding of an historical text is achieved through *wirkungs-geschichtliches Bewusstsein*. The structural aspects suggest, however, that it may be offering resources for *Wirkungsgeschichte* rather than modelling the full reflexive reprocess that Gadamer describes: under-standing as, essentially, a *wirkungsgeschichtliches* event.[127]

Judith Kovacs and Christopher Rowland, in the first volume of the Blackwell series, attempt to set parameters to the diversity with a *herme-neutical* framework, sampling 'different types of interpretation', in an effort to include representation of both 'the major figures' and 'the main types of interpretation'. The omission of much reception from the mod-ern period using historical criticism is referred to the availability of this in *other* publications, and because 'the main hermeneutical options were already well established...before the end of the eighteenth century'.[128]

In a discussion between participants from Blackwell Bible Commen-taries and the *Evangelisch-Katholischer Kommentar*, there is comment on the benefits of a 'catena' approach, which *might* be thought to organ-ize the diversity of interpretative possibilities, 'if somewhat woodenly': 'the quality of the "list" does enable the heterogeneity of the material to be apparent. One can see that there are merits in the "list" format in that it makes quick reference to masses of interesting and useful data very easy.' Subsequent discussion is revealing on the *principles of selection* that might still operate: 'There seemed to be some consensus that ethical and theological *criteria* should have a place in the process of selection, though little interest was expressed in ideological criticism of any kind (e.g. feminist, postcolonial etc.)'.[129] The compilers of these notes on the

127. Gadamer, *Truth and Method*, p.299, and *Wahrheit und Methode*, p.283. The *EBR* introduction's rendering of *Wirkungsgeschichte* (cited in §1.1.a) is 'study of effects' and not referred to Gadamer.

128. Kovacs and Rowland, *Revelation*, p.xiv.

129. John Sawyer and Christopher Rowland, 'Summary of the Discussion after Papers by John Sawyer and Christopher Rowland', *Evangelisch-Katholischer Kommentar* meeting, 2004 (http://www.bbibcomm.net/news/summary.doc, accessed 27 July 2010) (emphasis mine).

discussion were possibly using legitimate 'shorthand' for their in-house dissemination, but I am much less inclined to detach the ideological from the theological and ethical (see §§9.3 and §10.5). Indeed this would be hard to do with respect to the paraenetic texts in their relationship to the ideologies and ethics of household and state. It might even be considered an irresponsible act of interpretation, not reflecting authentically the Church's experience of the meaning and theology of these texts, to fail to respond to feminist and postcolonial reception of them.[130]

Whatever the principles of organization, 'histories of reception' are not, *simpliciter*, reception history. Indeed, they pose a question whether systematic enterprises 'do actually get us closer to a hermeneutical engagement with the text of the sort that Gadamer envisages'.[131] Roberts and Rowland pose this question about the *Evangelisch-Katholischer Kommentar*, the Blackwell Bible Commentaries and *Encyclopedia of the Bible and Its Reception*, in response to a critique of Luz by Mark Elliot.[132] Gadamer does indeed prioritise 'engagement with the text': 'I am not saying that historical enquiry should develop inquiry into the history of effect as a kind of enquiry separate from understanding the work itself'.[133] The reflexive enquiry he calls for, *integral* to 'understanding the work itself', is self-awareness in the operation of historical consciousness: 'that we should learn to understand ourselves better and recognise that in all understanding...the efficacy [*Wirklichkeit*] of history is at work'.[134] The subject of the final section in this chapter

130. For example, explicitly feminist reception is included here (§4.5.b, §5.3.b and samples from both 'first-wave' and 'second-wave' feminism in Chapter 8). Postcolonial reception of the submission of slaves (e.g. Tit. 2.9, ὑποτάσσεσθαι) forms part of the material researched for this project though omitted from the thematic selection made for this book.

131. Roberts and Rowland, 'Introduction', p.135 (cited in §2.3). Mark Knight also suggests (in the same publication) that 'the very idea of a series modelled on the "history of influence" conflicts with some of the comments Gadamer makes in *Truth and Method*' (Knight, '*Wirkungsgeschichte*', p.143). (This challenge was flagged up in §1.1.c.)

132. Elliott, 'Hermeneutics of Ulrich Luz', pp.161–73. Luz answers the question: Gadamer's idea would not have been 'the project of a Bible commentary oriented towards reception history, and surely not the idea of Bible commentaries that are twice as voluminous as normal commentaries'. He adds a footnote: 'This is what seemed to happen with the *EKK*!' ('Contribution of Reception History', pp.125 and 134n).

133. Gadamer, *Truth and Method*, p.299 (cited in §6.2.a, above).

134. Gadamer, *Truth and Method*, p.300.

concerns the role in this hermeneutics of the historical situation of the interpreter, their own 'horizon of the present'[135] which 'co-determines'[136] the meaning of a text.

6.4. The 'horizon of lived praxis'

[U]nderstanding always involves something like applying the text to be understood to the interpreter's present situation.[137]

The social function of literature manifests itself in its genuine possibility only where the literary experience of the reader enters into the horizon of expectation of his lived praxis...and...has an effect on his social behaviour.[138]

The third characteristic outlined by Thiselton, defining principles of selection of reception, was 'those effects which have held particular influence in theology[139] in the history of the daily life of the church'.[140] Thiselton's focus of 'daily life *of the church*' is an example of how *selection* is made from available reception. I am concerned here with the value given in biblical interpretation to contingent particularity, and to 'application' and 'lived praxis' (however this operates with parameters of 'Church' or 'culture').

Our attention in this chapter has been on reception as part a progressive process: as part of 'our relation to tradition' in Gadamer,[141] and in a series of literary instantiations in Jauss. The reader's own life horizon is also key to the process of understanding: to leave this out is to fail to recognise that 'subjective criteria, such as choice, perspective and evaluation, have been introduced into a supposedly objective reconstruction of the past'.[142] We have seen this in operation in the case study.[143] For Jauss, interpreting Gadamer, 'It is the task of historical understanding to take *both* horizons into account through conscious effort'. The 'horizon of our present' includes the 'horizon of the past'.[144]

135. Jauss, 'Identity of the Poetic Text', p.8 (cited in §2.3).
136. Gadamer, *Truth and Method*, p.296 (cited in §2.4).
137. Gadamer, *Truth and Method*, pp.306–7 (cited in §§1.1.b, and 2.2).
138. Jauss, *Aesthetic of Reception*, p.39.
139. Chapter 9 will pursue the place of *theological* judgments in traditions of reception history.
140. Thiselton, *First Corinthians*, p.196 (cited in §6.2).
141. Gadamer, *Truth and Method*, p.293 (cited in §1.1.a).
142. Jauss, 'Identity of the Poetic Text', p.8 (cited in §2.4).
143. For example, Jewel, Hobbes, Milton and Klausner read Rom. 13 with a mediation of horizons of the past and their various horizons of the present (see §5.1.c).
144. Jauss, 'Identity of the Poetic Text', p.8 (emphasis mine) and p.7.

Some interpreters see in Jauss's concept of a 'differentiation' of horizons (which maintains a tension between the text of the past and the present experience of the reader) a remedy to Gadamer's concept of the 'fusion of horizons'. Gadamer's *Horizontverschmelzung* has sometimes been criticised as a 'passive merging of two image fields into one field of vision'[145] and therefore not really responsive to the reader's 'own horizon of the present'. I argued (see §2.2) that for both Gadamer and Jauss, understanding occurs within the dialectic relation of the text and its historically conditioned readers.

The converse can also be argued – that Gadamer better upholds the 'power' of contingent particularity than Jauss. Parris makes the distinction that where Gadamer's concept of the horizon 'refers primarily to the historical world in which we live and is constituted by the prejudices we inherit from our tradition', Jauss's horizon of expectation draws on experiences in art-history and resembles a 'system of references' or a 'mind-set'.[146] Rowland sees this as the 'problem' with Parris's attempt to establish the position of Jauss within the field of biblical hermeneutics: 'the abstract delineation of aesthetic engagement risks undermining the very power of the contingent particularity of each and every aesthetic engagement that is such a feature of Gadamer's epistemological analysis'.[147] It is thus possible to draw two different emphases from Jauss.

Gadamer's work too is open to different perceptions and emphases concerning the historical contingency of the reader. Indeed, it is a particular feature of Gadamer's work that a number of claims can be made reflecting different emphases found in its argument and analogies. Tensions, reflecting the relative weight given to the horizon of the present and the horizon of the past, appear in revisions of the English version (by the same translators revisiting their own work). In the first example,[148] the revisions give greater weight to the continuing legacy of the historical origins of the text:

---

145. Parris, *Reception Theory*, p.152 (cited in §2.4); also e.g. Anthony C. Thiselton, *Hermeneutics of Doctrine* (Grand Rapids: Eerdmans, 2007), p.101.

146. Parris, *Reception Theory*, p.151; citing Holub, *Reception Theory*, p.59.

147. Rowland, 'Review of Parris'.

148. Gadamer, *Truth and Method* (2004), p.138, cf. *Truth and Method* (1979), p.127. The phrases in question are '*die Bedeutung sich aus der gelegenheit, in der sie gemeint wird, inhaltlich fortbestimmt*'; and '*die gekennzeichnete Okkasionalität im Ansprung des Werkes selbst gelegen ist*' (Gadamer, *Wahrheit und Methode*, p.137).

Occasionality means that *their meaning is partly determined by the occasion* for which they are intended... The important thing is that *this occasionality is part of what the work is saying* and not something forced on it by its interpreter (1979).

Occasionality means that *their meaning and content is determined by the occasion* for which they are intended... The important thing is that *this occasionality belongs to the work's own claim* and not something forced on it by its interpreter (2004).

In the second,[149] the revised translation increases the significance of the historical contingency of the interpreter:

Every age has to understand a transmitted text in its own way, for the text *is part of the whole of the tradition in which the age takes an objective interest* and in which it seeks to understand itself. The real meaning of a text, as it speaks to the interpreter, does not depend on the contingencies of the author and his original audience. It certainly is not identical with them, for *it is always partly determined also by the historical situation of the interpreter* (1979).

Every age has to understand a transmitted text in its own way, for the text *belongs to the whole tradition whose content interests the age* and in which it seeks to understand itself. The real meaning of a text, as it speaks to the interpreter, does not depend on the contingencies of the author and his original audience. It certainly is not identical with them, for *it is always co-determined also by the historical situation of the interpreter* (2004).

These translators comment on 'the fact that Gadamer's language resists hardening into a terminology, a technical language with stipulated, univocal meanings'.[150] Joel Weinsheimer further describes (as a feature of the 'necessary and irreducible complexity' of *Truth and Method*) Gadamer's impulse to 'break...down distinctions without obliterating differences', leaving 'unresolved tension'.[151] The revisions I have highlighted indicate specifically that the importance of both parts of the dialectic, the horizons of text and reader, can be more strongly or weakly asserted in some readings of Gadamer.

The variations in practice that claim a debt to Gadamer and Jauss support this evaluation. Compilation-histories of reception constructed as a 'canon of exemplary commentators'[152] give attention to 'continuities'

149. Gadamer, *Truth and Method* (2004), p.296, cf. *Truth and Method* (1979), p.263. The phrases in question are '*den er gehört in das Ganze der Überlieferung*'; and '*er ist immer auch durch die geschichtliche Situation des Interpreten mitbestimmt*' (Gadamer, *Wahrheit und Methode*, p.280).

150. Weinsheimer and Marshall, in *Truth and Method*, p.xii.

151. Weinsheimer, *Gadamer's Hermeneutics*, pp.x–xi.

152. Parris, *Reception Theory*, p.217 (cited in §6.2).

and 'discontinuities'[153] that 'condition the process of the formation of literary tradition'.[154] In doing so, there can be less attention, and less room for attention, to the way 'the historical situation of the interpreter' is the co-determinant of the understanding of the text.[155] Attention to recovering neglected aspects of the interpretation of a text or challenging conservative traditions is likely to valorise the 'power of the contingent particularity'[156] in reception and application.

6.5. Interim summary

I conclude that both of the emerging, contending patterns which chart the reception of a text through history can be defended as expressions of *Wirkungsgeschichte* and reception history as described by Gadamer and Jauss: both 'structures of exemplary character' (such as those examined in §6.2), and 'aspects of traditions of interpretation which are less prominent' (as with some of those discussed in §6.3). The value given to contingent particularity, 'application' and 'lived praxis' in relation to a 'progressive process' of reception varies; and this may reflect different emphases found in parts of Gadamer's work. It does not, however, represent a transparent or categorical methodological distinction between what is or is not a demonstration of *Wirkungsgeschichte* or reception history.

The selection and identification of 'defining moments of a tradition's contours' involve categorical and value judgments about any one reader's tradition and their value within or in relation to a 'canon of exemplary commentators'. The valorizing of culturally diverse or neglected reception – or the construction of a different 'canon' – likewise involves value judgments. Both strategies represent selective judgment, and prejudgment, which will need to be further considered (Chapter 9) in relation to Gadamer's analysis concerning prejudgment, the interpreter's place in a 'tradition' and the ability of a tradition to be self-critical.

Chapters 7 and 8 sample the case study in two different patterns of compilation-history, different structures of the progressive process of reception. These are modelled in a conscious relationship with different trends in practice described in this chapter, and serve to illustrate and test these arguments further.

153. Thiselton, *First Corinthians*, p.196.
154. Jauss, *Question and Answer*, p.202.
155. Gadamer, *Truth and Method* (2004), p.138 (cited above).
156. Rowland, Review of David Parris, *Reception Theory and Biblical Hermeneutics* (cited above).

Chapter 7

THE CASE STUDY:
CONTOURS OF A TRADITION IN THE CHURCH

7.1. Introduction

One strand of my argument in Chapter 6 was that the current discourse and practice valorizing trajectories of interpretative tradition, seen as significant, exemplary or normative within an ecclesial or theological tradition, represent one type of construct consonant with the hermeneutics of Gadamer. The operation of further systematic methods, from Jauss, of 'paradigm shifts' and a 'summit dialogue' of authors, represents particular *principles of selection* within a tradition. These may be constructed using pragmatic or ideological/theological values which may lie outside of the methodology[1] but, even so, they may demonstrate the *Wirkungsgeschichte* paradigm. Further, the emphasis on the 'defining moments of a tradition's contours'[2] raises a key question about the relative weight given on the one hand to a tradition of interpretation in a progressive process, and on the other to the contingent particularity of each engagement with a text.

In this chapter, therefore, a sample from the history of reception of some of my case-study texts is selected to illustrate and test these matters. The reception is of Rom. 13.1 and the paraenesis to be subject to governing authorities. As we have noted (§1.2.a), reception of this text may also reference, implicitly or explicitly, Tit. 3.1 and 1 Pet. 2.13 (and Rom. 13.5).

The sample will seek to mirror some of the principles of selection articulated by (for example) Luz, Thiselton, Parris and Riches, particularly in the preference for 'principal commentators',[3] and for 'continuities and discontinuities of interpretation with specific traditions that influence

---

1. They may, however, be part of an interpreter's tradition: the Gadamerian concept of a tradition's ability to critique itself has yet to be explored in relation to such judgments (see §9.3).
2. Parris, *Reception Theory*, p.217 (§6.2).
3. Riches, *Galatians*, p.11 (§6.2).

interpretation' and that 'shape the "pre-understandings" of subsequent generations of interpreters'.[4] Mirroring the preference for earlier commentators, and the pattern of Parris's case study in particular, I sample reception in the patristic period including Origen and Augustine (§7.2), and then the influence of this through mediaeval reception to Reformation authors including Luther and Calvin (§7.3).[5]

A further selection (§7.4) then tests the argument that the history of reception of biblical texts illustrates the 'norm-forming power of texts' shaping church history,[6] with some challenges to the tradition and inclusion of some neglected aspects. This sample selects particular ecclesial and political 'applications' of the paraenesis, reception reflecting historical *particularity* – the 'interest that arises out of the present situation'[7] – as well as their relationship with *trajectories* of interpretation. These raise questions about the relative weight given to these two factors.

Chapter 8 will offer a different 'progressive process': a selection giving greater weight to recovering neglected aspects of the interpretation of a text, challenging conservative traditions, and attempting a different construction of what constitutes 'principal commentators' in a tradition of reception.

7.2. Patristic reception

As we have discussed (§6.2.a), and in opposition to the views of some theorists, it is not by the distinctive nature of *sources* (biblical commentaries and similar reception in the history of scholarship) that an ecclesial and theological *Auslegungsgeschichte* is methodologically distinguished from *Wirkungsgeschichte* and reception history. In the patristic period, reception of the subjection paraenesis is indeed in doctrinal and practical commentaries, homilies, apologias, letters and similar writings. Reception of these texts outside of these parameters has not survived, and is not easily conceived. The sample adumbrates many of the issues espoused and debated in later periods, which reflects the role of these authors in the 'contours of a tradition', in the formation of orthodoxy and orthopraxy (and indeed in exegetical method: see, e.g., §§7.2.a and 7.3.a). These may be construed as initial stages or the earliest iterations in the progressive processes of reception. There is some support here for the trajectory of a normative tradition.

4. Thiselton, *First Corinthians*, p.196 (§6.2).
5. Cf. Parris, *Reception Theory*, pp.222–74.
6. Parris, *Reception Theory*, p.301 (§6.2).
7. Jauss, *Aesthetic of Reception*, p.65 (§6.4).

7.2.a. Clement of Rome

Clement and Ignatius stand at the head of two different themes in the tradition of reception addressed to two different contexts. Clement reflects the duty of Christians to governing authorities in the context of apologetic against rebellion (seen next in Origen, §7.2.c below). Ignatius begins the application of Rom. 13.1-7 to ecclesial authorities (seen next in this sample in Origen, and picked up much later by Joseph Stevenson, §7.4.c below).[8]

In the conclusion of the first letter of Clement of Rome to the church of Corinth, there is a long prayer for civil government: 'Grant that we may be obedient [ὑπηκόους γινομένους]...to our rulers and governors on earth... You, Master, gave them imperial power...so that we, recognizing it was you who gave them the glory and honour, might submit [ὑποτάσσεσθαι] to them, and in no way oppose your will.'[9]

Reception of Paul's injunctions may be specifically represented here: ὑποτάσσεσθαι is used in Rom. 13.5 and Tit. 3.1 (though 1 Clement may have been written before Titus). However, the broader context of the exemption to Jews[10] is also a factor that might give rise to such a text. This exhortation is the more remarkable for being written either during or immediately after the reign of Domitian.[11] In 1963, F.F. Bruce (for example) will see this as testimony to the reception of the Pauline paraenesis: 'Whether the prayer from which these petitions are taken was Clement's own composition or a prayer in general use in the Roman church, it shows how effectively that church took to heart Paul's injunctions about the duty of Christians to the powers that be'.[12]

This trend continues in the reception, for example in Origen (§7.2.c), and Pelagius' commentary on Rom. 13.1 (§5.2.a). There are many references in the early patristic literature to the requirement to pray for those

---

8. Clement also advocates submission to clergy but refers this to Christ's commissioning of the apostles rather than Rom. 13: Clement of Rome, 'First Letter to the Corinthians', 42, in *Early Christian Fathers* (ed. and trans. C.C. Richardson; LCC, 1; London: SCM, 1953), pp.62–63. (Hereafter bracketed page references to 'Corinthians' are to the *Early Christian Fathers* edition.)

9. Clement of Rome, 'First Letter to the Corinthians', 60.4-61 (p.72); Greek text from *The Apostolic Fathers* (ed. T.E. Page, E. Capps and W.H.D. Rouse; trans. Kirslopp Lake; LCL, 1; London: Heinemann, 1930), p.114.

10. Jews were required (as a concession) to offer sacrifices 'for Caesar and the Roman nation' in lieu of offering sacrifices to the emperor as a deity; see, e.g., Oskar Skarsaune, *In the Shadow of the Temple: Jewish Influences on Early Christianity* (Nottingham: InterVarsity, 2002), p.57.

11. Cf. some responses to the perceived historical situation of Rom. 13 in §5.2.c.

12. F.F. Bruce, *The Epistle of Paul to the Romans: An Introduction and Commentary* (Wheaton: Tyndale, 1963), p.235.

in authority. It is a common feature in the apologists (e.g. Justin Martyr, Athenagoras, Tertullian).[13] There are protestations of loyalty, or at least of innocence of rebellion, in a number of the accounts of early martyrdoms, where Christians insist on their (qualified) submission to the pagan governing authorities.[14] The second-century *Martyrdom of Polycarp* uses a phrase that may have reference to Rom. 13.1, with a qualificatory phrase. Polycarp defends himself to the Proconsul, saying, 'we have been taught to render honour, as is befitting, to rulers and authorities appointed by God so far as it does us no harm'.[15]

7.2.b. Ignatius of Antioch
In 1834 Joseph Stephenson (§7.4.c below) will cite Ignatius with approbation as evidence of the interpretation of Rom. 13.1-7 as referring to *ecclesiastical* relations and duties. Ignatius expounds a pattern of subordination which has a christological model but which is focused on the bishop. It is possible to see this, as Stephenson does, as reception of Romans 13. Ignatius exhorts the Christians of Ephesus: 'How much more do I count you blessed who are so united with him [your bishop] as the Church is with Jesus Christ, and as Jesus Christ is with the Father. Let us then be careful not to oppose the bishop, that we may be subject to God [ἵνα ὦμεν θεῷ ὑποτασσόμενοι].'[16]

The subjection to God reflects the eschatological pattern of 1 Cor. 15.28,[17] but the parallel of the relationship of the Church with Jesus could be an echo of the subordination paraenesis of Eph. 5.24. If the hermeneutical principle of scriptural unity is operating here (see §1.2.a), a number of different texts might have an influence (1 Cor. 16.16; Heb. 13.17; 1 Pet. 5.5-6).

---

13. Justin Martyr, *Apologia* 1.17, in *Apostolic Fathers* (ed. and trans. Alexander Roberts and James Donaldson; ANF, 1; Buffalo: Christian Literature Company, 1885), p.168; Athenagoras, *Legatio* 37, in *Fathers of the Second Century* (ed. and trans. Alexander Roberts and James Donaldson; ANF, 2; Grand Rapids, Michigan: Eerdmans, 1977) p.148; Tertullian, *Apologia* 30.39, in *Latin Christianity* (ed. and trans. Alexander Roberts and James Donaldson; ANF, 3; Buffalo: Christian Literature Company, 1885), pp.42 and 46.

14. Cf. Elliott, *Liberating Paul*, p.225.

15. 'Martyrdom of Polycarp' 10.2, in *Early Christian Fathers* (ed. and trans. C.C. Richardson; LCC, 1; London: SCM, 1953), p.153.

16. Ignatius, *Letter to the Ephesians* 5.3, in *The Apostolic Fathers* (ed. T.E. Page, E. Capps and W.H.D. Rouse; trans. Kirsopp Lake; LCL, 1; London: William Heinemann, 1930) pp.178–79. (Hereafter bracketed page references to works by Ignatius are to the *Apostolic Fathers* translation.)

17. Cf. §4.2. This would also be true for the alternative reading: ἵνα ὦμεν θεοῦ ὑποτασσόμενα, 'by our submission we may belong to God'.

Ignatius writes to the Christians of Tralles: 'For when you are subject [ὑποτάσσησθε] to the bishop as to Jesus Christ, you appear to me not to live according to humankind, but according to Jesus Christ who died for us'.[18] Exhortation to be subject to the bishop 'as to Jesus' is a new element. The parallel in the subordination paraenesis is Eph. 5.22, the injunction to wives to be subject to husbands 'as you are to the Lord'. It is a recurring feature of the reception (beyond the general principle of scriptural unity) that one Pauline paraenetic text using 'subjection' may have an impact on the interpretation and application of others (e.g. §4.6.a). An exhortation to the Christians of Magnesia, of submission to the bishop, contains an exhortation for mutual submission (cf. Eph. 5.21), and refers it to the christological subjection of 1 Cor. 15.28: 'Be subject to the bishop and to one another [ὑποτάγητε τῷ ἐπισκόπῳ καὶ ἀλλήλοις], even as Jesus Christ was subject to the Father, and the apostles were subject to Christ and to the Father, in order that there may be a union both of flesh and of spirit'.[19]

Ignatius makes no reference to the bishop of Rome but refers with some reverence to the Church of Rome.[20] Later reception of the paraenesis will also refer to papal authority (e.g. Hincmar, ninth-century Archbishop of Reims).[21]

In 1983 Schüssler Fiorenza will attribute to Ignatius a theologising of the *patriarchal* order: 'While 1 Clement justifies the patriarchal order with respect to nature and creation, Ignatius legitimises it theologically and christologically'.[22] The reception of Ignatius might therefore be characterised as a semiotic 'micro-shift'[23] in the reception. Schüssler Fiorenza sees the interpretative move made by Ignatius as formative for subsequent interpretation (and finds it illegitimate).

7.2.c. Origen

The appeal to a *normative* interpretative tradition comes as early as Origen (see §4.4.a). However, his reference to a 'generally received

18. Ignatius, *Letter to the Trallians* 2.1 (pp.212–23).

19. Ignatius, *Letter to the Magnesians* 13.4–5 (pp.208–9); and see §10.5 for the paraenesis interpreted by Christ's subjection in 1 Cor. 15.28.

20. Ignatius, *Letter to the Romans*, the greeting, in *Apostolic Fathers*, p.224. This almost certainly precedes exertion of episcopal supremacy or assent to the primacy of Rome. 'Paul and Ignatius do not know of any [monarchical episcopate]': Mark Edwards, 'The Development of Office in the Early Church', in *The Early Christian World* (ed. P. Esler; London: Routledge, 2000), pp.316–29 (319).

21. Hincmarus, *Epistola II*, p.33 (cited in §4.1).

22. Fiorenza, *In Memory*, p.294 (cited in §4.5.a).

23. Parris, *Reception Theory*, pp.198–202.

acceptation'[24] of Rom. 13.1-2 (such as the interpretation of Clement, §7.2.a) makes the single early instance, in this case study, of reception where a 'conscious appropriation and reassessment of a predecessor's work' (a judgment that plays a significant role in the construction of reception as a 'summit-conference') is explicit.

Celsus exhorts Christians to 'accept public office'. Origen counters with an account of the Church as 'another sort of country', with its own authorities and obligations to exercise authority:

> They keep themselves for a more divine and necessary service in the Church of God... Here it is both necessary and right for them to be leaders... Celsus exhorts us also to accept public office in our country if it is necessary to do this for the sake of the preservation of the laws and of piety. But we know of the existence in each city of another sort of country, created by the Logos of God. And we call upon those who are competent to take office...to rule over the churches.[25]

The introduction of this concept and its application to the reception is another candidate for a 'semiotic shift' in the reception history. Wilken suggests that the exchange between Celsus and the Christians is a debate about a new concept of 'religion':

> Celsus senses that Christians had severed the traditional bond between religion and a "nation" or people... [T]here was no term for *religion* in the sense we now use it to refer to the beliefs and practices of a particular group of people or of a voluntary association divorced from ethnic or national identity.[26]

The parallel explicitly extends the idea of 'the authorities that exist... instituted by God' (Rom. 13.1) to those instituted in the Church. It suggests that for Origen the 'generally received acceptation' might reflect the reception seen first in Ignatius. However, it also means that two quite different 'semiotic shifts' (theologising of the patriarchal order or a new concept of 'religion') might lead to the same features in the reception of a text.

One of the distinguishing features of the parallel structure of 'another sort of country' is a proper reluctance, in humility, of those called to lead: 'We do not accept those who love power'.[27] This emerges strongly later with Gregory I (§7.2.f below).

24. Origen, *Contra Celsum* 8.65 (p.502).
25. Origen, *Contra Celsum* 8.75 (p.510).
26. Robert Wilken, *The Christians as the Romans Saw Them* (New Haven: Yale University Press, 1984), p.124.
27. Origen, *Contra Celsum* 8.75 (p.510).

7.2.d. John Chrysostom

We saw how Chrysostom contributes to both hierarchical and anti-hierarchical application of the paraenesis (§4.4.a), and that his support of secular authority may be referred to his own historical situation (§5.2.a). He argued that Paul's assertion of God's appointment of rulers is not about each ruler individually, but about the institution of government, the 'power', not the person.[28] This subjection does not subvert spiritual authority. The authority of civil government is a mediation of God's providence. His reading paves the way for many later commentators, in a way that might earn him a place in a construct of 'summit dialogue'.

He is also among the first to figure in the debate over whether the subjection of Rom. 13.1 includes the subjection of clergy to civil authorities:

> And to show that these regulations are for all, even for priests, and monks and not for men of secular occupations only, he hath made this plain at the outset, by saying as follows: 'Let every soul be subject unto the higher powers', if thou be an Apostle even, or an Evangelist, or a Prophet, or anything whatsoever, inasmuch as this subjection is not subversive of religion.[29]

The Geneva Bible will later cite him on this inclusive interpretation, with its further assessment and application: 'Therefore the tyranny of the Pope over all kingdoms must down to the ground'.[30]

7.2.e. Augustine of Hippo

Like many churchmen of his era (354–430), with public affairs being administered by Christians, Augustine leaned to a social and political conservatism, and tended to explain away any apparently antinomian tendencies in the early Church. He seems not to have been attracted by projects of legal or administrative reform in either Church or state.[31] His commentary on Romans sets the tone of much of the exegesis and application of Romans 13 in Christian tradition – a reading with subsequent influence.

Augustine could claim, with reference to Romans 13 and 1 Peter 2, that a Christian's loyalty to the 'City of God' had never implied a political insubordination but rather obedience to civil powers. He warns Christians, in his exposition of Rom. 13.1, that though called to liberty they must not be exalted by pride, but should keep their place [*servandum*

---

28. Chrysostom, 'Homily on Romans 23', p.511.

29. Chrysostom, 'Homily on Romans 23', p.511.

30. Marshall Foster and Gary DeMar (eds.), *1599 Geneva Bible* (White Hall, WV: Tolle Lege Press, 2006): note to 'every soul' Rom. 13.1 (unpaginated).

31. Cf. Christopher Kirnan, *Augustine* (London: Routledge, 1989), p.218.

esse ordinem suum] and be subordinate to those higher authorities who, for the time being, may govern temporal things. The appropriate action is the payment of taxes and tribute, and the appropriate attitude is respect.[32] He makes the distinction, that many have made since (e.g. Aquinas, see §7.3.a), between temporal and spiritual authority, 'for we are both soul and body', and therefore,

> it behoves us in our temporal, physical aspect to be subject to [*subditos esse*]…the people who administer human affairs in some office… But concerning our spiritual selves…we should not submit [*non…esse subditos*] to any one desiring to destroy that very thing in us through which God deigned to give us eternal life.[33]

It follows that if insubordination is error, a greater error is for a Christian to be so submissive to someone administering temporal affairs as to hold that this officer is authoritative even over the Christian's faith.[34] The obedience rendered is to God, rather than to the office holders.[35]

He draws the analogy, again often made in subsequent reception, between this civic obedience to government and the domestic obedience of servants to their masters, noting that Paul 'in another place' (Eph. 6.6) urges the latter also.[36] Institutions of government and of slavery are corollaries of a fallen world in which the harmonious order of natural relationships is distorted.[37] These structures of obedience are a remedy of sin and do not correspond to the order of creation in which God made humankind – to be servant neither to sin nor to human beings. However, slaves can, by serving with loyalty and love rather than with fear, 'make their servitude a form of freedom'.[38] This is in line with the separability of temporal and spiritual noted above, 'for we are both soul and body', but might sit uncomfortably with the Pauline eschatological injunction (from the key christological subjection passage in 1 Cor. 15.24 and 28) that is brought to bear on it: 'till injustice pass away and every human principality and power be brought to nothing [*euacuetur omnis principatus et potestas humana*], so that God shall be all in all [*sit Deus*

32. Augustine, *Propositions* 72.1 and 72.4 (pp.41–42).
33. Augustine, *Propositions* 72.2 and 72.3 (p.41).
34. Augustine, *Propositions* 72.5 (p.42).
35. Augustine, *Propositions* 72.6 (p.42).
36. Augustine, *Propositions* 74.3 (p.42).
37. Cf. R.A. Markus, *Saeculum: History and Society in the Theology of St. Augustine* (Cambridge: Cambridge University Press, 1970), p.93.
38. Augustine, *City of God* 19.15, in *Saint Augustine's City of God and Christian Doctrine* (ed. Philip Schaff; trans. Oxford revd; NPNF, 1.2; Grand Rapids: Eerdmans, 1956), p.411. (Hereafter bracketed page references to *City of God* refer to Schaff's edition.)

omnia in omnibus]'.[39] Servitude here is to be valued, but it is also an 'injustice' [*iniquitas*] incompatible with Christ's rule, something not yet subjected to him (1 Cor. 15.24-28).

Augustine suggests that that the key is to distinguish between temporal and spiritual authority, while Pelagius suggests an alternative reading, '"Higher authorities" can mean ecclesiastical authorities'.[40] I have noted that this is a feature of some later reception (e.g. Stephenson, §7.4.c below, who cites Ignatius, §7.2.b above). These two 'semiotic trajectories' do not, as they do in Parris's examples, replace one another in a chronological sequence of shifts, but rather seem more responsive to historical contingency.

7.2.f. Gregory I

Gregory I gives an account of government, both civil and ecclesial, and applies it to abbots and bishops as well as kings and emperors: he was involved with the defence of the Empire and its relations with Germanic kingdoms, and had episcopal oversight within and beyond the Empire. He may have been the first to refer to popes with the title *Servus servorum Dei*.[41] 'He bore a deep suspicion of those in power, whether they were secular rulers or clergy.'[42] Outside of the disciplinary role, the ruler's relations with others should all be within 'a communion of equality': 'we have not dominion over your faith...for we are your equals'.[43]

Reception of the paraenesis of subjection to governing authorities appears as pastoral application in his *Commentary on Job*. Here Gregory offers some different restrictions or qualifications in obeying governing authorities, an example of reciprocity in applying the exhortation, and an early example of the *subversions* that the paraenetic submission texts can inspire. He does not subvert the ruling itself: rulers rule by 'the arrangements of providence',[44] but he anticipates faults in the governors, and

39.   Augustine, *City of God* 19.15 (p.411); cf. 1 Cor. 15.24 and 28 in the Vulgate: 'cum evacuaverit omnem principatum et potestatem et virtutem...cum autem subiecta fuerint illi omnia tunc ipse Filius subiectus erit illi qui sibi subiecit omnia ut sit Deus omnia in omnibus'.

40.   Pelagius, *Romans*, p.137 (§5.2.a).

41.   'Vita Gregorii', in *Opera Omnia* (ed. J.P. Migne; *PCCSL*, 75; Paris, 1862), p.126.

42.   Carole E. Straw, *Gregory the Great: Perfection in Imperfection* (Berkeley: University of California Press, 1988), p.24.

43.   Gregory I, *Pastoral Rule* 2.6 (ed. P. Schaff; trans. Oxford revd; NPNF, 2.12; Grand Rapids: Eerdmans, 1976), p.606.

44.   Gregory I, *Commentary on Job*, also known as *Magna Moralia* 25.16.38; trans. O'Donovan and Lockwood Lockwood from *Corpus Christianorum, Series Latina* 143; in *From Irenaeus to Grotius: A Sourcebook in Christian Political*

criticism from the governed. The governed are exhorted to a submission that is characterised by forbearance: 'Provided that it is in good faith...it is a mark of virtue to put up with superiors' faults'.[45] There is recognition of reciprocity in the relationship (cf. §4.6.a), and an exhortation matching Chrysostom's analysis (§7.2.d above) that the submission is directed to the office not the person:

> These wrongs take on specific forms: there are those commonly committed by subjects against their rulers, and those committed by rulers against their subjects... But even when the conduct of rulers may be justly criticised, it is the duty of subjects to respect them, though they may not admire them. In criticising his masters' deeds, the subject's attitude should show no lack of respect for the master's position. Good subjects while offended at their superiors' misdeeds, conceal them from others.[46]

Gregory follows this with a striking insight for the governed: God appoints people to rule in material matters who are temperamentally fitted for the administrative drudgery involved. Those who govern are insensitive folk, burdened by God with material responsibilities so as to liberate the more sensitive and spiritual for better things. In this reading, submission to such authorities is a provision of grace, with tangible advantages for the one who submits:

> But some who have made a small beginning in the spiritual life, seeing their rulers engaged with worldly business and material projects, quickly become discontented with the arrangements of providence, and think it pointless to expect senior officials to rule well, since their life is a model of trivial involvement... Since the exercise of governing authority requires attention to worldly responsibilities, Almighty God, in a marvellously caring provision to liberate sensitive and spiritual minds from material cares, often imposes the burden on insensitive and preoccupied hearts. So the one group is better protected from this world, while the others exert themselves enthusiastically over material supplies. To discharge this burden, assumed for their subjects' welfare and not only their own, is a mundane drudgery, hard going indeed![47]

This is a reception that has had little explicit influence on subsequent tradition. It does not readily form part of a 'summit dialogue' of authors, though it shares the rejection of the love of power in those who lead that we saw with Origen (§7.2.c above). It does not present a shift, paradigm

Thought (ed. Oliver O'Donovan and J. Lockwood O'Donovan; Grand Rapids: Eerdmans, 1999), p.203. (Hereafter bracketed page references to *Magna Moralia* refer to O'Donovan and Lockwood's edition.)

45. Gregory I, *Magna Moralia* 25.16.36 (p.201).
46. Gregory I, *Magna Moralia* 25.16.37 (pp.202–3).
47. Gregory I, *Magna Moralia* 25.16.38 (p.203).

or semiotic, in reception. Nor is it 'disruptive' to a stable core of continuity.[48] However, it stands early among the subversions of a coercive application of the text which, variously, offer solutions or limitations to what may otherwise be held to be a problematic injunction. It bears the hall-mark of lived praxis: the characterisation of those who 'exert themselves enthusiastically over material supplies' is surely drawn from life. A key factor, in terms of reception theory and my case study, might be Gregory's *theological prejudgment* in favour of humility and in opposition to structures of power – a focus of analysis in Chapter 9.

7.3. Scholastic and Reformation reception

The model of civil government in relation to the Church undergoes major change in the eighth century, with the 'watershed' decision of the papacy to support the Franks against the Byzantines, and Charlemagne crowned emperor of the Roman Empire in the West by Leo III in 800. It was 'the beginning of a long, tortuous and stormy relationship with the dominant power in Western Europe' with papal dependence on a powerful secular ruler.[49]

In the thirteenth century, Aquinas (§7.3.a below) married Augustinian theology with an Aristotelian world-order of natural hierarchies.[50] Matters of social order, economic and domestic, were broadly in the realm of natural law. Although this is a major conceptual construct, it represents a (semiotic) *continuity* of the conservative world-view operating in the earlier period. Troeltsch's summary is sweeping but apposite: 'To the Early Church social reform was too difficult; to the Mediaeval Church it seemed superfluous.'[51]

In terms of historical situation, the reception sample engages with tensions between papal, ecclesial and civil authority. Though the Protestant Reformation opposed papal claims and established new ecclesial structures, it did not at first bring radical changes in Christian attitudes to governing authorities except in some radical sects and movements.[52]

48. Thiselton, *First Corinthians*, p.xvii.
49. Hill, *Ministry and Authority*, p.45.
50. Aquinas, *Summa* 96, 4 Reply (in §5.2.a).
51. Troeltsch, *Social Teaching*, p.303.
52. E.g. the Anabaptists, and the Peasants' Revolt in Germany (1524–26), which represents one manifestation of the radical democratic claim, stimulated by the teaching of some of the Reformers, especially Thomas Münzer, whose demands included radical social as well as religious reform. Before the revolt was fully suppressed, its aims included the destruction of all religious and civic authority; see, e.g., Christopher Rowland, *Radical Christianity: A Reading of Recovery* (Cambridge: Polity, 1988), p.95.

A significance of this for my case study is that there is *not* the sort of epistemological crisis here that could be credited with a 'paradigm shift' in the reception history of Rom. 13.1. Mainstream Reformation Christianity 'retained (or rather established more strongly than before) the control of the church by civil authority'.[53] Calls for reform within the Catholic Church led to the Council of Trent, which was beset by struggles of authority between the papal bishops and the imperial (Spanish and French) bishops, and interrupted by the revolt of the princes against the Emperor Charles V.[54]

7.3.a. Thomas Aquinas

The influence of Thomas Aquinas in the issues of authority and politics is extensive. (See also his reception of the paraenesis to wives and the 'natural law' governing family life, §8.2). This influence extends to English legal theory in the fourteenth and fifteenth centuries, Protestant and Catholic resistance theories, and systems of international law and federalism in the sixteenth and seventeenth centuries.[55] Since Leo XIII (1878–1903), Thomist theology and ethics have official standing in the Catholic Church.

Politically, Aquinas combined hierarchical and democratic elements. On the one hand, law is 'the business of the whole people or their vice-regent';[56] and on the other hand, government by a monarch is best for the sake of unity and because it is patterned on God's monarchical government of all things.[57] On obedience and authority, he cites a particular feature of the subordination paraenesis of Rom. 13.1-7:

> obedience is connected with the obligation to such observance. But such obligation derives from the order of authority which carries with it the power to constrain, not only from the temporal, but also from the spiritual point of view, and in conscience [citing Rom. 13.5] and this because the order of authority derives from God.[58]

53. John Howard Yoder, *The Priestly Kingdom* (Notre Dame: University of Notre Dame Press, 1984), pp.106–7. This is true of radical movements too: Rowland notes that in the history of Anabaptism 'backlash' into civil authoritarianism is evident as much as 'the inability to manage routinization': *Radical Christianity*, p.154.

54. Cf. James H. Burns and Thomas M. Izbicki, *Conciliarism and Papalism* (Cambridge: Cambridge University Press, 1997), p.v.

55. Cf. O'Donovan and Lockwood O'Donovan, *Irenaeus to Grotius*, p.322.

56. Aquinas, *Summa* 1a2æ.90, 3 (vol. 28, p.13).

57. *De regimine principum* 2, in Thomas Aquinas, *On the Governance of Princes* (ed. and trans. G.B. Phelan; Toronto: St Michael's College, 1935), pp.38–39.

58. Aquinas, *Commentary on the Sentences of Peter Lombard*, Book 2.44.2 (trans. J.G. Dawson), in *Irenaeus to Grotius*, p.328.

On the relative authorities of Church and state he makes Augustine's distinction (§7.2.e above) between temporal and spiritual authority, 'for we are both soul and body'. The Pope leads the Church to a higher spiritual goal of humanity, but with conditions on his intervention in temporal affairs: 'The secular power is subject [*subditur*] to the spiritual power as body is subject to soul. And so judgement is not usurped when a spiritual authority enters into temporal matters on points where the secular authority is subordinate [*subditur*] to it or has left them to its jurisdiction.'[59]

The frameworks of authority and submission therefore reflect the submission paraenesis, but they are really an expression of Aristotelian order and natural law: 'Consequently there is a parallel between the natural necessity with which the lower in nature are subject to the higher by reason of the natural pattern established by God, and the necessity arising out of natural and divine law that in the course of human affairs subordinates are bound to be obedient to their superiors'.[60]

Aristotle provides the language in which the concepts are expressed, but it is not easy to frame this as a 'semiotic shift' in the reception. The association of a patriarchal order with nature and creation comes in the reception of the paraenesis as early as Clement (§7.2.a above). Aquinas' reading, though very influential, does not provide 'new answers', nor 'disrupt' a previous tradition of reception.

7.3.b. William of Ockham
The Aristotelian world-order similarly informs William of Ockham's reception. Ockham draws on all the Pauline subjection texts in his polemics on papal, civil and ecclesial government (with the household texts used in close analogies with civil structures). For example, in *A Short Discourse on Tyrannical Government over things divine and human, but especially over the Empire and those subject to the Empire, usurped by some who are called highest pontiffs* (of which the title provides an admirably succinct account of both scope and perspective), Ockham cites 1 Pet. 2.13-14, 18; Rom. 13.1, 5; 1 Tim. 6.1, 2; Eph. 6.5; Col. 3.22; Tit. 2.9; 3.1. He concludes: 'From these and many other texts we gather that since the pope cannot annul apostolic teaching he cannot take subjects away from kings and secular rulers.[61]

59. Aquinas, *Summa* 2a2æ.60, 6 (vol. 37, pp.84–85).
60. Aquinas, *Summa* 2a2æ.104, 1 (vol. 41, p.49). The *Secunda Secundae* of the *Summa* may represent scholastic reception of Aristotle's *Nichomachean Ethics* (cf. O'Donovan and Lockwood O'Donovan, *Irenaeus to Grotius*, p.321).
61. William of Ockham, *A Short Discourse on Tyrannical Government etc.* [c.1340] (ed. A.S. McGrade; trans. J. Kilcullen; Cambridge: Cambridge University Press, 1992), Book 2, Chapter 10, p.38.

He repeatedly uses Romans 13 to establish the 'true and ordained' power of secular authorities over temporal things – ordained, not merely permitted.[62] He uses 1 Pet. 2.13 (in the Vulgate translation: *subiecti estote omni humanae creaturae*) to argue that the pope has no more right over the Roman Empire than over any other kingdoms.[63]

In an incorporation of the *household* submission texts (see also §8.2), Ockham illustrates the holistic aspect of some interpretation of the submission paraenesis: it is what a Christian understands as submission that governs the reading of the texts and the view of civil, ecclesial and domestic institutions; and what is applied to one such text impacts on how the others are read (see §§4.6.a and 10.2). With Ockham, as with Aquinas, this owes more to Aristotle than to their perception of a distinctive Pauline pattern: 'Royal government is...like the natural rule by which the head of the household rules his offspring [and]..."constitutional" rule is like the rule by which the head of the household rules his wife'.[64] This use of cumulative or multiple texts can be a feature of the reception of the paraenesis,[65] and one associated feature is that the exhortations of the different texts, on *household* submissions and *civil* subjection, are drawn together. This gives the trajectory of interpretation of Rom. 13.1 an influence on patterns of reception of the household paraenesis (e.g. Shakespeare, Dickens and Gaskell, §§8.4.a, 8.5.a and 8.5.b).

This analogy of power and equality drawn from the household and applied to forms of governance (Ockham is writing here on 'the Power of the Pope and Clergy') closely follows distinctions made by Aristotle,[66] but Ockham makes no reference to Aquinas conforming to the same semiotic framework. The 'dialogue'[67] characteristic of the construct of the summit conference might be posited of Ockham and Aquinas in this feature of their reception but it is not, though they have such a thorough conceptual commonality, an explicit conversation.

62. Ockham, *Tyrannical Government*, Book 2, Chapter 3, p.79.
63. Ockham, *Tyrannical Government*, Book 4, Chapter 14, p.129.
64. William of Ockham, *A Letter to the Friars Minor* [1334], *and Other Writings* (ed. A.S. McGrade and J. Kilcullen; trans. J. Kilcullen; Cambridge: Cambridge University Press, 1995), p.147.
65. With the proviso (see §1.2.a) that it is a common early hermeneutical principle.
66. Cf. Aristotle, *Politics* 1.7 (pp.19–20).
67. Riches, *Galatians*, p.2 (cited in §6.2).

7.3.c. Martin Luther

Luther and Calvin interpret Pauline texts in relation to sixteenth-century challenges to ecclesial authority and in questions of liberty with respect to secular power. Luther accepted a sharp separation between civil and spiritual authorities, but with religion still the directing influence in the state.

His commentary on Rom. 13.1-7 follows one of the best defined 'contours' in this tradition of interpretation, in the distinction of temporal submission from spiritual; concerning which, as Augustine put it, 'we should not submit to any one desiring to destroy that very thing in us through which God deigned to give us eternal life'.[58] Though Luther 'can cite many passages of [Paul's] letters in which he upholds liberty and rejects servitude',[69] he places the discourse of subordination thoroughly in the framework of Paul's christology (1 Cor. 15.27-28; see ch. 4.1):

> Why does he say 'every soul' and not 'every [person]'?[70]... [T]he soul is in between the body and the spirit. He wants to point out, therefore, that a believer is exalted once for all above all things and yet is subject to all things. Just as Christ does, he bears two forms in himself, for he is a dual being. For according to the Spirit, he is lord of all things... By faith the believer makes all these things subject to himself in the sense that he does not let himself be affected by them in any way and does not put his trust in them but compels them to serve him towards his glory and salvation. To serve God means to rule in his manner.[71]

The use of Ps. 8.6 as applied to Christ is then drawn out more clearly: 'The spirit of believers...is not or cannot be subject to anyone, but it is raised up with Christ in God and it has all these things under its feet'.[72] The horizon of ecclesial authority in his own day explicitly colours the comment:

> Now, there is no better way to triumph over the world and to subject it to spiritual rule than to despise it. But nowadays this spiritual Kingdom is so little known that there prevails the almost unanimous opinion that the temporal things that have been given to the church are spiritual ones. And so the spiritual rulers regard only these as important and exercise their government in them, except that they still administer jurisdiction, fulminate

68. Augustine, *Propositions* 72.2 and 72.3, p.41 (cited in §7.2.e).

69. Luther, *Romans*, p.365.

70. Later commentators will refer the phrase 'every soul' to a Semitic idiom; see, e.g., Barrett, *Romans*, p.245.

71. Luther, *Romans*, pp.359–60.

72. Luther, *Romans*, p.360.

> their decrees, and hold the power of the keys, but with much less care and
> zeal than they expend on these 'spiritual', i.e., temporal, concerns of
> theirs.[73]

This submission of 'soul' to the 'higher powers' is related to the paraenesis of mutual submission, using not Eph. 5.21 but (the Vulgate translation of) 1 Pet. 2.13: 'The "soul"…must "be subject to every human
creature for God's sake"… By being thus subject it obeys God and wills
what he wills; thus it overcomes even now the temporal world.'[74]

The above is followed by a digression (in terms of exegesis) to
comment explicitly on the historical context of ecclesiastical rulers and
clerics claiming legal immunities and privileges but 'truly serving neither
God nor [people]'. A bishop remains unpunished for corruption because
there is a tradition that the churches must not be profaned. Then Luther
makes explicit the differentiation of horizons: 'But enough of this. We
must go back to the apostle.'[75]

There is an echo of Gregory's view (§7.2.f above) of officials, whose
life 'is a model of trivial involvement…worldly responsibilities…
material cares':[76] 'A person loses his liberty if he engages with others in
temporal matters and business transactions… Thus people of this sort are
somehow one another's prisoners. Completely occupied with temporal
affairs, they cannot devote attention to God.'[77]

He then relates the theological ethics of freedom, service and mutual
submission to Paul's theology of love:

> There is still another kind of servitude and this he calls the best of all: 'By
> love serve one another' (Gal 5.13). It is this servitude he has in mind
> when he says that though he was free, he made himself the servant of all
> [= 1 Cor. 9.19]… This, then, is the good kind of spiritual servitude: all
> things serve them that have it and all things work together for good to
> them, but they themselves are the servants of none.[78]

Returning to Romans 13, he clarifies that this does not embody 'that
spiritual kind of servitude', and here the 'apostle does not raise the
question of liberty with respect to secular power'.[79]

73. Luther, *Romans*, pp.360–61.
74. Luther, *Romans*, p.362. Elsewhere and in his own translation of the Bible
(1545), he gives, '*Seid untertan aller menschlichen Ordnung*' (cited in §4.7).
75. Luther, *Romans*, pp.363–64.
76. Gregory I, *Magna Moralia* 25.16.38, p.203.
77. Luther, *Romans*, p.365.
78. Luther, *Romans*, p.366.
79. Luther, *Romans*, p.366.

He uses Rom. 13.1-7 in other places in discussion of temporal authority, and again there is an explicit link of this paraenesis to the mutual service of Christians (Eph. 5.21) and the common good.

> But you say: if Christians do not need the temporal sword or law, why does Paul say to all Christians in Romans 13.1: 'Let all souls be subject to the governing authority', and St Peter: 'Be subject to every human ordinance' (1 Pet 2.13)... Answer... Because the sword is most beneficial and necessary for the whole world in order to preserve peace, punish sin, and restrain the wicked, the Christian submits most willingly to the rule of the sword, pays his taxes, honours those in authority, serves, helps, and does all he can to assist the governing authority... Although he has no need of these things for himself...he concerns himself about what is serviceable and of benefit to others, as Paul teaches in Ephesians 5.21–6.9.[80]

Again this is applied to Luther's perspective on the ecclesial context: 'our fine gentlemen, the princes and bishops, will see what fools they are when they seek to coerce the people with their laws and commandments into believing this or that'.[81] And again there can be no submission in *spiritual* matters, where submission can only be to God:

> St Paul is speaking of governing authority. Now you have just heard that no one but God can have authority over souls. Hence, St Paul cannot possibly be speaking of any obedience except where there can be corresponding authority...he prescribes limits for both authority and obedience (Rom. 13.7).[82]

Luther's influence in theological traditions of biblical interpretation is far-reaching. In the 'contours' I later examine (§10.5) Käsemann effectively nominates Luther's *theologia crucis* as a 'macro' (methodological paradigm) shift in interpretative tradition: 'The Reformers were indisputably right when they appealed to Paul for their understanding of evangelical theology as a theology of the cross... Paul has to be understood in the light of the Reformation's insight.'[83]

7.3.d. Jean Calvin
Calvin set up a theocratic government in Geneva where the life of the city was closely supervised by clergy, in a thoroughgoing subjection of

---

80. Martin Luther, 'Temporal Authority: To What Extent it Should Be Obeyed', in *Luther's Works*, vol. 35 (ed. E.T. Bachmann; trans. J. Schindel; rev. W.I. Brandt; Philadelphia: Fortress, 1960), p.253.

81. Luther, 'Part 2: How Far Temporal Authority Extends', in *Luther's Works*, 35, p.261.

82. Luther, 'Part 2', p.265.

83. Ernst Käsemann, *Perspectives on Paul* (London: SCM, 1971), p.32.

the temporal to the spiritual. In respect of this, 'when his enemies styled him a "Pope" they exactly hit off a similarity to his many mediaeval precursors'.[84] There were, however, to be more radical shifts in later Calvinism. We have seen (§5.2.b above) that Calvin stands near the head of generations of interpreters who seek in historical circumstances of Paul's exhortation to the Christians in Rome a reason why he might have urged their submission to the governing authorities. Calvin's suggestion is that the Jewish Christians of Rome might share the sense of 'Jewish impatience' under a 'Gentile yoke'.[85]

He is insistent that the higher authorities are secular not spiritual, and like Luther applied the text to his ecclesial context: 'This whole disputation is of civil government; therefore, in vain go they about by this place to establish their abominable tyranny, which exercise authority over men's consciences'.[86] He has a high view of civil authority, which in the *Institutes of the Christian Religion* he describes as 'in the sight of God, not only sacred and lawful, but the most sacred, and by far the most honourable, of all stations in mortal life [citing Rom. 13.1]'.[87]

In his commentary on Romans 13 there is no reference to the paraenetic use of ὑποτασσέσθω (or *subdita sit*) for the mutual submission of Christians, but his commentary on Eph. 5.21 exhorts 'mutual servitude' as a result of the reign of 'love' (cf. Luther, §7.3.c above): 'God has so bound us to each other, that no [one] ought to avoid subjection. And where love reigns, there is a mutual servitude. I do not except even kings and governors, for they rule that they may serve.'[88] The ethic is universal – a trajectory that might be traced back to Jerome ('also these who appear to be greater may be subject to those lesser').[89] Calvin's explicit inclusion of 'kings and governors' responds to his historical horizon. He also applies the ethic of mutual service elsewhere, for example in *Writing of Pastoral Piety*, to 'masters' and 'servants', two of the addressees of the *Haustafeln*, and then by extension to 'rich' and 'poor.'[90]

---

84.   Walter James, *Christian in Politics* (Oxford: Oxford University Press, 1963), p.58.

85.   Calvin, *Romans*, p.364 (cited in §5.2.b).

86.   Calvin, *Romans*, p.368.

87.   Calvin, *Institutes of the Christian Religion*, Book 4, Chapter 20.4 (trans. Henry Beveridge) in *Irenaeus to Grotius*, p.671.

88.   John Calvin, *The Epistles of Paul the Apostle to the Galatians, Ephesians, Philippians and Colossians* (trans. T.H.L. Parker; Edinburgh: T. & T. Clark, 1965), p.204.

89.   Jerome, 'Ephesians', p.232 (cited in §4.6.a).

90.   John Calvin, *Writing of Pastoral Piety* (ed. and trans. Elsie Anne Mckee; New York: Paulist, 2001), p.260.

Again, as with Luther, subsequent theological traditions explicitly reference Calvin's readings, and may give them a normative or paradigm status.

7.3.e. Johannes Althusius and Francisco Suárez

In late-mediaeval scholastic contribution, Johannes Althusius (1557–1638) can be viewed as a transitional figure, a Calvinist, straddling late-mediaeval and early modern developments.[91] He has a theo-political conception of church-commonwealth, and seeks to suppress tensions between the ecclesiastical and civil orders. In *Politica Methodice Digesta* (1603) he argues that social order as well as political order is covenantal, and that relations in the family as well as the commonwealth are a balance of natural necessity and human will. However, subjection to superiors is fundamental to all order, social, domestic, civic:

> All government is held together by imperium and subjection... God made Adam master and monarch of his wife, and of all creatures born or descendant from her (Gen 1.26-27; 3.16). Therefore all power and government is said to be from God (Rom. 13.1)...[citing Cicero on natural law].[92] If the consensus and will of rulers and subjects is the same, how happy and blessed is their life! 'Be subject to one another in fear of the Lord' (Eph. 5.21).[93]

The patriarchal reading of Genesis gives the pattern for all forms of dominion, and Eph. 5.21 is read as exhorting only subjection in the pattern of patriarchal stratification. (The appeal to Genesis as defining natural hierarchy is common in reception of the paraenesis of women's submission, see, e.g., Tertullian and Aquinas, §8.2; Council of Trent, §8.4; and a counter argument by Astell, §8.4.d.)

Francisco Suárez (1548–1617), a Spanish Jesuit scholastic, similarly makes an argument that obedience to civic authority, to laws, is a combination of a voluntarist response to externally imposed commands with what is also (the Thomistic view) a rational judgment about good and evil.[94] His argument combines headship in marriage from 1 Cor. 11.3 with Romans 13:

> The general opinion appears to be that this power [to make human laws] is given immediately by God as author of nature... The argument for this one I have already made: given that men decide to come together in a

91. Cf. O'Donovan and Lockwood O'Donovan, *Irenaeus to Grotius*, p.757.
92. Cicero, *De Legibus* 3.1.3.
93. Johannes Althusius, *Politica Methodice Digesta* [1603], Chapter 1.11 (trans. F.S. Carney), in *Irenaeus to Grotius*, p.761.
94. Cf. O'Donovan and Lockwood O'Donovan, *Irenaeus to Grotius*, pp.725–26.

single state, it is not in their power to prevent their being such a jurisdiction; which is an indication that it does not flow directly from their decision as its efficient cause. It is like marriage: the husband is the head of the wife, we suppose, by grant of the author of nature himself, not by the wife's decision. Their decision to marry may be free; but once they marry, they cannot prevent this order of precedence arising. In support of this view, we quote St Paul (Rom 13.1f)… In that case, this power is from God; and immediately from God, since there is not other more proximate or more immediate source.[95]

The association of one paraenesis with another, and the analogy of household with kingdom, recurs here (cf. Ockham, discussed in §7.3.b above). For Suárez, in both marriage and state, the 'order of precedence' and subordination are rationally non-negotiable: the voluntarism, in marriage at least, is in entering into that relationship. The analogy from marriage applied to Romans 13 gives the husband the 'proximate' role in marriage that God has without mediation ('immediately from God') in the second case. This is a theologising of the husband's authority that matches Eph. 5.22: 'Wives, [be subject] to your husbands as [you are] to the Lord.'

The Calvinist Althusius has a theo-political conception of church-commonwealth, and the Jesuit Suárez operates with a Thomistic view of rational judgment. However, for both, subjection to superiors is fundamental to all order. These two transitional figures, 'rethinking the mediaeval heritage in the light of contemporary positions'[96] give us a tacit continuity with a common 'tradition' of interpretation rather than an interpretative shift reflecting these conceptual differences. The 'corrective' insights from different denominational traditions pursued by Luz, and which Parris did not unearth as paradigm shifts in Reformation reception in his case study (see §6.2), are not apparent here.

7.4. Subsequent tradition and application

[T]he Bible's practical effect on history and culture often becomes most clearly visible where it moves out of the hands of the scribes and scholars into the life of Church and society. The scope of this field is thus potentially very far reaching.[97]

95. Francisco Suárez, *De legibus ac Deo legislatore*, Book 3, Chapter 3 (trans. O'Donovan), in *Irenaeus to Grotius*, p.734.

96. O'Donovan and Lockwood O'Donovan, *Irenaeus to Grotius*, p.757.

97. Bockmuehl, 'Commentator's Approach', p.62 (§6.2.a).

The contestation, from the Reformation onwards, over scriptural authority, papal and monarchical authorities, democracy, class and gender, and all forms of rights and authority, make the potential sample from these later centuries particularly eclectic. To this point my selection has attempted an adherence to the Thiselton/Parris principles of selecting what might be thought 'the most influential' reception in a construct of a 'summit dialogue', and a weighting to patristic, scholastic and reformation reception, and the commentary genre. The value judgments operating in such a construct, already evident, are still more apparent in the later periods. Whose tradition, what 'influence', does my compilation privilege? The samples chosen concern ecclesial and parliamentary authority before and after the English Civil War; the British constitution and the established Church in the nineteenth century; 'State theology' and apartheid in South Africa; and taxation and civil resistance in twentieth-century Mennonite tradition. They are selected as instances of applications that are both *distinctively historically contingent*, and that stand in a *self-conscious relationship to a history of reception*.

Aspects of the subsequent reception of Rom. 13.1 are also charted in other samples from the case study.[98] These did not suggest, perhaps surprisingly, that historical-critical method operates as a 'paradigm shift' in the reception of the paraenesis to governing authorities.[99] Rather, hermeneutical options of the later periods were already well established in the earlier ones.[100]

The samples of reception here are selected for application in specific contexts and with identifiable interests. Consequently (see §6.4), they contribute to a questioning of the constructs which claim to establish 'contours' by such hermeneutical shifts, or which valorise only 'influential' reception. These later instances can rarely claim significant influence shaping subsequent reception (but see the discussion in §7.4 on the impact of the Kairos document).

7.4.a. John Milton
In the seventeenth and eighteenth centuries there are competing claims of papal and royal absolutisms in European monarchies.[101] In England, questions of civil subordination and liberty are the subject of sermons and pamphlets in the context of kingship and the legal constitution. The

98. E.g. §§3.2, 4.4, and 5.2.
99. See too the observation in §7.4.
100. Cf. Kovacs and Rowland, *Revelation*, p.xiv (§6.3.a).
101. E.g. Klaus Schatz, *Papal Primacy: From its Origins to the Present* (trans. John Otto and Linda Maloney; Collegeville: Liturgical, 1996), p.189.

espousal by James I of the twin doctrines of the divine right of kings and non-resistance to authority, and the trial of Charles I and the abolition of the monarchy, were accompanied by vehement debate about the right of rule and liberties of the subject. The Civil War saw the overthrow and execution of a king and the creation of a Republic; then the 'Glorious Revolution' of 1688 saw the creation of modern constitutional monarchy. Both Royalists in the Civil War, and Tories and adherents of the 'High Church' at the Restoration, referred their position to theories of the divine right of the monarch. For many years after the Reformation, it was widely held that the Churches had a right to voice an opinion in political (and economic) concerns. By the eighteenth century this idea was less tenable in England, though the Law and the Church remain popularly linked.[102]

John Milton (1608–1674) published pamphlets against the *ecclesial* authority of the episcopacy, and in defence of the *civil* authority of those who had deposed King Charles. He held that the king or magistrate holds authority 'of the people', and the people can choose or reject him as seems to them best. He had a hatred of compulsion in religious matters.[103] In his first political publication, 'The Tenure of Kings and Magistrates' (published in 1649, within a fortnight of the King's execution), Milton uses the submission texts from Romans and 1 Peter in conjunction with one another and with the contrasting portrait of power from Revelation that often figures in interpretations of the civil submission texts.[104] Interpretations of historical events appealing to Revelation were commonplace in this period, and Milton's use was 'more temperate than most'.[105] He writes:

> Kingdom and Magistracy, whether supreme or subordinat, is without difference, call'd *a human ordinance*, 1 Pet. 2.12 &c. which we are there taught is the will of God wee shold alike submitt to, so farr as for the punishment of evildoers, and the encouragement of them that doe well. *Submitt*, saithe he,' *as free men* [1 Pet. 2.16]. But to any civil power unaccountable, unquestionable, and not to be resisted, no not in wickedness, and violent actions, how can we submit as free men? *There is no power but of God*, saith Paul, Rom. 13 as much to say, God put it into mans heart to find out that way at first for common peace and preservation, approving the exercise

102. Cf. David Forrester, *Young Doctor Pusey* (London: Mowbray, 1989), p.167.
103. Cf. Edgell Rickword, 'Milton: The Revolutionary Intellectual', in *The English Revolution* (ed. Christopher Hill; London: Lawrence & Wishart, 1985), p.120.
104. The case study does not focus on these because of the chosen constraint of the texts using ὑποτάσσειν and cognates, which do not appear in Revelation.
105. Patrides, *Milton*, p.26n.

therof; els it contradicts Peter who calls the same authority an Ordinance of man. It must be also understood of lawfull and just power, else we read of great power in the affaires and Kingdoms of the world permitted to the Devil [Rev. 13.2].[106]

This contains an interesting application of the multiple attestation noted in other reception: the paraenesis in 1 Peter constrains the reception of Romans 13. (Schüssler Fiorenza later challenges the 'reversal' of a trajectory of interpretation from an earlier text to a later one; see §5.3.b).

Milton's exposition of Romans 13 and 1 Peter 2 makes the distinction, recorded in Chrysostom (§7.2.d above), between the fact of individual rulers and the institution of government. Milton cites the interpretation of 'holy Chrysostom' whose exposition (it is in the Homily 23 on Genesis) 'on the same place dissents not':

> And it may bee well observed that both these Apostles, whenever they give this precept, express it in terms not concrete but abstract…, that is they mention the ordinance, the power, the authoritie before the persons that execute it; and what that power is, least we should be deceav'd, they describe exactly. So that if the power be not such, or the person execute not such power, neither the one nor the other is of God, but of the Devil, and by consequence to bee resisted.[107]

Milton uses Rom. 13.3-4 to argue that submission is not required to any powers that are not described by these verses (only to those that are not a terror to the good but to the evil). This is a repeated feature of the reception that seeks limits, variously, to the application of the paraenesis (e.g. Gregory, §7.2.f, and Fleetwood, §7.4.b). These tend to be grounded in theological and ideological prejudgments about coercive authority and voluntarism in subordination (see §10.5). I have not been able to characterise them as 'semiotic shifts'.

'The Tenure' also addresses a development in *ecclesiastical* authority since the abolition of episcopacy in 1646: the tendency, as Milton saw it, of the victorious Presbyterians to imitate the abuse of authority for which they had deposed the episcopacy. The individual conscience, for Puritan Milton, was under no-one else's authority, and yet the Presbyterians would 'sit closest & the heaviest of all Tyrants, upon the conscience, and fall notoriously in the same sins, wherof so lately and so loud they accus'd the Prelates'.[108] The profession of Presbyterian faith, later called the Westminster Confession (1646–48), set out by the Westminster Assembly, the synod appointed by the Long Parliament in 1643 to

---

106. John Milton, 'The Tenure of Kings', in Patrides, *Milton*, p.261.
107. Milton, 'Tenure', p.262.
108. Milton, 'Tenure', p.284.

reform the English Church, had given a higher role than this to civil authority: 'Infidelity, or difference in religion, doth not make void the magistrates' just and legal authority, nor free the people from their due obedience to them: from which ecclesiastical persons are not exempted, much less hath the Pope any power or jurisdiction over them'.[109] Later Protestant commentators cite this statement in relation to Rom. 13.1 (e.g. Murray, §4.4.a).

Religious freedom from civil authority in Milton's 'A Treatise of Civil Power in Ecclesiastical Causes' was discussed above (§5.2.c) with its appeal to authorial intention and the circumstances of first reception, deemed by Milton to have a strong measure of control on the subsequent application. If interpreters cannot 'prove' that Paul historically referred to governing authorities who justly intervened in ecclesial matters, the text cannot be used to endorse that power in magistrates.[110] The text does not licence what Paul did not 'mean'.[111]

In this reception of the New Testament paraenesis, the historical (political and ecclesial) contingencies are distinct and explicit in the co-determinacy of meaning discovered. The same historical contingencies do not lead deterministically to the same constructions of meaning: an evolving Puritan tradition brings a different ideology to bear than does its parent Presbyterian tradition. The role of ideological and theological 'foundations' in Gadamerian hermeneutics is the subject of §9.3.

There is an explicit intra-denominational dialogue. The Westminster Confession has the more 'influential' long-term role in subsequent tradition, and viewed from within such a tradition (the one, as it were, that 'won') Thiselton's language of a 'stable core of continuity' and 'a disruptive paradigm'[112] might be used to describe the contours of a history of interpretation. The principle that 'validity' in interpretation is 'tradition-constituted'[113] is explored in §9.3.b.

7.4.b. William Fleetwood

In debate about the right of rule and the liberties of the subject, the doctrine of passive obedience was particularly disputed in the legal fiction of succession 'by conquest' of King William and Queen Mary,

---

109. 'The Westminster Confession of Faith' [23.4], in *The Creeds of the Evangelical Protestant Churches* (ed. H.B. Smith and P. Schaff; London, 1887), pp.598–673.

110. Milton, 'Treatise', pp.305–6; see §5.2.c.

111. Cf. concern for this by Bultmann, Thiselton and others; see §9.2.a and §10.3.

112. Thiselton, *First Corinthians*, p.196 (cited in §6.2).

113. Parris, *Reception Theory*, p.193.

which secured the Protestant succession. Here, 'the very parsons and gentry who preached passive obedience to constituted authority in 1660, united to expel James II in 1688, when he made the mistake of taking these theories at face value and threatened to restore the old absolutist monarchy'.[114] In this context, William Fleetwood published a pamphlet[115] (1710) to refute a sermon from 'the High Church party', which he believed to be primarily about securing preferment for Tory adherents of the party. It is an apologia of Paul that drives his argument: 'that which gave me most trouble, in all our Bickerings, was, methought, that obstinate, vexatious citation of the 13th Chapter to the Romans, which was thrown at my Head upon all occasions'.[116]

Fleetwood's argument is constitutional: Paul tells every soul to be 'subject to the Higher Powers' but does not tell us who these are. What they are can only be a directive from the laws of the constitution. It follows that Romans 13 cannot be cited to accuse those who push the claims of the Commons against the King, and who protest against 'the Slavery of the Subject, and the Prince's Arbitrary Power'.

> The 13th Chap. to the Romans is…a much *quieter* Chapter than most People imagine. It *changed* no government: It *settled* none unalterably; It made no Freemen *Slaves*; It made no Slaves *Freemen*. It left every Nation to be governed by its own Law; and if they could *mend* those laws, they might. And if they should part with them for worse, it did not forbid them doing so… This innocent Chapter, to my mind, says nothing of [rebellion and resistance] – it leaves us to learn from the Laws and Constitution of each Government, what Obedience is required of the Subjects Hands: what it is to be a Rebel; and *what Resistance* is adjudged Rebellion… That the Law of the land must teach us.[117]

Fleetwood claims that it is right interpretation of scripture that concerns him more than the issues wrongly interpreted:

> I do not therefore intreat you, Not to be slaves yourselves; nor intreat you not to court Oppression, Tyranny, and Arbitrary Power; nor intreat you, not to abuse your Fellow Subjects for maintaining their Liberties and

114. Rickword, 'Milton', p.80.
115. William Fleetwood, 'The Thirteenth Chapter to the Romans, Vindicated from the Abusive Senses put upon it. Written by a Curate Of Salop; And Directed to the Clergy of that County, and to the Neighbouring Ones of North-Wales' (London: A. Baldwin, 1710), p.2. It seems not to have been republished: I accessed this in the archives of the University of Liverpool; however, a facsimile reproduction of the 1710 pamphlet has appeared in July 2010.
116. Fleetwood, 'Thirteenth Chapter', p.3.
117. Fleetwood, 'Thirteenth Chapter', pp.6–8.

Privileges which the Laws of the country have allowed them; I do not
now so much intreat in these Matters, as I intreat you, not to abuse *the
Word of God*; not to traduce S. *Paul*; not to speak evil of the *Christian
Doctrine*; as though these did not only barely favour, but encourage, and
commend, the Slavery of the Subject, and the Prince's Arbitrary Power, if
he should please to assume it. Let *the Scriptures* alone, and make not
them subservient to the base and villainous Designs of wicked Men that
would enthrall their Country.[118]

His espousal of parliamentary authority leads him to a position that
seems to weaken his 'vindication' of Paul. In denying that Paul has made
slaves of the 'Britons' to a sovereign, he gives the power to do this to the
'Lawful Powers' of Parliament. If they should do so, Paul's doctrine will
enforce it:

If they in whose Hands the *Legislative Power* is lodged, shall now or
hereafter, give up the Liberties and Privileges we now enjoy as *English-
men*, it will be time enough then to submit to our accursed Fortune. *That*
is a Power we know not how to disallow or disobey. *There* we shall...feel
the Weight of S. *Paul*'s Authority, pressing Submission to the Lawful
Powers, and calling for Obedience to the Rulers, that are set over us.
Resistance in that Case, shall be accounted damnable. Let *the Laws of our
Country* first bind our *Hands*, and then S. *Paul* will bind these Laws upon
our *Consciences*. But do not wrong that *Saint*, by saying that he hath
made us slaves, before *the Laws of our Country* have made us so. In this,
I intreat you to spare the *13th Chapt. to the Romans*.[119]

Fleetwood does not resolve the dilemmas of many readers of Romans
13 about corrupt rulers or bad laws: he seems reluctant to acknowledge
the reality or likelihood of circumstances 'where the Commands are
unreasonably Hard and Cruel, and so insupportable, that they cannot be
actually obeyed and complied withal': 'As to the Doctrines of *Passive
Obedience* and *Non-Resistance*, I seldom meddle with them, because
they always suppose some very hard Proceedings of the *Crown*, some
notorious Infringement of the *Liberties* of the People, or violent Invader
of their Right and Property'.[120]

---

118. Fleetwood, 'Thirteenth Chapter', p.9.
119. Fleetwood, 'Thirteenth Chapter', p.9.
120. Fleetwood, 'Thirteenth Chapter', p.14. The reference is to Jacobean and
Caroline bishops who held that Rom. 13 supported the doctrine of 'Passive
Obedience'; e.g. Bishop Berkeley, *Passive Obedience or the Christian Doctrine of
not Resisting the Supreme Power, Proved and Vindicated upon the Principles of the
Law of Nature, in a Discourse Delivered at the College Chapel* (Dublin: Francis
Dickson, 1712).

In later eighteenth-century contestations against the doctrine of non-resistance, Romans 13 – and 'notorious Infringement of...Liberties' – is used on both sides in the American Revolution. In a sermon in 1775, Jacob Duché (a supporter of the British, and defending the position of the 'Founding Fathers') qualifies submission in Romans 13 with other scriptural imperatives (and with 'reason' and 'humanity'):

> Whenever...rulers abuse their sacred trust by unrighteous attempts to injure, oppress, and enslave those very persons from whom alone, under God, their power is derived – does not humanity, does not reason, does not Scripture, call upon the man, the citizen, the Christian of such a community to 'stand fast in that liberty wherewith Christ...hath made them free!' [Gal. 5.1] The Apostle enjoins us to 'submit to every ordinance of man for the Lord's sake', but surely a submission to the unrighteous ordinances of unrighteous men, cannot be 'for the Lord's sake'.[121]

This is still a live debate: the texts and the arguments of the Founders are rehearsed in twenty-first century web-based polemic.[122]

A key influence on Fleetwood's reception must be contextual, his espousal of Parliamentary authority. However, his explicitness about what *not* to expect from the text prefigures an attitude taken in later biblical criticism. Fleetwood argues that the text leaves the reader 'to learn from the Laws and Constitution of each Government...*what Resistance* is adjudged Rebellion',[123] and he complains that other interpreters demand more from the text itself. This is a characteristic – perhaps a 'paradigm' – observable in later exegetical method: Käsemann in 1980 will argue that, in Romans 13 rightly understood, 'the basis of what [Paul] demands is reduced to a minimum, while exegesis usually seeks to take from it a maximum'.[124]

7.4.c. Joseph Stephenson

Secularism and the secular state advanced in the nineteenth century: the absolute monarchies, with an assertion of royal rights over national Churches, and rejection of a papal absolutism, did not survive much

---

121. Jacob Duché, *The Duty of Standing Fast in Our Spiritual and Temporal Liberties, A Sermon Preached in Christ Church, July 7, 1775. Before the First Battalion of the City and Liberties of Philadelphia* (Philadelphia: James Humphreys, 1775), pp.13–14.

122. E.g. the online postings on 'The American View Forum': http://www.theamericanview.com/2010/10/a-discourse-concerning-unlimited-submission-and-non-resistance-to-the-higher-powers/, accessed 13 August 2012).

123. Fleetwood, 'Thirteenth Chapter', pp.6–8 (cited above).

124. Käsemann, *Romans*, p.354 (cited in §5.2.d).

beyond the French revolution. However, like Fleetwood in 1710, though with a different exegesis, Joseph Stephenson in 1834 finds that Romans 13 endorses the legal constitution of a national Church. He published a pamphlet using Romans 13 in an argument in favour of the established Church and against Dissenters.[125] The spirit of loyal obedience, he says, is the essence of Christianity, and of its prevalence 'a more striking proof is not needed, than the very limitation which Christian loyalty alone has led all commentators, in all ages, without a single known exception, to put upon the passage referred to'.[126]

All modern commentators, according to Stephenson, have missed the reference of 'the higher powers' which is not to civil government but to 'spiritual governors' (in contrast with 1 Pet. 2.3 where the reference is to human creations). These are not cosmic forces but holders of office in the church. He finds the military etymology in ὑποτάσσειν as other commentators do, but includes a church hierarchy in this frame of reference: 'Being subordinated' is not strictly a civil, but either *a military or an ecclesiastical* duty.[127] It represents a claim to recover an earlier semiotic insight: 'There is ample evidence that the text was understood in the age in which it was written, as exclusively referring to ecclesiastical relations and duties'.[128] Unlike later commentators, the early Christians were, Stephenson asserts, aware of this, though he cites only Ignatius (*Epistle to the Magnesians* 13, and the *Epistle to the Trallians* 2, 7, 13; see §7.2.b).

Titus 3.1, he argues, exactly coincides with Romans 13 in this where 'Not a word is said of civil magistrates' – in contrast to the KJV which, as noted above (§4.4.a), renders the unpredicated πειθαρχεῖν as 'to obey magistrates'. Stephenson identifies the superordinates differently: 'To be subordinate to whom? To Titus himself…and to the presbyters and bishop ordained in every city by Titus.'[129]

125. Joseph Adam Stephenson, *The Sword Unsheathed: The Polity of the Church of England, the Polity Enforced by St. Paul, Romans XIII, 1–8* (London: Seeley, 1834). This seems not to have been republished and not to have been discussed in available secondary literature. I accessed this in the archives of the University of Liverpool. *Wirkungsgeschichte*, according to some theorists and practitioners, 'entails acknowledgment that…there is a rich tradition of biblical interpretation which lies unstudied and perhaps unread in libraries and archives': Roberts and Rowland, 'Introduction', p.132 (cited in §6.3).

126. Stephenson, *Sword Unsheathed*, p.9.

127. Stephenson, *Sword Unsheathed*, p.9.

128. Stephenson, *Sword Unsheathed*, p.19.

129. Stephenson, *Sword Unsheathed*, p.20n.

The historical setting thus constructed, Stephenson shows how he applies it within his context. The Dissenters withdraw their allegiance from the ecclesiastical kingly power (ordained by God). In doing so they think they can maintain their allegiance to the civil kingly power (ordained by humans). However, this civil power is 'not superseded, it is sustained, and sustained immeasurably' by the ecclesiastical power, and indeed the British Constitution makes no distinction between the one and the other.[130] Romans 13.1-7, properly interpreted, endorses the established position of the Church of England: 'It is evident that the polity in the text...is utterly at variance with modern Congregationalism..., modern Presbyterianism,... modern Popery [but] splendidly in union with the polity of that Church...of which the distinguishing character is constitutional liberty'.[131] Legally constituted authority derives its authority from spiritual, ecclesial, authority, and his conclusion is that disestablishment is logically indefensible on this basis: 'Omnipotent as parliament is, it cannot unchurchify itself'.[132]

This is a particularly *local* strand in the reception, though there is an explicit engagement with an 'alternative' trajectory of tradition, traced to Ignatius. It is difficult to see this in terms of 'a disruptive paradigm' introduced to a 'stable core of continuity' by 'fresh hermeneutical questions'.[133] Once again the key hermeneutical factors may be the lived praxis and the prejudgments of the reader.

Stephenson writes in a period when biblical interpretation is methodologically much contested. A key element is the flourishing and decline of 'liberal theology' with its roots in Schleiermacher (1768–1834), and associated with scholars such as Ritschl (1822–1889) and Harnack (1851–1930). In biblical interpretation, liberal theology espoused historical-critical method.[134] The questions it asks in terms of authorial intention and historical setting demonstrate considerable *continuity* with the reception of its predecessors – in method, if not in the particularities in Stevenson's reception of lexis and application.[135]

130. Stephenson, *Sword Unsheathed*, p.29.
131. Stephenson, *Sword Unsheathed*, p.22.
132. Stephenson, *Sword Unsheathed*, p.30.
133. Thiselton, *First Corinthians*, p.196 (cited in §6.2).
134. Baird notes the role of reception of Paul in this: 'It is ironic that the fatal blow to nineteenth-century liberalism was dealt by Harnack's most famous student, Karl Barth [1886–1968], in the name of Paul. This only reminds us that variety and conflict have been the pattern in the history of Pauline interpretation': Baird, 'Fate of Paul', p.274.
135. I noted above that modern historical-critical method seems not to operate as a radical 'paradigm shift' in reception of the paraenesis.

7.4.d. The Kairos Document
In the twentieth century, the scholarly location of much of the reception available, in a context of ready access to earlier and contemporary published materials, offers a more sustained awareness by the authors of agreement and variance in the interpretation of the primary texts.[136] There is a fairly consistent consciousness here of a 'history of interpretation' (explicit earlier, for example, in Origen's reference to a 'generally received acceptation', and in Milton's citation of Chrysostom).

In the decades from 1960 the challenges to authorities and to the very nature of authority lead up to and include post-modern perspectives of fragmentation and individualisation. A culture emerges in which 'it is not at all clear that submission is always healthier or more virtuous than self-determination nor that superiors in virtue of their office represent the will of God in all cases'.[137] Some political, cultural movements (O'Donovan refers to them collectively as 'late-modern liberalism') thoroughly espouse autonomy, rights, democracy and voluntarism. These may challenge the prerogatives of 'natural' (or coercive) structures like the family or a hereditary monarchy, in favour of 'voluntary' societies, constituted by agreement and seeking the consent of their members. They may also lead to espousal of economic choices of individual consumers in free-market capitalism.[138]

In this global environment, Latin American liberation theology first appeared around 1960, facing strong opposition from Church hierarchy, and gained prominence in the 1970s and 1980s. The criticism in the Catholic Church focused particularly on Gustavo Gutierrez' *Theology of Liberation* (1973) and on the use of Marxist analysis.[139] The *absence*, largely, of much use of Paul and the Pauline tradition in this movement is a significant gap in the history of reception: 'the epochal emergence of Latin American liberation theology, which occasioned a dramatic

---

136. E.g. Kallas' objection to Klausner, or Elliot's to Dunn (§§5.2.c and 5.2.d).

137. Sandra M. Schneiders, 'Obedience', in *The Oxford Companion to Christian Thought: Intellectual, Spiritual and Moral Horizons of Christianity* (ed. Adrian Hastings, Alistair Mason and Hugh Pyper; Oxford: Oxford University Press, 2000), p.493.

138. O'Donovan, *Desire of Nations*, p.276.

139. For example, John Paul II in his first social encyclical, criticises Latin American liberation theologians for using a conflict model of social analysis and especially for references to 'class struggle': *Laborem exercens* (1981) 3.11, in *Catholic Social Thought: The Documentary Heritage* (ed. David J. O'Brien and Thomas A. Shannon; Maryknoll: Orbis, 2001), p.366.

political reinterpretation of Jesus, has not ushered in a corresponding new understanding of Paul'.[140] Liberation theology uses the subordination paraenesis principally in a critique of a perceived, prevalent *history of interpretation* of Romans 13.[141]

The Kairos Document is liberation theology written from and to the system of apartheid. It was a statement distributed in 1985 by an anonymous group of South African theologians, principally from the black townships of Soweto. The immediate catalyst was the declaration in July 1985 of a State of Emergency under which organizations were banned and some thousands of people detained.[142] The document commented, centrally, on the interpretation of Romans 13 in providing a theological justification for such systems and policies. It described as 'State theology' a theological justification of the *status quo*, 'with its racism, capitalism and totalitarianism. It blesses injustice, canonises the will of the powerful and reduces the poor to passivity, obedience and apathy... It does it by (e.g.)...the use of Rom. 13.1-7 to give an absolute and "divine" authority to the State.'[143]

The authors comment on the widespread 'misuse' of this text: 'Throughout the history of Christianity totalitarian regimes have tried to legitimise an attitude of blind obedience and absolute servility toward the state by quoting this text'.[144] They cite Oscar Cullman and Ernst Käsemann[145] in support of their position: 'What has been overlooked here is one of the most fundamental of all principles of biblical interpretation:

140. Elliott, *Liberating Paul*, p.227.

141. Neil Elliott advocates a reading strategy of Rom. 13 drawn from liberation theology, claiming that 'Only the arrogant presumptions of our own privilege have allowed us to hear these verses as a sacred legitimation of power': *Liberating Paul*, p.226.

142. It was anticipated by the Western Province Council of Churches' publication of 'A Theological Rationale and a Call to Prayer for the End to Unjust Rule': reprinted in Allan Boesak and Charles Villa-Vicencio, *A Call to an End to Unjust Rule* (Edinburgh: St Andrew Press, 1986), pp.25–29.

143. Kairos Theologians, *The Kairos Document: A Theological Comment on the Political Crisis in South Africa* (Catholic Institute for International Relations: British Council and Churches, 2nd edn, 1985), p.56.

144. *Kairos Document*, p.56.

145. 'As soon as Christians, out of loyalty to the gospel of Jesus, offer resistance to a State's totalitarian claim, the representatives of the State or their collaborationist theological advisers are accustomed to appeal to this saying of Paul, as if Christians are here commended to endorse and thus to abet all the crimes of a totalitarian State': Oscar Cullman, *The State in the New Testament* (London: SCM, 1957), p.56. For Käsemann, see §5.2.d.

every text must be interpreted *in its context*[146] (cf. the varied arguments of §5.2). They refer to the literary and the historical contexts of a text, giving the historical context as 'the most revealing', and pronouncing confidently on the religious and political position of Paul's correspondents in Rome:

> They were not revolutionaries. They were not trying to overthrow the State. They were not calling for a change of government. They were, what has been called, 'antinomians' or 'enthusiasts' and their belief was that Christians, and only Christians, were exonerated from obeying any State at all, any government or political authority at all, *because* Jesus alone was their Lord and King.[147]

They describe such a belief as 'heretical' (cf. competing claims for theological orthodoxy in §10.5). Paul therefore must point out to these Christians that before the second coming of Christ 'there will always be some kind of State, some kind of secular government and that Christians are not exonerated from subjection to some kind of political authority'.[148] They also appeal to the *canonical* context, and the Christian hermeneutic that different parts of the Bible cannot be a contradiction of any other part.[149]

Like Chrysostom (§7.2.d), Fleetwood (§7.4.b) and many others, they conclude that Paul is not addressing the issue of a just or unjust state or the need to change one government for another. Their conclusion (like Fleetwood's) is that those using the text to answer questions that were not Paul's are 'doing a great disservice' to him. They also conclude that it is the *interestedness* of the reader that constructs the (false) meaning from the text: 'The use that "State theology" makes of this text tells us more about the political opinions of those who construct this theology than it does about the meaning of God's Word'.[150] (The theo-political prejudgment of the reader is the focus of the discussion in §9.3, and of the case study in §10.5.)

The Kairos Document provoked intense secular and ecclesial debate, and influenced other parts of the Church in South Africa to publish responses to Apartheid.[151] Beyond this national setting, it also inspired

146. *Kairos Document*, p.56.
147. *Kairos Document*, p.56.
148. *Kairos Document*, p.56.
149. *Kairos Document*, p.56.
150. *Kairos Document*, p.56.
151. E.g. A. Balcomb, *Third Way Theology: Reconciliation, Revolution, and Reform in the South African Church during the 1980s* (Pietermaritzburg: Cluster Publications, 1993).

other documents by theologians challenging the attitudes of the churches to immediate socio-political issues.[152]

7.4.e. Willard Swartley

Willard Swartley writes (1984) from a Mennonite tradition of commitment to non-violent civil resistance, and a tradition more recently committed also to active involvement in peace and social justice issues.[153] In a study of Rom. 13.1-7 for a journal targeted at 'Christians for Justice and Peace', and countering a perceived reception where the text 'has generated more uncritical acceptance of the powers, indeed specific governments, than any other',[154] he exercises a method of exegesis and application developed in a recent, earlier work, *Slavery, Sabbath, War and Women* (1983). He seeks to elucidate both 'what the text meant in its first context' (a 'Reformation principle') and how the text helps 'us become faithful followers..., [and offers] learning outcomes to guide us in...social ethical issues'.

His *lexical* work on 'be subject' argues that a distinction between 'subjection' and 'obedience' should be maintained. We saw earlier (§4.4.a) that these distinctions can be maintained to different effects, or denied. Swartley's analysis leads to a conclusion that Christians may sometimes refuse to obey:

> Obedience is used to describe response to the authority of Jesus...or to a person's command or authority... In light of this larger profile the use of 'obey' for slaves to masters in Eph. 6.5 has likely in mind specific and personal brother-to-brother relationships in the Christian community. Not an order but relationship is here accented. Hence subjection should not be confused with obedience... Rather, Christians are to be subject to the order that in turn is ordered by God. This distinction recognizes that Christians sometimes need to refuse to obey the authorities because of their higher allegiance to God (Acts 5.29); subjection then means not rebelling nor resisting with evil (i.e. with violence), but bearing rather the consequences of disobedience.[155]

---

152. E.g. 'The Road to Damascus', written by Central American theologians and published in 1988; *Kairos: Three Prophetic Challenges to the Church* (ed. R. McAfee Brown; Grand Rapids: Eerdmans, 1990).

153. See, e.g., Willard M. Swartley and Cornelius J. Dyck (eds.), *An Annotated Bibliography of Mennonite Writings on War and Peace: 1930–80* (Kitchener: Herald Press).

154. Swartley, 'How to Interpret', p.28.

155. Swartley, 'How to Interpret', p.29; cf. Yoder's analysis on this point: John Howard Yoder, *The Christian Witness to the State* [1968] (Eugene: Wipf & Stock, 1997), p.75.

The *literary* context, particularly the immediately preceding verse, 'overcome evil with good', when linked to 13.6-7 suggests that Paul was addressing a practical issue, the payment of tax. The *historical* context is referred to the tax revolt under Nero (cf. 4.2.2) and Romans 13 represents Paul's counsel not to join this revolt but to pay the taxes. 'In light of the emphases in chapters 12–13, it is clear that Paul considered this counsel to serve best the expression of love, that he considered the early reign of Nero as favourable for good to flourish, and that he hoped the Christian church in Rome would flourish.'[156]

A *canonical* perspective is offered, considering other biblical texts on civil authorities, kings as God's servants, tax payment and Christian response to evil. Swartley then implements a priority over 'specific counsel on particular topics' of '*theological principles* and basic moral imperatives' (see the discussion in §9.3.b):

> This study indicates that Paul's word on tax payment was occasioned by specific circumstances but the support he cites for this, subjection to authorities, is an appeal to theological principle found throughout the Bible. Likewise, overcoming evil with good and owing only love are basic moral imperatives. The [method]…would lead us to conclude that these points are normative for us, while the specific counsel on tax payment is instructive but not binding so as to apply to all situations at all times.[157]

The next phase of the study is its *application* in the reader's life, which entails an examination of an interpreter's own biases and prejudices – cultural, economic, political and religious – and an assessment of the distance 'between the situations of the text and of us as interpreters and the history in between'. The theological and moral imperatives (to be subject to the authorities, interpreted as the tax laws and officials, but also 'to witness against the evil') are then *applied*, in 'letters to the tax officials, to the charitable organizations to whom I try to send the military percentage of my tax, and to the politicians', in the operation of which 'I must image possibility for good and not be imprisoned by the evil'.[158] There are tangible 'effects' in this reception. A final (or iterative) stage is an *ecclesial testing* of this interpretation and application with fellow believers. Swartley comments on the plurality of reception among members *of his own tradition* exposed by this: 'Counsel that I have received has not been consensual'.[159]

---

156. Swartley, 'How to Interpret', p.29.
157. Swartley, 'How to Interpret', p.31.
158. Swartley, 'How to Interpret', p.31.
159. Swartley, 'How to Interpret', p.31.

This is self-consciously a reception that considers historical distance, ongoing Christian tradition, the interestedness of the reader and a potential plurality of possible understandings and applications. It represents one model of the method to which my arguments concerning Christian biblical interpretation as *Wirkungsgeschichte* will lead (§§9.3.a and 9.3.b).

7.5. Interim case-study evaluation

The aim of the chapter was to use a sample from the case study to investigate interpretations and applications of a biblical text as part of a 'progressive process' of reception. The focus is on trajectories of interpretative tradition – seen as significant, exemplary or normative within an ecclesial or theological tradition – and therefore on possible indications of 'paradigm shifts' and a 'summit dialogue' of authors. It has certainly been possible to trace some 'continuities and discontinuities of interpretation with specific traditions'. It has been possible to suggest instances where some reception shapes 'the "pre-understandings" of subsequent generations of interpreters' or has 'held particular influence' in theology and the life of the church.[160] A secondary focus was on the indications which might form a challenge to the normative trajectory, where the contingent particularity of each engagement with a text is manifestly a key co-determinant of the meaning discovered.

The patterns of reception do not readily suggest (simply) 'a stable core of continuity within tradition with more disruptive paradigms introduced by fresh hermeneutical questions'.[161] It might still be possible to present a sample exhibiting such a pattern, constructed with value judgments about 'the most influential interpretations', and the 'percentage of best evidence' and perhaps a different pragmatic about the 'amount of time to invest in this type of study'.[162] Such judgments would not have *methodological* foundation in the reception theory discussed. Likewise, sampling a wider or different body of reception, using different value judgments, might produce a different account of the impact of the texts and their trajectories in history.

The 'paradigm shifts' traced by Parris in his case study concerned the literary genre of parable. Comparable shifts in the understanding of a different *genre*, paraenesis, were not discovered in the reception sampled.

---

160. Thiselton, *First Corinthians*, p.196.
161. Thiselton, *First Corinthians*, p.xvii.
162. Parris, *Reception Theory*, p.219.

I have been able to suggest that some features could be described in terms of 'semiotic shifts', but these were parallel rather than sequential, not often in dialogue with one another, and two quite different conceptual 'shifts' might lead to the same features in the reception of a text (§7.2.c). The process of formation is a plural pattern, where the 'exemplary' structures of one commentator are the 'misuse'[163] of others. So if there are structures of exemplary character, they may be directly antithetical. It is demonstrable that shifts can emerge in directly oppositional *applications*. Ignatius (§7.2.b) interprets Rom. 13.1 as exhorting submission to bishops, but the Geneva Bible (§7.2.d) reads it as meaning: 'the tyranny of the Pope...must down to the ground'.[164] It is the key text supporting the exhortation of Jewel's Homily 'Against... Rebellion',[165] but Fleetwood reads that it says nothing about 'what it is to be a Rebel; and what Resistance is adjudged Rebellion'.[166]

My sample was not strongly characterised by distinctions focusing on ecumenical insight (favoured by Luz: see §6.2), though some reception certainly reflects different, definable, ecclesial confessions. There are denominational factors evident in the reception here (e.g. Luther's digression on ecclesiastical rulers or the Geneva Bible's citation of Chrysostom, §§7.3.c and 7.3.d), but these may not amount to distinctive denominational trajectories (e.g. the correspondences between Calvinist Althusius and Jesuit Suárez, §7.3.e).

In the construct of this as a 'summit' activity, there is little objectively to distinguish the reception of the 'principal commentators' in method or significance as being at a 'level at which an active and reflective conversation within a tradition occurs' or as 'defining moments of a tradition's contours'.[167] Indeed, Gregory I (§7.2.f) makes a striking reading of the subordination paraenesis which has probably had minimal impact on any tradition of reception. The sample of earlier reception might be deemed to have some characteristics of the summit dialogue with its focus on 'principal commentators'. However, in the construct of this as a 'dialogue' between commentators, there is again little to distinguish their 'conscious appropriation and reassessment of a predecessor's work' in method or significance from the similar reassessments in, for example, Fleetwood's reception (§7.4.b) challenging a tradition. The

---

163. *Kairos Document*, p.56 (§7.4.d).
164. *1599 Geneva Bible*, note to 'every soul' Rom. 13.1.
165. Jewel, 'Against Disobedience', p.562 (§5.2.c).
166. Fleetwood, 'Thirteenth Chapter', pp.6–8 (§7.4.b).
167. Parris, *Reception Theory*, pp.216–17.

earlier commentators, apart from Origen (§7.2.c), do not make explicit a consciousness of participating in a *dialogue* or constructing/challenging the contours of an interpretative tradition. The five later commentators who do, are not usually regarded as 'principal' or 'classic'.

For *particular readers*, perhaps, with particular political and/or theological investments, some of these later five might be included within a 'canon of exemplary commentators' (Swartley is certainly in *my* 'canon',[168] for example). However, the criteria for identifying such a canon are as historically contingent and as ideologically interested as other judgments. The 'primary consideration…given to the most influential interpretations'[169] may have a pragmatic foundation but not a methodological one, and not one free from value judgments lying outside the method (or within a dialectic of a reader's own tradition, §9.3).

Collectively, these characteristics do not question the validity of constructions of compilation-histories of reception valorizing classic readings, prioritising principal commentators and identifying paradigm shifts. However, they do problematise these principles, suggesting that value judgments are operating, and that other constructs, other selections, might validly be offered *within the same methodology*.

Further, two dimensions of my case study may problematise, distinctively, the methods under review. First, my case study is of the reception of *paraenetic* texts. This genre is a suasive locution, a perlocutionary speech act, with an explicit attention to application and the practical orientation of a reader's situation (a central aspect of Gadamerian hermeneutics, taken up by Jauss).[170] Where Thiselton articulates a principle of *selection* of reception that demonstrates particular influence in daily life,[171] *all* of the reception in my case study has an immediate relationship with lived praxis, daily life. The relation between literature and pragmatic history is characterised by Jauss as one in which a text is understood not only as a result of social forces but also as a cause of social transformation.[172] This, for Jauss, is mediated in a 'literary evolution' that 'discovers' the 'properly socially formative function that belongs to literature'.[173] In the interpretation and application of paraenetic biblical

168. 'Gadamer's canon is made up of texts…which draw the reader into conversation': Lawn, *Gadamer*, p.128 (cited in §6.2).

169. Parris, *Reception Theory*, p.219 (cited in §6.3).

170. Readers ask questions of the text that are 'decided first and foremost by an interest that arises out of the present situation': Jauss, *Aesthetic of Reception*, p.65.

171. Thiselton, *First Corinthians*, p.196 (cited in §6.2).

172. Jauss, *Aesthetic of Reception*, pp.45, 74.

173. Jauss, *Aesthetic of Reception*, p.45.

texts, this relationship is likely to be *immediate*, not evolutionary. This may diminish the impact of a developing 'tradition' of interpretation in this case study, and enhance the impact of the particular historical situatedness of the reader.

I have suggested that Thiselton's characterisation of the Jaussian dialectic operating 'by comparing a stable core of continuity within tradition with more disruptive paradigms introduced by fresh herme-neutical questions'[174] may not be a sufficient description of the patterns of this reception. Paraenesis may also elicit types of response that attempt to *delimit* the application (e.g. Luther, §7.3.c; Milton, §7.4.a; Fleetwood, §7.4.b) or *subvert* the authority (Gregory, §7.2.f) – without a semiotic or paradigm shift disrupting a tradition of interpretation. (Patterns of limitation and subversion are revisited in Chapter 8.)

The second distinctive dimension of my case study is the *theological and ideological* theme of subordination (and its potential challenge to social hierarchy). I have chosen texts from the Pauline corpus that allow an exploration of the relative interpretative weight given to ecclesial tradition, cultural context and theological hermeneutics, which I hope will test the methods that other commentators apply to other texts. I shall pursue this in relation to the hermeneutical priority Gadamer assigns to prejudgment in Chapter 9.

Hermeneutical insights from the case study in this chapter need to be seen alongside similar or different hermeneutical patterns in a different construction of reception of the paraenesis to women (Chapter 8). Together they contribute to evaluation of the arguments made in Chapter 6, and to further arguments concerning prejudgments and 'tradition' in Chapter 9.

174. Thiselton, *First Corinthians*, p.xvii.

Chapter 8

THE CASE STUDY:
CONTOURS OF A TRADITION IN LITERATURE

8.1. Introduction

This chapter attempts a different structure of progressive process or 'contours of a tradition' from those used in Chapter 7. Here the selection and organization of the sample will *not* focus primarily and predominantly on reception reflecting 'the formation of the traditions of creedal orthodoxy',[1] nor that from 'principal commentators' and in 'the commentary form'.[2] It seeks to respond instead to the discourse and practice (discussed in §6.3) that sees in reception history a method of challenging conservative traditions and recovering neglected aspects of the interpretation of a text.[3] It seeks to apply to a (short) compilation-history of reception the insight that 'interpreters are formed by traditions much more diverse and eclectic than can be easily encapsulated by this or that theological label... [A tradition is] inevitably a fluid constellation of ideas and events at a particular time and place that condition particular readings of biblical texts'.[4]

Some bounds must be set (see §6.3.a), and this is methodologically problematic. Reception in commentaries and confessional tradition is already manifold, and the hermeneutical challenge here is still less boundaried, potentially responding to reception 'whenever and wherever the divine Word finds flesh'.[5] Although I seek to respond to the arguments that find in reception history an impulse to question the conservative impulse in the structures of compilation-histories of reception, and the

---

1. Bockmuehl, 'Commentator's Approach', p.61 (cited in §6.3).
2. Riches, *Galatians*, pp.11 and 2, respectively (cited in §6.2).
3. Some neglected reception was also sampled in the previous construct in Chapter 6: for example Fleetwood, §8.4.b; Stevenson, §8.4.c; and perhaps more surprisingly not 'influential', Gregory, §8.2.f.
4. Rowland, 'Review of Parris (cited in §6.2).
5. May and Meyer, 'Unity of the Bible', p.149 (cited in §6.3).

emphasis on normative tradition, I also wish to avoid a mere 'tracing of random texts in their history of exposition',[6] if only to test the claim that avoiding this is possible outside of an ecclesial 'summit dialogue' of reception.

Jauss's development of Gadamer's paradigm seeks to reveal (or construct) 'structures of exemplary character that condition the process of the formation of literary tradition'.[7] One question posed by the contestations in Chapter 6 concerns how far patterns of reception may reveal 'defining moments of a tradition's contours' *without* primary recourse to a summit dialogue of ecclesial voices (reception exemplary or normative within an ecclesial or theological tradition). To test this, the reception needs to be sampled within some construct of a 'tradition' of interpretation and/or in a literary series.

We have seen that some practitioners claim that *Wirkungsgeschichte* 'acknowledges literature, art, music and actualizations of the text as modes of exegesis just as important as the conventional explanatory writing of Judaism and Christian theology'.[8] Visual or musical reception is hard to claim, specifically and explicitly, for the subordination paraenesis in the same way as for some narrative texts and other biblical genres.[9] However, the exhortations contribute to demonstrable social and political manifestations. They also provoke responses in a range of literary sources – drama, poetry, polemic, fiction, film. Should we judge such instances to be part of a progressive process of interpretation, a literary tradition, or merely 'random texts in…a bewildering zigzag course' governed by the particularity of their social and literary context? It is part of the aim of this chapter to pose and answer this question.

The (much contested) canonising impulses in areas of anglophone literary criticism may offer alternative models of 'tradition' to suggest a framework for my selection of reception. For example, F.R. Leavis famously valorised a strand of the development of the English novel as 'the Great Tradition'. Though he offers limited theoretical definition of the project, he claims that a focus on a few pre-eminent figures is the way to understand what a tradition is,[10] and this has some parallels with

---

6. Froehlich, 'Church History', p.10 (cited in §6.3).

7. Jauss, *Question and Answer*, p.202 (cited in §6.2).

8. Roberts and Rowland, 'Introduction', p.132 (cited in §6.3).

9. Jane Boyd and Philip Esler come closer to the social issues of my texts in discussion of a different, and narrative, text: *Visuality and Biblical Text: Interpreting Velázquez' 'Christ with Martha and Mary' as a Test Case* (Florence: Leo Olschki, 2004).

10. F.R. Leavis, *The Great Tradition: George Eliot, Henry James, Joseph Conrad* (London: Chatto & Windus, 1948), p.3.

the Jaussian construct of a *Höhenkamm der Autoren*.[11] Leavis is particularly elitist in his selection. Other programmes in English literature, with 'contours' of influential works and authors, put a slightly lower bar on what constitutes pre-eminence; for example, in Annette Rubinstein's account of 'the great tradition in English literature', she includes twenty-two 'major literary figures' in 300 years of English drama, poetry and prose.[12]

Espousal of a secular 'canon' of authors or texts can be related not only to aesthetic concerns – 'the possibilities of art for practitioners and readers'[13] – but to ethics and ideology, and this offers further stimulus to my attempt to explore a non-ecclesial 'tradition' of the reception of my texts. For example, Leavis argued for serious moral purpose as a criterion for great writing, and held that the significance of his authors lies not only in their contribution to the possibilities of the genre but also to 'the possibilities of life' and the 'human awareness they promote'.[14] Similarly, Rubinstein focused, from a Marxist perspective, on the relationship of political and social movements to 'major literary works'.[15]

The forms of literary genre I sample below (e.g. two recurring strands are the English novel, and polemical tracts in a strand of the *Querelle des Femmes*) particularly engage with moral and political issues. I noted differences (§6.4) in the attention given in patterns of interpretation, or in compilations of reception, to contingent particularity of reception. Some of the intensity of moral engagement, which attracts critical attention in literary genres, is related to possibilities of psychological and social realism, 'contingent particularity', in drama and the novel. In a major strand of development of the *novel* especially, the complex relationship between individual lives, social norms and moral choices are central preoccupations.[16] For my case study, sampling sources like this will offer reception where contingent particularity and the 'horizon' of lived praxis may figure strongly as components of interpreting and applying the texts (see, e.g., §8.6.b).

Concepts of a Great Tradition in English Literature, contestable in any era, are particularly hard to sustain in the development of the twentieth

11. Jauss, *'Der Leser'*, pp.326–40 (cited in §6.2).

12. Annette Rubinstein, *The Great Tradition in English Literature: From Shakespeare to Shaw* (New York: Citadel, 1962).

13. Leavis, *Great Tradition*, p.1.

14. Leavis, *Great Tradition*, p.2.

15. Rubinstein, *Great Tradition*, e.g. p.5.

16. E.g. Thomas G. Pavel, *The Lives of the Novel: A History* (Princeton: Princeton University Press, 2013), pp.169–98.

century and after. The selection here might be made in order to illustrate the trajectory of certain trends observed in earlier treatment of the Pauline paraenesis, rather than because these are works in an established literary 'canon'. Indeed, my researches suggest that reception of my texts in the period is more likely to appear in 'backwaters and underbellies'[17] of literary expression rather than in any quasi-canonical tradition.

Additionally or alternatively, I might appeal, for my purposes in this chapter, to the different construction of 'canon' that Gadamer makes, which depends on 'their power to address those in search of under-standing, which is, ultimately, self-understanding'.[18] This allows a claim that where works may not constitute a widely accepted cultural canon, they may still constitute 'my canon': that is, works that speak to me as a partner in dialogue. This accords with contemporary practice in the field of biblical interpretation where reception history 'usually' consists of collating reception 'in accordance with the particular interests of the historian concerned'.[19] Accordingly, the sources for the sample will be drama, poetry and prose in English literature, with representation of some of the quasi-canonical authors (Chaucer, Shakespeare, Milton, Dickens, Brontë) but also of some much less-studied texts.

The texts from my case study that lend themselves most readily to this construct of literary reception in various forms and over several centuries are those urging the submission of women or wives. The reception in these sources is often not explicit about the text, and may be allusive, or infer a nexus of texts on the subordination and silencing of women.[20] Therefore, the texts in view will be Col. 3.18 and Eph. 5.22, but also 1 Pet.3.1, 1 Cor. 14.34, 1 Tim. 2.11 and Tit. 2.5 (see §1.2.a). This also accords with arguments relating to a distinctive Pauline lexis (§§8.5.1 and 10.2).

The shift from a structure, Chapter 7, which sampled reception of the paraenesis concerning Christians and civil authorities, to one sampling reception of the paraenesis concerning husbands and wives, also reflects a feature of my case study, and of the associated hermeneutical analysis, where a canonical and theological 'pre-understanding' may be at stake.

17.   Sherwood, *Afterlives*, p.208 (cited in §6.3).
18.   Lawn, *Gadamer*, p.128, discussed in §6.2.
19.   Roberts, *Oxford Handbook*, p.1; there is further evaluation of the principle in §8.7.
20.   At the beginning of each section, therefore, I have included a footnote, flagging up which texts may be reflected, beyond the reception of an often unattributed subjection or silencing of women. The evaluation includes the 'sliding of reception' into 'history of ideas' (see §8.7).

In this chapter, for example, the trajectory of interpretation of Rom. 13.1 has an influence on patterns of reception of the household paraenesis. The authors cited in the contours of the earlier tradition correspond in large measure to the Patristic, Scholastic and Reformation reception in §§7.2 and 7.3. Thereafter, John Milton, with a major role in an English literary tradition as well as in theo-political history, is the only author common to both constructs; but the civil paraenesis continues to appear in interpretation of the domestic paraenesis (e.g. in Shakespeare, §8.4.a; Astell, §8.4.d; Gaskell, §8.5.b and Brontë, §8.5.c).

8.2. Contours of the earlier tradition

> The norm-forming power of texts helps to explain how the reception of biblical texts and previous interpretations of the Bible have shaped church history.[21]

The weight of this compilation is not the earlier periods as with Chapter 7. The purpose of this preliminary section is therefore to indicate some features of the earlier tradition of reception of the paraenesis of the submission of women, which inform or prefigure some later reception.

Patristic, Scholastic and Reformation reception revealed (§5.3.a) some tenacious assumptions concerning the structure of the family. The *Haustafeln* through many centuries could be called upon to witness that Christian domestic life supported the *status quo*.

Clement of Rome praises the Corinthian male heads of households for keeping 'God's ordinances', in the language of the civil paraenesis: 'You obeyed your rulers [ὑποτασσόμενοι τοῖς ἡγουμένοις]'.[22] He exhorts the men further with sentiments paralleled in the household paraenesis, particularly Tit. 2.5: 'You instructed your women to do everything with a blameless and pure conscience, and to give their husbands the affection they should. You taught them too to abide by the rule of obedience [τῷ κανόνι τῆς ὑποταγῆς] and to run their homes with dignity and thorough discretion'.[23] The exhortation to women's moderation in speech, 'By their reticence let them show that their tongues are considerate',[24] is an injunction to silence comparable to 1 Tim. 2.12.

21. Parris, *Reception Theory*, p.301 (cited in §6.2).
22. Ὑποτασσόμενοι is used in 1 Pet. 2.18 (addressed to slaves) and Eph. 5.21 ('one another'); but τοῖς ἡγουμένοις ὑμῶν is from Heb. 13.17 (where they are ecclesial rulers).
23. Clement of Rome, 'First Letter to the Corinthians', 1.3 (pp.43–44); Greek text in *Apostolic Fathers*, p.114.
24. Clement of Rome, 'First Letter to the Corinthians', 21.7 (p.54).

Clement of Alexandria expresses some of the tension, and some of the misogyny, that is an enduring feature of gender discourse through the centuries. Women are spiritually and morally equipped to live as Christians (and 'candidates' equally with men 'for the martyr's crown'), but physically they are suited for a domestic role: 'As then there is sameness, as far as respects the soul, she will attain to the same virtue; but as there is difference as respects the peculiar construction of the body, she is destined for child-bearing and housekeeping'.[25] Women may even philosophise ('though the males are preferable at everything, unless they have become effeminate').

Tertullian's argument, that the Pauline paraenesis (citing Eph. 5.22-23 and 28-29) conforms to the teaching of Genesis, is a forerunner of much reception that makes primary use of Genesis 1–3 and only secondary use of the *Haustafeln* in discourse about gender relations. The relationship of husband and wife is that adumbrated in the creation story in Gen. 2.24 to which Paul himself alludes (Eph. 5.31) as 'a great mystery'. The analogy of Christ and the Church is to be read as 'an interpretation, not a setting aside, of the mystery'.[26] (Astell, §8.4.d below, will later make the Genesis account *secondary* to the analogy in Ephesians.)

The model of household relationships and the injunctions of the Codes are laid out in the argument of Augustine's *The City of God* and much repeated in the subsequent tradition. The household must be the beginning or the cell of the city, and the head of the household should derive rules from the city's laws in order to govern the household. The *paterfamilias* should care for everyone in their household 'as regards the worship and service of God' precisely as they care for their children. There is, however, a material distinction in their care for children and slaves: the equality of care refers to spiritual matters and not 'temporal goods'. It is the context of the household that invariably brings an emphasis on hierarchical relationships. Augustine uses the double love-command, of God and neighbour, to outline an ordered obedience of faith governed by the eternal law, and this leads to an inclusive and also reciprocal pattern of care: 'From which it follows, that we must take care for our neighbour's love of God, in that he or she (wife, children, servants, anyone else) is to be loved as we love ourselves; and that we desire our neighbour to take care for us, if we need it, in just the same way'.[27]

25. Clement of Alexandria, *Stromata* 4.8, in *Fathers of the Second Century* (ed. and trans. Alexander Roberts and James Donaldson; ANF, 2; Grand Rapids: Eerdmans, 1977), p.420.

26. Tertullian, *Against Marcion* 5.18, in Tertullian, *Adversus Marcionem, Books 4–5* (ed. and trans. E. Evans; Oxford: Clarendon, 1972), pp.626–27.

27. Augustine, *City of God* 19.16 (p.412).

However, he then cites 1 Tim. 5.8 and extrapolates, in the pairs of the household codes, that the relationships are not mutual and equal as the earlier neighbour-model of care might have suggested. Some are caring and so command; others are cared for and so should be obedient: 'Commands are the business of those who take care: husband for wife, parents for children, masters for servants. Obedience is the responsibility of those who receive care: wives to husbands, children to parents, servants to masters.'[28]

This is the enduring ethos, later described as love-patriarchalism or benevolent patriarchalism.[29] (Right into the nineteenth century, the parallel of the status and responsibility of workers with those of children will be explicitly made;[30] and this impacts on reception of the paraenesis in Gaskell, §8.5.b below.) Social and institutional forms of subjection, of the citizen to the state or of slaves to their owners, are not 'natural' in the way that female subordination is to the 'naturally' superior male, or child to parent, which is a subordination of lesser to greater like the subordination of bodily things to the spiritual.[31]

Scholastic discourse on a woman's subordination builds on this but makes much more use of Genesis 1–3 than of the subordination paraenesis. Aquinas refers patriarchal authority to nature[32] rather than to the *Haustafeln*, and it is the prime authority, the only natural dominion. All other dominion and supremacy [*praelatio*] were introduced by human law, not natural law:

> Subjection is of two kinds; one is that of slavery, in which the ruler manages the subject for his own advantage, and this sort of subjection came in after sin. But the other kind of subjection is domestic or civil, in which the ruler manages his subjects for *their* advantage and benefit. And this sort of subjection would have obtained even before sin. For the human group would have lacked the benefit of order had some of its members not been governed by others who were wiser. Such is the subjection in which woman is by nature subordinate to man, because the power of rational discernment is by nature stronger in men.[33]

---

28. Augustine, *City of God* 19.16 (p.412).

29. See §5.3.b.

30. Cf. Paul Misner, 'Paternalism', in Dwyer (ed.), *Catholic Social Thought*, pp.712–13.

31. Augustine, *De Genesi ad litteram* 8.23, in Augustine, *De Genesi ad litteram libri duodecim etc.* (ed. J. Zycha; CSEL, 28.1; Vindobonae: Tempsky, 1894), p.262.

32. Cf. §5.3.a.

33. Aquinas, *Summa* 1a.92, 1 (vol. 13, pp.37, 39).

Ockham uses the household codes, citing Col. 3.20, 22; Eph. 6.5; 5.24 and 1 Tim. 2.11, as instances of what scripture means when it speaks of power and subjection:

> In these general statements, and in countless others found in sacred Scripture, the general words should not be taken generally with no exception. In many things, children are not bound to obey their parents, since they are not slaves but free, or wives their husbands, since they are not maidservants but are judged to be entitled to equality in many things..., and slaves are not bound to obey their masters in all things without any exception.[34]

Ockham here argues that power is partial and that subjection also embraces equalities. His analogy of power and equality drawn from the household and applied to forms of governance includes recognition of women as 'entitled to equality in many things' and acknowledges their freedom even in respect of the highest (male) ecclesial authority.

It was, however, a long time before there were social reforms affecting women's roles. The convent declined as an alternative to marriage for women: 'the church increasingly restricted female institutional life by insisting on closer male supervision'.[35] Women sought other options, in communities of laywomen arising in the thirteenth century in Western Europe, especially in Flanders and Italy; or in some heretical movements flourishing in the late Middle Ages 'whose anticlerical and sometimes anti-family positions particularly appealed to women'.[36] The Lollards, for example, in the late fourteenth and fifteenth centuries promoted some equality of the sexes and included women preachers. These were exceptional, but contribute to the potential *Erwartungshorizont* of literary representations of women's roles.

8.3. Middle English drama and poetry

8.3.a. Towneley Mystery Play[37]
The distinctive English tradition of biblical interpretation in the Mystery Cycles offers the first of several examples in this chapter of a subversion amounting to a rejection of the paraenesis concerning women or wives, and problematising the figure of Paul in Christian tradition. In the

---

34. Ockham, *Tyrannical Government* II, p.147, and cf. §7.4.2.
35. King and Rabil, 'The Other Voice', p.xvii.
36. King and Rabil, 'The Other Voice', p.xvii.
37. The reception is of 1 Tim. 2.12 (the silencing of women) and 1 Tim. 5.13; 2 Tim. 3.6.

fourteenth-century Towneley Cycle of Mystery Plays, one of the episodes, 'Thomas of India', is a representation of Mary Magdalene's witness, to the male disciples, of Christ's resurrection. There is often a negative presentation of women (played by male members of the Guilds) in the cycles – famously, Noah's wife in 'The Second Shepherds' Play' within this cycle. This pattern is untypically subverted in 'Thomas of India', where Mary Magdalene is treated scornfully by the disciples but then vindicated by Christ.

Paul appears, unscripturally, as one of the disciples to whom Mary brings her proclamation of Christ's resurrection, with assurances of truth and charged by Christ himself:

> Trist ye it and knawe,
> He is risen the soth to say…
> He bad me tell it you.[38]

Like Peter, and also later Thomas, Paul tells Mary that her word, as a woman, is not trustworthy:

> And it is wretyn in oure law
> 'Ther is no trust in womans saw
> No trust faith to beleefe'
> …
> In womans saw affy we noght,
> ffor thay ar fekill in word and thought,
> This make I myne avowe.[39]

In so far as this is 'written', it is in 1 Tim. 2.12 and 5.13, and perhaps particularly 2 Tim. 3.6. The 'silly women, overwhelmed by their sins and swayed by all kinds of desires, who…can never arrive at a knowledge of the truth' are aptly described as 'fekill'. The significance of this for reception of the Pauline paraenesis is the ascription to Paul of judgments about women (which he swears to, 'As Crist me lowse of sin')[40] that the play reveals to be demonstrably false. The course of the play, and the manifestation of the risen Jesus, reveal Paul to have been wrong in this ascribed estimation of women. There *is* 'trust in woman's saw'. A twentieth-century literary critic writes,

---

38. Anonymous, 'Thomas of India', in *The Towneley Plays* (ed. George England; London: Oxford University Press, 1897), pp.337–52, ll.113–16.

39. 'It is written in our law, "There is no trust in what a woman says…"'; 'In a woman's word we put no confidence, for they are fickle in word and thought: I make this my declaration': Anonymous, 'Thomas of India', ll.29–31, 50–52 (translation mine).

40. 'So may Christ release me from sin': 'Thomas of India', l.46.

> [Paul's] appearance is important, for Paul was the apostle whose letters command women to keep silent and to be submissive to men. Paul has been accused of misogyny, and is sometimes blamed for misogyny in the Christian Church. His anachronistic appearance as a disciple is appropriate for showing how mistaken wholesale condemnation of women is.[41]

Identification of Paul as the source of a strand of misogyny in Christian tradition emerges strongly in some later reception (Burdekin and Flagg, §§8.6.a and 8.6.b). This is an early instance of it, and a remarkable subversion of a tradition of interpretation: Paul's attempt to silence this woman is trounced, implicitly but demonstrably, by the appearance of Christ in fulfilment of her discredited proclamation.

8.3.b. Geoffrey Chaucer[42]

Chaucer's established role in the 'canon' of English literature, and the strand of story-telling in *The Canterbury Tales* (1387–1400) that focuses on male or female dominion in marriage, calls for his inclusion as part of a formative tradition. The *absence* of explicit citation of the household codes in the debate is an early instance of an avoidance that is found elsewhere in the reception that follows (Shakespeare, §8.4.a; Milton, §8.4.c), but also a reflection of the scholastic attribution of domestic hierarchy to natural law (cf. §8.2 above).

As with the character of Mary in the Towneley play, Chaucer gives a dramatised voice to a woman through the dialogue of his characters, and in a framework of contestation. Women's own authorial voices were soon to be heard in such conversations.[43] The demands for social reform, which were later to have expression in radical Protestant movements like the Anabaptists, and the Peasants' Revolt in Germany,[44] had already had literary expression in the *Roman de la Rose*.[45] De Meung links the portrayal of love with an exposition of the new rationalist philosophy of the thirteenth century, proclaiming egalitarian democratic ideals as those of the 'primitive state'. The *Roman* remained a powerful literary influence all through the later Middle Ages in France and beyond, including on Chaucer in England. In *The Canterbury Tales*, two of the Tales are

41. Mary P. Freier, 'Woman as Termagant in The Towneley Cycle', in *Essays in Medieval Studies* 2 (1985), pp.155–67 (165).
42. The reception (but see the discussion) concerns the submission of wives and 1 Tim. 2.12.
43. E.g. Christine de Pizan, *Book of the City of Ladies* [1405] (trans. E.J. Richards; New York: Persea, 1982) (see §8.4.b).
44. See, e.g., Rowland, *Radical Christianity*, p.95.
45. Begun by Guillaume de Lorris c.1240 and extended by Jean de Meung c.1280: Guillaume de Lorris, *Le Roman de la Rose* (Naples: A. Morano, 1947).

given over wholly to the theme of subordination in marriage, and are precursors of the *Querelle des Femmes* (see §8.4.b). Chaucer stands just on the cusp of this 'paradigm shift' in humanist debate: he is still within the framework of the Scholastic tradition, but this is presented in such a way as to subvert the received tradition. He also participates, creatively, in the revisionary debates on biblical authority prevalent in late mediaeval culture.[46]

Chaucer gives the Wife of Bath, in the Prologue to her Tale, some fairly close exegesis of 1 Corinthians 7.[47] Her Prologue is effectively a condemnation of celibacy. She is explicitly anti-clerical, and condemns clerical and scholastic misogyny ('Thou likest eek wommenes love to helle').[48] She privileges, hermeneutically, life-experience (in a prophetic act of proto-feminism[49]) over the standing of such scholars, in her opening lines:

> Experience, though non auctoritee
> Were in this world, is right ynogh for me.[50]

The clergy, first represented by the Friar, speak approvingly of her 'scole-matere' and exegesis but he advocates that she should leave citing scholastic authorities to clergy.[51]

In the Wife of Bath's Tale, based on Gower's story of Florent in *Confessio Amantis*, a knight of the court of King Arthur is required to answer the question: 'What thing it is that women moost desire'.[52] He will be subject to the judgment of the Queen, who is presiding at this event. The answer is that

---

46. See, e.g., Lawrence L. Besserman, *Chaucer's Biblical Poetics* (Norman: University of Oklahoma Press, 1998).

47. Geoffrey Chaucer, 'The Wife of Bath's Prologue', in *The Works of Geoffrey Chaucer* (ed. F.N. Robinson; London: Oxford University Press, 1966); e.g. the absence of commands from Christ for forbidding sexual relations, 1 Cor. 7.6 [ll.64–65]; Paul's celibacy, 1 Cor. 7.8 [l.79]; the right of a wife to have sex with her husband, 1 Cor. 7.3 [ll.129–30]. This exegesis in the Prologue contrasts with the *avoidance* of explicit citation of the household codes in the tale itself.

48. Wife of Bath's Prologue, l.371: 'You [the Friar] also compare love of women to hell'.

49. The privileging of experience in relation to cited, authoritative, tradition in biblical interpretation is of course a feature of much twentieth-century feminist biblical hermeneutics: cf., e.g., Deborah Middleton, 'Feminist Interpretation', in Coggins and Houlden (eds.), *Dictionary of Biblical Interpretation*, pp.231–34 (233).

50. Wife of Bath's Prologue, ll.1–2: 'Though there were no authority in the world, experience is right enough for me'; see also ll.172–74.

51. The Friar's Prologue, ll.1271–77.

52. Wife of Bath's Tale, l.1007.

Wommen desiren to have sovereynetee
As wel over hir housbond as hir love,
And for to been in maistrie hym above.[53]

He can then live in 'parfit joye'[54] governed by his wife. 'As wel over hir housbond as hir love' points to two different paradigms of subordination in gender relationships. While a man woos a woman, he is under her dominion in the (literary) tradition of 'courtly love'.[55] When he marries her, the Church's model of the husband's dominion operates instead. The Wife of Bath, who has undergone this transition five times, is calling for the literary paradigm to overrule the ecclesial one, and with it the ruling of 1 Tim. 2.12 that a woman should not 'usurp' a man's authority.

The Clerk follows with a tale of Patient Griselda (taken from Boccaccio's *Decameron* 10.10 [1349–51], which Petrarch translated into Latin). The Clerk of Oxford is characterised as an Aristotelian scholar, too unworldly to receive a benefice.[56] His heroine, Griselda, is commended for patient humility in the trials imposed by her husband. She insists that she is a 'humble servant' to her husband, not mistress of her household.[57] At the end of the tale, the Clerk insists that the moral is not one urging women's subjection to their husbands – because they could never do what she achieved – but rather one of constancy in adversity, and of universal application, to people, men and women, of every rank:

This storie is seyd, nat for that wyves sholde
Folwen Grisilde as in humylitee,
For it were inportable, though they wolde;
But for that every wight, in his degree,
Sholde be constant in adversitee
As was Griselde...[58]

The broader narrative gives the tale, and the whole sovereignty debate, a sequence of deconstructions. First the Clerk dedicates a song (and he cannot be taken at face value):

---

53. Wife of Bath's Tale, ll.1038–40: 'Women desire to have sovereignty over their husband as well as over their lover, and to be in mastery above him'.

54. Wife of Bath's Tale, l.1258.

55. E.g. Andreas Capellanus, *De Amore* (1184–1186), printed as *The Art of Courtly Love* (ed. P.G. Walsh; New York: Columbia University Press, 1960).

56. Prologue to the Tales, ll.291–95.

57. The Clerk's Tale, ll.820–24.

58. The Clerk's Tale, ll.1142–47: 'This story is told, not so that wives should imitate the humility of Griselde for this would be unachievable, even if they wished it; but rather that every person in their social rank should be constant in adversity like Griselde'.

...for the Wyves love of Bathe –
Whos lyf and al hire secte God mayntene
In heigh maistrie.[59]

Then, at the close, the Host unravels this, and with it the application the Clerk had given his tale that it was not about the submission of wives but about the constancy in adversity of 'every wight'. The Host makes a fervent wish that his own *wife* had heard this tale of Griselda:

Me were levere than a barel ale
Me wyf at hoom had herd this legende ones![60]

The Host's life experience of a wife's subordination evidently does not match the tale (cf. Dickens's Bumble in §8.5.a below)

The absence of *explicit* reference in this debate to Col. 3.18 or Eph. 5.22 is one of the noisiest silences in literature, bearing in mind the audience of Friar, Clerk, Pardoner and Nun's Priest, and the confident display of Pauline exegesis in the Wife of Bath's Prologue. It would be hard to maintain that their 'legacy' is not present in the *Erwartungshorizont* of the first audience to these representations of subordinate and insubordinate women. If *The Canterbury Tales* is deemed not to represent reception of the paraenesis, it does provide a precedent in (a tradition of) English literature for a particular comedic tension: between the rhetoric of womanly subordination and the narrative or dramatic presentation of women. This is a recurring feature of later literary reception (e.g. Dickens, Flagg, and West Wing: §§8.5.a, 8.6.b and 8.6.c). In *The Canterbury Tales*, there is a saturnalian aspect to the intratextual reception of the debate about gendered hierarchy (and some of the other tales turn other hierarchies topsy-turvy) that demonstrably challenges the *Erwartungshorizont* of the reader. The reader is offered a bizarre world where a merry widow prays for short-lived husbands, over whom she has mastery, and is applauded for it by the clergy.[61]

8.4. Early modern drama, poetry and polemic

The Reformation built to some extent on the possibility of a more positive evaluation of marriage and family life than the monastic ideal had encouraged, and humanists proposed 'a profound change in focus

59. The Clerk's Tale, ll.1169–71: '...for love of the Wife of Bath, whose life and her whole sect may God maintain in high mastery'.
60. The Clerk's Tale, ll.1214–15: 'Rather than a barrel of ale, I would prefer my wife at home to have heard this legend!'
61. The Clerk's Tale, ll.1260–61.

from otherworldliness to social responsibility, from renunciation and withdrawal to self-discipline and achievement in a world where family and productive labour were combined'.[62] However, Christian assumptions about the structure of the family changed very little. 'Protestantism engendered an ideal of marriage as a heroic endeavour and appeared to place husband and wife on a more equal footing. Sermons and treatises, however, still called for female subordination and obedience.'[63]

Exhortation, of course, is only necessary where alternatives are being exercised: if there were calls for subordination, it was because some women were living lives that did not express full subordination and obedience. Argula von Grumbach leaves a record of struggle with a vocation to public witness to the Gospel, in participation in disputes of the Reformation, alongside the paraenesis for women's submission and silence. The impact of the paraenesis is outweighed for her by *other* New Testament injunctions for speech and witness – and the inadequacy of men in obeying these: 'I cannot see any man who is up to it, who is either willing or able to speak'.[64] (One of Charlotte Brontë's characters will later lament the absence of any man who 'makes me sincerely feel that he is my superior': §8.5.c below).

The Catechism of the Council of Trent (Pius V, 1566) provides the first significant statement by the Magisterium on 'The Duties of Married People'. This draws on Genesis 2 (Eve 'was not formed from [Adam's] head, in order to give her to understand that it was not hers to command but to obey her husband'; cf. Aquinas and some patristic authors) and on the *Haustafel* of 1 Peter 3. The wife's submission from the latter is interpreted as an exhortation to the wife to yield to the husband, 'in all things not inconsistent with Christian piety, a willing and ready obedience'.[65]

8.4.a. William Shakespeare; and the scold's bridle[66]

Against this background of a continuously promoted ethic, the work by Shakespeare that most explicitly handles dominion and submission between spouses is *The Taming of the Shrew* (1594). It is notoriously hard to pin down the authorial perspective in Shakespeare's plays. There

62. Farley, 'Family', p.374.
63. King and Rabil, 'The Other Voice', p.xvii.
64. Argula von Grumbach, 'Letter to the University of Ingolstadt', in *Argula von Grumbach: A Woman's Voice in the Reformation* (ed. P. Matheson; Edinburgh: T. & T. Clark, 1995), p.79.
65. Catholic Church, *The Catechism of the Council of Trent* (London: G. Routledge, 1852), p.217.
66. Reception is (in *The Taming of the Shrew*) of 1 Cor. 11.3, and Rom. 13.1; and (regarding the scold's bridle) of 1 Tim. 2.11 and Rom. 13.1.

is a lack of resolution of key questions raised in many of the plays – a quality that Keats called 'negative capability'[67] – which matches the indeterminacy of the *Erwartungshorizont* in Chaucer. This is certainly true of *The Taming of the Shrew*, and directors and actors in recent decades have had to make choices about how sincere or ironic, or even tragic, is Katherine's final speech of submission to her husband, played to the shifting *mores* of their audiences. (We can only guess at what the boy or young man made of it when he first played the role in 1594 – we have no access to this 'first reception'.)

The closing sequence of the play, after a comic and savage 'taming' of Katherine, presents a reversal of the turbulence of her earlier scenes, and she wins her husband's wager with two other husbands as the man 'whose wife is most obedient'.[68] The headship of husbands (1 Cor. 11.3) forms part of tamed Katherine's rebuke to the other wives:

> Thy husband is thy lord, thy life, thy keeper,
> Thy head, thy sovereign.[69]

The key element in her argument is the analogy of the subjection of wife to husband being like that of subject to ruler (which has been part of this debate from Aristotle onwards):

> Such duty as the subject owes the prince,
> Even such a woman oweth to her husband.[70]
> Therefore, when she is not obedient,
> what is she but a foul contending rebel
> and graceless traitor to her loving lord?[71]

Threats of rebellion were a matter of common civic anxiety in the late sixteenth century.[72]

The analogy of wife/husband and subject/lord is a common one in the tradition (which includes explicit links between the paraenesis of Rom. 13.1 and the household codes). However, it lacks the distinction here (which Ockham makes) between the 'natural' rule of royal government

---

67. '[T]hat is, when a man is capable of being in uncertainties, mysteries, doubts, without any irritable reaching after fact and reason': John Keats, 'Letter to George and Thomas Keats, 21st December 1817', in *Letters of John Keats* (ed. Frederick Page; London: Oxford University Press, 1954), pp.51–54 (53).

68. *The Taming of the Shrew*, V.ii. 67; William Shakespeare, *The Complete Works* (ed. P. Alexander; London: Collins, 1951).

69. *The Taming of the Shrew*, V.ii, 146–47.

70. *The Taming of the Shrew*, V.ii, 155–56.

71. *The Taming of the Shrew*, V.ii, 158–60.

72. E.g. Jewel, 'Against Disobedience', p.571 (cited in §5.2.c).

'as to fullness of power', and that of 'constitutional' government which 'is like the rule by which the head of the household rules his wife' without that 'fullness of power'.[73]

The Shrew is actually a play within a play: there is a framing device or 'Induction' whereby the main action is staged for other characters to watch. In the frame drama, a tinker is taken up, drunk, by a lord and his huntsmen and, when revived, is persuaded that he is a wealthy lord who has been out of his mind for fifteen years. This tinker-lord then watches a play, 'The Taming of the Shrew', as a 'pleasant comedy', 'household stuff',[74] accompanied by a page pretending to be his wife. The framing drama is a saturnalia based on social reversal (cf. the Clerk's satirical praise for the Wife of Bath, 2.b above), and a deception, including a man or boy pretending to be someone's wife. The closing scene of the main play also represents a reversal, and here too a young man or boy would have been playing Katherine: is this scene a genuine *apologia* for domestic submission or another saturnalia and another deception? In the 'Great Tradition' of some of the most prized English writers, Chaucer and Shakespeare, a woman's subordination in marriage is not an unquestioning reproduction of Scholastic or Reformation reception.

The legal contingencies of the issues raised by Katherine's speech are significant to this reception and to the continuing tradition. A husband had the legal right to his wife's submission and obedience, and matrimonial law remained one of the areas of the Church's jurisdiction. Canon law, which had jurisdiction over matrimonial causes, was based on Roman civil and canon law as determined by church scholars and was administered by the ecclesiastical courts.[75] Legal theorists such as Blackstone[76] in the eighteenth century continued to use scriptural language when discussing the law, assuming that English law is at its best divinely inspired and that offences against the law are offences against God.

The most obvious way in which the law and church teaching reinforced each other was the legal right a husband had to 'correct' his wife's behaviour. A wife had no separate identity in law (it was subsumed into that of the husband): there is no voluntarism in her coercive subjection

---

73. Ockham, *A Letter to the Friars Minor*, p.147 (cited in §7.3.b).

74. 'Shrew', Induction, ii. 127, 137.

75. Examples in William S. Holdsworth, *A History of English Law*, vol. 1 (London: Methuen & Co., 3rd edn, 1922).

76. William Blackstone, *Commentaries on the Law of England* [1764–1769] (Chicago: University of Chicago Press, 1979).

by law. John Dove argued in a sermon in 1601, that a woman who sought a divorce was analogous to a servant who sought to dissolve his bond with his master.[77] William Whateley's early seventeenth-century sermon on female subordination in marriage claims that God will never allow a wife to cast off 'this yoke of subjection' even if she is beaten, and allows for an abusive husband as for an abusive jailer: 'if a woman be so yoked, she must keep her place and show patience. It is not for a prisoner to break prison at his pleasure because he hath met with a rough Jailer.'[78]

One of the key descriptions of Katherine is as 'an irksome brawling scold'.[79] A form of punishment for women addicted to abusive language and called 'scolds' (a term rarely applied to men in the period[80]) was the scold's bit or scold's bridle, called 'branks' in sixteenth-century Scotland. It is a startlingly physical enforcement of 1 Tim. 2.11, used to silence and humiliate women who would not learn 'in silence with full submission'. The bridle is a peculiarly British phenomenon, used in sixteenth- and seventeenth-century England but 'in active use in Scotland many years before their introduction into England'.[81] The instrument consisted of an iron framework to enclose the head, with a sharp metal gag or bit that entered the mouth and restrained the tongue.[82] It was coupled with a public exposure of the victim: the woman was publicly silenced and subjected; so she might be carried in a scold's cart wearing the branks (in Newcastle in 1595) or be pilloried in the market-place (in Dumfermline in 1652).[83] Magistrates could impose the penalty on women who spoke

77. John Dove, *Of Divorcement, a Sermon Preached at Paul's Cross the 10th of May 1601* (London: Printed by T. C[reede], 1601), p.33.

78. William Whateley [1583–1639], 'Directions for Married Persons: Describing the Duties Common to Both, and Peculiar to Each of Them' (Bristol: William Pine, 1768). This position is challenged later in the period. Locke suggested that a wife's subordination was part of a contract, which could be broken by tyrannical behaviour on the part of her husband, just as Whigs argued that subjects could resist their king if he violated the contract by tyrannical behaviour: John Locke, *Two Treatises*, in Christopher Flint, *Family Fiction: Narrative and Domestic Relations in Britain, 1688–1798* (Stanford: Stanford University Press, 1998), p.42.

79. 'Shrew', I.ii, l.88.

80. *OED*, vol. 9, p.231: 'Scold'.

81. T.N. Brushfield, 'On Obsolete Punishments with particular reference to those of Cheshire: part 1', *Journal of the Architectural, Archaeological, and Historic Society for the County, City, and Neighbourhood of Chester* 2 (1855–1862), pp.31–48 (35).

82. *OED*, vol. 1, p.1057: 'Branks'.

83. *OED*, vol. 1, p.1057: 'Branks', citing *Municipal Accounts of Newcastle*, and E. Henderson, *Kirk-Session Records of Dumfermline*, respectively.

against national or local government – in what is effectively a juridical coupling of 1 Tim. 2.11 with Rom. 13.1 – and there are recorded instances of its use on Quaker women who spoke 'doctrine'.[84] The punishment is not merely directed to the lack of a woman's subjection in the domestic sphere; it is a civic punishment for a civic crime. It is one of the starkest instances of the idea of a woman's submission as *involuntary*, a matter for enforcement rather than exhortation, in the reception of the submission texts.

8.4.b. Rachel Speght[85]

The sample so far has been of constructs of women's speech authored by men (Mary Magdalene, the Wife of Bath, Katherine), and it is 1617 before I have uncovered a woman's reception in English of the household paraenesis, in a polemical pamphlet. Attacks on women (and defences of them) were an established pamphlet genre in sixteenth-century England. These were part of a broader phenomenon, a debate about the nature and capacity of women, and the household and civic roles of women are central to the debate.

This had its origin in Renaissance humanism, a movement led by men who shared both the evaluation of women made in ancient classical texts and 'the misogynist perceptions of their [own] culture', but who 'regarded the Scholastic philosophy of mediaeval universities as out of touch with realities of urban life'.[86] Humanist Churchmen drew regularly on patristic authors (Tertullian, *On the Apparel of Women*; Jerome, *Against Jovinian*; and Augustine, *The Literal Meaning of Genesis*) to confirm the subordination of women. Giovanni Bocaccio's treatise, *Concerning Famous Women* (1365),[87] drew on classical texts to praise women: solely those who possess the virtues of chastity, silence and obedience. In the yoking of these three (which are all reflected in the exhortations of 1 Tim. 2.9-15) it is the imposition of silence on women (the key injunction of the submission paraenesis in 1 Tim. 2.11) which dominates, so that chastity is submerged in it as a metaphor. To keep silence is to be chaste, and speaking out is a form of unchastity. Responding to this and other works in 1405, the female humanist author Christine de Pizan, in the *Book of*

---

84. Cf. John Miller, '"A Suffering People": English Quakers and Their Neighbours c.1650–c.1700', *Past and Present* 188 (2005), pp.71–103.

85. Reception is of Eph. 5.23; 1 Cor. 11.3; 1 Pet. 3.7 and Col. 3.19.

86. King and Rabil, 'The Other Voice', p.xviii.

87. *De Mulieribus Claris*: Giovani Bocaccio, *Famous Women* (trans. V. Brown; Cambridge, Mass.: Harvard University Press, 2003).

the City of Ladies, makes a defence of the female sex, and a construction of an ideal community of women. This precipitated a literary deluge of Latin and vernacular texts, by women as well as men. The genre was known as the '*Querelle des Femmes*' and extended from the fourteenth into the eighteenth century.

An unscholarly but very popular item in this genre was Joseph Swetnam's pamphlet first published in 1615, 'The Arraignment of Lewde, Idle, Froward and Unconstant Women'.[88] It provoked many replies, including four extant which are ostensibly written by women.[89] The one that makes most use of the Pauline paraenesis is by Rachel Speght, one of the earliest female English polemicists.[90] In 'A Mouzell for Melastomus', Speght links Eph. 5.23 with 1 Cor. 11.3 and defines the headship as not validating a domineering authority: 'Man is the Woman's Head; by which title yet of Supremacie, no authoritie hath been giuen him to domineere, or basely command and imploy his wife, as a seruant'. She cites both 1 Pet. 3.7 and Col. 3.19 with their exhortation to husbands to be lenient, and with the comparison of husband to Christ being spelled out: if a wife is to submit to her husband as to Christ, then the husband may only command what Christ would command:

> women are enjoined to submit themselves vnto their husbands no other waies then as to *the Lord*; so that that from hence, for man, ariseth a lesson not to bee forgotten, that as the Lord commandeth nothing to be done, but that which is right and good, no more must the husband.[91]

This contrasts with the advice given in Juan Vives's manual, *The Instruction of a Christen Woman* (1523), one of the many 'conduct' books published in this period. Vives offers instruction on every aspect of a woman's life, all based on the idea that she should be subject to her husband. He advised beaten women to consider that they are being corrected by God, and in this way are expiating their sins, for 'good and

---

88. Joseph Swetnam, *The Arraignment of Lewde, Idle, Froward and Unconstant Women* (London: Thos. Archer, 1615); reprinted in *Female Replies to Swetnam the Woman-Hater* (ed. Charles Butler; Bristol: Thoemmes, 1995).

89. Ester Sowernam, 'Ester hath hang'd Haman' (1617); Rachel Speght, 'A Mouzell for Melastomus' (1617); Constantia Munda, 'The worming of a mad dog' (1617); Anonymous, 'Swetman the Woman-hater, Arriagned by Women' (1620), reprinted in Butler, *Female Replies*: at least two of these works were authored by men.

90. Cf. Helen Speight, 'Rachel Speght's Polemical Life', *Huntingdon Library Quarterly* 65 (2002), pp.449–63 (449).

91. Speght, 'A Mouzell', p.17.

prudent wives are rarely beaten by their husbands'.[92] *The Instruction* ran into several editions and was influential into the seventeenth century and beyond.

Swetnam's tract similarly was reprinted many times throughout the seventeenth and eighteenth centuries. Speght's and the other replies to Swetnam are considerably more learned than the piece they attack, but these were not reprinted. This highlights one of the problems for selection based on any criteria that valorise *continuities* of interpretation and the 'percentage of the best evidence'.[93] A counter-tradition may have found it difficult to make itself heard, and more difficult still to be reproduced. This is compounded when an influential interpretation of a text requires women receiving it to be silent.[94]

8.4.c. John Milton[95]

Milton's place in the tradition of English literature, and his concern for the exegesis and application of the Pauline paraenesis to civil authorities (see §§5.2.c and 7.4.a), make him a potential source of reception marking the contours of the tradition we are pursuing. He gave attention to the institution of marriage, in a challenge to some accepted traditions of interpreting scripture. The principle of Christian freedom (a strong 'contour' in the earlier tradition, e.g., Augustine and Luther, §§7.2.e and 7.3.c) which Milton directs to the reform of the state (§7.4.a),[96] is also applied to the reform of marriage. The title page of 'The Doctrine and Discipline of Divorce' (first published in 1643, the first of four tracts on the topic) announces the programme:

> The doctrine and discipline of divorce: restored to the good of both sexes, from the bondage of Canon law, and other mistakes, to Christian freedom, guided by the Rule of Charity. Wherein also many places of Scripture, have recover'd their long-lost meaning. Seasonable to be now thought of in the Reformation intended.[97]

---

92. Vives, *Christian Woman*, p.204.

93. Parris, *Reception Theory*, p.19 (cited in §6.2).

94. Cf. Schüssler Fiorenza's comment on the absence of first-reception of some Pauline injunctions: 'The theological counterarguments by slaves or women have not survived in history' (*In Memory*, p.217).

95. Reception is of Col. 4.14; 1 Cor. 11.3; Col. 3.18–19(?) and Eph. 5.22–28.

96. Milton, 'Civil Power', p.305.

97. John Milton, 'The Doctrine and Discipline of Divorce' [1643], in Patrides, *Milton*, p.112.

In recovering 'lost meaning from some biblical texts', he avoids the household paraenesis. However, his argument that the sentence of Christ concerning divorce must be expounded as a command of perfection is characterised with a text from the verses that lead up to the Colossians Code: 'it partakes of charity, which is the bond of perfection'.[98] This casts the paraenesis as a call to perfection, and needing to be applied with charity. His focus is the husband's prerogative: divorce should not be prevented by law because 'the freedom and eminence of man's creation gives him to be a Law in this matter to himselfe'. The Pauline scripture used is 1 Cor. 11.3: because the husband is 'the head of the other Sex which was mad[e] for him'.[99] If the household paraenesis appears, it is in the exhortation to husbands not to be bitter against their wives (Col. 3.19), and this is qualified by the priority of the husband's well-being: a man's wife 'was mad[e] for him; whom therefore though he ought not to injure, yet neither should he be forc't to retain in society to his own overthrow'.[100]

Within the broad historical context,[101] the personal circumstances influencing reception are diverse and perhaps untraceable, but may be very significant within the 'interest that arises out of the present situation':[102] Milton's first wife had left him after six weeks of marriage (returning some years later). The prime theological principle of 'freedom from authority' is not applied to *women* in Milton's exegesis (while Mary Astell will do just this: §8.4.d below).

It is his epic poem *Paradise Lost* (first printed in 1667) that gives Milton an acknowledged role in shaping the contours of the reception of a biblical text, the narrative of the Fall. He offers a reading of Eve's submission to Adam that has confirmed and defined a mainstream tradition of interpretation. The description, which centres on the hair of the man and of the woman, owes much to 1 Cor. 11.2-16, but also something to the submission texts, and the result is something that recurs later in more explicit application of Col. 3.18-19 and Eph. 5.22-28. Adam's look is 'sublime', and indicates 'rule':

98. Milton, 'Divorce', p.157: Col. 3.14, 'the bond of perfectness' (Tyndale, Geneva, KJV), 'the bond of perfection' (Wycliffe, Douay-Rheims).

99. Milton, 'Divorce', p.172.

100. Milton, 'Divorce', p.172.

101. The unusual continuance in Protestant England of Catholic canon law meant that it was 'lacking either formal controls over marriage or satisfactory legal means of breaking it': Lawrence Stone, *Road to Divorce* (Oxford: Oxford University Press, 1990), p.11.

102. Jauss, *Aesthetic of Reception*, p.65 (cited in §6.4).

> His large front and eye sublime declared
> Absolute rule; and hyacinthine locks
> Round from his parted forelock manly hung
> Clustering, but not beneath his shoulders broad.

Eve's look is 'wanton' and indicates 'subjection' and 'submission':

> She, as a veil down to the slender waist,
> Her unadorned golden tresses wore
> Dishevelled, but in wanton ringlets waved,
> As the vine curls her tendrils, which implied
> Subjection, but required with gentle sway,
> And by her yielded, by him best received,
> Yielded with coy submission, modest pride,
> And sweet reluctant amorous delay.[103]

It is the infusion of a woman's submission with a sexual connotation that appears in subsequent reception, in negative portrayals, in contrast to the positive authorial perspective here (see §§8.6.a and 8.6.b).

8.4.d. Mary Astell[104]

The claims made for Mary Astell as 'first English feminist'[105] sit interestingly with her High Tory Anglican views and her advocacy of the Divine Right of Kings. The first edition of her tract, 'Some Reflections Upon Marriage' analyses marriage from women's perspective, leading to the reflection that ' if a Wife's case be as it is her[e] represented, it is not good for a Woman to Marry, and so there's an end of [the] Human Race'.[106] Like a tyrannical sovereign – the analogy with the different forms of submission familiar from other parts of the paraenesis reception (e.g. Augustine and Shakespeare, §§8.2 and 8.4.a above) – a husband who has unlimited authority over his wife makes his wife into his slave.

The tract is wholly secular, and Astell uses Reason, rather than scripture, to make her argument, as do many writers in the humanist tradition and in the long *Querelle des Femmes*.[107] Many of her ideas parallel those of the same period where *men* claim the right to self-rule, 'to be a Law...

---

103. John Milton, 'Paradise Lost' [1667], in *The English Poems of John Milton* (ed. H.C. Beeching; Oxford: Oxford University Press, 1913), Book IV, ll.300–11.

104. Reception is of 1 Tim. 2.11-15 and Eph. 5.22-33, esp. 32.

105. E.g. Bridget Hill, *The First English Feminist: 'Reflections Upon Marriage' and Other Writings by Mary Astell* (Aldershot: Gower Publishing, 1986).

106. Mary Astell, 'Reflections Upon Marriage', in *Political Writings* (ed. Patricia Springborg; Cambridge: Cambridge University Press, 1996), pp.77–78.

107. E.g. up to and including Mary Wollstonecraft, *Vindication of the Rights of Woman* [1792] (ed. Miriam Brody; London: Penguin, 1988).

to himselfe', just as Milton claims this theologically.[108] However, for the third edition of this work, in 1706, Astell added a preface, justifying on scriptural grounds her right to write the tract. She uses one biblical passage to interpret another, exposing the parallel of the subordination of women with slavery. She juxtaposes Adam's ruling over Eve with Jacob's making a servant of Esau, and asks, Why is one of these held to be 'a Command' while the other is 'a Prediction'? This leads to her question (famous in some feminist traditions): 'If all men are born free, how is it that women are born slaves?'[109] She also notes a parallel with the parenesis to civil authorities in order to *contrast* the nature of authority commonly ascribed to husbands or men with the more qualified authority ascribed to civil authorities:

> Holy Scripture … speaks of Women as in a state of Subjection, and so it does of the Jews and Christians when under the dominion of the Chaldeans and Romans, requiring of the one as well as of the other a quiet submission to them under whose Power they lived. But will anyone say that these had a Natural Superiority and Right to Dominion?[110]

She goes on to challenge the prevailing interpretation of women's subjection, through the patristic and scholastic device of allegory. Her reading combines 1 Tim. 2.11-15 with the reading of Eph. 5.22-33, (especially 5.32, mediated through the words of introduction to the 'Solemnization of Matrimony'):[111]

> But, it will be said perhaps, that in I Tim. ii, 13, &c. St. Paul argues for the Woman's Subjection from the Reason of Things. To this I answer, that it must be confessed, that this (according to the vulgar Interpretation) is a very obscure Place, and I should be glad to see a natural, and not a Forced Interpretation given of it by those who take it Literally: Whereas if it be taken Allegorically, with respect to the Mystical Union between Christ and his Church, to which St. *Paul* frequently accommodates the matrimonial Relation, the Difficulties vanish.[112]

She demolishes the support Genesis is claimed to give to a woman's subjection though 'natural order' (and so runs counter to Tertullian's harmonising of Genesis and Ephesians, see section 1 above) by prioritising (Paul's) identification of Christ with Adam, and consequently the Church, male and female believers both, with Eve:

108. Milton, 'Divorce', p.172 (3.c above).
109. Astell, 'Preface', in *Political Writings*, p.18.
110. Astell, 'Preface', p.14.
111. Cf. 'the mystical union that is betwixt Christ and his Church': *The Book of Common Prayer* [1662] (London: Cambridge University Press, 1955), p.176.
112. Astell, 'Preface', p.21.

> For the Earthly Adam's being formed before Eve, seems as little to prove her Natural Subjection to him, as the living Creatures, Fishes, Birds, and Beasts being formed before them both, proves that mankind must be subject to these Animals... But it is very true, that the Second Adam, the man Christ Jesus, was first formed, and then his spouse the Church. He was not in any respect Deceived, nor does she pretend to Infallibility. And from this second Adam, promised to Eve in the Day of our first Parents Transgression, and from Him only, do all their Race, Men as well as Women, derive their Hopes of Salvation.[113]

In Astell's reading, 1 Tim. 2.11 therefore urges that *the Church* should learn in silence, and be subject to Christ. One of Brontë's characters will say (in 1849) of this same text: 'It would be quite possible, I doubt not, with a little ingenuity, to give the passage quite a contrary turn'[114] and indeed applies it by a 'contrary turn' to the younger Clergy (§8.5.c). Where Brontë suggests a reading that would uncover the lexis and occasion of first reception, Astell's distaste for the 'Forced Interpretation given of it by those who take it Literally' leads her in a different direction than attempted historical reconstruction.

Speght's reading (§8.4.b above) is closer to better known 'contours' of traditional readings than Astell's, but both suffer the fate of having little apparent influence in subsequent traditions, and Astell analyses a particular 'Disadvantage' contributing to this silencing of women. Brontë (§8.5.c below) will point up the circumstance of an individual woman, who says, 'I daresay, if I could read the original Greek, I should find that many of the words had been wrongly translated, perhaps misapprehended altogether'.[115] Astell argues, stingingly, that such 'Ignorance' is imposed on all women by male retention of the critical tools: 'Women without their own Fault, are kept in Ignorance of the original, wanting Languages and other helps to Criticise on the Sacred text, of which they know no more, than men are pleas'd to impart in their Translations'. Nevertheless, 'Scripture is not always on their side who make parade of it, and thro' their Skill in Languages and the tricks of the Schools, wrest it from its genuine sense to their own Interventions.'[116] Astell's ingenuity in fact turns on a 'trick of the Schools', allegorical interpretation, as well as a canonical and theological hermeneutic. These can be among the strategies to which interpreters have recourse to produce a 'change of horizons'[117]

113. Astell, 'Preface', p.21.
114. Charlotte Brontë, *Shirley* [1849] (London: Gresham, n.d.), p.258 and 210.
115. Brontë, *Shirley*, p.258.
116. Astell, 'Preface', p.14.
117. Jauss, *Aesthetic of Reception*, p.23 (§1.1.b).

when the 'more obvious and generally received acceptation'[118] is at odds with the reader's prejudgments and life horizon.

8.5. Nineteenth-century novels

8.5.a. Charles Dickens[119]

For Leavis, Dickens is not part of the Great Tradition of the English novel because his genius was that of 'a great entertainer'. He claims that Dickens (except in *Hard Times*) 'had for the most part no profounder responsibility as a creative artist than this description suggests'.[120] Without subscribing to Leavis's particular perspective on the nature of the novel, we can accept that entertainment will be at least as important as an ethical agenda in any reception of the paraenesis in Dickens. This was true in Chaucer too (§8.3.b above), and will be in later novels, for instance those by Flagg (§8.6.b below).

Dickens marries a religious sentiment concerning the family, with a mixture of realism and caricature in the lives of a stratified social hierarchy. In *Oliver Twist* (1837–38), Bumble the beadle contracts a marriage with the matron of the workhouse, and then finds his authority challenged. The household paraenesis is mediated through the norms in law and religion of the relative roles of husbands and wives, rather than being explicitly referred to Paul's letters (unless one refers the 'obedience' of wives to Tit. 2.5). It is also associated with the world order of the submission to civil authority, an implicit operation of what is explicit in, for example, Ockham (§7.3.b).

Bumble argues with his wife:

> 'The prerogative of a man is to command.'
> 'And what is the prerogative of a woman, in the name of Goodness?' cried the relict of Mr. Corney deceased.
> 'To obey, ma'am', thundered Mr. Bumble.[121]

His wife's response is to beat him. Bumble reflects on the loss of authority – beyond his marriage – that this 'reversal' of the *status quo* produces: 'He had lost caste and station before the very paupers; he had fallen from all the height and pomp of beadleship, to the lowest depth of the most snubbed hen-peckery'.[122]

---

118. Origen, *Contra Celsum* 8.65 (p.502) (§4.4.a).

119. Reception (obedience of wives) may reflect Tit. 2.5 (and Rom. 13.1).

120. Leavis, *Great Tradition*, p.30.

121. Charles Dickens, *The Adventures of Oliver Twist* [1837–38] (London: Chapman & Hall, n.d.), p.168.

122. Dickens, *Oliver*, p.69.

The beadle's authority as a parochial appointment, an instrument of 'the powers that be' that 'are ordained of God' (Rom. 13.1, KJV), is brought into question because of the challenge to his authority as a husband. The status in nineteenth-century law of Bumble's authority as a husband is illustrated when he is later charged with a crime for which he blames his wife; and he is not permitted to parry the charge. His response is famous:

> '...for the law supposes that your wife acts under your direction.'
> 'If the law supposes that', said Mr. Bumble... 'the law is a ass... If that's the eye of the law, the law is a bachelor; and the worst I wish the law is, that his eye may be opened by experience.'[123]

Experience, for the implied reader, is that such wives are not, in fact, submissive to their husbands, and that such husbands do not, in fact, love their wives. This representation, that the household code paraenesis is challenged by life-experience, is a recurring feature in the reception sampled: we have seen it in the Towneley play and in Chaucer (§§8.3.a and 8.3.b above) and in all of the sample below there is a similar experiential subversion (§§8.5.b, 8.5.c, 8.6.a, 8.6.b), or dismissal (§8.6.c) of patriarchal gender-relations.

8.5.b. Elizabeth Gaskell[124]
Elizabeth Gaskell's fictions in the 1850s and 60s were often retrospectives of forty to sixty years previously. Her societies are settled, incipiently a little disturbed by social changes, and often viewed by the narrators as old-fashioned, with an affectionate humour about fashion and style but with admiration for an age of stronger principles. There is a conscious romanticising of social subordination, but it is viewed from a distance, with a conscious 'differentiation of horizons', in a more liberal present. In the opening paragraphs of her last novel she writes:

> a very pretty amount of feudal feeling still lingered, and showed itself in a number of simple ways, droll enough to look back upon, but serious matters of importance at the time. It was before the passing of the Reform Bill, but a good deal of liberal talk took place occasionally between two or three of the more enlightened freeholders.[125]

---

123. Dickens, *Oliver*, p.248.
124. Reception is of the household codes (esp. Col. 3.22), and 1 Pet. 2.13-15.
125. Mrs. Gaskell, *Wives and Daughters: An Every-day Story* [1864–66] (London: Smith, Elder & Co., 1907), p.2.

This is still in a context where Church teachings (until the late nineteenth century) tended to view hierarchical class divisions as 'natural'.[126] The distance between the author and her readers on the one hand, and the events she depicts on the other, includes the continental upheavals of 1848, which 'had shaken the social order, and the resultant reaction had established it more firmly than ever'.[127] In the same year, 1848, Karl Marx and Frederick Engels in the *Manifesto of the Communist Party* made an analysis that suggested a less stable pattern of authority and domination:

> The history of all hitherto existing society is the history of class struggles. Freeman and slave, patrician and plebeian, lord and serf, guild master and journey man, in a word, oppressor and oppressed, stood in constant opposition to one another, carried on an uninterrupted...fight that each time ended, either in a revolutionary re-constitution of society at large, or in the common ruin of the contending classes.[128]

It is an analysis that makes a positive interpretation of Romans 13 even more problematic. Louis Cazamian cites Gaskell as one of three novelists in whose work one of the components of 'idealistic [social] interventionism' was exemplified better than anywhere else: 'this was the spontaneous repugnance felt by anyone of a religious disposition for the industrial system that violated scriptural teaching'.[129]

Gaskell scrutinises the paternalistic model in the nineteenth century workplace alongside a changing *Erwartungshorizont* of representations of the role and education of women. (We have seen that this combination of the Pauline paraenesis on civil authorities and the household codes is a repeated feature of the tradition.) Gaskell's writing is also contemporaneous with an attempt, in 1857, to reform the laws preventing married women holding property or making wills, and the attempt to include votes for women in the Reform Act of 1867. *The English Woman's*

126. Cf. Arthur F. McGovern, 'Class', in Dwyer (ed.), *Catholic Social Thought*, p.4.

127. Louis Cazamian, *The Social Novel in England, 1830–1885* (trans. M. Fido; London: Routledge & Kegan Paul, 1973), p.226. The re-establishment of most of the ruling houses (except in France) makes this the 'turning point' which 'failed to turn': A.J.P. Taylor, *The Course of German History: A Survey of the Development of German History Since 1815* (London: Routledge, 1961), p.69.

128. Karl Marx and Frederick Engels, 'Manifesto of the Communist Party' [1848], in *The Marx–Engels Reader* (ed. R. Tucker; New York: Norton, 2nd edn, 1978), pp.473–74.

129. Cazamian, *Social Novel*, p.211.

Journal was published in the same period (1858–64) with an agenda for education, employment, and reform of marriage laws.[130]

In 'Cousin Phillis', the portrait of the minister Holman reflects old-fashioned values (it is cast in the narrator's youth). As a portrait of a dissenting minister, 'an Independent', he represents something more extreme, but (and this is acknowledged with slight reluctance on the narrator's part) also more admirable than the fashionable and the main-stream. (The author, distinguishable here from the narrator, was herself the daughter and wife of Unitarian ministers.) Holman is a gentleman farmer who ministers without a stipend on weekends; his household is benevolently patriarchal, the wife and daughter submissive, the farm-hands respectful and loyal. Household codes are made of such as these.

An explicit citation of the Pauline texts (Col. 3.22) is made in an application of the Colossians Code referring to slaves/servants [οἱ δοῦλοι]. Holman takes the paraenesis to 'servants' (KJV) to apply to a 'clerk under the engineer' on a railway-building project. The narrator and said clerk, Paul Manning, has to explain the reasons for a longer than usual absence, namely:

> ...business and the necessity of attending strictly to the orders of a new superintendent, who had not yet learned trust, much less indulgence.
> The minister nodded his approval of my conduct, and said – 'Right, Paul! "Servants, obey in all things your masters according to the flesh." I had my fears lest you had too much licence under Edward Holdsworth.'[131]

Edward Holdsworth, Paul's first superintendent, has been attractive to the narrator's youthful perceptions; but it is his 'too much licence' that is later the source of grief in the family. The hierarchical household code that operates in the home and fields is seen here to be no less applicable, by the minister at least, in industrial and commercial settings, and to be part of an ordered universe that causes suffering when it is disturbed.

In contrast, in Gaskell's 'My Lady Ludlow' the central portrait is of an aristocrat whose character is sympathetically treated but whose views are nevertheless shown to be inadequate, and from the narrator's perspective in the mid-nineteenth century, old-fashioned. The narration is again a retrospect of some fifty years previously. Submission from the people on

---

130. See, e.g., Sarah Dredge, 'Opportunism and Accommodation: *The English Woman's Journal* and the British Mid-Nineteenth-Century Women's Movement', *Women's Studies* 34 (2005), pp.133–57. It is the movement associated with *The English Woman's Journal* that has retrospectively been referred to as First-Wave Feminism.

131. Mrs. Gaskell, 'Cousin Phillis' [1863–64], in *Cousin Phillis and Other Tales* (London: J.M. Dent, n.d.), p.55.

the estate to their masters and to the Lady of the Manor is demanded and on the whole given, yet the characters who flourish at the end of the tale are those, women and men, who are bold and self-assertive, challenging the social hierarchy, though also respectful to its representatives. This reflects an ethos where the distinction of modern socio-economic relations from 'feudal' ones was not yet realized, or was rejected as illegitimate.[132] As these stories show, members of an economic enterprise could be treated as the moral equivalent of a family, and a paternal authority would distribute tasks and benefits.

Lady Ludlow's hierarchical world order is explicitly of submission under God, the king and those in authority. There are clear resonances of the Household Codes (or 1 Pet. 2.13-15) in her stated world order (and also of 1 Cor. 7.20-21):

> I believe...that education is a bad thing, if given indiscriminately. It unfits the lower orders for their duties, the duties to which they are called by God; of submission to those placed in authority over them; of contentment with that state of life to which it has pleased God to call them, and of ordering themselves lowly and reverently to their betters.[133]

It is particularly in the matter of education that Lady Ludlow is most opposed by other characters, and by the author in the outcome of the tale. Two women are permitted by the narrative, followed by the reluctant acceptance of Lady Ludlow, to 'usurp' an authority not belonging to their sex, or to their sex and social station. Miss Galindo takes on clerical and accounting work, and Bessie Gibson, the illegitimate daughter of one of Lady Ludlow's servants, receives an education and teaches at the local school. We learn the consequences of this in a final, short, extraordinary paragraph: 'I never saw my dear lady again. She died in eighteen hundred and fourteen... As I dare say you know, the Reverend Henry Gregson is now vicar of Hanbury, and his wife is the daughter of Mr Gray and Miss Bessy.' That is, the illegitimate but educated Bessie has married the Vicar; and the poacher's son, also 'indiscriminately' educated, succeeds as Vicar, and marries the daughter of that marriage. *This* is the surviving, flourishing household, sanctioned by the Church, at the end of the narrative, while Lady Ludlow's nine aristocratic children have predeceased her. This is a subtle, but thorough, subversion of the 'unchanging' hierarchical social and political world-order upheld by a

132. Cf. Misner, 'Paternalism', pp.712–13.

133. Mrs. Gaskell, 'My Lady Ludlow' [1858], in *Cousin Phillis and Other Tales*, p.203.

strong tradition of interpretation of the Pauline paraenesis.[134] The implied author is not sympathetic, in the rewards given to her characters, to Lady Ludlow's interpretation of scripture, in so far as this oppresses or stunts the lives of these people. There is no fundamental challenge to the hierarchies of the institutions, scripturally defined – of Church, Society and Marriage – within which they live, but some patterns of that retrospective world order have, the novelist demonstrates, passed away.

This interpretative strategy of consciously engaging positively with a tradition of interpretation, and at the same time asserting or demonstrating its falseness or inadequacy, appears again, more explicitly, in Brontë (§8.5.c below). The construct of the 'summit dialogue' between authors valorised by some commentators (see §6.2, etc.), where one reception consciously responds to an earlier instantiation, has not been easy to discover in either of my compilations – neither in Chapter 7 nor here. By choosing some quasi-canonical authors such as Chaucer, Shakespeare and Milton, there may be some assumptions of influence or 'trajectory'. Between Gaskell and Brontë this might be further defended: Gaskell wrote *The Life of Charlotte Brontë* (1857) at the request of Charlotte's father, and the connection is credited with a role in her own literary development.[135] Gaskell also corresponded with Dickens, and most of her shorter works were published serially in *Household Words*, edited by Dickens. That they knew each other's works does not, of course, establish a 'trajectory' in their reception of the Pauline paraenesis, but the 'summit dialogue' is often not more explicit than this in other constructs of a 'tradition of reception'.[136]

8.5.c. Charlotte Brontë[137]

Differences over the submission of women to men, of laity to the clergy, and of workers to mill-owners run throughout Charlotte Brontë's *Shirley* (1849), with explicit reference to Pauline texts and an indication of questions about the nature of biblical interpretation. It is a retrospect of about forty years previously. This is a recurring device in novels of the period (cf. Gaskell's fiction, §8.5.b above, that allows for reflections on changing attitudes to, for example, social and domestic order. Katharine

---

134. In England in 1909, a commentator can still refer to the 'divinely founded' and 'unchanging institution' of social life, which includes 'servants and masters': Robinson, *Ephesians*, p.170 (cited in §4.6.b).

135. Cf. Nancy S. Weyant, *The Cambridge Companion to Elizabeth Gaskell* (Cambridge: Cambridge University Press, 2007), pp.xi–xx.

136. See the reflections on this in, e.g., §§7.2.b and 7.5.

137. Reception is of 1 Tim. 2.11-12.

Burdekin (§8.6.a below), conversely, uses the setting of a dystopic future. Both devices allow for a conscious realignment of the *Erwartungs-horizont.* In *Shirley*, the retrospective setting places some hierarchical values before an implied reader whose more 'modern' perspective is more liberal, but who nevertheless respects social and religious tradition.

The two central characters, Caroline Helstone and Shirley Keeldar, are two independently minded gentlewomen. Shirley is a mill-owner at a time of industrial unrest and threats to the livelihood of the mill workers. The role of the clergy is in flux too, though the author looks back on the period as more fortunate in its *scarcity* of the new type of clergy (of whom, more later):

> 'Of late years…an abundant shower of curates has fallen upon the north of England; but in eighteen-hundred-eleven-twelve that affluent rain had not descended… The present successors of the apostles, disciples of Dr. Pusey and tools of the Propaganda, were at that time being hatched under cradle-blankets or undergoing regeneration by nursery-baptism in wash-hand basins.'[138]

By portraying thus, in their undignified infancy, those who will later make claims of authority, the narrator suggests that these claims may be unwarranted and risible – a suggestion later made explicit.

Biblical interpretation is raised as an explicit debate in one passage. Joe Scott, overseer at the mill, says to Caroline and Shirley: 'I think women are a kittle and a forward generation; and I've a great respect for the doctrines delivered in the second chapter of St. Paul's first Epistle to Timothy… "Let the women learn in silence, with all subjection".' When asked to apply this, he says, 'Women is to take their husbands' opinion, both in politics and religion; it's wholesomest for them'. The women protest and he asks, 'And what is your reading, Miss Helstone, o' these words o' St. Paul's?' Caroline appeals to possibilities of lexical distinction and historical circumstance: just those resources, or resorts, which we saw operating in exegetical analyses in Chapters 4 and 5:

> 'Hem! I – I account for them in this way; he wrote that chapter for a particular congregation of Christians, under peculiar circumstances, and besides, I daresay, if I could read the original Greek, I should find that many of the words had been wrongly translated, perhaps misapprehended altogether.'

She then hypothesises some radical readings on this basis:

138. Brontë, *Shirley*, pp.3–4.

'It would be quite possible, I doubt not, with a little ingenuity, to give the passage quite a contrary turn; to make it say, "Let the woman speak out whenever she sees fit to make an objection";– "It is permitted to a woman to teach and to exercise authority as much as may be. Man, meantime, cannot do better than hold his peace" – and so on.'
'That willn't wash, Miss.'[139]

Caroline's assertion, that the author 'wrote that chapter for a particular congregation..., under peculiar circumstances' without being able to say what those circumstances were, is by no means an unfair parody of exegetical endeavour. Barrett (and others) assert just such an importance of the occasionality of Rom. 13.1, but without being able to identify the nature of the occasion: 'and there may well have been good reasons, unknown to us...'[140] (Some of Barrett's readers too may think, 'That willn't wash'.)[141] In *Shirley*, this alternative exegesis is represented, with conscious humour, as speculative and not securely founded. Nevertheless, *this* is the reading that effectively operates in the novel, and for the author. The novel itself, published under an un-gendered name, is a didactic act of a woman directed to men and women readers in contravention of the cited verse, 1 Tim. 2.12.

Moreover, Caroline later makes an application of this verse, in very much the way she speculates that one might do 'with a little ingenuity'. It is made in the face of what she perceives as an oppressive, unwarranted exercise of authority, of 'a tyranny', and in relation to subjection clergy – who 'talk to poor folk fair as if they thought they were beneath them'.[142] Miss Ainley is a poor, elderly spinster maid who is conscripted to administer a fund, provided by Shirley Keeldar, for the alleviation of the poor. Miss Ainley wishes to consult the clergy – to whom she is wholly deferential. Shirley trusts the rectors – 'they had some experience, some sagacity' – but will not let Miss Ainsley consult the curates. The authorial perspective here is Shirley's: submission is impossible to the curates 'who in their trivial arrogance, were hardly worthy to tie [Miss Ainley's] patten-strings'. It is to them that Caroline applies the paraenesis of younger to 'elder' (1 Pet. 5.5), but also, more strikingly, the paraenesis to women of 1 Tim. 2.11: 'they must be set aside, kept down, and taught that subordination and silence best became their years and capacity'.[143]

---

139. Brontë, *Shirley*, p.258.
140. Barrett, *Romans*, p.244 (cited in §5.2.d).
141. E.g. (though differently expressed) Guerra, *Romans*, p.161.
142. Brontë, *Shirley*, p.254.
143. Brontë, *Shirley*, p.210.

There is some external evidence of such an ethos of clerical tyranny, and from Edward Pusey himself – who was seen by Brontë as author or inspirer of some it.[144] In fact, Pusey supported the Anglican sisterhoods (parish workers) and their independence from the male clergy, and accused Arthur Stanton of being 'very much wedded to the modern idea of the clergy, to have everything in their parishes under their own control'. His own view was that for the clergy 'to interfere or check or wish to control any work, which religious women wish to set about in their parish [would] be the most horrible tyranny'. He especially deprecates young clergy giving orders to older women: 'I think that it is a wrong ambition of men, to wish to have the direction of the work of women. I should fear that it would be for the injury of both.'[145] That Brontë and Pusey with their different perspectives both protest at an inappropriate submission of women to clergy suggests that this was indeed part of mid-Victorian life-experience.

The two women, Shirley and Caroline, are represented as ones who respect the order of creation of Genesis, and want to find themselves in the ethos of the household codes, but lived praxis – specifically the lack of superiority in men (cf. Argula von Grumbach, §8.4), and life-observation of actual marriages – prevents these women playing the role scripture sets out and which they would like to fulfil:

> 'When they *are* good, they are the lords of creation... Indisputably a great, good, handsome man is the first of created things.'
> 'Above us?'
> 'I would scorn to contend for empire with him – I would scorn it. Shall my left hand dispute for precedence with my right?...'
> 'Men and women, husbands and wives quarrel horribly, Shirley.'
> 'Poor things! – poor, fallen, degenerate things! God made them for another lot – for other feelings.'
> 'But are we men's equals, or are we not?'
> 'Nothing ever charms me more than when I meet my superior – one who makes me sincerely feel that he is my superior.'
> 'Did you ever meet him?'
> 'I should be glad to see him any day; the higher above me so much the better; it degrades to stoop – it is glorious to look up. What frets me is, that when I try to esteem, I am baffled; when religiously inclined, there are but false gods to adore.'[146]

144. Brontë, *Shirley*, p.4, cited above.

145. George W.E. Russell, *Arthur Stanton: A Memoir* (London: Longman, Green, 1917), pp.153–70, cited in John Shelton Reed, *Glorious Battle: The Cultural Politics of Victorian Anglo-Catholicism* (Nashville: Vanderbilt University Press, 1996), p.208.

146. Brontë, *Shirley*, p.170.

There is a parallel here with the way reception struggles with Romans 13 in the light of corrupt rulers or bad laws (e.g. the Kairos theologians, §7.4.d).

Caroline Helstone at one stage concludes that, unexpectedly, she will not be married, which is 'the ordinary destiny', and so wonders what her 'duties' will be. (We shall see comparable questions in Flagg, §8.6.b below.) Caroline asks 'Where is my place in the world?', and reflects as follows:

> That is the question which old maids are puzzled to solve: other people solve it for them, by saying, 'Your place is to do good to others, to be helpful where help is wanted.' That is right in some measure, and a very convenient doctrine of the people who hold it; but I perceive that certain sets of human beings are very apt to maintain that other sets should give up their lives to them and their service, and then they requite them by praise… Does virtue lie in abnegation of self? I do not believe it. Undue humility makes tyranny: weak concession creates selfishness, submission to others…[147]

This analysis of submission causing tyranny appeared in Speght and Astell (§§8.4.b and 8.4.d above), and appears again in Elizabeth Cady Stanton,[148] and in Katherine Burdekin's 'crime against life' (§8.6.a below). Fanny Flagg's protagonist (§8.6.b below) attempts a number of ways of acting out humility, submission and abnegation which that narrative presents as both terrible and risible. We may not have in these iterations a real 'dialogue' between the authors – indeed, we do not – but these successive instantiations, by women, of the biblical paraenesis construct a repeated pattern of protest against other, 'normative' trends in its reception and application. In Brontë and Flagg there is another correlation: that their characters would attempt to obey the paraenesis if their life experiences offered the possibility: historical contingency is, observably, a major factor in co-determining how these texts are received in this 'tradition'.

8.6. Twentieth-century novels and a twenty-first-century TV drama

Church teaching maintained into the twentieth century a theology of the family and of marriage that associated them with the whole of an ordered, hierarchical society. Though the Church could no longer

---

147. Brontë, *Shirley*, p.138.

148. E.C. Stanton, 'The Christian Church and Women', *Index* (30 October, 6 November and 4 December 1884), p.1, cited by Gifford de Swarte, 'Politicizing the Sacred Texts', p.54.

maintain its claim to control marriage and education, women's (and children's) interests were understood to be protected and promoted by defending the rights of 'the family'. It was assumed that the order of the family included both the primacy of the husband in relation to the wife and their children, and the willing subjection and obedience of the wife, based on their different 'natures'. So, for example, the fourth encyclical of Leo XIII, on Marriage (1880), argues for this on scriptural grounds using Genesis (2.21-23) and the Pauline paraenesis:

> the mutual duties of husband and wife have been defined, and their several rights accurately established... The woman, because she is flesh of his flesh, and bone of his bone, must be subject to her husband and obey him; not, indeed, as a servant, but as a companion, so that her obedience shall be wanting in neither honour nor dignity [and citing Eph. 5.23-24].[149]

This teaching is effectively repeated in the later encyclical (1930) of Pius XI with its teaching that the order of the family: 'included both the primacy of the husband with regard to the wife and her children, and the ready subjection of the wife and her willing obedience [again citing Eph. 5.23-24]'.[150]

In Britain, the century begins with the violent clash over women's suffrage, and contested perceptions of behaviour appropriate for women:

> True to their word, the Suffragists marched on the House of Commons yesterday [18 November 1910], and the scenes witnessed exceeded in violence the utmost excesses of which even these militant women had previously been guilty. It was an unending picture of shameful reckless-ness. Never before have otherwise sensible women gone so far in forget-ting their womanhood.[151]

8.6.a. Katharine Burdekin[152]

Katharine Burdekin's dystopia, *Swastika Night* (1937), was written during the height of the Third Reich in Germany, and before the outbreak of the Second World War. It depicts a world some hundreds of years after the Nazi party has been globally victorious, and Hitler deified.

149. Leo XIII, *Arcanum divinae sapientiae*, On Christian Marriage [1880] (http://www.vatican.va/holy_father/leo_xiii/encyclicals/documents/hf_l-xiii_enc_ 10021880 _ arcanum_en.html), 11.

150. Pius XI, *Casti Connubii*, On Christian Marriage [1930] (http://www. vatican.va/holy_father/pius_xi/encyclicals/documents/hf_p-xi_enc_31121930_casti-connubii_en.html), 26.

151. *Daily Sketch*, Saturday 19 November 1910.

152. Reception is of the submission of women explicitly referred to 'St Paul'; including Tit. 2.4-5 and 1 Cor. 11.5-6.

It was almost certainly drawn on by George Orwell, an inveterate borrower, in the much more famous dystopia *Nineteen-Eighty-Four*.[153] Where Orwell offers no explanation of his regime's preoccupation with domination, power and violence, Burdekin does. She roots these firmly in a gender ideology of her ruling caste, and refers to this as the 'cult of masculinity'. In 1934, Goebbels, Nazi propaganda minister, gave an account of the gender ideology of Nazi Germany: 'The National Socialist movement is in its nature a masculine movement... While man must give to life the great lines and forms, it is the task of women out of her inner fullness and inner eagerness to fill these lines and forms with colour.'[154] The gender construct of Burdekin's totalitarian regime resembles that of the pre-fascist ideologue Otto Weininger, whose book *Geschlecht und Charakter* (1903) catalogues purported gender characteristics. He draws on Aristotle's characterisation of the male as perfected and active 'form', and the female as 'defective' and passive 'matter': woman therefore has a submissive 'nature', needing to be shaped by man.[155]

Burdekin projects a dystopia of a totalitarian subjugation of women, in the converse of the strategy where women promote or create *utopian* female communities, in literature or in life, to avoid subjugation (of which there are far more frequent examples).[156] Women are complicit in their own subjugation, in Burdekin's analysis, and so help to sustain the 'cult of masculinity'. They have been reduced in her dystopia to a level of breeding animals because they have believed in their own inferiority – and their 'submission' is their 'crime against life'.[157] This can be compared with Caroline Helstone's conclusion in *Shirley*.[158]

153. Cf. Daphne Patai, 'Introduction', in Katharine Burdekin, *Swastika Night* [1937] (London: Lawrence & Wishart, 1985), p.xii.

154. Cited in Clifford Kirkpatrick, *Germany: Its Women and Family Life* (Indianapolis: Bobbs-Merrill Co., 1938), p.116.

155. Otto Weininger, *Sex and Character: An Investigation of Fundamental Principles* (ed. Daniel Steuer; trans. Ladislaus Löb; Bloomington: Indiana University Press, 2005); cited in Patai, 'Introduction', p.ix; cf. Aristotle, *Physics* 1.9 192a, 20–24 (p.31) (cited in §4.5.a).

156. E.g. Sarah Scott creates a 'rational paradise' in *Millennium Hall* [1762] (ed. Gary Kelly; Peterborough: Broadview, 1995). In the real world, her sister Elizabeth Montagu was one of the originators of the protean feminist 'bluestocking' movement.

157. Burdekin, *Swastika Night*, p.107.

158. Brontë, *Shirley*, p.138 (§8.5.c above).

Like Cady Stanton, Burdekin traces the root of woman's subjection to the teachings of the institutional church.[159] Burdekin, however, presents citation of the Pauline paraenesis as a transparently 'unreliable' reception. The Christians in this dystopia are on the fringe of the social structure, in a role socially like that of the Roma or 'gypsies' in the early twentieth century but ideologically as 'a race of subhuman people, ranking even below women in general'.[160] One Nazi Knight has a fragment of tradition about Christians:

> Women had a very high place in the old Christian theology. Theoretically, their soul value was equal to the men's. Practically of course it was not... but when the Reduction of Women started the Christian men acquiesced in it, probably because there always had been in the heart of the religion a hatred of the beauty of women and a horror of the sexual power beautiful women with the right of choice and rejection have over men.[161]

Christians are the only other ones to have any tradition (with many clues to the reader that it is an unreliable tradition) of how things have come about. The code for households and gender relations, where women 'obey' and 'love' their husbands[162] (Tit. 2.4 and 5), is attributed to Paul: 'The Christian way of treating women [*they live submissive but at home, in contrast to the women's compounds of the "infidels"*] is the only possible way. It was laid down once and for all by the blessed Paul, brother of our Lord, and even in a thousand years of Error, Christians did not depart from it.'[163]

One custom in particular marks an inverted 'reception' of 1 Cor. 11.2-16, and again there is an attribution to Paul of the ethic:

> 'Why do you think women have their heads shaved, Joseph?'
> 'I don't know why *your* infidel women, whom you keep shut up in pens like bitches on heat, have their heads shaved, for a superficial following of the blessed Paul the brother of our Lord will not save any of you in the Judgement. But *our* women are shaved because the blessed Paul said, "A woman's hair is her shame, therefore let her be shorn." And its truth is evident in the fact that a man's hair is his glory and his strength lies in it, like Samson in the den of lions.'[164]

---

159. Stanton sees it as a subversion of Jesus' own message of equality, and is explicit in pointing an accusing finger to the *Haustafeln*, and to 1 Tim. 2: 'Christian Church and Women', p.1.

160. Burdekin, *Swastika Night*, p.71.

161. Burdekin, *Swastika Night*, p.73.

162. Burdekin, *Swastika Night*, p.184.

163. Burdekin, *Swastika Night*, p.184.

164. Burdekin, *Swastika Night*, p.175.

The same identification of *submission* with *servility* is made by Klausner, in the same period of Nazi dominance, in a reception of Rom. 13.1 (§5.2.c).

As we have seen, the conscious disparity between the reader's horizon and a tradition of interpreting the paraenesis has parallels in Gaskell and Brontë (§§8.5.b and 8.5.c above). The identification of Paul as the source of a strand of misogyny in Christian tradition was adumbrated in the Towneley play (§8.3.a above) and will appear again in Flagg (§8.6.b below).

8.6.b. Fannie Flagg[165]

In 1963, in an encyclical on 'justice' and 'liberty', John XXIII identifies three 'signs of our times: the rise of the working class, the participation of women in public life, and the emergence of new nations'[166] (in an interesting echo of Gal. 3.28). In the second half of the twentieth century, the language of 'complementarity' rather than inequality is sponsored both among conservative Evangelicals (see Piper and Grudem below) and in the Catholic Church. Pope Paul VI supports some political solutions to discrimination against women but qualifies this by saying, 'We do not have in mind that false equality which would deny the distinctions laid down by the Creator himself and which would be in contradiction with women's proper role, which is of capital importance, at the heart of the family as well as within society'.[167] Feminist analysis of culture, politics and religion establishes itself in the period,[168] published alongside popular and academic work that responds to, opposes or ignores it. Its impact in some areas is profound.

Fannie Flagg's novel *Fried Green Tomatoes at the Whistle Stop Café* (first published in 1987) includes a comedic representation of anti-feminist movements in the United States that developed in the 1980s. At the centre of the novel is a middle-aged woman, Evelyn Couch, who

165. Reception is of 1 Tim. 2.11–12.

166. John XXIII, *Pacem In Terris*, On Establishing Universal Peace in Truth, Justice, Charity, and Liberty [1963], (http://www.vatican.va/holy_father/john_xxiii/encyclicals/documents/hf_j-xxiii_enc_11041963_ pacem_en.html, accessed 14 April 2012).

167. Paul VI, 'Octogesima Adveniens' (A Call to Action), Apostolic Letter 1971, 13 (http://www.vatican.va/holy_father/paul_vi/apost_letters/documents/hf_p-vi_apl_19710514_octogesima-adveniens_en.html, accessed 14 May 2012).

168. This is part of what is termed 'second-wave' feminism; see, e.g., Imelda Whelehan, *Modern Feminist Thought: From the Second Wave to 'Post-feminism'* (Edinburgh: Edinburgh University Press, 1995). 'First-wave feminism' was noted as contemporaneous with Gaskell's work (§8.5.b above).

moves from oppression through anger to some sense of wholeness, partly through her friendship with an old woman who recounts tales of her youth in the overtly racist and sexist South, with some astonishing subversions of those public values.

Evelyn, when her husband is having an affair, 'wondered where her group was, the place where she would fit in'.[169] This has a resonance with Caroline Helstone's question in Brontë's novel *Shirley*, who wonders, *if* she is not to be married, 'Where is my place in the world?'[170] If the security of 'the household', as the Codes define it, leaves you *outside* of it, where else in society is there a place, a role? So Evelyn attends a group called 'The Complete Woman' to try to save her marriage. This organization believed that women 'could find complete happiness if they, in turn, would dedicate their entire lives to just making their man happy... Their leader had informed them that all the rich and successful career women out there who appeared to be so happy were, in reality, terribly lonely and miserable and secretly envied them their happy Christian homes.'[171]

The fictional organization has a number of parallels in American society,[172] and there are some close expressions to its ideology from the biblical interpretation of John Piper and Wayne Grudem, contemporary with the publication of this novel. Piper and Grudem offer readings of the scriptural injunctions as 'a response to Evangelical Feminism' and to *recover* 'Biblical Manhood and Womanhood'. They too believe that 'there are roles that strain the personhood of man and woman too far to be appropriate, productive and healthy for the overall structure of home and society. Some roles would involve kinds of leadership and expectations of authority and forms of strength as to make it unfitting for a woman to fill the role.'[173]

In *Fried Green Tomatoes*, the Pauline submission texts explicitly operate as a support of this worldview, even when they are not its only basis: 'Of course, even though [Evelyn] was not religious, it was a

169. Fannie Flagg, *Fried Green Tomatoes at the Whistle Stop Café* [1987] (London: Vintage, 1992), p.42.

170. Brontë, *Shirley*, p.138 (cited in §8.5.c above).

171. Flagg, *Fried Green Tomatoes*, p.42.

172. E.g. Laura Doyle, *The Surrendered Wife: A Practical Guide to Finding Intimacy, Passion, and Peace with Your Man* (New York: Simon & Schuster, 1999). Doyle recommends that wives 'give up unnecessary control and responsibility' and 'trust their husbands in every aspect of marriage, from sexual to financial'.

173. John Piper, 'A Vision of Biblical Complementarity: Manhood and Womanhood Defined According to the Bible', in Piper and Grudem (eds.), *Recovering Biblical Manhood*, pp.25–55 (51).

comfort to know that the Bible backed her up in being a doormat. Hadn't the apostle St. Paul said for women not to usurp power over the men, but to be in silence?'[174] It is 1 Tim. 2.11-12 ('to usurp authority over the man', KJV) that has fed this secular response most strongly, and once again this is explicitly identified as Paul's legacy. The comedic deconstruction in Evelyn's response has correspondences in the deconstruction of the ethic of female subordination in Chaucer and Dickens (§§8.3.b and 8.5.a above).

In a portrait of the *negativity* of women's submission to men, common to feminist perspectives, Flagg's Evelyn is characterised as a woman who has been terrified of displeasing men:

> She had stayed a virgin so she wouldn't be called a tramp or a slut; had married so she wouldn't be called frigid; had children so she wouldn't be called barren; had not been a feminist because she didn't want to be called queer and a man-hater; never nagged or raised her voice so she wouldn't be called a bitch...[175]

Piper, indeed, asserts that it 'puts a strain on the humanity' of both men and women when there is not the right ranking of women under men. He does not thereby give a justification for the above degradation of women by men, but does endorse the masculist view that sees women's power as a *disorder* that needs correcting. His advocacy of a form of submission as the fulfilment of scriptural injunctions includes this (cf. Milton's description of the primal relationship in *Paradise Lost*, §8.4.c above):

> There are ways for a woman to interact even with a male subordinate that signal to him and others her endorsement of his mature manhood. Her demeanour – the tone and style and disposition and discourse of her ranking position – can signal clearly her affirmation of the unique role that men should play in relationship to women owing to their sense of responsibility to protect and lead.[176]

Conversely, men's competitive display of power (which is part of the ethos that frightens women like Evelyn) is God-given for Piper, Grudem and other contributors to *Recovering Biblical Manhood and Womanhood*. Women should not seek to control 'heated disputes among men'; this male behaviour is 'not necessarily owing to male egotism, but to a natural and good penchant given by God'.[177]

---

174. Flagg, *Fried Green Tomatoes*, p.43.
175. Flagg, *Fried Green Tomatoes*, pp.236–37.
176. Piper, 'Biblical Complementarity', p.50.
177. Piper, 'Biblical Complementarity', p.52.

The Ten Steps to Complete Happiness recommended by the fictional group, 'The Complete Woman', in Flagg's novel are characterised by explicitly sexual submission. Evelyn tries greeting her husband at the door, 'nude, wrapped in Saran wrap': her husband is appalled. Advocacy of sexual submission is countered in the novel not by argument but by mundane realities of lived experience:[178] 'pretty soon, the group leader, Nadine Fingerhutt, got a divorce and had to go to work, so the group just sort of fizzled out. Then, after a while, Ed stopped seeing that woman and things settled down.'[179]

These contingent factors ensure the demise of the group and the survival of Evelyn's marriage. In this novel, these are, in the end, more substantial and more reliable, than acting out patterns of gender submission derived from the Bible or other sources. Where Piper and Grudem derive gender roles that are 'productive and healthy for the overall structure of home and society' (substantially) from a tradition of reception of the *Hasutafeln*, it is Evelyn's 'lived praxis' that, in the end, is determinant for applying (what she receives as) the teaching of 'the apostle St. Paul'.

8.6.c. *The West Wing*[180]

Contemporary story-telling is as much in televisual or cinematic form as novels, and there are some instances where these combine reception of biblical texts with something like the moral seriousness[181] of a strand in English literature. A contemporary American reception of the Ephesians household-code and the exhortation to mutual submission comes from Alex Graves's series for television about a fictional American administration, *The West Wing*.

The ethos of the presidency and the character of the President are established in the series as in the liberal wing of the American establishment – with concerns for justice and radical possibilities but awareness of the constraints of expediency and the pressure of majority opinion and the *status quo*. Matters of religion and ethics are regularly part of the material. Relationships within the White House are robust but also deferential. The president is courteous to subordinates, respectful of the

---

178. Historical contingency has had a similar prevalence over contested interpretation of other parts of the paraenesis: for example, 'The abolitionists did not persuade the slave-owners; slavery ceased to have an ethical claim in American society because a war was won and lost': Meeks, 'American Slavery', p.248.

179. Flagg, *Fried Green Tomatoes*, p.43.

180. Reception is of Eph. 5.21, 22 and 25.

181. Cf. Leavis, *Great Tradition*, p.1 (cited at the beginning of this chapter).

opinions of female officials, and of his wife, but his personal authority and status is never fundamentally in doubt. The ethos is hierarchical with liberal aspirations – this is a 'benevolent patriarchy'.[182]

From the third series (2000), in an episode called 'War Crimes', an opening scene[183] is of the President and his wife, Jed and Abbey Bartlett, coming into the office after a church service, in dispute over the homily – 'a perfectly lovely homily on Ephesians 5.21' according to Abbey who cites 5.25, 'Husbands, love your wives...', with approval. Her husband complains,

> J.B.   She skipped over the part that says, 'Wives, be subject to your husbands'.
> A.B.   I do skip over that.
> J.B.   Why?
> A.B.   Because it's stupid.[184]

The President's criticism of the homily is directed at style (the 'hackery' of the sermon) rather than substance. He privileges the paraenesis to *mutual* submission (see the discussion on the transformative force of Eph. 5.21 on 5.22, in §4.6.a). He says, 'I have no problem with Ephesians... It has nothing to do with husbands and wives: it's all of us. Be subject to one another.' He applies it to the predatory style of journalism prominent in one of the episode's storylines: he asks, 'How do we end this cycle? – "Be subject to one another".' He shortly after meets his Vice President and asks him, 'What can I do to be of subject [*sic*] to you?' This solecism is presumably made, in the writer's conscious or unconscious mind, by analogy with the more usual (and grammatical) phrase, 'How can I be of service?' If so, this is a sub-merged correspondence of one who submits with one who serves, which corresponds to the strategies that link the lexis with other Pauline expressions (examples in §§4.6.c and 10.2).

The episode is one where there are competing interests, and the necessity of co-operation, but no self-sacrificial submission to the other's interest. This is a reading that ostensibly privileges the universal

182. Cf. discussion in §5.3.b.

183. This scene can be accessed online (YouTube): browse for 'Ephesians' and 'West Wing'.

184. Alex Graves (director), Allison Abner (story), Aaron Sorkin (teleplay), 'War Crimes', *The West Wing*, 3rd Season, Episode 6 (Warner Bros, 2000). There are parallels in academic reception to this verdict of 'stupid': Käsemann (*Romans*, p.355) argues that the thesis which makes Rom. 13.1 a 'universal apostolic decree' is 'absurd' (when it attempts to combine *theologia crucis* with submission to authorities; see §10.5).

application over a household hierarchy, and the injunction for the love of a husband over that for the subjection of a wife (examples in §4.6.a); but it is a reading that is perhaps as unresolved as the ethos of this White House.

The husband–wife paraenesis is not pursued: 'it's stupid' gets the last word on this. It is also the last word in something of a trajectory of deconstruction in the drama and fiction sampled. In the Towneley play the submission paraenesis is undermined in its estimate of women; in Chaucer, Dickens and Flagg it is subverted comedically; in Burdekin it is distorted in a savage parody; here, it is simply rejected.

8.7. Interim case-study evaluation

This second construction of a compilation-history of reception was undertaken to evaluate some contrary claims about *Wirkungsgeschichte* and reception history. It responds to the question of what is *forfeited* if the selection does not valorise reception, in a progressive process of interpretation, which is 'largely determined by the major voices of the Christian theological tradition'.[185] It responds to the question of what is *achieved* if the selection valorises instead reception that challenges conservative traditions and recovers neglected aspects of the interpretation of a text.

The selection here of moments in English literary 'tradition' fulfils some of the characteristics of the construct of a 'progressive process': that is, a Jaussian strategy of a diachronic series, with synchronic 'cross-sections', moments in a literary series, with analysis of genre and context 'to make the literary horizon of a specific historical moment comprehensible'.[186] Conversely, several of its shortcomings highlight *the fragility of claims* about such constructs, including those privileging a 'summit dialogue' of exemplary or normative ecclesial voices, 'principal commentators'. Both the successes and failures of the venture offer a useful, partial, critique of the claims made about the *Wirkungsgeschichte* of biblical texts. It is by no means wholly successful, but nor, I suggest, are constructs like those of Parris or Riches wholly successful.

The chapter *succeeds* in supporting the insight that 'the Bible's practical effect on history and culture often becomes most clearly visible where it moves out of the hands of the scribes and scholars into the life of

---

185. Rowland, Review of David Parris, *Reception Theory and Biblical Hermeneutics* (cited in §6.2).

186. Jauss, *Aesthetic of Reception*, pp.36 and 37 (cited in §2.2).

Church and society'.[187] There is evidence here that understanding a text and its influence through trajectories of its reception can benefit from investigation of 'political or economic appropriations of the Bible..., literary...re-imaginings, and...everyday application of Scripture by the Christian laity...considered among the more focused insights of specialist scholars'.[188] The 'application', which for Gadamer is always involved in understanding,[189] is in most cases 'clearly visible'.

The chapter also succeeds in illustrating Gadamer's insight that when tradition conditions our thinking, the *disorientation provided by a challenging perspective* provides a way more clearly to understand our own reading perspective: 'we can open our eyes on a new perspective and experience detail invisible to the stationary observer'.[190] Luz's emphasis on renewal through *denominational* perspectives was not prominent: for example, Brontë's anti-Oxford-Movement perspective on patterns of subordination was actually endorsed by Pusey (§8.5.c above). The chapter does, however, respond to May and Meyer's challenge to seek to listen to 'silenced or stifled' voices rather than 'serve a dominator tradition'[191] and includes some of the reception characterised by Sherwood as 'backwaters and underbellies', traditions that use the text in ways subversive to a mainstream Christian tradition of reception. Material in this chapter could support the claim that this forms 'one of the vibrant uses of the "biblical" in Western culture' that can 'animate... biblical texts precisely by questioning their relevance'.[192]

It offers an opportunity to identify some reception that has 'held particular influence in...the daily life of the church, or more broadly in the history of ideas'.[193] The *iteration* of strategies for avoiding or subverting an (oppressive) reception of the paraenesis[194] contribute to an appreciation of the impact of the text through history. To this extent, it may be possible to use the language of 'contours' of a (literary) tradition in respect of these instantiations, but the field is too large and too diverse to refer to them as 'defining moments of a tradition's contours'.

187. Bockmuehl, 'Commentator's Approach', p.62 (cited in §6.2.a).
188. Knight, '*Wirkungsgeschichte*', pp.138–39 (§6.2.a).
189. Gadamer, *Truth and Method*, p.306 (§1.1.a).
190. Nicholls, '*Parkour*', p.11 (cited in §6.2).
191. May and Meyer, 'Unity of the Bible', p.148 (§6.3).
192. Sherwood, *Afterlives*, p.208 (§6.3).
193. Thiselton, *First Corinthians*, p.196 (§6.2).
194. There is a comparable subversion of a tradition in popular, cultural reception of Rom. 13: these are particularly characterised by subversive or cynical reference to authorities as 'the powers-that-be'.

The same assessment can be made of the sample in the previous chapter (§7.3), the later applications of Rom. 13.1. The judgments that identify 'principal', 'exemplary' and 'normative' reception in compilation-histories are part of the construction of meaning made by the compiler, as well as discoverable patterns in the tradition. In the process of selection and construction, these judgments reflect *prejudgments* as part of a legacy of the historical trajectory. When interpretation is 'largely determined by the major voices of the Christian theological tradition' there are prejudgments operating on the concepts of 'theology', the selection of 'exemplary' voices and the nature of 'tradition'.

Here in Chapter 8, what has been (further) problematised is the endeavour to offer 'examples which instantiate continuities and dis-continuities of interpretation with specific traditions'.[195] The chapter illustrates the complexity, plurality and fluidity of what constitutes a 'tradition' of reception, and the relationship that an example of reception may have to its predecessors. Jauss worked with a much tighter, much more restricted model, of a series of receptions.[196] Moreover, I have pushed the question still further. Not only have I allowed 'reception' to embrace a *nexus of several texts* on the silencing or subordination of women (because this is how they are received in this 'tradition'), I have also included as 'reception' some allusive treatment of the (dis)obedi-ence of wives (e.g. Chaucer and Dickens, §§8.3.b and 8.5.a) where 'reception of biblical texts' may be sliding into a still less identified 'history of ideas'. If reception history concerns the legacy of traditionary texts, *this is the way* that that legacy is reflected in this 'tradition'.

The construction of reception here (in the present chapter and also in §7.4) must still be vulnerable to Froehlich's warning about the 'tracing of random texts in…a bewildering zigzag course'. It confirms the impor-tance of Rowland's observation that 'actual interpreters are formed by traditions much more diverse and eclectic than can be easily encapsu-lated by this or that theological label'.[197] Even more must this be the case where a number of traditions is operating: for example, the pattern of humanist polemic, which undergoes many configurations in a particular centuries-long debate (the *Querelle des Femmes*), and is fitted with a scriptural preface in Astell's tract (§8.4.d). The twentieth-century recep-tion introduces a further indeterminacy, which Callaway describes as that

195. Thiselton, *First Corinthians*, p.196 (§6.2).

196. E.g. his account of the changing reception of Flaubert's *Madame Bovary* from 1857 to mid-twentieth century: Jauss, *Aesthetic of Reception*, pp.27–28 (cited in §1.1.b).

197. Rowland, 'Review of Parris' (cited in §6.2).

of 'a culture grappling with an identity shaped by the Bible but not versed in it'.[198] The problem with Froehlich's warning is that it advises avoidance of what may actually be the case: reception through history may indeed offer interesting details and a bewildering course. We saw that Parris concedes that a tradition of interpretation is 'a serpentine path, with twists, turns, and dead ends' rather than 'a steady march towards a higher, "truer" understanding of a text or the past'.[199] My sample is destabilizing for a systematic management of reception. It points to the inevitability that pragmatic attempts to make the hermeneutical process manageable *impose methodological or ideological frameworks*, and *these do not arise spontaneously* from the full reception of the texts in history, but from the compilers of the reception and the traditions in which they themselves live and read.

It is difficult to produce, from this body of material, reception that demonstrably 'shapes the "pre-understandings" of subsequent generations of interpreters'.[200] Equally difficult is the identification of 'paradigm shifts', which depends on being able to identify single changes in systematic or chronological sequence. Constructions that achieve this more convincingly operate with much more restricted principles of selection (e.g. Parris's case study and Riches's commentary). Parris defines the task as a programme for identifying *mediation* of differences, and *continuity* within a tradition: 'The summit-dialogue is a heuristic tool that allows us to identify the competing trajectories of interpretation and at the same time observe the history of mediation within that tradition that creates continuity'.[201] This agenda, which also describes the core of other practice (including Luz, Thiselton and Riches), is not one for investigating, and valorizing, *diffuse reception, disrupted process or subverted tradition*. It is, however, a programme that offers an iterative engagement with the horizon of expectation of hypothetical first-reception, engaging much more with the tools of historical-critical exegesis, notably absent from much of *this* chapter.

One further reflection is necessary. *Wirkungsgeschichte* is an account of how we construct meaning from texts. The work of hermeneutics (for Gadamer) is 'not to develop a procedure of understanding, but to clarify the conditions in which understanding takes place'.[202] If this compilation

198. Callaway, 'What's the Use?', p.14.
199. Rowland, Review of David Parris, *Reception Theory and Biblical Hermeneutics*, pp.19–20 (cited in §6.2).
200. Thiselton, *First Corinthians*, p.196 (cited in §6.2).
201. Parris, *Reception Theory*, p.221 (cited in §6.2).
202. Gadamer, *Truth and Method*, p.295 (cited in §1.1.a).

is only a 'study of effects',[203] the effects can be observed without our subjective involvement, because the object of it is 'dead enough to have only historical interest'.[204] *Wirkungsgeschichte* describes a process where historical consciousness should '*make conscious the prejudices governing our own understanding* so that the text, as another's meaning, can be isolated and valued on its own'.[205] In Gadamerian hermeneutics, we 'produce [tradition] ourselves inasmuch as we understand, participate in the evolution of tradition and hence further determine it ourselves'.[206] In compilation-histories of reception, there must be a key question about the understanding, historical contingency and 'tradition' of the *compiler* of reception.[207] Nguyen, reviewing *Galatians Through the Centuries*, comments: 'it is interesting to ponder how Riches' commentary…affects or influences the ongoing literary history of the text'.[208] A chapter such as this one in my case study is constructing meaning, not merely uncovering it, and it reflects, in some measure, 'the commonality that binds' *me*, as editor and interpreter of it, in traditions of reception of the Pauline paraenesis, and influences my own reception of the texts.[209] Indeed, the 'progressive progress' of reception in this chapter, and its legacy, is coherent to me in a way unlikely to be equalled by many other readers – it is, formatively, part of my tradition. This is a key feature of Gadamer's hermeneutics, which Jack Mendelson summarises:

> One's interpretation of a particular subject matter stands in traditions of previous interpretations of the same subject. The totality of such 'effects' [*sic*] and ultimately the whole historical process linking subject and object constitute the hermeneutical situation of the knower. Effective history is the chain of past interpretations through which the preunderstanding of the interpreter is already linked with his object.[210]

Further evaluation of the practice represented by Chapters 7 and 8 (and also Chapters 3, 4 and 5) needs more investigation of Gadamer's concepts of tradition and prejudgment, and we move to this next (Chapter 9).

203. The (inadequate) rendering of '*Wirkungsgeschichte*' given by the *EBR* editors: Klauck *et al.*, 'The Project, Introduction', *EBR* (cited in §1.1.c).
204. Gadamer, *Truth and Method*, p.297 (cited in §1.1.a).
205. Gadamer, *Truth and Method*, p.298 (emphasis mine; cited in §1.1.a).
206. Gadamer, *Truth and Method*, p.293 (cited in §1.1.a).
207. Cf. Riches, *Galatians*, p.65 (cited in §6.2).
208. Nguyen, Review of John Riches, *Galatians Through the Centuries*, p.15.2.
209. Gadamer, *Truth and Method*, p.293 (cited in §1.1.a).
210. Mendelson, 'Habermas–Gadamer Debate', p.55.

Chapter 9

RECEPTION HISTORY AND THEOLOGICAL HERMENEUTICS

9.1. Introduction: whose tradition?

> The anticipation of meaning that governs our understanding of the text is
> not an act of subjectivity, but proceeds from the commonality that binds
> us to the tradition.[1]

The third group of hermeneutical issues for consideration in this work
are those reflecting on the prejudgments, interestedness and place in a
'tradition' of the interpreter, in contestations about 'subjectivism',
'conservatism', 'validity' and 'ideology' in biblical interpretation using
reception-historical methods. The criticisms made against Gadamer and
an assessment of how they can be answered – particularly in relation to
hypothetical first-reception and to aspects of theological hermeneutics in
biblical studies – form the basis of this chapter. (There is more on these
issues in Gadamer than in Jauss, but there is some consideration of Jauss
and deconstruction in §9.3, and of Jauss and ideology in §9.3.b.)

There are criticisms of Gadamer that find two quite different tendencies in his work. One is that Gadamer's position is 'subjectivist', because
he emphasises the variability, and plurality, of textual understanding
according to historical circumstances, rather than a (claimed) singularity
of authorial consciousness as the focus of 'validity' and 'objective'
meaning. This criticism, first made by E.D. Hirsch, is considered in §9.2.

The second is that in attempting to avoid such subjectivism, the
tendency of Gadamer's hermeneutics is inevitably conservative. If tradition determines the nature of interpretation, there is no basis from which
to critique 'normative' interpretation, and so, it is claimed, Gadamer
'ignores the fact that traditional interpretations can be ideologically
distorted'.[2] This challenge, made by Jürgen Habermas and others, is
considered in §9.3.

---

1. Gadamer, *Truth and Method*, p.293 (cited in §1.1.a).
2. Georgia Warnke, *Gadamer: Hermeneutics, Tradition and Reason* (Cambridge:
Polity, 1987), p.x.

These two criticisms have a close match with features of the contested practice in biblical interpretation analysed in Chapters 2 and 6: the contested validity and role of historical-critical methods, and the selection and organization of reception in relation to normative traditions of interpretation *or* privileging plurality, neglected reception and challenges to conservative traditions. A positive evaluation of diversity of perspective, and interpretation governed more by historical contingency than by a continuity with one tradition, can support the 'determination to recover aspects of traditions of interpretation which are less prominent',[3] and contest 'one single meaning...identified with the author's original intention'.[4] This may appear to other critics as 'subjectivist'. Conversely, if validity is held to be constituted by a tradition of interpretation, or by a primary datum established through historical-critical analysis, these investments may support the conservative impulse to valorise the 'most influential interpretations'[5] or a 'canon of exemplary commentators',[6] and/or a claimed continuity with a construction of first reception. Such investments may seem to offer no critique of conservative or 'normative' tradition.

The critique and (partial) defence of Gadamerian hermeneutics offered in §§9.2 and 9.3 is followed by their application to specifics of biblical interpretation in §§9.2.a, 9.3.a and 9.3.b. Some of the key issues are further tested in relation to reception of the case-study texts, in Chapter 10.

9.2. Subjectivism, and authorial intention

Key arguments levelled at Gadamer's 'subjectivism' relate to matters discussed in Chapter 2 concerning the perceived attempt of historical-critical commentaries to identify the 'original meaning' of texts, 'as intended by their authors'.[7] Such a location of 'meaning' has indeed,

3. Rowland, 'Pragmatic Approach', p.5 (cited in §6.3).
4. Sawyer, Rowland and Kovacs, 'Series Editors' Preface', in Kovacs and Rowland, *Revelation*, p.xi.
5. Parris, *Reception Theory*, p.219 (cited in §6.3).
6. Parris, *Reception Theory*, p.217 (cited in §6.2).
7. Luz, *Matthew in History*, p.7; cf. (e.g.) Nigel Watson: 'It is surely no exaggeration to say that the quest for authorial intention represents the fundamental aim of historical-critical exegesis... [U]ntil the rise of the so-called New Criticism in Britain and America some sixty years ago the quest for the meaning intended by the author was generally accepted as the fundamental aim of all literary studies': 'Authorial Intention: Suspect Concept for Biblical Scholars?', *Australian Biblical Review* 35 (1987), pp.6–13 (6).

in some quarters of biblical interpretation, survived or ignored the challenges of reader-response theory, socio-rhetorical criticism and deconstruction. Gadamer challenges the restriction of meaning by authorial intention or first reception. He makes a critique of Schleiermacher's 'psychological interpretation', which he characterises as ultimately a divinatory process, a placing of oneself within the whole framework of the author, an apprehension of the 'inner origin' of the composition of a work, a recreation of the creative act.[8]

As we have seen, for Gadamer the meaning of a text is 'always co-determined also by the historical situation of the interpreter':[9] he writes, 'Thus the reference to the original reader, like that to the meaning of the author, seems to offer only a very crude historic-hermeneutical criterion that cannot really limit the horizon of the text's meaning'.[10] It is this insight in Gadamer's hermeneutic that the editors of *Relegere* find determinative for reception history, which 'must actively interrogate the taken-for-granted idea that foundational texts are somehow fixed, that their essential natures can be distinguished from their subsequent reception'.[11]

E.D. Hirsch (one of the earliest English-language commentators on *Truth and Method*)[12] interprets the insight as advocating indeterminacy of meaning. Hirsch has been, and in some quarters remains, an influential voice in biblical studies in the rejection of plurality of meaning and the identification of the author as the focus of legitimacy and 'objective' meaning. 'Meaning' for Hirsch is properly determined by the author's intention. The range of 'meaning possibilities' that a text can represent is not defined by the interpreter but by the 'imaginative construction of the speaking subject'. The 'speaking subject' is the authorial consciousness that has shaped the text: 'to verify a text is simply to establish that the author probably meant what we construe his text to mean'. The task of the interpreter is 'to reproduce in himself the author's 'logic', his attitudes, his cultural givens, in short his world'.[13]

8. Gadamer, *Truth and Method*, p.186.
9. Gadamer, *Truth and Method*, p.296 (cited in §2.1).
10. Gadamer, *Truth and Method*, p.397.
11. Harding, Repphun and Sweetman, 'Focus and Scope'.
12. Hirsch, 'Gadamer's Theory of Interpretation', in his *Validity*, pp.245–64.
13. E.D. Hirsch, 'Objective Interpretation', *Publications of the Modern Language Association of America* 75.4 (1960), pp.463–79 (478).

Many scholars find Hirsch's hermeneutics conceptually inadequate and dated,[14] though Hirsch's influence in biblical interpretation is still 'praised by many scholars of diverse traditions'.[15] Donald Hagner's critique of Luz includes a Hirschean response, that Luz places 'new meanings' on the same level as the 'original sense', so that 'what the author may have intended...is regarded as having no special importance'.[16]

Hirsch's claim for the location of an 'objective' meaning in authorial intention presents a clear contrast with Gadamer, but does not make the case that Gadamer's hermeneutics can be characterised as subjectivist.[17] Certainly, Gadamer rejects appeals to any guarantee of objective meaning, which he sees as a rationalist principle brought into hermeneutics by Schleiermacher,[18] but he denies the identification of situatedness-of-interpretation with subjectivity. For Gadamer, both author and reader share an understanding of the subject-matter of the text. The author is another 'interpreter' of his own work:

> As an interpreter he has no automatic authority over the person who is simply receiving his work. Insofar as he reflects on his own work, he is his own reader. The meaning that he, as reader, gives his own work does not set the standard. The only standard of interpretation is the sense of his creation, what it 'means'. [This]...collapses the distinction between interpreter and author.[19]

Gadamer's analogies for this mutual participation in understanding (or 'total mediation'[20]) of author and reader focus on those of play and performance. He asserts 'the primacy of the play over the consciousness of the player':[21] 'to start from subjectivity here is to miss the point. What no longer exists is the players – with the poet or the composer being considered as one of the players'.[22]

14. E.g. Thiselton, *On Hermeneutics*, p.613.

15. David Dockery, 'Study and Interpretation of the Bible', in *Foundations for Biblical Interpretation* (ed. D. Dockery, K. Matthews and R. Sloan; Nashville: Broadman & Holman, 1994), p.46.

16. Donald A. Hagner, 'Review: Matthew 8–20 by Ulrich Luz', *JBL* 121.4 (2002), pp.766–69 (768).

17. Cf. Warnke, *Gadamer*, p.x: 'The question is whether the ideas of tradition of interpretation and truth and prejudice need to be given the subjectivist twist Hirsch gives them'.

18. Gadamer, *Truth and Method*, p.193.

19. Gadamer, *Truth and Method*, p.192.

20. Gadamer, *Truth and Method*, p.110.

21. Gadamer, *Truth and Method*, p.105.

22. Gadamer, *Truth and Method*, p.111.

This is a hermeneutics distinguished from Hirsh's and from the location of meaning in the author, but it is also distinguished from reader-response criticism and the location of meaning in the reader.[23] It is the key element of *wirkungsgeschichtliches Bewusstsein,* 'consciousness of being affected by history',[24] that offers to interpreters of the Bible an analysis that is not available in more exclusively reader-centred reception theory. Knight cites three recent authors who highlight the inadequacy of reader-response criticism, specifically for *Christian* reception. Their insistence, variously expressed, is focused on *historical consciousness*: not just that 'elevating the reader at the expense of the text is problematic' but that 'a more theorised approach to reception should not leave history behind'.[25] (They also argue that Christian theology must 'set the terms' for thinking about the nature of interpretation – a matter to which I shall return in §9.3.b, below.)

Gadamer offers a hermeneutics which, defensibly, meets these concerns. Textual meaning cannot be located in the author's intentions, but neither is it located in the experience of the reader – neither the 'ideal' reader of some reception theory, nor the first readers constructed by historical-critical researches.[26] Yet understanding an historical text demands (as I argued in Chapter 2) a reconstruction of hypothetical first-reception, not as *precondition* of understanding, but inextricably within the process of understanding. Gadamer writes,

> We may wonder...whether it is possible to distinguish...between identifying with the original reader and the process of understanding. Actually this ideal precondition of understanding – identifying with the original reader – cannot be fulfilled prior to the effort of understanding proper but rather is inextricable from it.[27]

Understanding is dialectic, 'neither subjective nor objective'; it proceeds from the 'interplay of the movement of tradition and the movement of the interpreter. The anticipation of meaning that governs our understanding

---

23. E.g. the 'affective stylistics' of Stanley Fish, *Is There a Text in This Class? The Authority of Interpretive Communities* (Cambridge, Mass.: Harvard University Press, 1980), pp.21–67.

24. Gadamer, *Truth and Method*, p.301.

25. Knight, '*Wirkungsgeschichte*', p.141, citing Gerard Loughlin, *Telling God's Story: Bible, Church and Narrative Theology* (Cambridge: Cambridge University Press, 1996); Watson, *Text and Truth*; and Kevin Vanhoozer, *First Theology: God, Scripture and Hermeneutics* (Downers Grove: InterVarsity, 2002).

26. E.g. Gadamer, *Truth and Method*, p.396 (cited in §2.1).

27. Gadamer, *Truth and Method*, p.190.

of the text is not an act of subjectivity, but proceeds from the common-ality that binds us to the tradition'.[28]

The model is not of one agent's subjectivity, but a form of negotiation between two agents. It is a dialectic that 'makes understanding appear to be a reciprocal relationship of the same kind as a conversation'.[29] This is explicit in a reflection by Gadamer (in 1997) on his own philosophical journey: 'It is the other who breaks into my ego-centredness and gives me something to understand'.[30] We have seen that he makes a connection between *Verstehen* [to understand] and *Verständigung* [coming to an understanding with someone].[31] Thiselton comments:

> Gadamer is concerned to challenge and to correct the individualism and brash over-confidence that seeks understanding…in the basis of individ-ual self-reflection and consciousness alone, especially 'consciousness' only of a single point in time. 'Method'…cannot be imposed upon under-standing of texts or of life in advance of genuine engagement with 'the other'.[32]

A key distinction between Hirsch and Gadamer is that Hirsch distin-guishes 'meaning' (singular, 'objective', meaning: what 'the author probably meant') from 'significance' (the plural, historically contingent applications of a text).[33] This remains an influential distinction among some biblical interpreters,[34] though a large body of contemporary schol-arship challenges Hirsch's notion that 'meaning' is accessible in isolation from interpretative appropriation.[35]

28. Gadamer, *Truth and Method*, p.293.
29. Gadamer, *Truth and Method*, p.370.
30. Hans-Georg Gadamer, 'Reflections on my Philosophical Journey', in *The Philosophy of Hans-Georg Gadamer* (ed. Lewis Hahn; Chicago and La Salle: Open Court, 1997), p.46. 'For Gadamer dialogue and conversation, in their various forms, are constitutive of what the world is for people': Dieter Misgeld, 'Poetry, Dialogue and Negotiation: Liberal Culture and Conservative Politics in Hans-Georg Gadamer's Thought', in *Festivals of Interpretation: Essays on Hans-Georg Gadamer's Work* (ed. Kathleen Wright; Albany: State University of New York Press, 1990), pp.161–81 (166).
31. Cf. Weinsheimer and Marshall, 'Translators' Preface', p.xvi (cited in §1.1.a).
32. Thiselton, 'Can "Authority" Remain Viable in a Postmodern Climate?', in *On Hermeneutics*, p.626.
33. E.g. Hirsch, *Validity*, p.8.
34. E.g. (in 2007), 'A given meaning in the text persists over time even when its significance is differently perceived': Barton, *Nature of Biblical Criticism*, p.99, citing Hirsch, *Validity*, pp.86–88.
35. E.g. David Hoy, *The Critical Circle: Literature and History in Contem-porary Hermeneutics* (Berkeley: University of California Press, 1978), pp.11–40.

For Gadamer, interpretation always involves application.[36] It is this feature that Emilio Betti identifies as opening Gadamer's analysis to *subjectivity* and arbitrariness, and unable to offer criteria for 'valid' interpretation.[37] Thiselton similarly regrets the absence in Gadamer's analysis of 'room for hermeneutical norms of a kind which would help us decide what might constitute *responsible* interpretation in any given case'.[38] Responsibility defined in what terms, by what pre-judgements? Thiselton explicitly rejects Hirsch's dichotomy of 'meaning' and 'significance', but the perceived deficiency he finds in Gadamer's hermeneutics is comparable to Hirsch's complaint that this is unable to 'enunciate a principle for distinguishing between an interpretation that is valid and one that is not'.[39] If understanding a text includes its application to the interpreter's historical situation, what are the constraints in deeming any interpretation 'adequate'? Gadamer's position is that his paradigm describes 'what is' and not a prior conception of what ought to be,[40] but he also claims not to 'open the door to arbitrariness in interpretation but to reveal what always takes place'.[41] It is his identification of 'truth' as part of the hermeneutical process itself which may be judged to have a corollary: that the 'truthfulness' or validity or responsibility of any interpretation cannot be challenged.[42]

One of the features of Gadamer's hermeneutics that possibly offers such a constraint, a measure of 'adequacy', is his emphasis on 'the rightness of the question'. An historical text 'puts a question to the interpreter... To understand a text means to understand this question.'[43]

36. 'This fusing of understanding and interpretation, of which I am accused by writers like E. D. Hirsch, I derived from Schleiermacher': Gadamer, *Truth and Method*, p.257n.

37. Emilio Betti, *Die Hermeneutik als allgemeine Methodik der Geisteswissenschaften* (Tübingen: Mohr, 1962), p.49.

38. Thiselton in Roger Lundin, Clarence Walhout and Anthony Thiselton, *The Responsibility of Hermeneutics* (Grand Rapids: Eerdmans, 1985), p.110.

39. Hirsch, *Validity*, p.251.

40. 'My real concern was and is philosophic: not what we do or we ought to do, but what happens to us over and above our wanting and our doing' (Gadamer, *Truth and Method*, pp.xxv–xxvi). Gadamer responds to early critics that 'They fail to recognize that reflection about practice is not methodology': 'Afterword', in *Truth and Method*, p.559.

41. Gadamer, *Truth and Method*, p.367.

42. This is Lawrence Hinman's argument in '*Quid factis or Quid Juris*? The Fundamental Ambiguity of Gadamer's Understanding of Hermeneutics', *Philosophy and Phenomenological Research* 40 (1980), pp.512–35. See the discussion (Habermas's critique of prejudged truths) in §9.3.

43. Gadamer, *Truth and Method*, p.363.

Questions operate within both of the 'horizons' (past and present, of the text and of the reader), and these achieve, in the process of understanding, 'fusion'. The reconstruction of the questions 'to which the text is presumed to be an answer' takes place 'within' another process of questioning 'through which we try to answer the question that the text asks us'.[44]

There is both 'openness' and 'limitation' in this operation.[45] Questions imply more than one possible answer. Weinsheimer extrapolates: 'insofar as the text depends on the question it addresses, it possesses…a horizon of unasserted possibilities of meaning, which are the possibilities of interpretation that exceed what is stated in the text'.[46] The possibilities of addressing questions to which the text offers 'answers', Gadamer argues, exceed what the author has stated: 'it is a hermeneutical necessity always to go beyond mere reconstruction. We cannot avoid thinking about that which was unquestionably accepted, and hence not thought about, by an author, and bringing it into the openness of the question.'[47]

Understanding is neither merely the reconstruction of the author's view nor an assertion of the reader's. Understanding takes place in 'dialogue', in which to reach understanding (as a fusion of horizons) means 'being transformed into a communion in which we do not remain what we were'.[48] In this construction, 'truth', 'tradition' and 'prejudgement' are dialectically, not subjectively, conceived. (We return to this concept of communion or commonality in §§9.3 and 9.3.a below and to the transformative, rather than merely confirmatory, potential of the fusion of horizons in §§9.3 and 9.3.b.)

The engagement with what is 'not thought about' by an author but 'unquestionably accepted' (as part of her/his 'horizon') is an important feature of some perceived constraints to subjectivity and criteria for validity. This is of particular relevance to my case study because of an appeal to the mind of the author in the (contested) hermeneutical principle that 'Pauline exegesis is rooted in "Pauline theology"'.[49]

44. Gadamer, *Truth and Method*, p.367.
45. Gadamer, *Truth and Method*, p.357.
46. Weinsheimer, *Gadamer's Hermeneutics*, p.210.
47. Gadamer, *Truth and Method*, p.367.
48. Gadamer, *Truth and Method*, p.371.
49. Thiselton's description of a principle of his own and of James Dunn: *On Hermeneutics*, p.303.

9.2.a. 'Beyond the mind of the author'

Thiselton expresses a constraint of authorial intentionality as 'caution about going beyond the mind of Paul'. He suggests (for instance) that the 'varied agendas brought to our attention by some patristic writings may serve to explicate what is often presupposed in Pauline texts'.[50] 'What is presupposed' matches Gadamer's 'that which was unquestionably accepted'. Thiselton refers the psychology of intentionality not only to Schleiermacher's maxim that interpretation 'may go beyond the conscious awareness of an author',[51] but also to Theissen's work on psychological aspects of Pauline theology,[52] 'which penetrates beneath the surface of Pauline texts to explore concepts of which Paul himself might scarcely have been fully conscious as conceptual tools or categorisations'.[53]

Such 'conceptual tools or categorisations' form part of what, in Gadamer's terms, is the horizon of the text: 'It is not the author's reflective self-interpretation but the unconscious meaning of the author that is to be understood'.[54] This corresponds to a considerable range of theory and practice in hermeneutics in general, including some constructs of *Sachkritik* (see below, §9.3.b), and to the interpretation of Paul in particular. Luther refers to 'what Paul intended'.[55] Bultmann regularly makes a distinction between Paul's words and his 'intention'.[56] Paul Ricoeur writes that to understand an author 'better' than he could understand himself is to 'display the power of disclosure implied in his discourse beyond the limited horizon of his own existential situation'.[57] Weinsheimer comments on this: 'If "better" is defined in this way,

---

50. Thiselton, *On Hermeneutics*, p.303. This matches his agenda of using reception history to further elucidate historical-critical reading of the text.

51. F.D.E. Schleiermacher, *Hermeneutics: The Handwritten Manuscripts* (Missoula: Scholars Press, 1977), p.246n, cited in Thiselton, *On Hermeneutics*, p.303.

52. Gerd Theissen, *Psychological Aspects of Pauline Theology* (trans. John Galvin; Edinburgh: T. & T. Clark, 1997).

53. Thiselton, *On Hermeneutics*, p.303.

54. Gadamer, *Truth and Method*, p.192.

55. E.g. Martin Luther, *A Commentary on St. Paul's Epistle to the* Galatians (ed. P. Watson; London: James Clarke, 1953), p.11.

56. E.g. R. Bultmann, *Theology of the New Testament I* (New York/London: SCM, 1951), p.259; cf. Räisänen, *Beyond New Testament Theology*, p.41. (*Meinung* semantically covers both 'meaning' and 'intention'.)

57. Paul Ricoeur, 'The Model of the Text', *Social Research* 38 (1971), pp.529–62 (558).

Gadamer and Ricoeur are not far apart, though Gadamer resists the implications of progress connoted by any notion of "better understanding"'.[58]

Thiselton's next step in reflection on contingent application and the exegetical quest involves a hypothetical reversal of the trajectory of historical consciousness: 'if he were given a retrospective [= prospective?] understanding [of modern notions of the unconscious and of related mechanisms of self-deception,] might not Paul have said..., "Yes, this is the kind of thing that I wish to convey"'.[59] Such a description of an interpretative principle may not escape Gadamer's rejection of 'psychological interpretation' and the possibility of an apprehension of the 'inner origin' of a text or 'placing of oneself within the whole framework of the author'.[60] ('The whole framework' [*die ganze Verfassung*] was 'the mind' of the author in the earlier English translation.)[61]

What, as I have argued, Gadamer and Jauss describe, is an approach to the likely origin of the text or the framework of the author with tools (such as an understanding of the genre and lexis) that construct the *Wirkungsbedingungen*[62] and a 'system of expectations that arise for each work in the historical moment of its appearance'. Jauss offers this analysis of interpretation (in thesis 2) specifically as a way to avoid 'the threatening pitfalls of psychology'.[63] This is a very common strategy in contemporary New Testament interpretation (illustrated in Chapters 3, 4 and 5), which construes 'the questions to which the text is an answer' as the meaning or meanings accessible to the first readers.[64]

'Authorial intention' and 'the mind of Paul' are particularly problematized by my case-study texts. Rowland writes, 'Many biblical texts are not written expressions of a direct communication between author and reader' but notes, 'the Pauline letters are something of an exception to this'.[65] They are from 'letters', expressions of a direct communication

58. Weinsheimer, *Gadamer's Hermeneutics*, p.142n.

59. Thiselton, *On Hermeneutics*, pp.303–4.

60. Gadamer, *Truth and Method* (2005), p.186.

61. Gadamer, *Truth and Method* (1979), p.164; Gadamer, *Wahrheit und Methode*, p.175.

62. Jauss, *Alterität und Modernität*, p.129 (cited in §1.1.b).

63. Jauss, *Aesthetic of Reception*, p.22.

64. For example, Hooker (without any appeal to reception theory): 'By asking questions about the *original audience*...we hope to keep in contact with the *author and his intentions*': Morna D. Hooker, *A Commentary on the Gospel according to St Mark* (London: A. & C. Black, 1991), p.4.

65. Rowland, 'Pragmatic Approach', p.12.

between author and reader, 'illocutionary' speech acts[66] that *intend* interaction with the receiver. Further, they are paraenetic, 'perlocutionary'
utterances that attempt to effect a change in the behaviour of the reader.
Some reception associates the paraenetic use of ὑποτάσσειν with a
specifically Pauline theological use of the word elsewhere (see §4.2).

One of Gadamer's illustrations of the hermeneutical demand, to
understand a text in terms of the specific situation in which it was written
(cf. reception in Chapter 5), uses an illustration of 'command' (another
perlocutionary utterance). Gadamer writes:

> To understand the order means to apply it to the specific situation to which
> it is relevant… If we now imagine an historian who regards a traditionary
> text in this way as an order and seeks to understand it, he is, of course, in a
> situation quite different from that of the original addressee. He is not the
> person to whom the order is addressed and so cannot relate it to himself…
> It may be difficult for the historian to reconstruct the original situation in
> which the order arose. But he will understand it fully only when he has
> thus made the order concrete.[67]

Thiselton makes a similar argument (in relation to texts like those of my
case study):

> in the case of many biblical texts (not all) it is necessary to include the
> work of historical reconstruction… This model operates characteristically
> in cases in which biblical texts serve primarily as transmissive and com-
> municative vehicles to express the thought of an author towards a given
> directedness.[68]

My case study therefore provokes a return to the question focusing on
the interpretative weight of the original setting, and, further, the interpretative 'control' of Pauline theology: how far, and for what 'community
of readers', the ethical paraenesis should be considered *within the framework of a theological hermeneutic, derived from Paul.* (This is pursued
in relation to the case study in §§9.3.b below and 10.5.)

9.3. Participation in the evolution of tradition

> Tradition is not simply a precondition into which we come, but we produce
> it ourselves, inasmuch as we understand, participate in the evolution of
> tradition and hence further determine it ourselves.[69]

66. Another term from Searle, *Speech Acts*, p.24 (cited in §1.2.b).
67. Gadamer, *Truth and Method*, pp.329–30.
68. Part of a clarification of the expression 'Author's Intention' in Thiselton, *On Hermeneutics*, pp.352 and 354.
69. Gadamer, *Truth and Method*, p.293 (cited in §1.1.a).

If Gadamer is deemed to *avoid* the 'subjectivism' of offering an equal validation to any and all understandings of a text, a second criticism holds that this avoidance is achieved by subscribing to what is effectively a *different form of subjectivism*: one where a reader merely affirms the interpretations of a text made by the tradition to which that reader belongs. In this view, 'Gadamer's position reduces to a subjectivist glorification of an interpretive community's or tradition's prejudices'.[70]

Gadamer identifies the conditions of understanding a text as lying *within* such traditions. The 'prejudices of the individual' (the anticipations or pre-understandings that are the conditions of the possibility of historical knowledge) 'far more than his judgments, constitute the historical reality of his being'.[71] Gadamer does not see these prejudices as subjectivist: what we bring to the process of interpretation are not merely our individual concerns but the *issues that have developed within the historical tradition to which we belong*. Pre-judgments are intrinsic to our *Geworfenheit* ['thrownness' or human finitude] and to our historical consciousness. We are limited and qualified in various ways, 'set within various traditions', and so 'subject to prejudices and limited in [our] freedom'.[72] Our understanding of a 'traditionary work' is conditioned by the way that text has previously been understood in a history of interpretation, and our prejudgments are part of its legacy. In comparison to the substantive role of these 'fore-structures' of understanding, the (mere) 'focus of subjectivity', in Gadamer's assessment, 'is a distorting mirror. The self-awareness of an individual is only a flickering in the closed circuits of historical life.'[73] This is, in essence, *Wirkungsgeschichte*, the principle of history-of-effect:

> If we are trying to understand a historical phenomenon from the historical distance that is characteristic of our hermeneutical situation, we are always already *affected by history* [*unterliegen...den Wirkungen der Wirkungsgeschichte*]. It determines in advance both what seems to us worth enquiring about and what will appear as an object of investigation.[74]

To operate with a subjectivism that would take the 'immediate appearance' as the whole truth of a text is to 'forget half of what is really there' – and to 'miss the whole truth' of the phenomenon of how we understand. Conversely, the conservatism of taking 'the tradition' as the measure of

70. Warnke, *Gadamer*, p.x.
71. Gadamer, *Truth and Method*, p.278 (cited in §1.1.a).
72. Gadamer, *Truth and Method*, p.277 (cited in §1.1.a).
73. Gadamer, *Truth and Method*, p.278.
74. Gadamer, *Truth and Method*, p.300 (emphasis mine), and *Wahrheit und Methode*, p.284.

correct interpretation is countered by the dialectic or 'interplay' of tradition and interpreter. Gadamer holds that understanding as the 'fusion of horizons' is neither an appropriation by the interpreter of the prejudgments of the text, nor an imposition on the text of the interpreter's prejudgments. There is a transformation of the initial positions of each in a consensus of meaning, a *new* stage of the tradition of interpretation, but which 'proceeds from the commonality' binding interpreter to tradition.[75]

This creative, generative legacy of texts in the prejudgments of the reader is core to Gadamer's hermeneutics but often absent or not well represented in different types of current practice: in a 'study of effects' (the *EBR* translation of *Wirkungsgeschichte*); in a selection of the 'major' commentators, where there is not a reflexive account of what constitutes major and for whom; or in historical-critical methods, if these are assumed to offer singularity and certainty. What is often unacknowledged in these is the role of historical consciousness in reception history (that is, reflexive consciousness of the hermeneutical situation) to make 'conscious the prejudices governing our own understanding'.[76]

If theorists and practitioners are not working with a common vocabulary, in spite of appeals to *Wirkungsgeschichte*, variously understood, there is some excuse for this in the complexity of Gadamer's analysis. The dichotomous charges of subjectivism and conservatism may be responding to what Georgia Warnke terms 'a peculiar oscillation' in Gadamer's hermeneutics: the attempt to avoid both conformity to a tradition, on the one hand, and the 'opportunism' of interpretation in accordance with historical circumstances, on the other:

> To the original charge that his hermeneutics permits subjective arbitrariness in interpretation he replies by pointing to the need to anticipate the truth…of the object in question. To the charge that this solution simply reflects a prejudice in favour of the truth of the object he replies by pointing to the way in which understanding involves application and hence to the way in which interpretations of the truth of the object change in accordance with historical circumstances.[77]

This 'dilemma' has a significant correspondence with my analysis of two different trends in the contemporary practice of biblical interpretation, which, I have suggested, give different weights to (1) continuities and 'contours' of a tradition of interpretation and (2) contingent particularity in reception. It also reflects the two shifting 'poles' of emphasis noted in the revised translation of *Truth and Method* (see §6.4).

75. Gadamer, *Truth and Method*, p.293 (cited above, §9.2).
76. Gadamer, *Truth and Method*, p.298 (cited in §1.1.a).
77. Warnke, *Gadamer*, p.99.

The 'oscillation' reflects the duality in the hermeneutical task summarised by Ricoeur: 'Hermeneutics seems to me to be animated by this double motivation: willingness to suspect, willingness to listen'.[78] Roberts observes that Gadamer's rehabilitation of tradition, and his account of 'open-minded, benevolent dialogue' with tradition, has characteristics of a hermeneutics of trust that can be 'quite surprising to those schooled in a hermeneutics of suspicion'.[79] The question raised for some of Gadamer's critics is whether 'because of our historicity, we can never transcend the prejudices of the tradition to which we belong and evaluate them according to independent criteria of reason'.[80]

This is at the heart of Habermas's critique of Gadamer's hermeneutics in a two-decades-long debate.[81] Habermas accepts the idea of understanding as 'consensus' of meaning, but believes that Gadamer does not acknowledge the ways in which power and coercion operate in social life.[82] Hermeneutics is not an end in itself: it is a means towards the greater end of the emancipation of the individual.[83] It should be concerned to determine when statements 'express ideologically frozen relations of dependence that can in principle be transformed', and the critique of ideology can access 'the level of unreflected consciousness'.[84] Gadamer, by sublimating 'social processes entirely to cultural tradition',[85] offers no acknowledgment, says Habermas, that the 'dialogue' may be distorted by

78. Paul Ricoeur, *Freud and Philosophy: An Essay on Interpretation* (trans. Denis Savage; New Haven: Yale University Press, 1970), p.27.

79. Roberts, *Oxford Handbook*, p.3.

80. Warnke, *Gadamer*, p.91.

81. The Gadamer–Habermas debate begins with Habermas's review of recent publications in a supplemental volume of the journal *Philosophische Runtschau* (1967), later developed and published as a book: Jürgen Habermas, *Zur Logik der Sozial Wissenschaften* (Frankfurt: Suhrkamp, 1982). Gadamer's response includes his essay, 'Rhetoric, Hermeneutics and the Critique of Ideology', in *The Hermeneutics Reader: Texts of the German Tradition from the Enlightenment to the Present* (ed. Kurt Mueller-Vollmer; Oxford: Blackwell, 1989), pp.274–92. Habermas responded in the same volume: 'On Hermeneutics' Claim to Universality', pp.293–319.

82. Habermas, *Zur Logik*, pp.306–10.

83. Jürgen Habermas, *Knowledge and Human Interests* (Boston: Beacon, 1971), pp.308–15.

84. Habermas, *Knowledge*, p.310.

85. Jürgen Habermas, 'A Review of Gadamer's *Truth and Method*' (trans. F.R. Dallmayr and T. McCarthy), in *The Hermeneutic Tradition: From Ast to Ricoeur* (ed. Gayle Ormiston and Alan Schrift; Albany: State University of New York Press, 1990), p.240.

oppressive forces, and no basis on which to assess how far the tradition is either rational or ideologically distorted. Gadamer is cleared of Hirsch's charge of subjectivism, but the 'objectivity of a "happening of tradition"…is not objective enough'.[86]

Gadamer himself takes an 'anti-utopian position', and this includes 'the rejection of emancipatory politics as a real possibility of social transformation',[87] but he explicitly disclaims an *antithesis* of authority, tradition and prejudice to reason and freedom.[88] The question he poses is, 'What distinguishes legitimate prejudices from the countless others which it is the undeniable task of critical reason to overcome?'[89] Our prejudices are tested 'in encountering the past and in understanding the tradition from which we come'.[90] There is, arguably, an internality to this process, which does not challenge the shared tradition from a position of critical distance – but, again, Gadamer's purpose is to analyse the process of understanding, not to offer criteria for 'responsible' interpretation. Moreover, his polemic is rooted in an opposition to historical objectivism: Habermas's appeal to a form of universal consensus as the true arbiter of moral validity[91] seems to propose a construct that offers a comparable access to independent criteria.

There *is* a self-critical, reflexive process in Gadamer's hermeneutics.[92] Indeed, it is key to his analysis that hermeneutics has little or nothing to do with 'preserving one's own position'.[93] For Gadamer the precondition for understanding is the willingness of the 'conversation partners' (which is how he conceives, hermeneutically, the reader and the text) to be open to what the other has to say. Subsequent to their rather unsuccessful meeting in 1981,[94] Jacques Derrida wrote to Gadamer that he was 'not

86. Habermas, 'A Review of Gadamer's *Truth and Method*', p.239.
87. Misgeld, 'Poetry, Dialogue and Negotiation', p.170.
88. Gadamer, *Truth and Method*, pp.278–82, and see §1.1.a.
89. Gadamer, *Truth and Method*, p.278.
90. Gadamer, *Truth and Method*, p.305.
91. E.g. Jürgen Habermas, 'Justice and Solidarity', in *Hermeneutics and Critical Theory in Ethics and Politics* (ed. Michael Kelly; Cambridge: MIT, 1990), p.40.
92. Jauss hints at such a process too: the 'productive function of progressive understanding…necessarily also includes criticizing the tradition and forgetting it': Jauss, *Aesthetic of Reception*, p.32.
93. Gadamer, 'Philosophical Journey', p.17.
94. The encounter at a symposium on 'Text and Interpretation' at the Goethe Institute in Paris was not, many conclude, a meeting of minds. Derrida responded to Gadamer's presentation 'with several questions that…appear to have been misdirected': Michelfelder and Palmer, 'Introduction', p.3.

convinced' of the possibility and reality of dialogue or conversation, 'of knowing in a dialogue that one has been perfectly understood or experiencing the success of confirmation'.[95] Gadamer replied:

> Certainly I would not want to say that the solidarities that bind human beings together and make them partners in a dialogue always are sufficient to enable them to achieve understanding and total mutual agreement... Perhaps the experience of a text always includes...a moment of encountering limits... One must lose onself in order to find oneself... [O]ne never knows in advance what one will find oneself to be.[96]

These 'solidarities' are hermeneutically necessary to the process of *transformation* of meaning as well as confirmation of meaning. Biblical interpreters, such as those characterised by Roberts and Rowland as having 'a methodologically and historically agnostic position', may see in reception-historical approaches 'liberation from the boundary setting of any single tradition'. With this investment, there is sometimes an assumption that 'the relinquishment of the hermeneutic parameters established by a given tradition'[97] means a Derridean deconstruction of all historical, theological traditions, and a perpetual equivocation and undecidability of meaning. (Indeed, Gadamer writes that Jauss 'seized on' the relinquishment of unique, correct interpretation 'but so over-emphasised it that he comes close to Derrida's "deconstruction", contrary to his own wish'.)[98] That is to miss the real nature and role of tradition and prejudgment in Gadamer's thought: there are always, in the transmission of texts, 'solidarities that bind human beings together and make them partners in a dialogue'.[99] Critics have perceived in Derrida's non-engagement with Gadamer a refusal to affirm what Gadamer perceives as this necessary condition of dialogue, a shared 'language'.[100]

Within this Gadamerian 'dialogue', it is the readiness to have expectation thwarted that distinguishes 'historically effected consciousness'. It is because of this consciousness that readers can be conscious of the prejudices governing their own understanding 'so that the text, as

---

95. Jacques Derrida, 'Three Questions to Hans-Georg Gadamer' (trans. D. Michelfelder and R. Palmer), in *Dialogue and Deconstruction*, pp.52–54 (54).

96. Hans-Georg Gadamer, 'Reply to Jacques Derrida' (trans. D. Michelfelder and R. Palmer), in *Dialogue and Deconstruction*, pp.55–57 at 57.

97. Roberts and Rowland, 'Review Essay: *Encyclopedia of the Bible and Its Reception*' (cited in §6.3).

98. Gadamer, *Truth and Method*, p.164n (and p.118).

99. Gadamer, 'Reply to Derrida', p.57.

100. Cf. Michelfelder and Palmer, 'Introduction', in *Dialogue and Deconstruction*, p.10.

another's meaning, can be isolated and valued on its own'.[101] It is also because of this consciousness that it is possible to *understand* traditions in which the reader does not already participate: scholars who adopt a 'methodologically and historically agnostic position'[102] are still engaged in a negotiation of meaning involving prejudgments. Gadamer describes a need to distinguish appropriate prejudices, which lead to understanding, from 'false prejudices' that produce misunderstanding. 'Legitimate' prejudices are effects produced by the historical tradition that the reader seeks to understand. The prejudices or prejudgments by which a tradition is constituted have the potential to distort communication or to allow for a better understanding of the text.[103] Before false prejudices can be avoided, our prejudices must be raised to consciousness – provoked and irritated (cf. Luz's account of denominational 'correctives', in §6.2).

Critique of Gadamer in this matter focuses on the process of *assuming the truth* of a text or tradition as the position from which the reader can discriminate between different accounts of it: 'how can we ever learn to reject the truth we have assumed?'[104] Habermas outlines a self-correcting learning process where the aim of, for example, reading an historical text, is a disinterested pursuit of truth. In the 'ideal speech situation' (or a rhetorically adequate process) there should be a critical testing of competing arguments. This process requires conditions such as equality between the participants, an absence of both coercion and self-deception.[105] (Such conditions, surely, are rarely realizable and never empirically demonstrable.) For Habermas, the heart of the matter is that Gadamer permits tradition to be the only test of the validity of prejudgments. Even when prejudgments are recognised for what they are, they continue to function prejudicially, and permit no real critique. If the legacy of a traditionary text to a subsequent generation is not only its 'knowledge' but its 'authority', it *legitimates* the prejudgments it gives rise to in the recipients of that legacy.[106]

---

101. Gadamer, *Truth and Method*, p.298 (cited in §1.1.a).
102. Roberts and Rowland, 'Review Essay: *Encyclopedia of the Bible and Its Reception*'.
103. Cf. Parris, *Reception Theory*, p.108.
104. Warnke, *Gadamer*, p.106.
105. E.g. Jürgen Habermas, *Zwischen Naturalismus und Religion* (Frankfurt: Suhrkamp, 2005), pp.89–91.
106. 'A structure of pre-understanding or pre-judgment that has been rendered transparent can no longer function as a prejudice. But this is precisely what Gadamer seems to imply. That authority converges with knowledge means that the tradition that is effectively behind the educator legitimates the prejudices inculcated in the

What is at stake is exactly what is meant by agreement or consensus between differently situated people – and concerning this there is a particular ambiguity in Gadamer. The fusion of horizons is characterised by a necessary 'connection' of the two players: '[w]hen our historical consciousness transposes itself into historical horizons, this does not entail passing into alien worlds unconnected in any way with our own; instead, they together constitute the one great horizon'.[107] But this is also like the necessary connection in an intelligible 'conversation' where, 'when we have discovered the other person's standpoint and horizon, his ideas become intelligible without our necessarily having to agree with him.'[108]

Warnke judges that 'Gadamer fails adequately to distinguish these two senses of agreement, one of which entails a concrete unity of judgment and the other reflective and critical integration'.[109] On the one hand, agreement may be a 'common idea of what is true and valid'; on the other, it may be a 'fusion of horizons', that is, 'an integration of differing perspectives in a deeper understanding of the matters in question'.[110] This latter commonality means that the interpreter may not share the views constituting the first horizon of the text, *yet those views form an integral part of the interpreter's self-understanding*. We 'agree' with the tradition in the sense that we are part of it and it is part of us. If the second sense of critical and reflective agreement is merely identified with the first, Warnke suggests, we move from

> an investigation of the conditions of understanding to the basically conservative thesis according to which we are not only members of a tradition but also its ideological supporters. The suspicion that this thesis lies at the heart of Gadamer's position has motivated much of the criticism of his work.[111]

So Richard Rorty suggests that Gadamerian operation of commonality is a search for the 'all the comforts of consensus';[112] and Ronald Beiner

---

rising generation... [T]he act of recognition that is mediated through reflection would not at all have altered the fact that tradition as such remains the only ground of the validity of prejudices': Habermas, 'A Review of Gadamer's *Truth and Method*', p.237.

107. Gadamer, *Truth and Method*, p.303.
108. Gadamer, *Truth and Method*, p.302 (cited in §2.3).
109. Warnke, *Gadamer*, p.106.
110. Warnke, *Gadamer*, p.169.
111. Warnke, *Gadamer*, p.106.
112. Richard Rorty, *Consequences of Pragmatism* (Minneapolis: University of Minnesota Press, 1982), p.153.

judges that Gadamer's moral theory gives *primacy* to the concept of a shared ethos.[113]

If there is an effective answer in Gadamer to such criticism, it lies (as discussed above) in the *reflexive and dialogic character of understanding*: '[t]o understand a text is to understand oneself in a kind of dialogue'.[114] We do not have access to independent criteria of reason outside of an historical condition, and all assertions of authority, judgment, reason and freedom are made from historical and cultural experience. Such experiences 'make of us who we are and we cannot transcend them to evaluate them according to standards formulated independently of them'.[115] However, crucially, the characteristic of genuine dialogue is that those engaged in it move beyond their own initial positions, informed by other positions.

The reader thus 'participate[s] in the evolution of tradition'.[116] To the complaint that for Gadamer tradition 'remains the only ground of the validity of prejudices',[117] Gadamer's responses focus on rejection of any claims to universalism from which our historical situatedness can be critiqued, but also on the ability of new insights revealed in the dialogue with 'the authority' of the tradition. We do assess the values of a text in the light of 'prejudices' – the norms and principles that are its legacy to us – but we also assess it from our different historical circumstances: understanding *always* involves application. If this remains an operation in which a tradition is, partly, affirmed, it is also one in which readers are reflexively critical. Eagleton describes it (without endorsing it) thus: 'we enter into the alien world of the artefact [text], but at the same time gather it into our own realm, reaching a more complete understanding of ourselves'.[118]

The discussion in Chapter 6 included a critique of the summit-dialogue construct as self-limiting, and the 'canon' of exemplary commentators as having parameters designed by the same tradition that they are then used to define.[119] However, if the reader participates in the evolution of their own tradition, they may also be redefining the concept of the 'canon'.

---

113. Ronald Beiner, 'Do We Need a Philosophical Ethics? Theory, Prudence, and the Primacy of Ethos', *The Philosophical Forum* 21 (1989), pp.230–43.

114. Gadamer, *Philosophical Hermeneutics*, p.57 (cited in §1.1.a).

115. Warnke, *Gadamer*, p.169.

116. Gadamer, *Truth and Method*, p.293 (cited in §1.1.a).

117. Habermas, 'A Review of Gadamer's *Truth and Method*', p.237.

118. Eagleton, *Literary Theory*, p.72.

119. Cf. Roberts, *Oxford Handbook*, p.5 (cited in §6.2).

Gadamer's canon is in an endless process of redefinition. It 'is made up of texts, the voices of which draw the reader into conversation'. And the explanation of why some texts are in the canon and others are not lies in 'their power to address those in search of understanding, which is, ultimately, self-understanding'.[120]

My task here is not to attempt an adjudication of the full Gadamer–Habermas debate, or of similar challenges like those from Derrida, but specifically to consider how, in the light of challenges like these, Gadamer's hermeneutics operates within current theory and practice of interpretation of the Bible, and of the Pauline paraenesis in particular. Section 9.3.a therefore pursues, in relation to Christian biblical interpretation, the idea of commonality in a tradition; and §9.3.b pursues the roles of theology and ideology in 'distorting' interpretation or distinguishing 'legitimate prejudices' or 'responsible interpretation'.[121]

9.3.a. 'Lived affinity' between interpreter and text

Concerning the 'commonality' that binds us to 'the tradition',[122] Eagleton asks, 'It might be as well to ask Gadamer whose and what "tradition" he actually has in mind'.[123] Eagleton complains that Gadamer's analysis of understanding historical texts is predicated on a false construct of a unitary and 'mainstream' tradition, in which all 'valid' works participate, and of a seamless, uncontradictory progression of history,

> and that the prejudices which 'we' (who?) have inherited from the 'tradition' are to be cherished. It assumes, in other words, that history is a place where 'we' can always and everywhere be 'at home'; that the work of the past will deepen – rather than, say, decimate – our present self-understanding.[124]

We saw above that this is not how Gadamer characterises the operation of 'tradition' – and a transformation of one's self-understanding is in fact not outside the compass of Gadamer's understanding of our relationship to tradition.

Christian biblical interpretation, specifically, offers particular opportunities to consider the nature of what 'commonality' binds new readers to earlier readers, and to traditionary texts. The Pontifical Biblical

120. Lawn, *Gadamer*, p.128. Such a (re)definition of canon informed the choice of reception in Chapter 8.

121. Gadamer, *Truth and Method*, p.278; Thiselton, *Responsibility*, p.110.

122. Gadamer, *Truth and Method*, p.293 (cited above).

123. Eagleton, *Literary Theory*, p.72.

124. Eagleton, *Literary Theory*, pp.72–73.

Commission holds that the 'lived affinity' between the interpreter and the biblical text is 'the condition that makes the entire exegetical enterprise possible'.[125] For Gadamer, this is not because the Bible is, hermeneutically, a special case but rather, in some ways, a *clear* case of the conditions of how a traditionary text is understood, and of the hermeneutical requirement of 'fore-understanding'. Understanding the text *presupposes a relationship to what it says*. Gadamer cites Bultmann's assertion that the 'interpretation of the biblical writings is subject to exactly the same conditions as any other literature', and Hofmann's (cited by Bultmann) that 'scriptural hermeneutics presupposes a relationship to the content of the Bible'.[126] The examination of *these* texts 'is determined by a very precise fore-understanding'. Indeed, 'the hermeneutical significance of fore-understanding in theology seems itself theological' – that is, premised on recognising the 'alternative of belief or unbelief in the true God':

> This does not mean that such theological hermeneutics is dogmatically predisposed, so that it reads out of the text what it has put into it. Rather, it really risks itself. But it assumes that the word of Scripture addresses us and that only the person who allows himself to be addressed – whether he believes or doubts – understands.[127]

The premise is that there is real 'commonality' or 'solidarity' across different historical and cultural experience in an ongoing dialectic, where a tradition may be conceived, in MacIntyre's words, as 'an argument extended through time in which certain fundamental agreements are defined and redefined'.[128] For Gadamer, 'dialogue' and 'conversation' (in literal and metaphoric operation) constitute the human condition, and these rest, as Dieter Misgeld observes, on the importance of commonality: 'Having a world in common means living in solidarity and living in solidarity means openness to conversation and dialogue. The other becomes indispensable for us in this openness and for it'.[129]

125. Pontifical Biblical Commission, 'The Interpretation of the Bible in the Church', in *The Interpretation of the Bible in the* Church (ed. J. Leslie Houlden; London: SPCK, 1984), p.58.

126. Rudolf Bultmann, *Glauben und Verstehen*, vol. 2 (Tübingen: J.C.B. Mohr, 1965), p.231, cited in Gadamer, *Truth and Method*, p.327.

127. Gadamer, *Truth and Method*, p.328.

128. Alasdair MacIntyre, *Whose Justice, Which Rationality?* (Notre Dame: University of Notre Dame Press, 1985), p.12.

129. Misgeld, 'Poetry, Dialogue and Negotiation', p.166.

In biblical studies, Wayne Meeks and others (e.g. Richard Hays, Amy Plantinga Pauw)[130] use George Lindbeck's 'cultural-linguistic' model of religion which grounds religious experience in the *shared language and practices* of a religious community.[131] The concept of a shared language supports the possibility of 'dialogue' in understanding a traditionary text. This corresponds to Frank Kermode's observation that there is 'genuine continuity between the operations performed on the material by the evangelists, and the work of exegetes who, for almost two millennia, have continued their labours'.[132] It also supports my previous argument for the exercise of historical criticism within reception history, because it acknowledges (as Pauw notes) 'the importance of historical-critical questions for developing a "thick description"' of the contexts in which biblical texts were written and first received'.[133]

This reinforces the degree of engagement undertaken in biblical studies with hypothetical first-reception, not as a detached, and detachable, historical study but as part of an ongoing *theological* engagement, and an 'application' of the texts. It provides an affirmative answer to Riches' question: 'Is it perhaps for *theological* reasons that historical-critical study of the Bible has given so much of its attention to the reconstruction of the original meaning of the text?'[134] This is of course a matter of contention in contemporary biblical interpretation. Where, for example, Räisänen argues that 'historical and theological tasks…are to be kept apart,[135] Morgan holds that '[t]heological reflection on the biblical witness cannot begin where historical research stops. It begins with the texts themselves.'[136]

130. Meeks, 'Social Embodiment', pp.176–86; Richard B. Hays, *Echoes of Scripture in the Letters of Paul* (New Haven: Yale University Press, 1989); Amy Plantinga Pauw, 'The Word Is Near You: A Feminist Conversation with Lindbeck', *Theology Today* 50.1 (1993), pp.45–55.

131. George A. Lindbeck, *The Nature of Doctrine: Religion and Theology in a Postliberal Age* (Philadelphia: Westminster, 1984).

132. Frank Kermode, *The Genesis of Secrecy: On the Interpretation of Narrative* (Cambridge, Mass.: Harvard University Press, 1979), p.99. Weinsheimer suggests that Kermode may be influenced by Gadamer in reaching this conclusion: *Gadamer's Hermeneutics*, p.172n.

133. Pauw, 'Feminist Conversation', p.46, citing Geertz, *Interpretation of Cultures*, pp.3–30 (see §2.3).

134. John Riches, 'Why Write a Reception-Historical Commentary?', *JSNT* 29 (2007), pp.323–32 (330).

135. Heikki Räisänen, *Beyond New Testament Theology* (London: SCM, 2000), p.137 – in an endorsement of J.P. Gabler's (1787) similar dichotomy.

136. Robert Morgan with John Barton, *Biblical Interpretation* (Oxford: Oxford University Press, 1988), p.185.

For Gadamer, this latter position reflects the solidarity, in some measure, of new readers with first readers. Understanding depends on a disposition to agree, and tradition depends upon deep-seated agreements, where the legacy of a text is part of our self-understanding. Subsequent to *Truth and Method*, Gadamer makes little reference to 'traditions' and more, in various essays and interviews, to 'solidarity'.[137] Chris Lawn suggests: 'This gives rise to the suggestion that the idea of solidarity becomes either a replacement for the earlier "tradition", or a way of amplifying and expanding upon it'.[138] Lawn compares 'solidarity' in Gadamer and Rorty: where Rorty speaks of 'creating' solidarities,[139] Gadamer claims that we do not need to 'invent' solidarities, 'we merely have to make ourselves aware of them'.[140] Gadamer, indeed (as Walter Lammi notes), 'goes so far as to call the self-recognition of the faithful in the events of the past the real purpose of Scriptural interpretation and an "essential aspect" of Christianity'.[141] (There *may* be an undercurrent in Gadamer of a *distinctiveness* of the hermeneutics of scriptural interpretation in Christian community: he speaks of 'the Christian tradition which contains an unsolvable contradiction impossible to hide between reason and revelation'.)[142]

There is a wide range of expression in recent decades, contested but well attested, identifying interpretation of the Bible in a social embodiment[143] of Christian faith, which suggests that a body of interpreters make a fairly confident answer to Eagleton's question about whose and what 'tradition' is in mind.[144] Understanding can be conceived as proceeding from a commonality binding the readers to a tradition, in which, *pace* Eagleton, the readers may be, in some measure, 'at home'. This also reflects the 'social function' of texts, which for Jauss 'manifests itself in its genuine possibility only where the literary experience of the reader

---

137. Gadamer, *Gadamer in Conversation*, e.g. pp.34–35 and 80–82.

138. Lawn, *Gadamer*, p.106.

139. E.g. Richard Rorty, *Contingency, Irony and Solidarity* (Cambridge: Cambridge University Press, 1989), p.196.

140. Gadamer, *Gadamer in Conversation*, p.80.

141. Walter Lammi, *Gadamer and the Question of the Divine* (London/New York: Continuum, 2008), p.15, citing Hans-Georg Gadamer, 'Herméneutique et Théologie', *Revue des Sciences Religieuses* 51.4 (1977), pp.384–97 (391).

142. Hans-Georg Gadamer, 'The Philosophy and Religion of Judaism', in *Gadamer on Education, Poetry and History: Applied Hermeneutics* (ed. D. Misgeld and G. Nicholson; trans. L. Schmidt and M. Reuss; Albany: State University of New York Press, 1992), p.160.

143. This phrase is from Meeks, 'Social Embodiment', see esp. pp.176–86.

144. Eagleton, *Literary Theory*, p.72 (cited above).

enters into the horizon of expectation of his lived praxis, performs his understanding of the world, and thereby also has an effect on his social behaviour'.[145]

We have seen this in the recurring insistence in discussions concerning the interpretation and application of biblical texts in the priorities of *Auslegungsgeschichte* (§6.2.a), and the interpretation and application which goes beyond the reconstructions of the effective-conditions for meaning in historical-critical method (§2.1). Ebeling, for example, presented his programme of Church history as the 'History of the Exposition of Scripture', and identified 'interconnections of theological thinking and of the church situation' in the interpretation of the Bible. Wink sought 'new possibilities for personal and social transformation', and Swartley 'the rejoining of the text's message to the life-world of the interpreter'.[146]

Nicolas Lash develops the metaphor of *performance* of the text in the life of the church as the authentic biblical interpretation.[147] The concept is often referred to Alasdair MacIntyre[148] and has been used by several other theologians,[149] but is also a key analogy used by Gadamer.[150] The metaphor can be referred to realms of theatre or music, where 'performance' is different from 'expertise' in music history (a theoretical framework) or 'analysis' of the musical score (an analogy with some historical-critical competences). Performance is communally expressed, in worship, the eucharist and daily life. The analogy not only has resonances with Gadamer's account of the 'performance' of a text, but particular resonances in my case study where the observable expression of the texts are rooted in so much lived experience of legal provision and of political and domestic contingencies.

However, Rowland voices a concern about where a 'theologically self-conscious set of concerns' might lead:

145. Jauss, *Aesthetic of Reception*, p.39 (cited in §6.4).

146. Ebeling, *Word of God*, p.28, and *Word and Faith*, p.22; Wink, *Human Transformation*, pp.10–12; Swartley, *Slavery, Sabbath*, p.219.

147. Nicholas Lash, 'Performing the Scriptures', in *Theology on the Way to Emmaus* (London: SCM, 1986), pp.37–46.

148. Alasdair MacIntyre, *After Virtue* (London: Duckworth, 1981).

149. E.g. Frances M. Young, *Art of Performance: Towards a Theology of Holy Scripture* (London: Darton, Longman & Todd, 1990); Stephen C. Barton, *Life Together: Family, Sexuality, and Community in the New Testament and Today* (Edinburgh/New York: T. & T. Clark, 2001), pp.223–50 ('New Testament Interpretation as Performance').

150. E.g. Gadamer, *Truth and Method*, pp.115–17.

It would be a pity if reception history of the Bible followed in the footsteps of the historical-critical method and ended up with a kind of received wisdom of what counted as 'classic readings' or, indeed, an understanding of tradition that became a kind of academic theological equivalent of the *magisterium*.[151]

Compilations of reception that give primary consideration 'to the most influential interpretations'[152] may indeed be expressing such an understanding of tradition. In doing so, I have argued (see §6.5), these are still expressions of *Wirkungsgeschichte*, but so also may be those that privilege neglected reception and challenge conservative traditions. *Wirkungsgeschichte* is an account of how we construct meaning from texts, and not one method, nor one tradition, of so doing. Christian tradition, of course, is far from monolithic. Kathryn Tanner argues that an *ecclesiocentric approach* to scripture can span historical, geographical and cultural breadth, as 'a tradition that is self-critical, pluralistic, and viable across a wide range of geographical differences and historical changes of circumstance'.[153] However, one interpreter may identify the commonality and tradition through which *they* receive a text more narrowly than another.

For biblical interpretation, such considerations may have a *theological* foundation. I shall enquire (in §9.3.b below) how far the theology influencing such decisions may be internal or external to the subject matter of the texts. Here my argument is that *Wirkungsgeschichte* encompasses the theologically charged engagement of Christians with historical and contemporary reception of biblical texts. This is motivated (with a perlocutionary immediacy with some texts, such as those of my case study) by the perceived need 'to build a foundation for decisions concerning the use of Scripture today'.[154] Räisänen makes a case for the inclusion, in reception-historical approaches to a biblical text, of 'the totality of its various functions'; and he too identifies this as a 'theological concern': 'Should not the clarification of the actual role which Scripture has played in history be *one* necessary condition (among others) for making meaningful suggestions about its hoped for role today?'[155] I cited above Morgan's suggestion that the 'desire to understand what is

151. Rowland, Review of David Parris, *Reception Theory and Biblical Hermeneutics*.

152. Parris, *Reception Theory*, p.219 (cited in §6.3).

153. Kathryn Tanner, 'Theology and the Plain Sense', in *Scriptural Authority and Narrative Interpretation* (ed. Garrett Green; Philadelphia: Fortress, 1987), p.60.

154. Räisänen, *Challenge*, p.268.

155. Räisänen, 'Effective History', p.268.

going on in Christian reception of the Bible' is key to the operation of theological interpretation within reception-historical approaches.[156] The compilation of reception from my case study offered in Chapter 8, with its attention to some classic and some neglected literary texts, shares such a motivation: to clarify the 'actual role which Scripture has played in history'.

It is this *theological* foundation for a 'hermeneutics of consequences'[157] that may be seen, in forms of Christian biblical interpretation, as a compelling argument for seeking neglected reception or interpretation that challenges conservative traditions. (This is by no means to deny that there are other foundations providing the same impulse.)[158] Luz argues that 'Biblical texts whose consequences have been hatred, exclusiveness and injustice call for critical questioning'.[159] Schüssler Fiorenza refers to an 'ethics of accountability' that accepts responsibility for ethical consequences of the biblical text and its meanings: 'If scriptural texts have served not only noble causes but also to legitimate war, to nurture anti-Judaism and misogynism, to justify the exploitation of slavery, and to promote colonial dehumanization, then scholars must expose such effects'.[160]

It is the expressed intention of the series editors of the Blackwell Bible Commentaries that in those volumes 'the material will be presented in such a way that readers can make up their own minds on the value, morality and validity of particular interpretations'.[161] This may underestimate the role of the compilers in selection, and in their identification, implicit or explicit, of the 'tradition' that receives and transmits it.

Bockmuehl's comments (on Luz's expression of the hermeneutics of consequences) may be applied to these positions:

> One is left with the impression that the hermeneutical adjudication between text and effective history [*sic*] is plagued by conflicting ideological commitments... [I]s not the 'effect' of a text a kind of optical illusion, limitless in scope and complexity and forever receding beyond our grasp unless we impose on it some theological or ideological order?[152]

156. Morgan, '*Sachkritik*', p.189.

157. Cf. Dorothee Sölle, *Phantasie und Gehorsam: Überlegungen zu einer künftigen christlichen Ethik* (Stuttgart: Kreuz, 1968), p.16.

158. We saw examples of both in §6.3.

159. Luz, *Matthew in History*, p.92.

160. Elisabeth Schüssler Fiorenza, 'The Ethics of Biblical Interpretation: Decentering Biblical Scholarship', *JBL* 107 (1988), pp.3–17 (15–16).

161. Sawyer *et al.*, 'Series Editors' Preface', p.xii.

162. Bockmuehl, *Seeing the Word*, p.166. It is a feature of discourse on reception history that the terms are variously, conflictingly, used (see §1.1.c). There is, I

254 Reception History, Tradition and Biblical Interpretation

However, his suggestion seems to be that the role of theological and ideological factors is in distinguishing 'legitimate prejudices' or 'distorting' interpretation as *external* factors to the process of understanding. My case-study texts, with their participation in discourses of political, social and domestic relationships, leave me in no doubt that, with some texts at least, ideological commitments are *integral* to the historical contingencies of both text and reader. My question – raised in §6.2 but responding also to the critique of Habermas and others – is how far to characterise, as Bockmuehl may be doing, the selection of reception of texts as an external imposition of 'some theological or ideological order' or, with Gadamer, as something intrinsic to the hermeneutical operation, which foregrounds prejudgments (arising from the text and developed within the historical tradition to which the reader belongs). The next section seeks to clarify this, and particularly in relation to interpretation of the case-study texts.

9.3.b. 'The prejudices governing our own understanding'

In one place in his analysis, Parris judges that '"validity in interpretation" would appear to be something that is tradition-constituted' – where 'valid' characterises interpretations that have 'demonstrated their appropriateness across paradigm shifts or in several different paradigms'.[163] This may be vulnerable to the critique offered by Habermas and others that tradition as such remains the only ground of the validity of prejudices[164] and thus a designation of a conservative thesis 'according to which we are not only members of a tradition but also its ideological supporters'.[165] In order to avoid the undetected influence of force or domination, which he deems is what can happen if we rely solely on hermeneutic understanding, Habermas insists on the operation of a 'reference system' of relations of power and the conditions of social labour, that does not 'sublimate social processes entirely to cultural tradition'.[166]

In another part of his analysis, Parris refers to some such reference system, similarly drawn from outside of an historical text and a tradition of its reception. He judges that Jauss 'overcomes one of the 'major

suggest, no adjudication in Gadamerian hermeneutics between 'text' and 'effective history', and I would adjust this to: 'the hermeneutical adjudication of both a text and *its various reception* is plagued by conflicting ideological commitments'.

163. Parris, *Reception Theory*, p.193.
164. E.g. Habermas, 'A Review of Gadamer's *Truth and Method*', p.237.
165. Warnke, *Gadamer*, p.106 (§9.3).
166. Habermas, 'A Review of Gadamer's *Truth and Method*', p.361 (§9.2).

criticisms that has been persistently made against Gadamer, the need for some form of critique of ideology within hermeneutics'.[167] Jauss refers to 'the ideological-critical suspicion that literary transmission may not unfold in absolute freedom; it may be pseudocommunicatively constrained'.[168] Parris extrapolates that mediation between horizons should be preserved from 'the power of traditions to incorporate what is heterogeneous into it… The inclusion of a critique of ideology…is an extremely important aspect of reception theory's possible contribution to the fields of biblical interpretation and church history.'[169] This is not, however, demonstrated. The operation of such ideological-critical suspicion does not figure clearly or systematically either in Jauss or in Parris' case study – *other than by the operation of Gadamer's own principle* of historically effected consciousness and the process of dialectic.

A significant distinction seems to be made here between 'ideology' and 'prejudice'. For critics like Habermas – and, less explicitly, for Jauss and Parris too – ideological perspectives are characterised, in a manner foreign to Gadamerian thought, as not sharing the same experiential and historically situated characteristics as other prejudgments. Warnke, in a discussion of Habermas' thought, characterises 'ideological claims' as coming from an 'unarticulated source' different from the traditionary text being read (a sort of 'undue influence' that Jauss describes as a 'pseudo-communicative' constraint):

> The crucial point here is that ideology is not the same as prejudice, that there is a difference between calling a perspective ideological and recognizing its historical and social situatedness. What makes a claim ideological is not merely its connection to an unarticulated source, not its reliance on unexpressed norms and assumptions. Ideological claims do not simply leave the assumptions behind them implicit; they rather articulate them in such a way that it becomes difficult to disentangle the warranted part of the claims from the unwarranted.[170]

This is a contestable distinction. There are indeed interpretative strategies (and ones applied to the Pauline paraenesis of submission) that might be characterised in this way, though with radical revisions to this description. For example, some reading strategies in liberation and feminist

---

167. This is not a common judgment made concerning Jauss's achievement: see, e.g., Andrzej Warminski, in Paul de Man, *Aesthetic Ideology* (Minneapolis: University of Minnesota Press, 1996), pp.3 and 6.

168. Jauss, *Question and Answer*, p.226.

169. Parris, *Reception Theory*, p.164.

170. Warnke, *Gadamer*, p.115.

theologies may derive a compelling prejudgment from alternative sources, and other interpreters may find the resulting reading 'unwarranted'. Meeks notes that

> Schüssler Fiorenza and some other feminists...are quite candid in advocating an honest and overt adoption of an ideological position against the perceived patriarchy in any of the texts as well as in the tradition that interprets them. An ideology favouring the oppressed may justly displace the regnant ideology of the oppressors.[171]

Comparably, the focus in Latin American liberation theology on the role of praxis (a concept derived from Marxism) in shaping the pre-understanding that informs biblical interpretation, motivates Miguez Bonino's insistence on 'identification of the ideological framework of interpretation implicit in a given religious praxis'.[172]

The assertion is that 'ideology is not the same as prejudice', but it is difficult to see why such critiques of ideology are qualitatively different from Gadamer's principle of *wirkungsgeschichtliches Bewusstsein*, which 'can solve the question of critique in hermeneutics' and 'make conscious the prejudices governing our own understanding'.[173] Habermas and others refer to constraints of social and economic factors that are 'outside' the 'self-contained' traditions.[174] But any such factors, if they have anything to do with interpreting the text, are part of the lived experience within the origins of the text, or within its transmission, or within its current reception-and-application – prejudgments revealed through consciousness of the hermeneutical situation, *wirkungsgeschichtliches Bewusstsein*. Both the examples above, feminist and liberationist ideologies, reassert the 'co-determinant' role of the historical situatedness of the interpreter in understanding a text. Both examples may also reinforce a 'commonality', a shared ideology, binding new readers to earlier readers, and to an evolving tradition. The ideology can be challenged. Texts approached from different historical perspectives disclose new, different aspects of their meaning: values, commitments and claims that may be hidden from one point of view are revealed from another.[175] For Gadamer, as discussed above, commonality means that the interpreter may not share the views constituting the first horizon of

---

171. Meeks, 'American Slavery', p.248 (cited in §4.5.a).

172. J. Miguez Bonino, *Revolutionary Theology Comes of Age* (London: SPCK, 1975), p.94.

173. Gadamer, *Truth and Method*, p.298 (cited above).

174. Warnke, *Gadamer*, p.112; cf. Habermas, 'A Review of Gadamer's *Truth and Method*', p.361.

175. Cf. Warnke, *Gadamer*, p.114.

the text, even though those views form an integral part of the interpreter's self-understanding.

The implicit and explicit theological and ideological 'claims' made in many biblical texts raise a specific question about the origin of 'unwarranted' claims from an 'unarticulated source'. In particular Paul's own discourse of power, social relationships and gender may defy attempts to distinguish ideology from theology (see §10.5). Particular reception of my case-study texts suggests that, for some interpreters, an 'ideology favouring the oppressed' is not an incorporation of something 'heterogeneous' into the mediation of horizons. It may be a 'warranted' claim from an 'articulated' source, namely, Pauline texts, and part of what the historical tradition of reception of the texts has determined as 'what seems to us worth enquiring about and what will appear as an object of investigation'.[176]

The operation of theological prejudgments in understanding a text can be seen as a form of *Sachkritik*, a 'critical assessment of what a biblical text says in the light of the gospel that the author intended to communicate'.[177] This is related to the discussion in §9.2.a, above: Gadamer's citations of Bultmann and Hofmann that 'scriptural hermeneutics presupposes a relationship to the content of the Bible', and Thiselton's claim that 'Pauline exegesis is rooted in "Pauline theology"'. Though the term *Sachkritik* has expressed particular, contested strategies in the last nine decades,[178] the attempt to discern the key subject matter of a text is a widespread strategy in contemporary New Testament interpretation,[179] and one in which 'all historical-critical theologians claim either more or less continuity with their scriptures'.[180] How far such an identification then becomes a 'guide and even a criterion by which other aspects of the wider context in which the particular passage is to be found are assessed'[181] is variously undertaken, in Gadamerian terms, in the mediation of horizons that takes place in each reception of the text.

176. Gadamer, *Truth and Method*, p.300, cited in §9.3 above.

177. Morgan, '*Sachkritik*', p.175.

178. Robert Morgan's account of the variety of English translations of this term illustrates this: *The Nature of New Testament Theology* (London: SCM, 1973), p.42; cf. John Ashton, 'History and Theology in New Testament Studies', in Rowland and Tuckett (eds.), *Nature of New Testament Theology*, pp.1–17 (11).

179. The series editors of the New International Greek Testament Commentary suggest that, '[o]ne of the gains of recent scholarship has been the recognition of the primarily theological character of the books of the New Testament': I. H. Marshall and D. A. Hagner, 'Foreword', in Thiselton, *First Corinthians*, p.xv.

180. Morgan, '*Sachkritik*', p.145.

181. Roberts and Rowland, 'Introduction', p.135.

9.4. Interim summary

Gadamer denies the identification of situatedness-of-interpretation with subjectivity. Understanding is dialectic, 'neither subjective nor objective'; it proceeds from 'the commonality that binds us to the tradition'.[182] Understanding is neither merely the reconstruction of the author's view nor an assertion of the reader's but results from a dialogic encounter: and understanding depends on a disposition to 'agree'. All assertions of authority, judgment, reason and freedom are made from historical and cultural experience, and may be a legacy of a text and the tradition in which the reader receives it, in an operation where there is both 'openness' and 'limitation'.[183]

I conclude that reception-historical methods in biblical studies can demonstrate the aptness of Gadamer's hermeneutics for the description of biblical interpretation, including Christian interpretation of the New Testament. This can be characterised by solidarity or commonality in a tradition, variously delineated by the interpreter's experience of being formed by a tradition, and subject to the dialectic 'interplay of the movement of tradition and the movement of the interpreter'.[184] It may also be characterised by the role of theology in the horizon of the past and present – in the conscious and 'unconscious meaning of the author',[185] and the tradition contributing to the horizon of expectation of successive readers.

Wirkungsgeschichte, the history-of-effect principle, offers an account of how 'validity' in interpretation is, partly, 'tradition-constituted'. Traditionary texts have their legacy in the pre-judgments of the reader. Interpretative traditions exercise theological and ecclesial constraints, which may derive from the texts or from other texts in the traditions that have transmitted them. Gadamer's hermeneutics nevertheless do not describe a process of understanding that must merely affirm interpretations made by the tradition to which that reader happens to belong. This in particular will be tested in the case-study sample that follows.

However, the value given to neglected reception or interpretation that challenges conservative traditions will vary. This is an observed 'oscillation' rather than a systematically argued analysis in Gadamer's hermeneutics: the affirmation of some continuity in a tradition (and

182. Gadamer, *Truth and Method*, p.293.
183. Gadamer, *Truth and Method*, p.357.
184. Gadamer, *Truth and Method*, p.293.
185. Gadamer, *Truth and Method*, p.192.

avoidance of 'subjectivism') on the one hand, *and* the affirmation of the new reader's perspective, respecting historical contingency (and offering the possibility of critiquing the tradition) on the other.

The resulting weight given either to a 'canon of exemplary commentators', or to reception representing greater diversity and neglected aspects of biblical interpretation, may both be characterised as the operation of 'legitimate prejudices' within a Gadamerian hermeneutics. There are theological arguments – and these may be received as part of the legacy of the texts – for valorizing a 'hermeneutics of consequences', seeking to clarify the 'actual role which Scripture has played in history' and an 'ethics of accountability'.[186]

---

186. Räisänen, 'Effective History', p.268; Schüssler Fiorenza, 'Ethics of Biblical Interpretation', pp.15–16.

Chapter 10

THE CASE STUDY AND THEOLOGICAL HERMENEUTICS

10.1. Introduction

A final sample from the history of reception of my case-study texts is selected to illustrate and test key aspects of the arguments discussed in Chapter 9. The case-study texts, perlocutionary utterances where an author *intends* a particular interaction with the receiver, foreground questions of the interpretative 'control' of Pauline theology with respect to the co-determining influences of the original setting, the 'contours' of a tradition, and the historical contingencies of the interpreter. How far, and in what traditions of reception, is the ethical paraenesis considered within the framework of a theological hermeneutic, derived from Paul?

The arguments of some critics is that the role of theological and ideological factors in distinguishing 'legitimate prejudices' or 'distorting' interpretation is an *external* factor to the process of understanding. My contention is that, with some texts at least, ideological and theological commitments are *integral* to the historical contingencies of text or reader, and may be received as the legacy of a text to a reader. The desire of Gadamer's critics for an externality in this process (not available if Gadamer is right) is in order to have a basis from which to critique 'normative' interpretation, because traditional interpretations can be 'ideologically distorted'.[1] Does the case study offer evidence that, if tradition co-determines the nature of interpretation, reception merely confirms and conforms to a transmitted understanding, or does the *wirkungsgeschichtliches Bewusstsein* offer a dialectic and self-critical process, capable of transformation as well as confirmation?

In §§10.2 and 10.3, the examples are chiefly summary revisits to reception sampled in earlier chapters. In §10.2, the focus is reception that may constitute implicit or explicit appeals to *authorial intention*:

---

1.   Warnke, *Gadamer*, p.x (cited in §9.1).

'articulated' and 'warranted' opportunities of reading the texts in relation to other Pauline texts. In §10.3, the focus is the hermeneutical priority Gadamer assigns to prejudgment, and operations of a *Sachkritik*. In §10.4, with some new examples from the case study, reception reveals a confluence of the issues in §§10.2 and 10.3: convergence of a *Sachkritik* with speculation about 'the mind of Paul' and a construct of the author's intention. In §10.5 the focus is directed to reception that instantiates antithetical foundational prejudgments – a particular testing of the hermeneutical priority Gadamer assigns to prejudgment, using doctrinal or ideological positions that may be defended as part of the legacy of a text.

10.2. 'Specific warrants'

In earlier examples from the case study, we have seen the hermeneutical principle of a canonical univocality operating in patristic and mediaeval interpretation (and beyond), where 'commonality' extends to receiving the biblical writers as part, in some sense, of a unitary doctrinal tradition. Gadamer refers to this principle as a *departure* from Schleiermacher's 'psychological interpretation', noting that 'in the case of the Bible... interpreting each writer in terms of his individual psychology is of less moment than the significance of what is dogmatically uniform and common to them'.[2] The Bible is received in a tradition or traditions in which there is a prejudgment of a canonical coherence and a legacy of doctrinal instantiation of meaning.[3]

While this strategy may sometimes be characterised hermeneutically as introducing 'unwarranted' claims from an 'unarticulated source',[4] the interpretation of Pauline texts can offer specific *warrants* (in what may be received as 'a body of letters', see §3.2), and sources that are *articulated*, when one Pauline text is used to construct the horizon of expectation of another. We have seen this strongly represented in the case study. Indeed, the design of my case study around a repeated word and a nexus of texts, rather than a single text, establishes a principle of a canonical interpretation as part of the study (and makes it untypical of current writing in reception history). The frequency of use in the Pauline and post-Pauline tradition, and the infrequency of the word in Christian

2. Gadamer, *Truth and Method*, p.186 (cited in §9.3.a).
3. It is not my task here either to reject (cf. Räisänen, *Challenge*, pp.227–49) or to affirm (cf. Thiselton, *On Hermeneutics*, p.800) the Bible as providing the foundation for Christian doctrine.
4. Cf. Warnke, *Gadamer*, p.115 (cited in §9.3.a).

texts outside of this tradition (§4.7) – and the preference in the New Testament outside of Paul for other words in similar exhortation (e.g. Heb. 13.17) – suggests that Paul's use may be distinctive.[5] This offers particular, *articulated, warranted* opportunities of reading the texts in relation to other Pauline texts, such as the examples that follow here from the reception already sampled.

The role of Ὑποτασσόμενοι ἀλλήλοις (Eph. 5.21) as a lexical and hermeneutical key for other paraenetic uses of ὑποτάσσειν was illustrated in Chapter 4 (e.g. Jerome and Bilezikian, §4.5.a; Cranfield, §4.3.a). I described this as a transformative dynamic in terms of shaping the *Erwartungshorizont* of the interpreters.

Other texts, Pauline and non-Pauline, are used too: for example, Luther (§7.3.c) refers to the (Vulgate translation of) 1 Pet. 2.13 for a 'control' of meaning as applied to Romans 13, while Rachel Speght (§8.4.b) uses Paul's image of the Body (1 Cor. 12.26) to interpret the subordination of wives. Franz Leenhardt (§4.6) is one of very few commentators to use 1 Cor. 16.16 in the interpretation of Rom. 13.1. Barth, perhaps uniquely, and also problematically (§4.3), uses Rom. 8.20 to govern the paraenetic use in Rom. 13.1.[6] Multiple texts are used too, so Cranfield's use citing Eph. 5.21, referred to above, also cites Phil. 2.3 ('in humility regard others as better than yourselves').

A governing theology of mutual service and self-offering may be referenced to Christ's incarnation and ministry, or his death on the cross, often referencing Philippians 2. For example, in comment on Col. 3.18, Witherington (§4.6.c) notes, not the identification of the husband with Christ, but the mutual behaviour that is fitting 'in the Lord': he writes, 'This is presumably because Christ himself modelled this behaviour by taking on the form of a servant, submitting to serve others while on earth'.[7] Sydney Park, with closer attention to the key note of Jesus' death in this passage, roots the 'radical' implications for all Christian patterns of submission in the volitional and vicarious self-sacrifice of the cross of Christ[8] (and see below, §10.5, for a *theologia crucis* as the governing theology of submission).

---

5. This is by no means always accepted: e.g. Carrington, *Catechism*, pp.49–50.
6. Barth, *Romans*, p.485.
7. Witherington, *Paul Quest*, p.189. (He is taking Phil. 2.7 to reference the incarnation, rather than the 'death on a cross', Phil. 2.8.)
8. M. Sydney Park, *Submission within the Godhead and the Church in the Epistle to the Philippians: An Exegetical and Theological Examination of the Concept of Submission in Philippians 2 and 3* (London: T&T Clark International, 2007), p.163.

10.3. Pauline texts 'rooted in Pauline theology'

I have suggested (and the last examples illustrate) that in the case of understanding New Testament texts *Wirkungsgeschichte* may incorporate an operation of *Sachkritik*: an interpretative 'control' of a theological framework, in the sense that this provides a co-determinant of the meaning of the text in the tradition in which it is received. The identification of such a framework is subject, like every aspect of understanding, to contestation by different readers whose tradition is to any degree a legacy of the texts. This description has a particular correspondence with reception of Pauline texts 'rooted in Pauline theology'.[9] J.C. Beker notes that Paul's 'hermeneutic consists in the constant interaction between the coherent centre of the gospel and its contingent interpretation';[10] and Wayne Meeks argues that it is 'time that we took seriously the well-known fact that most of the New Testament documents, including the Pauline Epistles that have provided the central motifs of Protestant theology, were immediately addressed to problems of behaviour within the communities, of moral formation'.[11]

For my case-study texts, the description strongly corresponds to the case that can be made for Paul's rooting of ethical imperatives in theological indicatives, and for interpretation rooted in Pauline theology. It is possible to interpret these texts using *the framework of a theological hermeneutic, derived from Paul*, and to identify such a strategy with Gadamer's account of a hermeneutical operation that foregrounds *pre-judgments arising from the text, developed within the historical tradition* to which the interpreter belongs.

This is interpretation that may be regarded by other interpreters as governed by an ideology with an origin in 'unwarranted' claims from an 'unarticulated source'.[12] Dibelius, for example, explicitly denies a relationship of the paraenesis to Paul's theology: 'the hortatory sections of the Pauline epistles have nothing to do with the theoretic foundation of the ethics of the apostle, and very little to do with other ideas peculiar to him'.[13]

9. Thiselton, *On Hermeneutics*, p.303.
10. J.C. Beker, *Paul the Apostle* (Edinburgh: T. & T. Clark, 1980), p.11.
11. Meeks, 'Social Embodiment', p.185.
12. Warnke, *Gadamer*, p.115.
13. Dibelius, *James*, p.5 (and see §3.3).

A far more frequent analysis is that 'Paul integrated his ethical teaching into the context of his whole theology'.[14] In Chapter 4, I sampled commentators (e.g. Augustine, Barrett, Cranfield, Rowland, Ziesler, §10.3.b) who reference Pauline christology and eschatology for the semantic framework for ὑποτασσέσθω in Romans 13. Although Dunn criticises interpretation that tries to 'import too much theological freight in to the word',[15] he makes a theological reading in spite of this. While 'submission' is, he holds, a secular more than a theological term, and so does not carry the sense of 'recognising that one is placed below the authority by God',[16] the transformative doctrine, that a ruler's authority is God-given, is the point of the clauses that follow. The governing theology for Luther (§7.3.c) from the 'many passages of [Paul's] letters in which he...rejects servitude',[17] is the christological framework of 'submission' in 1 Cor. 15.27-28.

Two particular theological 'warrants' appealed to in interpretation of ὑποτάσσειν are (1) a *theologia crucis*, and (2) a trinitarian doctrine of the Son's subordination to the Father. Ignatius provides an example of each (§7.2.b). He writes to the Christians of Tralles, 'For when you are subject [ὑποτάσσησθε] to the bishop as to Jesus Christ, you appear to me not to live according to humankind, but according to Jesus Christ who died for us';[18] and his exhortation to the Christians of Magnesia references 1 Cor. 15.28: 'Be subject to the bishop and to one another [ὑποτάγητε τῷ ἐπισκόπῳ καὶ ἀλλήλοις], even as Jesus Christ was subject to the Father'.[19] Particular operations of these two doctrinal 'prejudgments' will be explored below in §10.5.

10.4. 'Conscious' and 'unconscious' authorial intention

There may be, with some authors, particular convergence of a *Sachkritik* with speculation about 'the mind of Paul', and a construct of the author's intention. This, as I have suggested (§§8.7 and 9.2.a), is not surprising in reception of letters, an illocutionary genre, and in paraenesis, a perlocutionary one.

14. Eduard Lohse, 'Changes of Thought in Pauline Theology? Some Reflections on Paul's Ethical Teaching in the Context of his Theology', in Lovering *et al.*, *Theology and Ethics*, pp.146–60 (160).
15. Dunn, *Romans 9–16*, p.760.
16. Cranfield, *Romans*, vol. 2, p.660.
17. Luther, *Romans*, p.365.
18. Ignatius, *Letter to the Trallians* 2.1 (pp.212–23).
19. Ignatius, *Letter to the Magnesians* 13.4–5 (pp.208–9).

So Witherington finds (in Eph. 5) a 'new approach to marriage', which is 'Paul's deliberate attempt to reform the patriarchal structure of his day'.[20] I suggested (§4.6.c) that other interpreters might well follow Witherington in his construction of Pauline theology, but balk at reading the *Haustafeln* as expressions of this. James Crouch, conversely, makes a distinction between Paul's intention, which is prescribed by shared cultural values (cf. Wedderburn, §3.4), and the true 'mind of the author'. This, Crouch says, is to be found not in the time-bound, culture-bound precepts but in the 'timeless message', which is that the *Haustafel* calls the reader 'to give oneself to one's neighbour within the limitations which the social order places on the relationship'.[21] The implication for Crouch is that Christians of his own day need not follow literally the command in Colossians (3.18–4.1) that wives and slaves be subordinate because his society, unlike that of the first century, does not demand the subordination of women and slaves. It is an example of the assumption, not often as explicitly articulated as in this example, that Paul or the deutero-Pauline authors were 'forced by their culture to make statements which in our culture they would not have made'.[22] Gadamer wrote, 'It is not the author's reflective self-interpretation but the unconscious meaning of the author that is to be understood'.[23] Crouch's analysis might be thought to accord with this, though it does not represent at all well the dialectic of understanding and the historically effected consciousness: 'the horizon of the present cannot be formed without the past' and understanding 'is always the fusion of these horizons supposedly existing by themselves'.[24]

Paul's *conscious* intention, even Paul's biography, may be seen as wholly determinant for interpretation of the paraenesis. Allan Boesak argues that the interpretation of submission (in Rom. 13) 'as blind obedience to civil authority is wrong', and references Paul's interaction with the magistrates of Philippi (Acts 16.37). He writes: 'For both Peter and Paul these were occasions where disobedience to civil authority was the only honourable way out for the Christian. Is it conceivable that Paul,

---

20. Witherington, *Genesis of Christianity*, p.156.
21. Crouch, *Colossian Haustafel*, p.160.
22. Bernadette J. Brooten, 'Jewish Women's History in the Roman Period: A Task for Christian Theology', in *Christians among Jews and Gentiles*, pp.22–30 (24). Thiselton may come close to this with his speculation of giving Paul a prospective understanding of modern notions: *On Hermeneutics*, pp.303–4 (cited in §9.2).
23. Gadamer, *Truth and Method*, p.192 (cited in §9.2.a).
24. Gadamer, *Truth and Method*, p.305 (cited in §9.2.a).

after having engaged in acts of disobedience himself, would now counsel Christians in Rome to blindly obey governmental powers?'[25] One answer to his question is that some people, with other prejudgments that are part of the legacy of the text in ecclesial and civil traditions, can apparently conceive something akin to this. The life-experiences of the readers, not just the biography of the author, participate in determining the understanding that is achieved.

Such receptions, Witherington's, Crouch's and Boesak's, seek or assume solidarity with a conscious or unconscious authorial 'meaning'. A too-ready equation in this process is what leads some commentators to prefer Jauss's *Horizontabhebung* over Gadamer's *Horizontverschmelzung*.[26] Both, however, describe any application as new, negotiated meaning (§§2.4 and 6.4). Understanding takes place in 'dialogue', in which to reach understanding, as a fusion of horizons, means 'being transformed into a communion in which we do not remain what we were'.[27]

10.5. The Trinity, the cross, and subordination

The purpose of this final interrogation of reception of the case-study texts is to illustrate and test the hermeneutical priority Gadamer assigns to prejudgment, as this applies to *a doctrinal or ideological position that may be defended as part of the legacy of a text*. The sample here represents antithetical foundational prejudgments: some reception holds that subordination is a prescribed, natural condition of some categories of human; other reception patterns subordination for all Christians on the voluntary self-offering of Christ.

The first example concerns the role of 1 Cor. 15.28 in doctrinal formulations of the Trinity: it is a key text in disputes about 'subordinationism', which characterises the Son as subordinate (in some way) to the Father. Gadamer's hermeneutics recognises such use of a text to answer a question not posed by the author, for a text possesses 'a horizon of unasserted possibilities of meaning...that exceed what is stated in the text'.[28]

25. Boesak, *Unjust Rule*, p.147.
26. E.g. '*Alienation* and *provocation* (or a challenge experienced on the basis of difference) are part of Jauss's hermeneutics of alterity': Thiselton, *Doctrine*, p.101.
27. Gadamer, *Truth and Method*, p.371.
28. Weinsheimer, *Gadamer's Hermeneutics*, p.210 (cited in §9.2).

A doctrine of economic subordination was accepted by the Council of Nicaea, construing as heretical the Arian teaching of ontological subordination. (A doctrine of ontological subordination of Son to Father is maintained today by Jehovah's Witnesses.) Such reception has not appeared in my case study, which is focused on the paraenetic use of ὑποτάσσειν, though the potentially transformative role of instances of the active voice (which are all christological, except Rom. 8.20) has been considered (§4.1). Some recent reception of 1 Cor. 15.28, however, appeals to its perceived support for subordinationist doctrines in the context of its implications for human hierarchies and women's subordination.

In 1977, the Anglican General Synod of Australia commissioned a report, 'The Ministry of Women', which recommended the ordination of women. The report concluded that an orthodox, credal christology leads to an understanding of subordination as 'voluntary and mutual':

> The Athanasian creed specifies that there is no ordered subordination or hierarchy within the Godhead. The only stated subordination is that Jesus is 'inferior to the Father, as touching his manhood'. Headship within the Trinity cannot mean 'subordinate to' or 'under the authority of'. Subordination is a matter of the freedom of the will, not of some imposed order.[29]

A one-person minority-position addendum by one of the Doctrine Commission's twelve members, D. Broughton Knox, was published with the report, denouncing its conclusions. Knox 'presented the full range of arguments against women's ordination still current in Sydney to this day'.[30] He writes,

> The principle of order, of headship and subordination, is clearly seen in 1 Cor. 15.23-28 where Christ is head over all things and yet himself is subordinate to the Father. Since Christ is both head of every man and himself subordinate to the Father he is the example (in perfect relationship) both of the exercise of headship...and obedience.[31]

In 1999, the (conservative evangelical) Diocese of Sydney commissioned its own report, 'The Doctrine of the Trinity and its Bearing on the Relationship of Men and Women'. This cites Knox's addendum to the

---

29. Church of England in Australia, General Synod, Commission on Doctrine, *The Ministry of Women: A Report of the General Synod Commission on Doctrine* (Reports to the General Synod of the Church of England in Australia 1; Sydney: St. Andrew's House, 1977), p.3.

30. Muriel Porter, *Sydney Anglicans and the Threat to World Anglicanism: The Sydney Experiment* (Farnham: Ashgate, 2011), p.123.

31. D.B. Knox in General Synod of Australia, *The Ministry of Women*, p.31.

General Synod's report. The Sydney report concludes that the submission of the Son (as in orthodox patristic and scholastic tradition) is
functional and not ontological, but (against this tradition) that this
submission is not temporary, for the incarnation, but eternal: 'As far as
revelation permits us to see in any temporal direction – ...forward to
consummation...and beyond (1 Cor. 15.28) – unity, equality and subordination characterise the life of the Trinity'.[32] On these grounds, the
1999 Sydney Doctrine Commission claims that the statement of the 1977
Australian General Synod Commission (cited above) 'misunderstands
the meaning of freedom. The will is not free from the order imposed by
the inner reality of personhood'. If subordination is not voluntary, neither
is it mutual: 'The Son does not ask the Father to submit to him...and
cannot do so if he is to have the liberty to be true to his...nature'.[33]

The corollary of a Son equal in being but below by order, eternally, is
that humanity may be construed to have the same pattern of equal being
but distinct order – not temporally in free and mutual acts of subordination, but permanently by 'nature'. The conclusion of the 1999 report is
as follows:

> The Doctrine Commission agrees that the concept of 'subordination' has
> significant implications. It concludes...that the concept of 'functional
> subordination', of equality of essence with order in relation...should...
> determine our commitment both to the equality of men and women in
> creation and salvation, and also to appropriately biblical expressions of
> the functional difference between men and women in home and church.[34]

The *eternal* subordination of the Son means the *permanent* subordination
of women. This is their conclusion, and the *quod erat demonstrandum*:
the text provides the doctrinal statement that is used as the foundational
principle for its interpretation. This is the sort of pattern that might attract
Habermas's critique of Gadamer, that 'tradition...remains the only
ground of the validity of prejudices'[35] – except that it itself counters a
different doctrinal prejudgement within the same tradition. (The division
of the Commission's report into first 'meaning' and then 'significance'
suggests the influence of the hermeneutics of Hirsch; see §9.2).

32. Diocese of Sydney Doctrine Commission, 'The Doctrine of the Trinity and
its Bearing on the Relationship of Men and Women' (http://www.sds.asn.au/
assets/documents/synod/TrinityDoctrineComm.pdf, accessed 27 March 12), 4.1, p.7.
33. Sydney Doctrine Commission, 'Trinity', 4.2, p.7.
34. Sydney Doctrine Commission, 'Trinity', 6.4, p.19. Reception of the subordination paraenesis to slaves offers interesting parallels concerning contested theologies of 'human nature': see Meeks, 'American Slavery', pp.232–53.
35. Habermas, 'Review of Gadamer', p.237.

The hierarchical, involuntary, non-reciprocal, model of submission has been popularised (among conservative evangelicals) in the 'complementarian' theology and ethics of 'The Council on Biblical Manhood and Womanhood', which sponsors John Piper and Wayne Grudem's collection of essays (drawn on earlier in the case study: §§4.6.b and 8.6.b). One of the authors, Thomas Schriener, uses the Son's subjection to the Father in 1 Cor. 15, and Trinitarian doctrine, in an advocacy of women's submission to men: 'Women are equal to men in essence and in being; there is no ontological distinction, and yet they have a different function or role in church and home'.[36]

Kevin Giles argues, against the Sydney Doctrine Commission and the complementarians, that the orthodox tradition of economic, temporal, subordination means that it is 'Christlike' willingly to subordinate oneself in the service of others 'and this is so for men and women'.[37] He refers this (which we have seen is a frequent strategy in the reception) to Paul's theology in Phil. 2.5-8 ('in humility regard others as better than yourselves…[for] Christ…humbled himself…to the point of…death on a cross').

As Habermas insisted, there are competing ideological positions at stake. Elizabeth Castelli, for example, interprets Paul's 'pastoral power' in terms of hierarchy and conformity. Paul is 'shaping relations of power' in a promotion of 'a hierarchical view of imitation'. His appeal to his own submission, in order to obtain the submission of others (1 Cor. 9.19-27), she argues, serves a purpose of social control in the interests of pre-ordained or 'natural' human and societal norms.[38]

Conversely, Theissen makes an analysis of Paul's ideology that is founded in Paul's own account of the *Sache* of his proclamation: 'Christ crucified' (1 Cor. 1.23) who is the 'power of God', characterised as God's 'foolishness' and 'weakness':

> The dominant system is to lose its power over Christians. The preaching is to make one independent from every external judgment. The decisive condition for learning is the model of Christ. In him the impotent is shown as powerful, and the powerful as weak. With a view to him one need not

36. Thomas Schreiner, 'Head Coverings, Prophecies and the Trinity', in Piper and Grudem (eds.), *Recovering Biblical Manhood*, pp.117–32 (120). Extracts from these essays were cited in §8.6.b.

37. Kevin Giles, *The Trinity and Subordinationism: The Doctrine of God and the Contemporary Gender Debate* (Downers Grove: InterVarsity, 2002), p.116.

38. Elizabeth A. Castelli, *Imitating Paul: A Discourse of Power* (Louisville: Westminster John Knox, 1991), pp.119, 113 and 117.

be impressed by the claims of the powerful, the respected, and the well-born... Only love has emancipated itself from all external authorities, consequences, and models, from all the extrinsic reinforcements whose functioning is inconceivable without power.[39]

We saw this emancipation by love in reception of the paraenesis, as, for example, Martin Luther (§7.3.c) on Romans 13: '"By love serve one another"... This...is the good kind of spiritual servitude: all things serve them that have it...but they themselves are the servants of none.'[40]

Giles, Theissen and Luther all give Paul's theology of the cross a hermeneutical priority, and this forms my second example (briefly illustrated, as it has already appeared throughout the sample) of a doctrinal/ideological prejudgment that may be defended as part of the legacy of inter-related or canonical texts. The term *theologia crucis* originates with Martin Luther and it was Ernst Käsemann who introduced the term into New Testament scholarship.[41] It is a move that is a candidate for a 'macro' (methodological paradigm) shift in interpretative tradition (see §6.2): 'The Reformers were indisputably right when they appealed to Paul for their understanding of evangelical theology as a theology of the cross... Paul has to be understood in the light of the Reformation's insight.'[42]

Käsemann explicitly makes the case for subordination being interpreted in the light of ταπεινοφροσύνη (Phil. 2.3) 'as the mark of a Christian life', and not according to a foundation of natural law and the order of creation, which does not play a large role in Paul's theology.[43] He therefore reads the exhortation of Romans 13 with the foundation principle of Paul's theology of the cross (the implications of which Theissen summarises above). Käsemann argues that the thesis that makes

---

39. Theissen, *Psychological Aspects*, pp.372–73. Other analyses include Clarke's, who contrasts coercive and hierarchical models of power with Paul's appeal to the pattern of Christ crucified: Andrew D. Clarke, *Secular Christian Leadership in Corinth: A Socio-historical and Exegetical Study of 1 Corinthians 1–6* (Leiden: Brill, 1993).

40. Luther, *Romans*, p.366.

41. Cf. Michael Wolter, 'The Theology of the Cross and the Quest for a Doctrinal Norm', in Rowland and Tuckett, *Nature of New Testament Theology*, pp.263–85 (263–64).

42. Ernst Käsemann, *Perspectives on Paul* (London: SCM, 1971), p.32.

43. Käsemann, *Romans*, p.356, citing (*contra*) Ulrich Duchrow, *Christenheit und Weltverantwortung: Traditionsgeschichte und systematische Struktur der Zweireichelehre* (Stuttgart: E. Klett, 1970). (This is in an extension of Käsemann's argument discussed in §5.2.d.)

Rom. 13.1 a 'universal apostolic decree' is clearly seen to be 'absurd' when it attempts to combine the theology of the cross with submission to the authorities.[44]

Others accept the theological foundation, Paul's theology of the cross, but see this as co-existing in Paul's texts with social ethics based on hierarchy and conformity – an ethos hard to distinguish from Castelli's view of Paul's promotion of hierarchy. So Schüssler Fiorenza argues that, although in Paul's thought the cross of Jesus 'applies to all human frailty and mortality' so that 'newness' of God's creation should transform the 'mind', Paul does not then say that it should change the social-political relationship of Christians.[45] Gerhardsson sees the paradox as between Paul's individual ethics which were 'so radical' and the 'little radicalism' apparent in his social ethics.[46] I have suggested that there is indeed an ideology and ethos in the post-Pauline Pastoral Letters now often characterised as 'love-patriarchalism' or 'benevolent patriarchalism':[47] an ideology that ameliorates coercive hierarchical power with good will to subordinates. In these texts, however, it is not apparent that the characteristically Pauline *theologia crucis* is foundational:[48] the love-patriarchal ethics of the Pastoral Letters can be held to match their less 'radical', less distinctively Pauline theology.[49] It is very problematic to read this love-patriarchalism back into the earlier letters, whether Pauline or deutero-Pauline, as Gerhardsson does,[50] and also the 'complementarians': it is problematic (even, with Käsemann, 'absurd') because the radicalism in Paul's theology of the cross puts the continuance of hierarchical power beyond 'amelioration'.

---

44. Käsemann, *Romans*, p.355. With respect to submission to imperial authorities, Richard Horsley argues that Paul's focus on the crucified Christ is 'the most blatantly anti-Roman imperial aspect of his gospel': Horsley, *Paul and Empire*, p.141.

45. Schüssler Fiorenza, *In Memory*, p.187.

46. Gerhardsson, *Ethos of the Bible*, p.88.

47. Theissen, *Social Setting*, p.107; Martin, *Slavery as Salvation*, p.128; cf. Troeltsch, *Social Teaching*, p.78 (cited in §5.3.b).

48. Cf. S.G. Wilson, *Luke and the Pastoral Epistles* (London: SPCK, 1979), pp.80–85; I. Howard Marshall makes a case for *some* 'theology of the cross' in these letters: 'The Christology of Luke–Acts and the Pastoral Epistles', in *Crossing the Boundaries: Essays in Biblical Interpretation in Honour of Michael Goulder* (ed. S.E. Porter, P. Joyce and D.E. Orton; Brill: Leiden, 1994), pp.167–82 (172–75).

49. Cf. Lincoln, *Later Pauline Letters*, p.141; Schüssler Fiorenza, *In Memory*, p.288 (cited in §5.3.b).

50. Gerhardsson, *Ethos of the Bible*, pp.84–85 (cited in §5.3.b).

The hermeneutical point here is that these contests about theology and ideology are not merely drawing on an external system of references. They do not require the moves offered by Crouch or Thiselton giving Paul a prospective view of *later* cultural or conceptual notions not available to him. They are not an importation or mediation from the reader's horizon, not present in the author's. They are not an 'unwarranted' claim from an 'unarticulated source'[51] but part of the dialectic 'interplay of the movement of tradition and the movement of the interpreter'.[52]

In my two key examples – the hierarchically subordinationist theology with a matching complementarian ethic (e.g. Knox, Sydney Doctrine Commission, Piper and Grudem), and the theology of the cross with a matching radical ethic of mutual subordination (e.g. Käsemann, Giles and my own position) – in both of these, the reader's theology claims a solidarity with Paul's. Throughout the sample of reception, neither the ideology of subordination by nature that permanently superordinates some human beings to others,[53] nor subordination as a voluntary and reciprocal act by each for the common good, is 'outside' the 'self-contained' traditions.[54] The ideologies may be specifically theological. They are christologically founded in Pauline texts (though differently): on the 'ordering' of Christ as 'eternally subordinate', or on the voluntary act of Christ who 'humbled himself'. The distinction made by critics of Gadamer (see §9.3.b) between 'ideology' and 'prejudgment' holds true for neither of these: each position is identified by the interpreter as part of the legacy of the text within the tradition in which they have received it. Both Giles and the Sydney Doctrine Commission represent their own position as the 'orthodox' one.

10.6. Interim case-study evaluation

The case study demonstrates, variously, how 'validity' in interpretation may be, partly, 'tradition-constituted'. Historical-critical analysis and theology can have roles in distinguishing what may be 'legitimate prejudices'[55] for any one biblical interpreter. Interpretative traditions

---

51. Warnke, *Gadamer*, p.115 (cited in §9.3.a).

52. Gadamer, *Truth and Method*, p.293 (cited in §1.1.a).

53. Cf. Delling ('Hupotassein', p.43): ὑποτάσσειν 'simply denotes...status...as such' (cited in §4.5.a). This position is reflected in the arguments from natural law (e.g. §5.3.a; §7.3.a).

54. Warnke, *Gadamer*, p.112; cf. Habermas, 'A Review of Gadamer's *Truth and Method*', p.361 (cited in §9.3.a).

55. Gadamer, *Truth and Method*, p.278.

exercise theological and ecclesial constraints, which may be construed as a legacy of a text itself in the tradition in which it is received.

The sample demonstrates the aptness of Gadamer's hermeneutics for the description of biblical interpretation, and Christian interpretation of New Testament paraenetic texts. This can be characterised by solidarity or commonality in a tradition, and by the role of theology in the horizon of the past and present – in the conscious and 'unconscious meaning of the author',[56] and within the tradition contributing to the horizon of expectation of successive readers.

The resulting variability of understanding in different historical circumstances, and by readers with different prejudgments, weighs against the conclusion that the tendency of Gadamer's hermeneutics is inevitably conservative, preserving the *status quo*. In none of the examples discussed in §10.5 does the reader merely affirm interpretations made by the tradition to which that reader happens to belong. Each interpretation is offered in debate with others: the 'structures of exemplary character' are plural, and may be antithetical, in the dialectic of a tradition. So the reception of 1 Cor. 15.28 by the Anglican Diocese of Sydney in 1999 challenges, from within the tradition, the reception of the General Synod of Australia 1977.

I recall, too, that after consultation with members of his own tradition on his understanding/application of Romans 13, Swartley reflects: 'Counsel that I have received has not been consensual'.[57] 'Unresolved tension'[58] is certainly a possible outcome in Gadamer's hermeneutics.

56. Gadamer, *Truth and Method*, p.192.
57. Swartley, 'How to Interpret', p.31 (cited in §7.4 e).
58. Weinsheimer, *Gadamer's Hermeneutics*, pp.x–xi (cited in §6.4).

Chapter 11

CONCLUSION

My own journey through this material has given me a considerable respect for Gadamer's articulation of *Wirkungsgeschichte* as a theoretical resource for understanding biblical interpretation, and what we are doing when we are reading, and finding understanding in, such texts. In an academic discipline that threatens to fragment with multiple contestations over focus and methodology, I find myself an advocate for Gadamerian hermeneutics as offering an integrity to the whole discipline. Contestations in academic biblical studies appeal on the one hand to the authority of the text and on the other to the culture of the reader; or to criteria for 'validity' in interpretation, referred variously to historical and/or theological impulses. Gadamer's hermeneutics offers a discourse that encompasses text and reader, their respective historical and cultural contingencies, and the traditions of interpretation that lie between them – all the elements at stake in the discipline. Therefore, the diverse range of practice and theory which claims a legacy in Gadamer or Jauss can, I suggest, contribute to dialogue and solidarity across the whole diverse discipline, rather than offering further confusion or fragmentation.

If I am defending and advocating reception-historical methods in biblical studies, this study has also led me to a critical defence of practices that some other advocates of reception history reject or avoid. My conclusions partly endorse a *status quo* in the discipline, including many of its diversities of practice. However, I have attempted also to clarify what is at stake between some of these divergences, with an analysis of the reception theory of Gadamer and Jauss that is often missing in relation to this practice.

The interim conclusions and evaluations made at the end of each chapter, and their cumulative argument, permit a fairly brief summary of the findings here, with some further reflections on their collective character and significance. My arguments principally affirm the strategies (as matching Gadamer's analysis) observed in recent publications:

these various ways of handling texts are indeed what he describes as *Wirkungsgeschichte*. My arguments also offer a particular critique of aspects of these, made from Gadamer's hermeneutics.

I have identified, in a long, diverse, tradition of Christian biblical interpretation, support for the way Gadamer describes the process of understanding/applying traditionary texts, in (varying) solidarity with their earlier and earliest readers. Practices of theological and ethical engagement intrinsic to this broad tradition, particularly in New Testament reception, and including forms of *Sachkritik*, demonstrably conform to the way Gadamer describes the way in which a text is understood and applied, *within a tradition that forms part of its legacy* to the readers concerned.

I have addressed divergent claims leading to espousal or avoidance of historical-critical analysis. My examination discovers a strong measure of support in the hermeneutics of Gadamer and Jauss, largely neglected in current discussion, for the role of historical-critical tools *within* the whole process of understanding historical texts. Strategies of historical analysis contribute to constructions of the 'horizon of expectation' in its first reception – which both Gadamer and Jauss insist on as co-determining meaning. I advocate the description of this construct as 'hypothetical first-reception' (picking up Mayordomo-Marín's neglected suggestion, with thanks to Morales Vásquez). This is useful for characterising these acts of interpretation as preliminary, plural and iterative – an 'application' rather than a claim for a definitive, singular 'meaning' (not available in Gadamerian hermeneutics). If a Jaussian model of a literary series of reception is used, hypothetical first-reception can be conceptually, methodologically, positioned as a synchronic 'cross section' within the diachronic perspective and processes of reception history. In this way the methodologies of historical-critical exegesis, and very common strategies in contemporary biblical commentaries, operate in a dialectic, not a dichotomy, with ongoing or iterative interpretation and application of the text.

I have identified a second apparent dichotomy in current practice, likewise concerning the range and nature of reception that is selected and valorized. On the one hand, there is an impulse toward establishing a 'canon of exemplary commentators'[1] in ecclesial traditions. On the other, there is an impulse toward a recovery of neglected reception, and a challenge to conservative traditions. This aspect of my evaluation (as a by-product of my aims) might be characterised as 'reception history of Gadamer's *Truth and Method*' – as itself a traditionary text received

1. Parris, *Reception Theory*, p.217 (cited in §6.2).

and applied in instantiations of biblical interpretation. The dichotomous practices identified might thus be seen as 'paradigm shifts' in a progressive progress, or a developing, self-critical tradition. They each represent defensible expressions of *Wirkungsgeschichte*, and I have identified some of the 'oscillations' in Gadamer's expression, and corresponding emphases in how he is read (including the application made of Gadamer by Jauss), which may contribute to different constructions of practice, each claiming a legacy in Gadamer.

This work nevertheless offers a particular critique of the 'canons of exemplary commentators' as one such 'reception of Gadamer'. These conform to Gadamer's description of how texts are understood, and are further shaped by Jauss's advocacy of 'structures of exemplary character'.[2] However, in their espousal of (only) the 'most influential'[3] receptions within a particular tradition, *they are vulnerable to charges that the tradition and the process are not self-critical.* This critique is characterised by theological impulses (such as a 'hermeneutics of consequences')[4] as well as the immanent impulses of the reflexive, dialogic characteristics of Gadamer's hermeneutics. As such, this critique may constitute an advocacy of one possible emphasis in Gadamer, rather than the identification of an inescapable imperative in his hermeneutics for all readers, with their different contingencies and prejudgments.

I have further offered a critique of practices in reception history, whether constructs of a summit dialogue, or the recovery of neglected or subversive reception, if *either* is made as 'a kind of enquiry separate from understanding the work itself'.[5] This might appear to privilege the reception-historical accounts of those 'sure of [their] own tradition',[6] and constitute a critique of projects which make a 'study of effects'[7] separate from the full process of engaging with meaning of a text within a tradition of interpretation. However, my argument makes the same challenge to the compilers of ecclesial traditions of reception as to those who seek 'liberation from the boundary setting of any single tradition'.[8] Gadamer's emphasis on the prejudgments that operate in understanding calls for

2. Jauss, *Question and Answer*, p.202 (cited in §6.2).
3. Parris, *Reception Theory*, p.219 (cited in §6.3).
4. Cf. Sölle, *Phantasie und Gehorsam*, p.16 (cited in §9.3.a); also Parris, *Reception Theory*, p.164.
5. Gadamer, *Truth and Method*, p.299 (cited in §2.3).
6. Roberts, *Oxford Handbook*, p.5 (cited in §6.3).
7. Klauck *et al.*, 'The Project, Introduction'. The critique applies to the hermeneutical concept, not to the *EBR per se* (but see §6.3.a).
8. Roberts and Rowland, 'Review Essay: *Encyclopedia of the Bible and Its Reception*' (§6.3).

reflexivity in the practitioners who are commenting on or compiling reception of a text. This may be held to be particularly the case with the interpretation of New Testament texts, where the *Erwartungshorizont* is characteristically theological and theo-ethical – but the different prejudgments operating will not make the verdict consensual.

This last argument, for foregrounding the investments and commitments of the interpreter, is a common element in all components of this work. It applies to an historical-critical exegete, to an historian of a denominational or inter-denominational *Auslegungsgeschichte*, and to editors of reception whether these focus on 'principal commentators' and 'the commentary form',[9] or offer analyses where, for example, the 'religious tradition' is 'completely open-ended'.[10] While I claimed above that this analysis potentially offers some support for the 'integrity' of the discipline of biblical studies, this aspect constitutes an advocacy that will not suit all its practitioners. My argument reinforces the identification of *Wirkungsgeschichte* as a process of understanding biblical texts (available in the divergent models of practice), rather than *either* the establishment of a dominant 'canon' of interpretation *or* the entertainment of an interesting, and 'disinterested', path through history. In reception-historical approaches, Gadamerian hermeneutics calls for reflexive criticism within the process of understanding, 'which is, ultimately, self-understanding'.[11] This applies (as a *description* of what is taking place, not a prescription or proscription of different approaches) not only to a consideration of the interestedness of the author of the reception being examined, but, necessarily, that of the editor of a compilation of reception, or of the commentator sampling an instance of someone else's reception (normative or subversive, canonical or neglected). It is the essential character of *wirkungsgeschichtliches Bewusstsein* that it makes 'conscious the prejudices governing our own understanding'.[12]

Finally, how does the case study contribute to these arguments? It is characterised by the *interrelation and integration* of the hermeneutic elements of *Wirkungsgeschichte* in a number of significant ways. It offers attention to particular historical-critical methods that contribute to the reception *made in different traditions*, and which has outcomes co-determined by historical contingencies of the interpreters. It provides a focus in social and political ethics, and the *impact of the texts beyond*

---

9. Riches, *Galatians*, p.2 (§6.2).
10. Roberts, *Oxford Handbook*, p.5 (§6.3).
11. Lawn, *Gadamer*, p.128 (§9.3).
12. Gadamer, *Truth and Method*, p.298 (§1.1.a).

the ecclesial discourse in social embodiment. It is characterised by mediation of horizons which may be either *conformist* or *transformatory.* It highlights ideological commitments and the *legacy of the tradition,* including *theological imperatives* in Christian biblical interpretation. It offers plurality and antitheses in interpretation – which are ascribable to the horizon of the past and the *prejudgments that are the legacy of the text,* or *historical contingencies in its reception.* These are not resolvable on objective criteria but illustrative of how texts are understood and how communities read.

Reflexively, undertaking a case study in reception history (selections from which have appeared here) has been both an interesting path through history and a testing of my prejudgments. I have referred (§§4.2 and 10.5) to my own theological prejudgment, that Paul's ethical paraenesis should be considered within the framework of a theological hermeneutic, derived from Pauline theology: that the paraenetic uses of ὑποτάσσειν, characterised as patterns of reciprocal or mutual submission, are governed by a transformative theology and ideology of the cross of Christ, with a semantic relationship to its use in 1 Cor. 15.28. This was the key impulse in first examining the history of reception of these texts. Reshaping the material here, to reflect elements of Gadamerian hermeneutics and contemporary practices, has demonstrated two aspects of his analysis of 'method' and 'truth'. On the one hand it has confirmed that my own reception constitutes an articulated, reflexive operation of the process of understanding that Gadamer describes. On the other hand, it also reveals my reception of the texts as one of the available ones, rather than confirming, methodologically, its claim for a greater validity in competition with others.

I have resisted a final and formal presentation of my own understanding/application of my case-study texts: how I myself would construct a hypothetical first-reception and maintain an iterative engagement with this; what solidarities I encounter and what legacy the texts transmit to me; how I enter into dialogue with Paul's theology and with a series of reception. The *processes* have been demonstrated throughout, and I have confessed to particular prejudgments. I choose to let the process stand rather than cap it with what can only be another partial and provisional demonstration of it. However, reflexive criticism is central to Gadamer's hermeneutics, and I shall indulge in two further reflections.

First, for a reader with my prejudgments, one of the gratifying discoveries of the study has been the range, variety and tenacity of challenges and subversions to coercive, hierarchical readings of the paraenesis. Though these did not always refer their prejudgment, as I do mine, to historical-critical investigation and a construction of Pauline theology (a theology of the cross) as co-determinants of their interpretation, they are a significant part of the legacy of the texts within my tradition, and contribute to my reception of Pauline paraenesis and, in the dialectic impact of text and reader, to my self-formation.

Second, the concept of understanding as a dialectic process has strong theological resonances in my own Christian tradition. I recognize that 'having a world in common means living in solidarity and living in solidarity means openness to conversation and dialogue':[13] listening to others is indispensable for living, understanding and changing. I also recognize the imperative to acknowledge 'authority whenever and wherever the divine Word finds flesh':[14] listening to the Other is a discipline and a grace. In this respect, the case study of the subordination paraenesis was an intriguing one to explore for the hermeneutical process. I hear the resonances of (what is for me) the key exhortation, 'Be subject to one another', not only in the instantiations of the texts but in the process by which human understanding takes place.

13. Misgeld, 'Poetry, Dialogue and Negotiation', p.166 (cited in §9.3.a).
14. May and Meyer, 'Unity of the Bible', p.149 (cited in §6.3).

BIBLIOGRAPHY

Biblical quotations in Greek are from *The Greek New Testament* (Stuttgart: Deutsche Bibelgesellschaft, 4th rev. edn, 1998), except where stated. Biblical quotations in modern English are from the *New Revised Standard Version*, except where stated. Biblical quotations in other languages are as stated.

Aichele, George, and Fred W. Burnett (eds.), *The Postmodern Bible* (New Haven: Yale University Press, 1995).

Aichele, G., P. Miscall and R. Walsh, 'An Elephant in the Room: Historical-Critical and Postmodern Interpretations of the Bible', *JBL* 128 (2009), pp.383–404.

Albl, Martin C., *'And Scripture Cannot Be Broken': The Form and Function of the Early Christian Testimonia Collections* (Leiden: Brill, 1999).

Alchin, A.M., *Silent Rebellion: Anglican Religious Communities 1845–1900* (London: SCM, 1958).

Alter, Robert, *The Art of Biblical Narrative* (London: George Allen & Unwin 1981).

Aquinas, Thomas, *On the Governance of Princes* (ed. and trans. G.B. Phelan; Toronto: St Michael's College, 1935).

—*The Summa Theologiae* (trans. Edmund Hill; Cambridge: Cambridge University Press, 2006).

Aristotle, *Physics* (trans. R. Waterfield; Oxford: Oxford University Press, 1996).

—*Politics* (trans. Ernest Barker; rev. R.F. Stalley; Oxford: Oxford University Press, 2009).

Asano, Atsuhiro, *Community-Identity Construction in Galatians: Exegetical, Social-Anthropological and Socio-Historical Studies* (London: T&T Clark International, 2005).

Ashton, John, 'History and Theology in New Testament Studies', in Rowland and Tuckett, *Nature of New Testament Theology*, pp.1–17.

—*Studying John: Approaches to the Fourth Gospel* (Oxford: Oxford University Press, 1994).

Astell, Mary, 'Reflections Upon Marriage', in *Political Writings* (ed. Patricia Springborg; Cambridge: Cambridge University Press, 1996), pp.1–80.

Athenagoras, 'Legatio', in *Fathers of the Second Century* (ed. and trans. Alexander Roberts and James Donaldson; ANF, 2; Grand Rapids: Eerdmans, 1977).

Augustine, *De Genesi ad Litteram Liber Imperfectus, De Genesi ad Litteram, Locutiones in Heptateuchum* (ed. J. Zycha; CSEL 28/1; Vindobonae: Tempsky, 1894).

—*Saint Augustine's City of God and Christian Doctrine* (ed. Philip Schaff; trans. Oxford revd; NPNP 1.2; Grand Rapids: Eerdmans, 1956).

Aune, D., *The New Testament in its Literary Environment* (Philadelphia: Westminster, 1987).

Baird, W., 'The Fate of Paul in Nineteenth Century Liberalism', in Lovering *et al.*, *Theology and Ethics*, pp.254–74.

Balch, D.L., *Let Wives be submissive: The Domestic Code in 1 Peter* (SBL Monograph Series, 26; Chico: Scholars Press, 1981).

Balcomb, A., *Third Way Theology: Reconciliation, Revolution, and Reform in the South African Church during the 1980s* (Pietermaritzburg: Cluster Publications, 1993).

Barr, James, *The Semantics of Biblical Language* (London: SCM, 1961).

Barrett, C.K., *The Epistle to the Romans* (London: A. & C. Black, 1957).

—*The First Epistle to the Corinthians* (London: A. & C. Black, 2nd edn, 1971).

Barth, Karl, *The Epistle to the Romans* (trans. from 6th edn by Edwyn C. Hoskyns; London: Oxford University Press, 1933).

Barth, Markus, *Ephesians, Anchor Bible Commentary* (New Haven: Yale University Press 1974).

Barthold, Lauren Swayne, *Gadamer's Dialectical Hermeneutics* (Plymouth: Lexington, 2010).

Barton, John (ed.), *The Cambridge Companion to Biblical Interpretation* (Cambridge: Cambridge University Press, 1998).

—*The Nature of Biblical Criticism* (Louisville: Westminster/John Knox, 2007).

Barton, John, and John Muddiman (eds.), *Oxford Bible Commentary* (Oxford: Oxford University Press, 2001).

Barton, Stephen C., *Life Together: Family, Sexuality, and Community in the New Testament and Today* (New York: T&T Clark, 2001).

Baur, F.C., *Paul the Apostle of Jesus Christ: His Life and Work, his Epistles and his Doctrine: A Contribution to a Critical History of Primitive Christianity* (trans. A. Menzies; London: Williams & Norgate, 2nd edn, 1876).

Beiner, Ronald, 'Do We Need a Philosophical Ethics? Theory, Prudence, and the Primacy of Ethos', *The Philosophical Forum* 21 (1989), pp.230–43.

Beker, J.C., *Paul the Apostle* (Edinburgh: T. & T. Clark, 1980).

Berger, Klaus, *Hermeneutik des Neuen Testaments* (Gütersloh: Gerd Mohn, 1988).

Berkeley, Bishop, *Passive Obedience or the Christian Doctrine of not Resisting the Supreme Power, Proved and Vindicated upon the Principles of the Law of Nature, in a Discourse Delivered at the College Chapel* (Dublin: Francis Dickson, 1712).

Besserman, Lawrence L., *Chaucer's Biblical Poetics* (Norman: University of Oklahoma Press, 1998).

Best, Ernest, *Essays on Ephesians* (Edinburgh: T. & T. Clark, 1997).

Betti, Emilio, *Die Hermeneutik als allgemeine Methodik der Geisteswissenschaften* (Tübingen: J.C. Mohr, 1962).

Bilezikian, Gilbert, *Beyond Sex Roles: What the Bible Says about a Woman's Place in Church and Family* (Grand Rapids: Baker, 1985).

Blackstone, William, *Commentaries on the Law of England* [1764–1769] (Chicago: University of Chicago Press, 1979).

Bocaccio, Giovani, *Famous Women* (trans. V. Brown; Cambridge, Mass.: Harvard University Press, 2003).

Bockmuehl, Markus 'A Commentator's Approach to the "Effective History" of Philippians', *JSNT* 60 (1996), pp.57–88.

—*Seeing the Word: Refocusing New Testament Study* (Grand Rapids: Baker Academic, 2006).

Boer, Roland, 'Against "Reception History"' (University of Newcastle, Religion and Theology, May 2011), Cited 3 July 2012. Online: http://www.bibleinterp.com/opeds/boe358008.shtml.

Boesak, Allan, and Charles Villa-Vicencio, *A Call to an End to Unjust Rule* (Edinburgh: St Andrew Press, 1986).

Bonino, J. Miguez, *Revolutionary Theology Comes of Age* (London: SPCK, 1975).

Borg, Marcus, 'A New Context for Romans XIII', *New Testament Studies* 19 (1972), pp.205–18.

Bornkamm, G., *Paul* (trans. M.G. Stalker; London: Hodder & Stoughton, 1971).

Boyd, Jane, and Philip F. Esler, *Visuality and Biblical Text: Interpreting Velázquez' 'Christ with Martha and Mary' as a Test Case* (Florence: Leo S. Olschki, 2004).

Braxton, Brad, 'Preaching, Politics and Paul in Contemporary African American Christianity', in Lieb *et al.*, *Oxford Handbook*, pp.557–75.

Brontë, Charlotte, *Shirley* [1849] (London: Gresham, n.d.).

Brooten, Bernadette J., 'Jewish Women's History in the Roman Period: A Task for Christian Theology', in Nickelsburg and MacRae, *Christians among Jews and Gentiles*, pp.22–30.

Brown, R. McAfee (ed.), *Kairos: Three Prophetic Challenges to the Church* (Grand Rapids: Eerdmans, 1990).

Bruce, F.F., *The Epistle of Paul to the Romans: An Introduction and Commentary* (Wheaton: Tyndale, 1963).

Brushfield, T.N. 'On Obsolete Punishments with Particular Reference to those of Cheshire: part 1', *Journal of the Architectural, Archaeological, and Historic Society for the County, City, and Neighbourhood of Chester* 2 (1855–62), pp.31–48.

Bryan, C., *A Preface to Romans: Notes on the Epistle in its Literary and Cultural Setting* (Oxford: Oxford University Press, 2000).

Bultmann, Rudolf, *Essays Philosophical and Theological* (trans. J.C. Grieg; London: SCM, 1955).

—*Existence and Faith: Shorter Writings of Rudolf Bultmann* (ed. and trans. S.M. Odgen; London: Hodder & Stoughton, 1960).

—*Glauben und Verstehen*, vol. 2 (Tübingen: J.C.B. Mohr, 1965).

—*Theology of the New Testament I* (New York/London: SCM, 1951).

Burdekin, Katharine, *Swastika Night* (London: Lawrence & Wishart, 1985).

Burns, James H., and Thomas M. Izbicki, *Conciliarism and Papalism* (Cambridge: Cambridge University Press, 1997).

Callaway, Mary Chilton, 'What's the Use of Reception History?'. Paper presented at SBL, San Antonio, 2004. Cited 26 August 2012. Online: http://bbibcomm.net/files/callaway2004.pdf.

Calvin, John, *Commentary upon the Epistle of Saint Paul to the Romans* [1539] (ed. H. Beveridge; trans. C. Rosdell; Edinburgh, 1844).

—*The Epistles of Paul the Apostle to the Galatians, Ephesians, Philippians and Colossians* (trans. T.H.L Parker; Edinburgh: T. & T. Clark, 1965).

—*Writing of Pastoral Piety* (ed. and trans. Elsie Anne Mckee; New York: Paulist, 2001).

Capellanus, Andreas, *The Art of Courtly Love* (ed. P.G. Walsh; New York: Columbia University Press, 1960).

Carrington, P. *The Primitive Christian Catechism* (Cambridge: Cambridge University Press, 1940).

Carter, T.L., 'The Irony of Romans 13', *Novum Testamentum* 46.3 (2004), pp.209–28.

Castelli, Elizabeth A., *Imitating Paul: A Discourse of Power* (Louisville: Westminster/ John Knox, 1991).

Catholic Church, *The Catechism of the Council of Trent* (London: G. Routledge, 1852).

Cazamian, Louis, *The Social Novel in England, 1830–1885* (trans. M. Fido; London: Routledge & Kegan Paul, 1973).

Chadwick, H., *Origen, Contra Celsum* (Cambridge: Cambridge University Press, 1965).

Chaucer, Geoffrey, *The Works of Geoffrey Chaucer* (ed. F.N. Robinson; London: Oxford University Press, 2nd edn, 1966).

Childs, Brevard, *The New Testament as Canon: An Introduction* (London: SCM, 1984).

Christianson, Eric S., *Ecclesiastes Through the Centuries* (Oxford: Blackwell, 2007).

Chrysostom, John, *Homilies on the Acts of the Apostles and the Epistle to the Romans* (ed. P. Schaff; trans. Oxford revd; *NPNF*, 1.11; Grand Rapids: Eerdmans, 1969).

—*Homilies on the Epistles to the Galatians, Ephesians, Philippians, Colossians, Thessalonians, Timothy, Titus, and Philemon* (ed. P. Schaff; trans. Oxford revd; *NPNF*, 1.13; Grand Rapids: Eerdmans, 1916).

Church of England in Australia, General Synod, Commission on Doctrine, 'The Ministry of Women: A Report of the General Synod Commission on Doctrine' (Reports to the General Synod of the Church of England in Australia, vol. 1; Sydney: St Andrew's House, 1977).

Church of England, The, *Book of Common Prayer, The* [1652] (London: Cambridge University Press, 1955).

—*Sermons or Homilies, Appointed to Be Read in Churches in the Time of Queen Elizabeth of Famous Memory: To Which Are Added, the Articles of Religion* (London: Ellerton & Henderson for The Prayer-book and Homily Society, 1824).

Cicero, Marcus Tullius, *De Re Publica, De Legibus* (trans. C.W. Keyes; LCL, 16; Cambridge, Mass.: Harvard University Press, 1928).

Clark, S.B., *Man and Woman in Christ: An Examination of the Roles of Men and Women in the Light of Scripture and the Social Sciences* (Ann Arbour: Servant, 1980).

Clarke, Andrew D., *Secular Christian Leadership in Corinth: A Socio-historical and Exegetical Study of 1 Corinthians 1–6* (Leiden: Brill, 1993).

Clement of Alexandria, 'Stromata', in *Fathers of the Second Century* (ed. and trans. Alexander Roberts and James Donaldson; ANF, 2; Grand Rapids: Eerdmans, 1977).

Clement of Rome, 'First Letter to the Corinthians', in *Early Christian Fathers* (ed. and trans. C.C. Richardson; LCC 1; London: SCM, 1953); and in *The Apostolic Fathers* (ed. T.E. Page, E. Capps, and W.H.D. Rouse; trans. Kirslopp Lake; LCL, 1; London: William Heinemann, 1930).

Coggins, R.J., and J.L. Houlden (eds.), *A Dictionary of Biblical Interpretation* (London: SCM, 1990).

Conzelmann, H., *1 Corinthians: A Commentary on the First Epistle to the Corinthians* (Philadelphia: Fortress, 1975).

Cranfield, C.E.B., *A Commentary on Romans 12–13* (Edinburgh/London: Oliver & Boyd, 1965).

—*A Critical and Exegetical Commentary on the Epistle to the Romans* (2 vols.; London: T&T Clark, 1975).

—*The Service of God* (London: Epworth, 1965).

—'Some observations on Romans 13:1-7', *New Testament Studies* 6.3 (1960), pp.241–48.

Crouch, J.E. *The Origin and Intention of the Colossian Haustafel* (Göttingen: Vanden-
    hoeck & Ruprecht, 1972).
Cullman, Oscar, *Christ and Time: the Primitive Christian Conception of Time and
    History* (trans. F. Filson; London: SCM, 1951).
Culpepper, R. Alan, *Anatomy of the Fourth Gospel: a Study in Literary Design* (Phila-
    delphia: Fortress, 1983).
Davids, Peter H., *The First Epistle of Peter* (New International Commentary; Grand
    Rapids: Eerdmans, 1990).
Davies, W.D., *Paul and Rabbinic Judaism* (London: SPCK, 1948).
Dawes, G.W., *The Body in Question. Metaphor and Meaning in the Interpretation of
    Ephesians 5.21-33* (Leiden: Brill, 1998).
Delling, Gerhard, *Römer 13, 1-7 innerhalb der Briefe des Neuen Testaments* (Berlin:
    Evangelische Verlagsanstalt 1962).
Derrida, Jacques, 'Three Questions to Hans-Georg Gadamer' (trans. D. Michelfelder and
    R. Palmer), in Michelfelder and Palmer, *Dialogue and Deconstruction*, pp.52–54.
Dibelius, Martin, *From Tradition to Gospel* (ed. W. Barclay; trans. B.L. Woolf; New
    York: Scribner, 1965).
—*James: A Commentary on the Epistle of James* (trans. M.A. Williams; Philadelphia:
    Fortress, 1975).
Dickens, Charles, *The Adventures of Oliver Twist* [1838] (London: Chapman & Hall,
    n.d.).
Dockery, David 'Study and Interpretation of the Bible', in *Foundations for Biblical
    Interpretation* (ed. D. Dockery, K. Matthews and R. Sloan; Nashville: Broadman &
    Holman, 1994), pp.36–54.
Diocese of Sydney Doctrine Commission, 'The Doctrine of the Trinity and its Bearing on
    the Relationship of Men and Women'. Cited 10 November 2013. Online:
    http://www.sds.asn.au/assets/documents/synod/TrinityDoctrineComm.pdf.
Dodd, C.H., *The Epistle to the Romans* (London: Fontana, 1959).
—*Gospel and Law: The Relation of Faith and Ethics in Early Christianity* (Cambridge:
    Cambridge University Press, 1951).
Dove, John, *Of Divorcement, a Sermon Preached at Paul's Cross the 10th of May 1601*
    (London: Printed by T. C[reede], 1601).
Doyle, Laura, *The Surrendered Wife: A Practical Guide to Finding Intimacy, Passion,
    and Peace with Your Man* (New York: Simon & Schuster, 1999).
Dredge, Sarah, 'Opportunism and Accommodation: The English Woman's Journal and
    the British Mid-Nineteenth-Century Women's Movement', *Women's Studies*
    34 (2005), pp.133–57.
Duché, Jacob, *The Duty of Standing Fast in our Spiritual and Temporal Liberties: A
    Sermon Preached in Christ Church, July 7, 1775, Before the First Battalion of the
    City and Liberties of Philadelphia* (Philadelphia: James Humphreys, 1775).
Dunn, James, 'Criteria for a Wise Reading of a Biblical Text', in *Reading Texts, Seeking
    Wisdom: Scripture and Theology* (ed. David F. Ford and Graham Stanton; Grand
    Rapids: Eerdmans, 2003), pp.35–52.
—*Romans 1–8* (Word Biblical Commentary 38a; Dallas: Word, 1988).
Dwyer, Judith A. (ed.), *A New Dictionary of Catholic Social Thought* (Collegeville:
    Liturgical, 1994).
Eagleton, Terry, *Literary Theory: an Introduction* (Oxford: Blackwell, 1983).
Ebeling, Gerhard, *Word and Faith* (trans. J.W. Leitch; Philadelphia: Fortress, 1963).

—*The Word of God and Tradition* (London: Collins, 1968).

Eco, Umberto, *The Role of the Reader: Explorations in the Semiotics of Texts* (ed. Thomas Sebeok; Bloomington: Indiana University Press, 1979.

Edwards, Mark, 'The Development of Office in the Early Church', in *The Early Christian World* (ed. P. Esler; London: Routledge, 2000), pp.316–29.

Elliott, Mark W. 'Effective-History and the Hermeneutics of Ulrich Luz', *JSNT* 33 (2010), pp.161–73.

Elliott, Neil, *Liberating Paul: the Justice of God and the Politics of the Apostle* (Sheffield: Sheffield Academic, 1994).

—'Romans 13: 1–7 in the Context of Imperial Propaganda', in Horsley, *Paul and Empire*, pp.184–205.

Ellis, E.E., 'The Silenced Wives of Corinth', in *New Testament Textual Criticism* (ed. E.J. Epp and G.D. Fee; London: Oxford University Press, 1981), pp.213–20.

Evans, Robert, *Judge for Yourselves: Reading 1 Corinthians* (London: Darton, Longman & Todd, 2003).

Fish, Stanley, *'Is There a Text in this Class?': The Authority of Interpretive Communities* (Cambridge, Mass.: Harvard University Press, 1980).

Fitzmyer, J.A., *Romans: A New Translation with Introduction and Commentary* (London: Geoffrey Chapman, 1992).

Flagg, Fannie, *Fried Green Tomatoes at the Whistle Stop Café* (London: Vintage, 1992).

Fleetwood, William, 'The Thirteenth Chapter to the Romans, Vindicated from the Abusive Senses put upon it. Written by a Curate Of Salop; And Directed to the Clergy of that County, and to the Neighbouring Ones of North-Wales' (London: A. Baldwin, 1710).

Forrester, David, *Young Doctor Pusey* (London, Mowbray, 1989).

Foster, Marshall, and Gary DeMar (eds.), *1599 Geneva Bible* (White Hall: Tolle Lege, 2006).

Freier, Mary P., 'Woman as Termagant in The Towneley Cycle', *Essays in Medieval Studies* 2 (1985), pp.155–67.

Friedrich, J., W. Pöhlmann and P. Stuhlmacher, 'Zur historischen Situation und Intention von Rom 13. 1-7', *ZTK* 73 (1967), pp.131–66.

Froehlich, Karlfried, 'Church History and the Bible', in *Biblical Hermeneutics in Historical Perspective* (ed. M.S. Burrows and P. Rorem; Grand Rapids: Eerdmans, 1991), pp.1–18.

Furnish, V.P., 'On Putting Paul in his Place', *JBL* 113 (1994), pp.3–17.

Gadamer, Hans-Georg, *Gadamer in Conversation: Reflections and Commentary* (ed. and trans. Richard E. Palmer; New Haven: Yale University Press, 2001).

—'Herméneutique et Théologie', *Revue des Sciences Religieuses* 51.4 (1977), pp.384–97.

—*Philosophical Hermeneutics* (ed. and trans. D.E. Linge; Berkeley/Los Angeles: University of California Press, 1977).

—'The Philosophy and Religion of Judaism', in *Gadamer on Education, Poetry and History: Applied Hermeneutics* (ed. D. Misgeld and G. Nicholson; trans. L. Schmidt and M. Reuss; Albany: University of New York Press, 1992).

—'Reflections on my Philosophical Journey', in *The Philosophy of Hans-Georg Gadamer* (ed. Lewis Hahn; Chicago and La Salle: Open Court, 1997), pp.3–63.

—'Reply to Jacques Derrida' (trans. D. Michelfelder and R. Palmer), in Michelfelder and Palmer, *Dialogue and Deconstruction*, pp.55–57.

—'Text and Interpretation' (trans. D.J. Schmidt and R. Palmer), in Michelfelder and Palmer, *Dialogue and Deconstruction*, pp.21–51.

—*Truth and Method* (trans. rev. by J. Weinsheimer and D.G. Marshall; London/New York: Continuum, 2nd rev. English edn, 2004). (An earlier translation, London: Sheen & Ward, 1979, is also cited where there are significant variants.)

—*Wahrheit und Methode: Grundzüge einer philosophischen Hermeneutik* (Tübingen: Mohr, 1972).

Gaskell, Mrs., *Cousin Phillis and Other Tales* [1864] (London: J.M. Dent, n.d.).

—*Wives and Daughters: An Every-day Story* [1859] (London: Smith, Elder & Co., 1907).

Geertz, Clifford, *The Interpretation of Cultures: Selected Essays* (New York: Basic, 1973).

—'Thick Description: Toward an Interpretive Theory of Culture', in *The Interpretation of Cultures*, pp.3–30.

Gerhardsson, B., *The Ethos of the Bible* (Philadelphia: Fortress, 1982).

Giles, Kevin, *The Trinity and Subordinationism: The Doctrine of God and the Contemporary Gender Debate* (Downers Grove: InterVarsity, 2002).

Gnilka, Joachim, Hans-Josef Klauck, Ulrich Luz und Jürgen Roloff (eds.), *Evangelisch Katholischer Kommentar zum Neuen Testament* (Düsseldorf/Zürich: Benziger, from 1978).

Gore, Charles, *St Paul's Epistle to the Ephesians: A Practical Exposition* (London: John Murray, 1898).

—*St Paul's Epistle to the Romans: A Practical Exposition* (London: John Murray, 1900).

Gowler, David B., 'Socio-Rhetorical Interpretation: Textures of a Text and its Reception', *JSNT* 33 (2010), pp.191–206.

Graves, Alex (dir.), Allison Abner (story), Aaron Sorkin (teleplay), 'War Crimes', *The West Wing* (3rd Season, Episode 6, Warner Bros, 2000).

Gregory the Great, *Pastoral Rule* (ed. P. Schaff, Oxford revd; *NPNF*, 2.12; Grand Rapids: Eerdmans, 1976).

—'Vita Gregorii' [anon.], in *Opera Omnia* (ed. J.P. Migne; PCC-SL 75; Paris, 1862), pp.41–460.

Grudem, Wayne, 'Wives Like Sarah, and the Husbands Who Honor Them', in Piper and Grudem (eds.), *Recovering Biblical Manhood*, pp.193–210.

Grumbach, Argula von, 'Letter o the University of Ingolstadt', in *Argula von Grumbach: A Woman's Voice in the Reformation* (ed. P. Matheson; Edinburgh: T. & T. Clark, 1995).

Guerra, Anthony J., *Romans and the Apologetic Tradition: The Purpose, Genre and Audience of Paul's Letter* (Cambridge: Cambridge University Press, 1995).

Habermas, Jürgen, 'Justice and Solidarity', in *Hermeneutics and Critical Theory in Ethics and Politics* (ed. Michael Kelly; Cambridge: MIT Press, 1990), p.32–52.

—*Knowledge and Human Interests* (Boston: Beacon, 1971).

—'A Review of Gadamer's *Truth and Method*' (trans. F.R. Dallmayr and T. McCarthy), in *The Hermeneutic Tradition: From Ast to Ricoeur* (ed. Gayle Ormiston and Alan Schrift; Albany: State University of New York Press, 1990), pp.213–44.

—*Zur Logik der Sozial Wissenschaften* (Frankfurt am Main: Suhrkamp, 1982).

—*Zwischen Naturalismus und Religion* (Frankfurt am Main: Suhrkamp, 2005).

Hagner, Donald A., 'Review: Matthew 8–20 by Ulrich Luz', *JBL* 121 (2002), pp.766–69.

Hayes, John H. (ed.), *Dictionary of Biblical Interpretation* (2 vols.; Nashville: Abingdon, 1999).

Harding, James E., Eric Repphun and Will Sweetman (eds.), 'Focus and Scope', in *Relegere: Studies in Religion and Reception.* Cited 3 April 2012. Online: http://www.relegere.org/index.php/relegere/about/editorialPolicies#focusAndScope.

Harnack, Adolf von, *What Is Christianity?* (trans. Thomas Bailey Saunders; New York: Harper, 1957).

Hartman, L., 'Some Unorthodox Thoughts on the "Household Code" Form', in *The Social World of Formative Christianity and Judaism: Essays in Tribute to Howard Clark Kee* (ed. J. Neusner, Peter Borgen, Ernest S. Frerichs and Richard Horsley; Philadelphia: Fortress, 1988), pp.179-94.

Hays, Richard B., *Echoes of Scripture in the Letters of Paul* (New Haven: Yale University Press, 1989).

Heard, Chris, 'In Defense of Reception History' (12 June 2011). Cited 3 July 2012. Online: http://bbibcomm.net /?p=216#more-216.

Heidegger, Martin, *Sein und Zeit* (Tübingen: Max Niemeyer, 2006).

Heine, Ronald (ed.), *The Commentaries of Origen and Jerome on St Paul's Epistle to the Ephesians* (Oxford: Oxford University Press, 2002).

Hill, Bridget, *The First English Feminist: 'Reflections Upon Marriage' and Other Writings by Mary Astell* (Aldershot: Gower, 1986).

Hill, Christopher, *The English Revolution* (London: Lawrence & Wishart, 1985).

Hill, Edmund, *Ministry and Authority in the Catholic Church* (London: Geoffrey Chapman, 1988).

Hincmarus, *Epistola II, ad Nicolaum Papam de vacatione sedis Cameracensis* (ed. J.P. Migne; PCC-SL 126; Paris, 1879).

Hinman, Lawrence, '*Quid factis or Quid Juris*? The Fundamental Ambiguity of Gadamer's Understanding of Hermeneutics', *Philosophy and Phenomenological Research* 40 (1980), pp.512–35.

Hirsch, E.D., 'Objective Interpretation', *Publications of the Modern Language Association of America* 75.4 (1960), pp.463–79.

—*Validity in Interpretation* (New Haven: Yale University Press, 1967).

Hobbes, Thomas, *Leviathan: The Matter, Form and Power of a Commonwealth* (ed. R. Tuck; Cambridge Texts in the History of Political Thought; Cambridge: Cambridge University Press, 1991).

Hock, R.F., *The Social Context of Paul's Ministry* (Philadelphia: Fortress, 1980).

Holdsworth, William S., *A History of English Law*, vol. 1 (London: Methuen & Co., 3rd ed., 1922).

Hollingshead, James R., *The Household of Caesar and the Body of Christ: A Political Interpretation of the Letters from Paul* (Lanham, Md.: University Press of America, 1998).

Holub, Robert C., *Reception Theory: A Critical Introduction* (London: Methuen, 1984).

Hooker, Morna D., *A Commentary on the Gospel according to St Mark* (London: A. & C. Black, 1991).

Horsley, Richard A. (ed.), *Paul and Empire: Religion and Power in Roman Imperial Society* (Harrisburg: Trinity Press International, 1997).

Houlden, J. Leslie, *The Interpretation of the Bible in the Church* (London: SPCK, 1984).

Hoy, David C., *The Critical Circle: Literature and History in Contemporary Hermeneutics* (Berkeley: University of California Press, 1978).

Ignatius, *Letters to the Ephesians, the Magnesians, the Romans and the Trallians*, in *The Apostolic Fathers* (ed. T.E. Page, E. Capps and W.H.D. Rouse; trans. Kirsopp Lake; LCL, 1; London: William Heinemann, 1930).

Iser, Wolfgang, *The Act of Reading: A Theory of Aesthetic Response* (Baltimore/London: Johns Hopkins University Press, 1978).

—*The Implied Reader: Patterns of Communication in Prose Fiction from Bunyan to Beckett* (Baltimore/London: Johns Hopkins University Press, 1974).

James, Walter, *Christian in Politics* (Oxford: Oxford University Press, 1963).

Jauss, Hans-Robert, *Alterität und Modernität der Mittelalterlichen Literatur: Gesammelte Aufsätze 1956–1976* (Munich: Wilhelm Fink, 1977).

—*Ästhetische Ehrfahrung und litarische Hermeneutik* (Frankfurt am Main: Suhrkamp, 1997).

—'The Identity of the Poetic Text in the Changing Horizon of Understanding', in *Reception Study: From Literary Theory to Cultural Studies* (ed. James L. Machor and Philip Goldstein; New York/London: Routledge, 2001), pp.7–28.

—*The Book of Jonah: A Paradigm of the 'Hermeneutics of Strangeness'* (Minneapolis: University of Minnesota Press, 1987).

—'Der Leser als Instanz einen Neue Geschichte der Literatur', *Poetica* 7 (1975), pp.326–40.

—'Limits and Tasks of Literary Hermeneutics', *Diogenes* 109 (1980), pp.92–119.

—*Question and Answer: Forms of Dialogic Understanding* (trans. M. Hays; Theory and History of Literature 68; Minneapolis: University of Minnesota Press, 1989).

—*Die Theorie der Rezeption: Rückschau auf ihre unerkannte Vorgeschichte: Ansprache anlässlich der Emeritierung von Hans Robert Jauss am 11 Februar 1987* (Konstanz: Universitätsverlag Konstanz, 1987).

—*Toward an Aesthetic of Reception* (trans. Timothy Bahti; Brighton: Harvester Press, 1982).

Jauss, Hans-Robert, and Elizabeth Benzinger, 'Literary History as a Challenge to Literary Theory', *New Literary History* 2.1, A Symposium on Literary History (1970), pp.7–37.

John XXIII, *Pacem In Terris*, On Establishing Universal Peace in Truth, Justice, Charity, and Liberty [1963]. Cited 14 April 2012. Online: http://www.vatican.va/holyfather/ john_xxiii/encyclicals/documents/hf_jxxiii_enc_11041963_pacem_en.html.

Josephus, Flavius, 'The Jewish War', in *The Works of Josephus* (trans. William Whiston; Peabody, Mass.: Hendrickson, 1995).

—*The Life, Against Apion* (ed. H.St.J. Thackeray; LCL, 1; Cambridge, Mass.: Harvard University Press, 1926).

Justin Martyr, 'Apologia', in *Apostolic Fathers* (ed. and trans. Alexander Roberts and James Donaldson; The Ante-Nicene Fathers 1; Buffalo: Christian Literature Co., 1885).

Kairos Theologians, *The Kairos Document: A Theological Comment on the Political Crisis in South Africa* (Catholic Institute for International Relations: British Council and Churches, 2nd edn, 1985).

Kallas, James, 'Romans XIII.1-7: An Interpolation', *New Testament Studies* 11 (1965), pp.365–74.

Kamlah, E., "Ὑποτασσέσθαι in den neutestmentlichen Haustafeln', in *Verborum Veritas: Festschrift für G. Stählin zum 70 Geburtstag* (ed. O. Bocher and K. Haacker; Wuppertal: Brockhaus, 1970), pp.237–43.

Karris, Robert M., 'The Pastoral Letters', in *The Oxford Companion to the Bible* (ed. Bruce Metzger and Michael D. Coogan; New York: Oxford University Press, 1993), pp.573–76.

Käsemann, Ernst, *Commentary on Romans* (ed. and trans. G.W. Bromiley; Grand Rapids: Eerdmans 1980).

—*Perspectives on Paul* (London: SCM, 1971).

Keats, John, 'Letter to George and Thomas Keats, 21st December 1817', in *Letters of John Keats* (ed. Frederick Page; London: Oxford University Press, 1954), pp.51–54.

Kermode, Frank, *The Genesis of Secrecy: On the Interpretation of Narrative* (Cambridge, Mass.: Harvard University Press, 1979).

Kidd, B.J., *Documents Illustrative of the Continental Reformation* (Oxford: Clarendon, 1911).

King, Margaret, and Albert Rabil, 'The Other Voice in Early Modern Europe: Editors' Introduction to the Series', in Vives, *Christian Woman*, pp.ix–xxviii.

Kirkpatrick, Clifford, *Germany: Its Women and Family Life* (Indianapolis: Bobbs-Merrill Co., 1938).

Kirnan, Christopher, *Augustine* (London: Routledge, 1989).

Klauck, Hans-Josef, Volker Leppin, Bernard McGinn, Choon-Leong Seow, Hermann Spieckermann, Barry Dov Walfish and Eric Ziolkowski (eds.), *Encyclopedia of the Bible and its Reception* (Berlin/New York: W. de Gruyter, 2009–).

Klauck *et al.*, 'The Project, Introduction', in *Encyclopedia of the Bible and its Reception*. Cited 2 September 2012. Online: http://www.degruyter.com/staticfiles/content/dbsup/EBR_02_Introduction.pdf.

Klausner, Joseph, *From Jesus to Paul* (London: Allen & Unwin, 1942).

Knight, George W., 'Husbands and Wives as Analogues of Christ and the Church', in Piper and Grudem (eds.), *Recovering Biblical Manhood*, pp.161–75.

Knight, Mark, '*Wirkungsgeschichte*, Reception History, Reception Theory', *JSNT* 33 (2010), pp.137–46.

Kovacs, Judith L., *1 Corinthians: Interpreted by Early Christian Commentators* (Cambridge/Grand Rapids: Eerdmans, 2005).

Kovacs, Judith, and Christopher Rowland, *Revelation Through the Centuries: The Apocalypse to Jesus Christ* (Oxford: Blackwell, 2004)

Kroeger, Catherine, 'The Classical Concept of Head as Source', in Gretchen Gabelein Hull, *Equal to Serve: Women and Men in the Church and Home* (London: Scripture Union, 1987), Appendix III, pp.267–83.

Kueh, Richard, 'Reception History and the Hermeneutics of *Wirkungsgeschichte*: Critiquing the Use of Gadamerian Hermeneutics in Biblical Reception History' (unpublished doctoral dissertation, University of Cambridge, 2012).

Kuhn, Thomas, *The Structure of Scientific Revolutions* (Chicago: University of Chicago Press, 1962).

Lammi, Walter, *Gadamer and the Question of the Divine* (London/New York: Continuum, 2008).

Landes, Paula Fredriksen, *Augustine on Romans: Propositions from the Epistle to the Romans and Unfinished Commentary on the Epistle to the Romans* (Chico: Scholars Press, 1982).

Lash, Nicholas, 'Performing the Scriptures', in *Theology on the Way to Emmaus* (London: SCM, 1986), pp.37–46.

Lawn, Chris, *Gadamer: A Guide for the Perplexed* (London: Continuum, 2006).

Leavis, F.R., *The Great Tradition: George Eliot, Henry James, Joseph Conrad* (London: Chatto & Windus, 1948).

Leenhardt, Franz J., *The Epistle to the Romans* (trans. H. Knight; London: Lutterworth, 1961).

Leo XIII, *Arcanum divinae sapientiae*, On Christian Marriage [1880]. Cited 29 July 2010.   Online: http://www.vatican.va/holy_father/leo_xiii/encyclicals/documents/hf_l-xiii_ enc_10021880_arcanum_en.html.

Lieb, Michael, Emma Mason and Jonathan Roberts (eds.), *The Oxford Handbook of the Reception History of the Bible* (Oxford/New York: Oxford University Press, 2011).

Lietzmann, Hans, *An die Römer* (Tübingen: Mohr Siebeck 1906).

Lincoln, Andrew T., *Ephesians* (Word Biblical Commentary 42; Nashville: Word, 1990).

Lincoln, A.T., and A.J.M. Wedderburn, *The Theology of the Later Pauline Letters* (New Testament Theology; Cambridge: Cambridge University Press, 1993).

Lindbeck, George A., *The Nature of Doctrine: Religion and Theology in a Postliberal Age* (Philadelphia: Westminster, 1984).

Loades, Ann, 'Elizabeth Cady Stanton's *The Woman's Bible*', in Lieb *et al.*, *Oxford Handbook*, pp.307–22.

Locke, John, *Two Treatises*, in Christopher Flint, *Family Fiction: Narrative and Domestic Relations in Britain, 1688–1798* (Stanford: Stanford University Press, 1998).

Lohse, Eduard, 'Changes of Thought in Pauline Theology? Some Reflections on Paul's Ethical Teaching in the Context of his Theology', in Lovering *et al.*, *Theology and Ethics*, pp.146–60.

—'Paraenese und Kerygma im 1 Petrusbrief', *ZNW* 45 (1954), pp.68–89.

Lorris, Guillaume de, *Le Roman de la Rose* (Naples: A. Morano, 1947).

Loughlin, Gerard, *Telling God's Story: Bible, Church and Narrative Theology* (Cambridge: Cambridge University Press, 1996).

Lovering, E.H., and J.L. Sumney (eds.), *Theology and Ethics in Paul and his Interpreters: Essays in Honour of Victor Paul Furnish* (Nashville: Abingdon, 1996).

Lundin, Roger, Clarence Walhout and Anthony Thiselton, *The Responsibility of Hermeneutics* (Grand Rapids: Eerdmans, 1985).

Luther, Martin, *A Commentary on St. Paul's Epistle to the Galatians* (ed. Philip Watson; London: James Clarke & Co, 1953).

—*Lectures on Romans* (trans. W. Pauck; London: SCM, 1961).

—*Luther's Works*, vol. 35 (ed. E.T. Bachmann; trans. J. Schindel; rev. W.I. Brandt; Philadelphia: Fortress, 1960).

Luz, Ulrich, *Matthew 1–7: A Commentary* (trans. James E. Crouch; Edinburgh: T. & T. Clark, 1989).

—*Matthew 8–20: A Commentary* (trans. James E. Crouch; Philadelphia: Fortress, 2001).

—*Matthew 21–28: A Commentary* (trans. James E. Crouch; Minneapolis: Fortress, 2005).

—*Matthew in History: Interpretation, Influence and Effects* (Minneapolis: Fortress, 1994).

—'Review of Michael Lieb, Emma Mason and Jonathan Roberts (eds.), *The Oxford Handbook of the Reception History of the Bible*', *Journal of Theological Studies* 63.1 (2012), pp.273–76.

—'*Zum Aufbau von Röm. 1–8*', *Theologische Zeitschrift* 25 (1969), pp.161–81.

Lyons, William John, 'Hope for a Troubled Discipline? Contributions to New Testament Studies from Reception History', *JSNT* 33 (2010), pp.207–20.

Macdonald, Margaret, 'Rereading Paul: Early Interpreters of Paul on Women and Gender', in *Women and Christians Origins* (ed. Ross Shephard Kraemar and Mary Rose D'Angelo; Oxford: Oxford University Press, 1999), pp.236–53.

MacIntyre, Alasdair, *After Virtue* (London: Duckworth, 1981).

—'Epistemological Crisis, Dramatic Narrative and the Philosophy of Science', in *Paradigms and Revolutions* (ed. Gary Gutting; Notre Dame: University Press, 1980), pp.54–74.

—*Whose Justice, Which Rationality?* (Notre Dame: University of Notre Dame Press, 1985).

Maier, Gerhard, *The End of the Historical-Critical Method* (trans. E.W. Leverenz and F.R.F. Norden; St Louis: Concordia, 1977).

Malina, Bruce J., *The New Testament World: Insights from Cultural Anthropology* (Atlanta: John Knox, 1981).

Man, Paul de, *Aesthetic Ideology* (Minneapolis: Minnesota Press, 1996).

Markus, R.A., *Saeculum: History and Society in the Theology of St. Augustine* (Cambridge: Cambridge University Press, 1970).

Marshall, I. Howard, 'The Christology of Luke–Acts and the Pastoral Epistles', in *Crossing the Boundaries: Essays in Biblical Interpretation in Honour of Michael Goulder* (ed. S.E. Porter, P. Joyce and D.E. Orton; Brill: Leiden, 1994), pp.167–82.

Martin, Dale, *Slavery as Salvation: the Metaphor of Slavery in Pauline Christianity* (New Haven: Yale University Press, 1990).

Marx, Karl, and Frederick Engels, '*Manifesto of the Communist Party*' [1848], in R. Tucker (ed.), *The Marx–Engels Reader* (New York: Norton, 2nd edn, 1978).

May, Melanie, and Lauree Hersch Meyer, 'Unity of the Bible, Unity of the Church: Confessionalism, Ecumenism and Feminist Hermeneutics', in Schüssler Fiorenza (ed.), *Searching the Scriptures*, vol. 1, pp.140–53.

Mayordomo-Marín, Moisés, *Den Anfang Hören: Leseorientierte Evangelienexegese am Beispiel von Matthaeus 1–2* (Göttingen: Vandenhoeck & Ruprecht, 1998).

Mayordomo-Marín, Moisés (ed.), *Die prägende Kraft der Texte. Hermeneutik und Wirkungsgeschichte des Neuen Testaments: Ein Symposium zu Ehren von Ulrich Luz* (Stuttgart: Katholisches Bibelwerk, 2005).

Meeks, Wayne A., *The First Urban Christians* (New Haven: Yale University Press, 1983).

—'The "Haustafeln" and American Slavery: The Hermeneutical Challenge', in Lovering et al., *Theology and Ethics*, pp.232–53.

—'A Hermeneutics of Social Embodiment', in Nickelsburg and MacRae, *Christians among Jews and Gentiles*, pp.171–86.

Mendelson, Jack, 'The Habermas–Gadamer Debate', *New German Critique* 18 (1979), pp.44–73.

Merriman, Brigid, 'Minutes of the colloquy of 27 February 1983', in W.R. Herzog (ed.), *Protocol of the Colloquy of the Center for Hermeneutical Studies in Hellenistic and Modern Culture* (Berkeley: Graduate Theological Union and University of California, 1983).

Michelfelder, Michelle P., and Richard E. Palmer, 'Introduction', in *Dialogue and Deconstruction*, pp.1–20.

Michelfelder, Michelle P., and Richard E. Palmer (eds.), *Dialogue and Deconstruction: the Gadamer–Derrida Encounter* (Albany: State University of New York Press, 1989).

Middleton, Arthur, *Fathers and Anglicans: The Limits of Orthodoxy* (Leominster: Gracewing, 2001).

Miller, John, '"A Suffering People": English Quakers and their Neighbours c.1650–c.1700', *Past and Present* 188 (2005), pp.71–103.

Milton, John, *The English Poems of John Milton* (ed. H.C. Beeching; Oxford: Oxford University Press, 1913).

Minear, Paul, *The Obedience of Faith: The Purpose of Paul in the Epistle to the Romans* (London: SCM, 1971).

Misgeld, Dieter, 'Poetry, Dialogue and Negotiation: Liberal Culture and Conservative Politics in Hans-Georg Gadamer's Thought', in *Festivals of Interpretation: Essays on Hans-Georg Gadamer's Work* (ed. Kathleen Wright; Albany: New York Press, 1990), pp.161–81.

Mitchell, Margaret M., *Paul and the Rhetoric of Reconciliation: An Exegetical Investigation of the Language and Composition of 1 Corinthians* (Westminster: John Knox, 1992).

Monro, W., *Authority in Peter and Paul: The Identification of a Pastoral Substratum in the Pauline Corpus and 1 Peter* (Cambridge: Cambridge University Press, 1983).

Morales Vásquez, Víctor Manuel, *Contours of a Biblical Reception Theory: Studies in the Rezeptionsgeschichte of Romans 13.1-7* (Göttingen: VandR unipress, 2012).

Morgan, Robert, *The Nature of New Testament Theology* (London: SCM, 1973).

—'*Sachkritik* in Reception History', *JSNT* 33 (2010), pp.175–90.

Morgan, Robert, with John Barton, *Biblical Interpretation* (Oxford: Oxford University Press, 1988).

Morrison, Clinton D., *The Powers That Be: Earthly Rulers and Demonic Powers in Romans 13.1-7* (London: SCM, 1960).

Mueller-Vollmerf, Kurt (ed.), *The Hermeneutics Reader: Texts of the German tradition from the Enlightenment to the Present* (Oxford: Blackwell, 1989).

Murray, James A.H., Henry Bradley, W.A. Craigie and C.T. Onions (eds.), *The Oxford English Dictionary*, vols 1 and 9 (Oxford: Clarendon, 1933),

Murray, John, *The Epistle to the Romans: The English Text with Introduction, Exposition and Notes* (New International Commentary; Grand Rapids: Eerdmans 1990).

Nguyen, V. Henry T., 'Review of John Riches, Galatians Through the Centuries', *The Bible and Critical Theory* 6.1 (2010), pp.15.1–15.3.

Nicholls, Rachel, 'Is *Wirkungsgeschichte* (or Reception History) a Kind of Intellectual *Parkour* (or Freerunning)?', British New Testament Conference, September 2005. Cited 2 August 2012. Online: http://issuu.com/revrach/docs/wirkungsgeschichte.

—'*Walking on the Water': Reading Matthew 14:22-33 in the Light of its Wirkungsgeschichte* (Leiden: Brill, 2008).

Nickelsburg, George W., and George W. MacRae (eds.), *Christians among Jews and Gentiles: Essays in Honor of Krister Stendahl on his Sixty-fifth Birthday* (Philadelphia: Fortress, 1986).

Nolland, John, 'Review of Moisés Mayordomo-Marín, *Den Anfang hören: Leserorientierte Evangelienexegese am Beispiel von Matthäus 1–2*', *Review of Biblical Literature* (2000). Cited 28 March 2012. Online: http://www.bookreviews.org/pdf/492_312.pdf.

O'Brien David J., and Thomas A. Shannon (eds.), *Catholic Social Thought: the Documentary Heritage* (Maryknoll: Orbis, 2001).

O'Brien, Peter T., *Colossians, Philemon* (Word Biblical Commentary 44; Dallas: Word, 1982).

—*The Letter to the Ephesians* (Cambridge: Eerdmans, 1999).

O'Donovan, Oliver, *The Desire of the Nations: Rediscovering the Roots of Political Theology* (Cambridge: Cambridge University Press, 1996).

O'Donovan, Oliver, and J. Lockwood O'Donovan (eds.), *From Irenaeus to Grotius: A Sourcebook in Christian Political Thought* (Grand Rapids: Eerdmans, 1999).

Ockham, William of, *A Letter to the Friars Minor* [1334], *and Other Writings* (ed. A. S. McGrade and J. Kilcullen; trans. J. Kilcullen; Cambridge: Cambridge University Press, 1995).

—*A Short Discourse on Tyrannical Government over Things Divine and Human, but Especially over the Empire and Those Subject to the Empire, Usurped by Some Who Are Called Highest Pontiffs* [c.1340] (ed. A.S. McGrade; trans. J. Kilcullen; Cambridge: Cambridge University Press, 1992).

Origen, *Commentaria in Epistolam Pauli ad Romanos* (ed. J.P. Migne; PCC-SGP 14; Paris, 1862), pp.1227–80.

Park, M. Sydney, *Submission within the Godhead and the Church in the Epistle to the Philippians: An Exegetical and Theological Examination of the Concept of Submission in Philippians 2 and 3* (London: T&T Clark, 2007).

Parris, David Paul, *Reception Theory and Biblical Hermeneutics* (Eugene: Pickwick, 2009).

Parry, Robin, 'Review of David Paul Parris, *Reception Theory and Biblical Hermeneutics*. Cited 28 March 2012. Online: https://wipfandstock.com/store/Reception_Theory_and_Biblical_Hermeneutics.

Patai, Daphne, 'Introduction', in Burdekin, *Swastika Night*, pp. iii–x.

Patrides, C.A. (ed.), *John Milton: Selected Prose* (Harmondsworth: Penguin, 1974).

Paul VI, '*Octogesima Adveniens*' (A Call to Action), Apostolic Letter 1971, 13. Cited 14 May 2012. Online: http://www.vatican.va/holy_father/paul_vi/apost_letters/documents/hf_p-vi_apl_19710514_octogesima-adveniens_en.html.

Pauw, Amy Plantinga, 'The Word Is Near You: A Feminist Conversation with Lindbeck', *Theology Today* 50.1 (1993), pp.45–55.

Pavel, Thomas G., *The Lives of the Novel: A History* (Princeton: Princeton University Press, 2013).

Pelagius, *Commentary on St Paul's Epistle to the Romans* (trans. Theodore de Bruyn; Oxford: Clarendon, 1998).

Philo, 'Hypothetica and De Providenti', in *Philo* (ed. F.H. Colson; LCL, 9; London: William Heinemann, 1941).

Piper, John, 'A Vision of Biblical Complementarity: Manhood and Womanhood Defined According to the Bible', in Piper and Grudem (eds.), *Recovering Biblical Manhood*, pp.25–55.

Piper, John, and Wayne Grudem (eds.), *Recovering Biblical Manhood and Womanhood: A Response to Evangelical Feminism* (Wheaton: Crossway, 1991).

Pitts, Andrew W., 'Philosophical and Epistolary Contexts for Pauline Paraenesis', in *Paul and the Ancient Letter Form* (ed. Stanley E. Porter and Sean A. Adams; Leiden: Brill, 2010), pp.270–306.

Pius XI, *Casti Connubii*, On Christian Marriage [1930]. Cited 26 August 2012. Online: http://www.vatican.va/holy_father/pius_xi/encyclicals/documents/hf_p-xi_enc_31121930_casti-connubii_ en.html.

Pizan, Christine de, *Book of the City of Ladies* [1405] (trans. E.J. Richards; New York: Persea, 1982).

Polycarp, 'Letter to the Philippians' and 'Martyrdom of Polycarp', in *Early Christian Fathers* (ed. and trans. C.C. Richardson; LCC 1; London: SCM, 1953).

Porter, Muriel, *Sydney Anglicans and the Threat to World Anglicanism: The Sydney Experiment* (Farnham: Ashgate, 2011).

Quinn, Jerome D., 'Paraenesis and the Pastoral Epistles: Lexical Observations Bearing on the Nature of the Sub-genre and Soundings on its Role in Socialization and Liturgies', in *Paraenesis: Act and Form* (ed. John Gammie and Leo Perdue; Semeia 50; Atlanta: SBL, 1990), pp.189–210.

Räisänen, Heikki, *Beyond New Testament Theology* (London: SCM, 2000).

—*Challenge to Biblical Interpretation, Essays 1991–2001* (Leiden: Brill, 2001).

Rasmusson, Arne, 'Historiography and Theology: Theology in the Weimar Republic and the Beginning of the Third Reich', *Kirchliche Zeitgeschichte* 20.1 (2007), pp.155–80.

Reed, John Shelton, *Glorious Battle: The Cultural Politics of Victorian Anglo-Catholicism* (Nashville: Vanderbilt University Press, 1996).

Riches, John, *Galatians Through the Centuries* (Oxford: Blackwell, 2008).

—'Why Write a Reception-Historical Commentary?', *JSNT* 29 (2007), pp.323–32.

Rickword, Edgell, 'Milton: The Revolutionary Intellectual', in *The English Revolution* (ed. Christopher Hill; London: Lawrence & Wishart, 1985), pp.100–32.

Ricoeur, Paul, *Freud and Philosophy: An Essay on Interpretation* (trans. Denis Savage; New Haven: Yale University Press, 1970).

—'The Model of the Text', *Social Research* 38 (1971), pp.529–62.

Robbins, V.K., *Jesus the Teacher: A Socio-Rhetorical Interpretation of Mark* (Minneapolis: Fortress, 1992).

Roberts, Jonathan, 'Introduction', in Lieb *et al.*, *Oxford Handbook*, pp.1–8.

Roberts, Jonathan, and Christopher Rowland, 'Introduction', *JSNT* 33 (2010), pp.131–36.

—'Review Essay: *Encyclopedia of the Bible and its Reception*', *Relegere: Studies in Religion and Reception* 1.2 (2011). Cited 3 April 2012. Online: http://www.relegere.org/index.php/relegere/article/viewFile/473/452.

Robinson, J. Armitage, *St Paul's Epistle to the Ephesians, an Exposition* (London: Macmillan, 1909).

Rorty, Richard, *Consequences of Pragmatism: Essays 1972–1980* (Minneapolis: University of Minnesota Press, 1982).

—*Contingency, Irony and Solidarity* (Cambridge: Cambridge University Press, 1989).

Rowland, Christopher, *Christian Origins* (Cambridge: Cambridge University Press, 1985).

—'"Open thy Mouth for the Dumb": A Task for the Exegete of Holy Scripture', *Biblical Interpretation* 1 (1993), pp.228–45.

—'A Pragmatic Approach to *Wirkungsgeschichte*: Reflections on the Blackwell Bible Commentary Series and on the Writing of its Commentary on the Apocalypse' [2004] (http://bbibcomm.net/files/rowland2004.pdf, 7.4.12).

—*Radical Christianity: A Reading of Recovery* (Cambridge: Polity, 1988).

—'Re-imagining Biblical Exegesis', in *Religion, Literature and the Imagination: Sacred Worlds* (ed. Mark Knight and Louise Lee; London: Continuum, 2010), pp.140–49.

—'Review of David Parris, *Reception Theory and Biblical Hermeneutics*', Review of Biblical Literature, 2010. Cited 26 August 2012. Online: http://www.bookreviews.org/pdf/7129_7747.pdf.

Rowland, Christopher, and Christopher Tuckett (eds.), *The Nature of New Testament Theology: Essays in Honour of Robert Morgan* (Oxford: Blackwell, 2006).

Rubinstein, Annette, *The Great Tradition in English Literature: From Shakespeare to Shaw* (New York: Citadel, 1962).

Sainte Croix, G.E.M. de, *The Class Struggle in the Ancient Greek World: From the Archaic Age to the Arab Conquests* (London: Duckworth, 1981).

Sampley, J.P., *'And the Two shall become One Flesh': A Study of Traditions in Ephesians 5.21-33* (Cambridge: Cambridge University Press, 1971).

Sanday, William, and Arthur C. Headlam, *A Critical and Exegetical Commentary on the Epistle to the Romans* (Edinburgh: T&T Clark, 5th edn, 1902).

Saussure, Ferdinand de, *Course in General Linguistics* (ed. C. Bally and A. Sechehaye; trans. W. Baskin; New York: McGraw-Hill, 1966).

Sawyer, John F.A., 'The Role of Reception Theory, Reader-Response Criticism and/or Impact History in the Study of the Bible: Definition and Evaluation'. Cited 2 August 2012. Online: http://bbibcomm.net/files/sawyer2004.pdf.

Sawyer, John, and Christopher Rowland, 'Summary of the Discussion after Papers by John Sawyer and Christopher Rowland', *Evangelisch-Katholischer Kommentar* meeting, March 2004. Cited 27 July 2010. Online: http://www.bbibcomm.net/news/summary.doc.

Sawyer, John, Christopher Rowland and Judith Kovacs, 'Series Editors' Preface', in Judith Kovacs and Christopher Rowland, *Revelation Through the Centuries* (Oxford: Blackwell, 2004).

Schatz, Klaus, *Papal Primacy: From its Origins to the Present* (trans. John Otto and Linda Maloney; Collegeville: Liturgical, 1996).

Schleiermacher, F. D. E. *Hermeneutics: The Handwritten Manuscripts* (Missoula: Scholars Press, 1977).

Schnackenburg, Rudolf, *The Epistle to the Ephesians: A Commentary* (trans. H. Heron; Edinburgh: T. & T. Clark, 1991).

Schneiders, Sandra M., 'Obedience', in *The Oxford Companion to Christian Thought: Intellectual, Spiritual and Moral Horizons of Christianity* (ed. Adrian Hastings, Alistair Mason and Hugh Pyper; Oxford: Oxford University Press, 2000), p.493.

Schrage, Wolfgang, *Der erste Brief an die Korinther*, vols. 1 and 3 (Zürich: Benziger; Neukirchen–Vluyn; Neukirchener Verlag, 1991).

Schreiner, Thomas R., 'Head Coverings, Prophecies and the Trinity', in Piper and Grudem (eds.), *Recovering Biblical Manhood*, pp.117–32.

—*Romans: Baker Exegetical Commentary on the New Testament* (Grand Rapids: Baker, 1998).

Schüssler Fiorenza, Elisabeth, 'The Ethics of Biblical Interpretation: Decentering Biblical Scholarship', *JBL* 107 (1988), pp.3–17.

—*In Memory of Her: A Feminist Theological Reconstruction of Christians Origins* (London: SCM, 1983).

Schüssler Fiorenza, Elisabeth (ed.), *Searching the Scriptures: A Feminist Introduction*, vol. 1 (London: SCM, 1993).

Scott, Sarah, *Millennium Hall* [1762] (ed. Gary Kelly; Peterborough: Broadview, 1995).
Searle, John Rogers, *Speech Acts: An Essay in the Philosophy of Language* (Cambridge: Cambridge University Press, 1969).
Selwyn, E.G., *The First Epistle of Peter* (London: Macmillan, 1969).
Shakespeare, William, *The Complete Works* (ed. P. Alexander; London: Collins, 1951).
Sherwood, Yvonne, *A Biblical Text and its Afterlives: The Survival of Jonah in Western Culture* (Cambridge: Cambridge University Press, 2000).
Skarsaune, Oskar, *In the Shadow of the Temple: Jewish Influences on Early Christianity* (Nottingham: InterVarsity, 2002).
Smith, H.B., and P. Schaff (eds.), *The Creeds of the Evangelical Protestant Churches* (London, 1887).
Sölle, Dorothee, *Phantasie und Gehorsam: Überlegungen zu einer künftigen christlichen Ethik* (Stuttgart: Kreuz, 1968).
Speight, Helen, 'Rachel Speght's Polemical Life', *Huntingdon Library Quarterly* 65 (2002), pp.449–63.
Standhartinger, A., 'The Origin and Intention of the Household Code in the Letter to the Colossians', *JSNT* 23 (2001), pp.117–30.
Stendahl, Krister, 'Biblical Theology, Contemporary', in *The Interpreter's Dictionary of the Bible*, vol. 1 (ed. G.A. Buttrick; Nashville: Abingdon, 1962), pp.418–32.
Stephenson, Joseph Adam, *The Sword Unsheathed: The Polity of the Church of England, the Polity enforced by St. Paul, Romans XIII, 1-8* (London: Seeley, 1834).
Sterne, Laurence, *The Life and Opinions of Tristram Shandy, Gentleman* (Harmondsworth: Penguin, 1967).
Stirewalt, M.L., *Paul, the Letter Writer* (Grand Rapids/Cambridge: Eerdmans, 2003).
Stone, Lawrence, *Road to Divorce* (Oxford: Oxford University Press, 1990).
Straw, Carole E., *Gregory the Great: Perfection in Imperfection* (Berkeley: University of California Press, 1988).
Strieder, Leon F., *The Promise of Obedience: A Ritual History* (Collegeville: Liturgical, 2001).
Strobel, A. 'Zum Verständnis von Römer 13:7', *ZNW* 47 (1956), pp.67–93.
Stuhlmacher, Peter, *Historical Criticism and Theological Interpretation of Scripture: Towards a Hermeneutics of Consent* (trans. R. A. Harrisville; London: SPCK, 1979).
Suetonius, *The Lives of Twelve Caesars* (trans. J.C. Rolfe; LCL, Latin Series 148; Cambridge, Mass.: Harvard University Press, 1959).
Swarte Gifford, Carolyn de, 'Politicizing the Sacred Texts: Elizabeth Cady Stanton and *The Woman's Bible*', in Schüssler Fiorenza (ed.), *Searching the Scriptures*, vol. 1, pp.52–63.
Swartley, Willard M., 'How to Interpret the Bible: A Case Study of Romans 13.1-7 and the Payment of Taxes Used for War', *Seeds* 3 (1984), pp.28–31.
—*Slavery, Sabbath, War and Women: Case Issues in Biblical Interpretation* (Kitchener: Herald, 1983).
Swartley, Willard M., and Cornelius J. Dyck (eds.), *An Annotated Bibliography of Mennonite Writings on War and Peace: 1930–80* (Kitchener: Herald).
Swetnam, Joseph, *The Arraignment of Lewde, Idle, Froward and Unconstant Women* (London: Thos. Archer, 1615); reprinted in *Female Replies to Swetnam the Woman-Hater* (ed. Charles Butler; Bristol: Thoemmes, 1995).
Tacitus, *The Annals of Imperial Rome* (trans. M. Grant; Harmondsworth: Penguin, 1975).

Kathryn Tanner, 'Theology and the Plain Sense', in *Scriptural Authority and Narrative Interpretation* (ed. Garrett Green; Philadelphia: Fortress, 1987), pp.59–78.

Tavard, George, 'Episcopacy and Apostolic Succession according to Hincmar of Reims', *Theological Studies* 34 (1973), pp.594–623.

Taylor, A.J.P., *The Course of German History: A Survey of the Development of German History since 1815* (London: Routledge, 1961).

Tertullian, *Adversus Marcionem, Books 4–5* (ed. and trans. E. Evans; Oxford: Clarendon, 1972).

—'Apologia', in *Latin Christianity* (ed. and trans. Alexander Roberts and James Donaldson; The Ante-Nicene Fathers 3; Buffalo: Christian Literature Co., 1885).

Theissen, Gerd, *Psychological Aspects of Pauline Theology* (trans. John Galvin; Edinburgh: T. & T. Clark, 1997).

—*Social Reality and the Early Christians: Theology, Ethics, and the World of the New Testament* (trans. Margaret Kohl; Minneapolis: Fortress, 1992).

—*The Social Setting of Pauline Christianity* (Edinburgh: T. & T. Clark, 1982).

Thiselton, Anthony C., *1 & 2 Thessalonians Through the Centuries* (Oxford: Blackwell, 2010).

—*The First Epistle to the Corinthians: A Commentary on the Greek Text* (Carlisle: Paternoster, 2000).

—*Hermeneutics of Doctrine* (Grand Rapids/Cambridge: Eerdmans, 2007).

—*New Horizons in Hermeneutics* (London: Harper Collins, 1992).

—'Reception Theory, H.R. Jauss, and the Formative Power of Scripture', *SJT* 65 (2012), pp.289–308.

—*Thiselton on Hermeneutics: Collected Works with New Essays* (Grand Rapids/Cambridge: Eerdmans, 2006).

'Thomas of India' (anon.), in *The Towneley Plays* (ed. George England; Early English Text Society; London: Oxford University Press, 1897), pp.337–52.

Torrance, Iain R., 'Gadamer, Polyani and Ways of Being Closed', *SJT* 46 (1993), pp.497–506.

Troeltsch, Ernst, *The Social Teaching of the Christian Churches*, vol. 1 (trans. Olive Wyon; New York: Macmillan, 1931).

Vanhoozer Kevin, *First Theology: God, Scripture and Hermeneutics* (Downer's Grove: InterVarsity, 2002).

Vives, Jaun Luis, *The Education of a Christian Woman: A Sixteenth-Century Manual* (ed. and trans. C. Fantazzi; Chicago: University of Chicago Press, 2000).

Warnke, Georgia, *Gadamer: Hermeneutics, Tradition and Reason* (Cambridge: Polity, 1987).

Watson, Francis, *Text and Truth: Redefining Biblical Theology* (Edinburgh: T. & T. Clark, 1997).

Watson, Nigel, 'Authorial Intention: Suspect Concept for Biblical Scholars?', *Australian Biblical Review* 35 (1987), pp.6–13.

Wedderburn, A.J.M., *Reasons for Romans* (London/New York: Continuum 2004).

Weinsheimer, Joel C., *Gadamer's Hermeneutics: A Reading of Truth and Method* (New Haven: Yale University Press, 1985).

Weyant, Nancy S., *The Cambridge Companion to Elizabeth Gaskell* (Cambridge: Cambridge University Press, 2007).

Whateley, William, 'Directions for Married Persons: Describing the Duties Common to Both, and Peculiar to Each of Them' (Bristol: William Pine, 1768).

Whelehan, Imelda, *Modern Feminist Thought: From the Second Wave to 'Post-feminism'* (Edinburgh: Edinburgh University Press, 1995).

Wilken, Robert, *The Christians as the Romans Saw Them* (New Haven: Yale University Press, 1984).

Williams, David J., *Paul's Metaphors: Their Context and Character* (Cambridge, Mass.: Henderson, 1999).

Wilson, S.G., *Luke and the Pastoral Epistles* (London: SPCK, 1979).

Wink, Walter, *The Bible in Human Transformation: Towards a New Paradigm for Biblical Study* (Philadelphia: Fortress, 1973).

Wire, Antoinette Clark, *The Corinthian Women Prophets: A Reconstruction through Paul's Rhetoric* (Minneapolis: Fortress, 1990).

Witherington, Ben, *The Paul Quest: The Renewed Search for the Jew of Tarsus* (Leicester: InterVarsity, 1998).

—*Women and the Genesis of Christianity* (Cambridge: Cambridge University Press, 1990).

—*Women in the Earliest Churches* (Society for New Testament Studies, Monograph Series 59; Cambridge: Cambridge University Press, 1988).

Wollstonecraft, Mary, *Vindication of the Rights of Woman* (ed. Miriam Brody; London: Penguin, 1988).

Wolter, Michael, 'The Theology of the Cross and the Quest for a Doctrinal Norm', in Rowland and Tuckett, *Nature of New Testament Theology*, pp.263–85.

Yoder, John Howard, *The Christian Witness to the State* (Eugene: Wipf, 1997).

—*The Priestly Kingdom* (Notre Dame: University of Notre Dame Press, 1984).

Young, Frances M., *Art of Performance: Towards a Theology of Holy Scripture* (London: Darton, Longman & Todd, 1990).

—*Biblical Exegesis and the Formation of Christian Culture* (Cambridge: Cambridge University Press, 1997).

Ziesler, John, *Paul's Letter to the Romans* (London: SCM, 1989).

INDEXES

INDEX OF REFERENCES

INDEX OF AUTHORS